ON THE SHORES
OF THE MEDITERRANEAN

On the Shores of
The Mediterranean

ERIC NEWBY

Little, Brown and Company
Boston   Toronto

FIRST AMERICAN EDITION

Library of Congress Cataloging in Publication Data

Newby, Eric.
    On the shores of the Mediterranean.
    Bibliography: p.
    Includes index.
    1. Mediterranean Region — Description and travel.
2. Newby, Eric. I. Title.
D973.N39   1984   910'.091822   84-21294
                ISBN 0-316-60422-4

MV

Map of the Mediterranean by Freda Titford

To Wanda, the only item of essential equipment – apart from a Rolex watch (boiled in a stew by Afghans to tests its waterproof qualities) – not lost, stolen or simply worn out in the course of some thirty years of travel together.

Contents

The drawings illustrating the text are by Jonathan Newby

Acknowledgements

I wish to take this opportunity to express my warmest thanks to the following: Joan Bailey of the London Library; Ann Etherington, who had the unenviable job of typing the book from my manuscript; Adrian House for his constant encouragement and constructive criticism; and all the other members of the Harvill Press – literally the whole lot – for their help. Also to Joy Law.

I should also like to thank the Tourist Boards of Italy, Turkey, Israel, Egypt, Tunisia and Morocco for their help and hospitality, and Colonel Muammar Qathafi for inviting us to be his guests in Libya.

E.N.

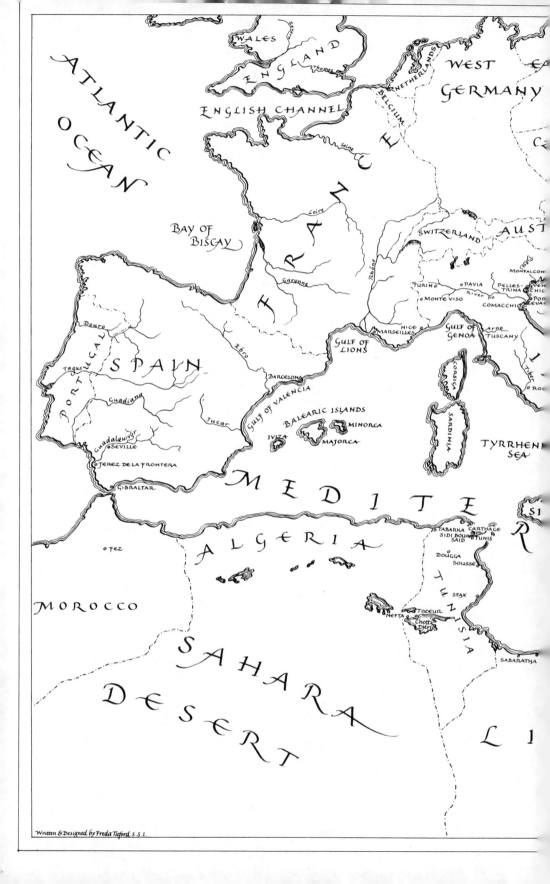

ATLANTIC OCEAN

WALES

ENGLAND

Thames

ENGLISH CHANNEL

Seine

NETHERLANDS

BELGIUM

WEST GERMANY

CZ

FRANCE

Loire

BAY OF BISCAY

Garonne

Rhone

SWITZERLAND

AUST

MONTFALCON

TURINO

PAVIA

MONTE VISO

River Po

PELLES-TRINA

COMACCHIO

CHIC

POR LEVA

Douro

PORTUGAL

SPAIN

Ibro

NICE

MARSEILLES

GULF OF LIONS

GULF OF GENOA

Arno

TUSCANY

CORSICA

Tiber

RO

Tagus

Guadiana

BARCELONA

GULF OF VALENCIA

Jucar

BALEARIC ISLANDS

IVIZA

MAJORCA

MINORCA

SARDINIA

TYRRHEN SEA

Guadalquivir

SEVILLE

JEREZ DE LA FRONTERA

GIBRALTAR

MEDITE

SI

R

FEZ

ALGERIA

TABARKA

SIDI BOU SAID

CARTHAGE

TUNIS

MOROCCO

DOUGGA

SOUSSE

SFAX

TUNISIA

TOZEUR

NEFTA

Chott Djerid

SABARATHA

SAHARA DESERT

LI

Written & Designed by Freda Tieford. S.S.I.

I
ITALY

A Tuscan Vineyard

When people in England and America ask about our house in Italy and we tell them that it is in northern Tuscany, their eyes light up, because Tuscany is one of the parts of Italy that the British and the Americans know about, or think they do. For most of them who have visited it, Tuscany conjures up that rather open-cast country permanently suffused in golden light that forms the background of so many fourteenth-century paintings, country in which Chianti is made. In their mind's eye they even think they know what sort of house it is we live in, though we stress the fact that it is very small and very ungrand. They immediately begin to think of the sort of house that appears with its name against it on a map, or in an architectural guide to Tuscany as a Villa, followed by the name of its past owner, often a hyphenated one, and that of its present owner, preceded by the word *ora*, meaning 'now'; for example, to invent one, Villa Grünberg-Tiffany, *ora* Newby, a place with a spacious terrace and lots of statuary, the sort of place at which Sitwells used to, and Harold Acton still might, drop in uninvited to tea.

In fact our house is in a part of Tuscany so far to the north of Florence, Pisa and Lucca that it ceases to conjure up the idea of Tuscany at all, either in its countryside or in the quality of its light. It is quite near Carrara, a place famous for its marble, where Michelangelo had enormous blocks of the stuff quarried, as did later Henry Moore and Noguchi; marble that is still used to make the sort of tombstones that are popular with the Mafia and the Camorra, the other criminal secret society. Carrara, probably because of the abundance of blasting material conveniently to hand, is also the headquarters of the Italian Anarchists and the place where they hold, or used to until recently – nothing is forever – their annual convention. The house certainly cannot be called a villa, or even a weekend *villetta*, let alone a Villa-whatever-it-was, *ora* Newby. Looking down on it from the upper part of our vineyard it resembles a *dun*, a prehistoric Irish fort, more than a dwelling, or else one of those enormous heaps of stone that people in limestone countries used to pile up in the process of making a field, before the coming of the bulldozer, which is what a lot of old peasant houses do look like in the Mediterranean lands. It does in fact appear as a small black blip on a sheet of the Italian 1:25,000 military maps, which look as if they had been drawn by a lot of centipedes with ink on their feet.

One of the reasons we had bought it was because it was exactly like almost any one of the various houses in which Italian peasants had hidden me high up in the Apennines in the winter of 1943–4 when I had been an escaped prisoner-of-war. It was in autumn 1943 that, emerging from my prison camp in the valley of the River Po, I had first met my wife, who lived in the nearby village and who had arranged for me, because I had a broken ankle, to be hidden in the maternity ward of the local hospital. Later, I had been recaptured and sent to Germany, but when I was finally released in 1945 I had gone back to Italy, and Wanda and I had subsequently married. And we still are married.

The house is in a little dell, and although it is hidden from almost every other point by the chestnuts, *i castagni*, from which it takes its name, and by olive trees and vineyards, it has a magnificent view over the valley in which the Magra, one of Italy's polluted rivers, flows into the Ligurian Sea, one of the numerous more or less polluted seas into which the Mediterranean is sub-divided.

We found the keys, all five of them, where our neighbours had hidden them in case we arrived late at night, as like many of the older country people, they went to bed as soon as it was dark and they had eaten their evening meal, which was what most country people did before the arrival of television. Three of the keys are very big, all of them are very old and shiny. On the first day the house became ours some twenty years ago I lost one of the big ones, a key that had been made when the house was built more than a hundred years before, and I never found it again. Luckily there was a spare key, but that was the only one. The doors of the house are made of slabs of chestnut cut by hand, and they are so full of cracks and holes that from the inside you can see the light of day shining through them in dozens of places. When I lose the rest of the keys, or if the huge locks give up, it will mean new doors, and the house will never look the same again.

With the doors open I switched on the current and turned the water on at the tap outside the bathroom; the water comes from a spring higher up the hill called la Contessa and is very good. The bathroom is in what had been the *stalla*, the byre in which the animals were kept, on the ground floor below the hay loft, and this means that when we want to visit it in the night from our bedroom, which is upstairs, we have to go down the staircase which leads to it. The staircase is in the open air, which is why visitors are provided with chamber pots in which they occasionally put their feet when getting out of bed in the darkness, with spectacular results.

Apart from some dust and fallen plaster and a few dead mice, there was nothing much wrong. Here, the mice are almost as big as rats. This time they had eaten the poison laid down for them the previous winter instead of our bedding, as they often do, gnawing their way through the backs of old chests-of-drawers to get at it, although one or two of them had taken some chunks out of a red shirt of mine from L. L. Bean, Freeport, Maine, to make what we subsequently found when we discovered one of their nests, to be blankets for their children.

While I turned things on and buried dead mice, Wanda began to remove the plastic sheeting which protected the mattresses on the old iron bedsteads which are painted with flowers, some of them inlaid with mother-of-pearl, beds she had bought, or had simply been allowed to cart away, years ago, when the local farmers' wives had decided to modernize their houses and had thrown them out to rust in their back yards.

Outside, in the vineyard on the side of the hill, the grapes looked healthy enough, having been sprayed with copper sulphate throughout the summer, and quite good, but not very numerous. It had been a very wet spring and had continued to be wet right into June, but what had then followed had been a phenomenally hot summer, even for Italy, with shade temperatures week after week up in the hundreds Fahrenheit, and absolutely no rain; and this weather had persisted into autumn, apart from a few short, welcome downpours. Down in central Tuscany, even as far north as Lucca, the grapes were abundant and it would be a good year. Here, where we lived, where often in early autumn it rained and rained when the sirocco blew from Africa, and the grapes then began to suffer from *muffa*, mildew, or a sudden hailstorm could destroy an entire crop in a few minutes, it was increasingly rare to have an outstanding year for what would never be, even if the grapes were outstanding, outstanding wines. Here, in an area which only appears on the most optimistic wine maps as being of moderate wine production, we and the neighbouring farmers make white and red wine, using as many varieties of grapes as possible, in our case about six, as a talisman principally against disease.

The end product is not what is known as DCG (*Denominazione Controllata e Garantita*), or DOC (*Denominazione Origine Controllata*), or even, until recently, DS (*Denominazione Semplice*), the humblest of all denominations, because in order to satisfy these minimal requirements, it would have to have a label stating the region in which it was produced, something I had never seen before 1983.

This wine can rarely, if ever, be found on sale even in local shops. When our neighbouring farmers sell what is surplus to their own enormous requirements, then it invariably finds its way into private houses or the sort of trattoria which announces its cooking as being *cucina casalinga*, the sort the best Italian mothers turn out every day for the whole of their working lives. This is because it fulfils the demand, which is becoming every year more difficult to satisfy, not only in Italy but in every other wine-producing country, for everyday drinking wine that has no additives, the sort of wine that has neither been pasteurized nor clarified with pills, although it is almost impossible to make white wine that can travel without any kind of help that will not change its colour. Wine that has been too generously assisted in this way, however, possibly with the addition of sodium bi-sulphate, looks like water, has a sickly aftertaste and gives the drinker a ferocious headache with its epicentre between the eyebrows.

The harvesting of the grapes, here where we live, hardly ever begins before the *festa* of San Remigio, which takes place on 1 October each year at Fosdinovo, a large village on the hill some nineteen hairpin bends above us. The stone effigy of San Remigio, the patron saint of the town, a saint who baptized Clovis, King of the Franks, stands high above the altar in one of the two churches. Also high up to one side of it is the tomb of one of the Malaspina family, feudal lords of this part of Italy, which is still called Lunigiana, after Luni, a Roman city and seaport now high and dry on what had been the northern borders of ancient Etruria. They still own and inhabit the castle which looms above the rooftops and in which Dante stayed.

For weeks before the *festa* there is bee-like activity everywhere and all the specialist shops along the terrible, traffic-ridden Via Aurelia, one of the great Roman roads to Rome, which sell barrels, hods, grape crushers and presses, have them prominently displayed outside their premises.

The actual *festa* begins to assemble itself early in the morning, long before dawn, when a procession of vans, lorries and motor cars starts groaning up the hill to the town loaded with merchandise which will later be displayed on the stalls in the open-air market place under the plane trees below the village. It is mostly cheap stuff, but some products of the pre-plastic age still persist: copper cauldrons, earthenware casseroles, mousetraps made of wood that look like lock-up garages, thick woollen socks and vests and the bed-warmers known as *preti*, priests, wooden frameworks which you put between the bedsheets on cold winter nights with an iron pot full of hot ashes inside them and which warm a bed in a way that no other kind of warmer can. Also on sale will be pack-mules, pigs and cattle. The animals are sold on the same patch of ground that has been used for this purpose as long as anyone can remember, although it has now been turned into a children's playground and is full of plastic gnomes. And there is plenty to eat. In the market you can also buy *panini*, big, crusty sandwiches filled with delicious slices of pork cut from a young pig that has been roasted on a spit. And there is also plenty to drink. Until recently there were open-air drinking booths under the plane trees at which you could sit and eat *panini* and drink last year's wine at tables with white cloths on them. Now, if you want to eat and drink you have to do it indoors because it is very rare, almost unknown, for it not to pour with rain on the *festa* of San Remigio. Last year was an exception. This is the day, too, when Wanda, and she did it for more than fifteen years, worked in one of the two hotels as a waitress, to help out with the farmers' lunches, invariably receiving an offer of marriage from one of them who had become a widower in his fifties.

This year we have arrived too early for San Remigio, but not too early to harvest our grapes and make our wine, or help others with their *vendemmia*, the harvesting and the wine-making. We always help four families with the *vendemmia*. The harvesting of the grapes usually takes one or two days; the fermentation takes about ten days. To be asked to help is an honour because it means that we are regarded as hard workers, and therefore earn the prodigious quantities of wine and food that are served throughout the *vendemmia*.

It takes several days to get ready for our own *vendemmia*. All the barrels have first to be washed and scrubbed and then kept standing upright with a hose running water into them until the seams swell and close and they no longer leak. So on the first morning when the *vendemmia* begins we start work with the family which owns the farm across the road from where the track leads down to our house. We have known them ever since we first came here. Their children have come to England and stayed with us and we have seen them grow up, get married and themselves have children.

Tomorrow, around seven-thirty, dressed in our oldest clothes, we will turn up at the big modern farmhouse they have built to replace the old, more beautiful one, armed with baskets with iron hooks on them so that we can hang them from the *pergole*, the horizontal wires on which vines are trained, while we cut the grapes with scissors, secateurs, or just sharp knives, all of which become equally painful to handle when you use them day after day.

If the family is an efficient one, and this one is highly efficient, there should be about a dozen people waiting outside, and the tractor should be warmed up and the trailer attached to it, already filled with the heavy hods called *bigonci*, sometimes made of plastic now and much lighter, in which the grapes are brought back to the house and poured into the *macchina da macinare*, the grape crusher. If they are an inefficient lot and no one else has turned up, which often means they have forgotten to ask them, a lot of screaming across valleys to other houses takes place – '*Maariaaa! Ahmaaandoh! Doveee seei?*' ('Maria! Armando! Where are you?') – just as they had screamed at one another across similar expanses up in the nearby Apennines when I was hiding from the Germans. Or they could still be scrubbing the barrels or even waiting for the barrel staves to swell sufficiently to stop the barrels leaking, which should have been done long before, or perhaps the man with the tractor hasn't arrived, in any of which cases we hang about and get cheesed off. The most inefficient people we know are the P . . . . s, who are never ready. One year the bottom literally fell out of their biggest barrel, which was really enormous, after we had quarter filled it with crushed grapes. Yet in spite of being highly inefficient, they make some of the best wine in the district.

We always start at the most distant vineyard, which may be a mile or more away from the house, up or down the hillside, often separated from it by other people's properties and usually only reached by the roughest and steepest of tracks.

In some of the vineyards the grapes are still trained on *pergole*, trellises, some of them extended out over steep banks which are anything up to eight feet high. *Pergole* are picturesque and shade you from the midday sun, but they no longer accord with modern wine-making theory. No more trellises are being constructed, and new vineyards are planted in regular, widely-spaced parallel rows in fields bulldozed out of the hillside, and the pretty terraced fields one above the other will soon be no more. It is difficult to cut the bunches of grapes under a pergola. If they are very high you have to use triangular, home-made step ladders, which everyone keeps for this purpose and for harvesting the olives later in the year, but often, when the ground underneath is too bumpy to set them up, I find myself swinging from the pergola, like one of the larger primates trying to reach some far-out bunches.

If it rains it is hell. If it rains heavily you have to stop work, because you get too much water with the grapes when you squash them in the press. A sack is the best thing to wear over the head and shoulders when it rains, cooler and less constricting than a waterproof. If the grapes are more or less a write-off, as they were in 1972, and it rains as well, it is indeed lugubrious, but whatever the conditions, the day passes in constant gossip, which seems to become more and more lubricious as the day goes on; some of the more hair-raising stories being recounted by respectable-looking ladies dressed in the deepest black. From time to time, gusts of laughter sweep through the vineyard as a result of some particularly coarse remark. Some of the time I don't harvest the grapes. Instead I am given the job of heaving the *bigonci*, filled with grapes, on to the trailer which will take them back to the press. This is because I am one of the few grown men here who haven't yet had a hernia from lifting enormous weights.

At about ten o'clock, after we have worked for a couple of hours or more, we have a *merenda*, a picnic, in whichever field we happen to be in, brought there by the farmer's wife; a very un-English breakfast spread out on a white cloth on the grass, with lots of fresh pecorino, cheese made with ewe's milk, prosciutto, and what is here called mortadella but which is nothing like real mortadella di Bologna – more like salami – bread baked in the outside wood oven which every house possesses, and wine. We go on having swigs of wine throughout the day, to keep us going, not much but enough, always white.

At about a quarter to one we go back to the house for the midday meal, by which time we have, temporarily at least, had enough. All the morning a band of women have been sorting the bunches that they take from the baskets at tables set up in the various fields, cutting off long stalks, removing leaves which would give the wine a bad taste and rejecting unripe grapes or those covered with mildew, before putting the rest into the *bigonci*. Sometimes, if it is hot, we eat at a long table outside in the yard, but usually we are in the parlour with great black and white photographs of ancestors on the walls. We never drink before the meal, apart from the occasional swig we have already had in the fields, and we never mix white with red, because drinking on an empty stomach and mixing white with red is thought to be injurious to health.

We eat *brodo*, broth, made with beef or chicken stock, with pasta in it, followed by *manzo bollito*, boiled beef, stuffed with a mixture of spinach, egg, parmigiano cheese and mortadella; and also roast or boiled chicken chopped up with a chopper and the bones broken, the chickens being the best sort that have scratched a living in the yard, roast potatoes, the bitter green salad called *radici*, mixed with home-produced olive oil and vinegar, and plates of delicious tomatoes eaten with oil, salt and pepper.

The afternoon seems longer and harder and, if it is hot, much hotter than the morning, and the work goes on in the fields until it is so dark that it is no longer possible to see anything. It goes on longer back at the house where there is usually a last trailer-load of *bigonci* full of grapes that have to be fed into the *macchina da macinare*, from which they fall into full ones which you hoist on your shoulder before staggering away with them and pouring the contents into one of the *barili* in which it will eventually become wine.

Now, after a good wash at a tap in the yard, we all sit down again, with the children home from school, to eat a dinner: a home-made ravioli (each house has a special piece of furniture called a *madia*, a sort of dough tray, for making pasta), more meat and chicken, but never for some reason pork, then cheese and lots of walnuts, with which we drink the stronger, sweeter wines of which the owner is usually very proud, and coffee.

Then we all reel home under the stars, or through wetting rain, sometimes, if we have indulged too freely, falling into ditches which some thoughtless fellows seem to have dug since we passed that way in the morning; and the next day will be the same, and the next.

This time, we had not come here only to make the wine or simply to drink it while at the same time enjoying the heat of the Mediterranean sun. This time, we were using I Castagni as the point of departure for other, some of them wilder, shores of the Mediterranean. Now it was August. This year, to do our *vendemmia* we would have to return from wherever we happened to be.

What we were hoping to do was to travel around the shores of the Mediterranean, or as many as we felt inclined to travel round (some of them being at that time – as they still are – either difficult or undesirable places to visit unless you have to), with the idea of seeing people, places and things that we had either never seen before or had not seen for so long that we both wanted to see them again and to discover – though we were less anxious about this – what changes time had wrought in them.

'Shores' were something we were going to interpret liberally. I knew, from visiting our own neighbouring shores in the Gulf of Spezia and almost the entire Tuscan littoral south of it as far as Livorno, that if I slavishly traversed the entire coastline of the Mediterranean I would end up either as a topographical bore or as one of those prophets of doom and pollution who is actually confronted with what he has been prophesying, rather as Smollett was when he travelled to Rome by way of the Riviera in the eighteenth century. For what has happened to enormous tracts of the Mediterranean was, as we later found out if we did not know it already, too awful for anyone but the most insensitive traveller to contemplate. All the coasts of the Mediterranean, from the east coast of Spain in the latitude of the Balearic Islands to Albania, including the coasts of France, Italy and Yugoslavia, Corsica, Sardinia, Sicily and the Balearics, are so badly polluted that swimming and eating fish caught in these waters is said to be dangerous, and the same applies in the eastern Mediterranean from northern Syria to the borders of Egypt and Libya.

'Shores' were something we interpreted to include places that might be far inland – such as Fez in Morocco where I had long wanted to go, or the edge of the Sahara – providing that they were part of the Mediterranean world. History was something I proposed not to delve into too deeply, even though in order to pay for this land-borne Odyssey I was going to write a book about it. The thought of attempting to chronicle in more or less detail the peoples who had dwelt on its shores, sometimes merely as a passing whim, made my mind reel: Minoans, Egyptians, Greeks, Macedonians, Israelites, Phoenicians, Romans, Dacians, Etruscans, Carthaginians, Persians, Arabs, Assyrians, Albanians, Jews, Vikings, Crusaders of various nationalities, Byzantines, Vandals, Genoese, Turks, Venetians, Dutch, English, French, Spaniards, Slovenes and Croats and Montenegrins, Barbary pirates of various sorts and goodness knows who else, like a cast of billions in some colossal, crazy Cecil B. de Mille film of the thirties. It was no wonder that many of the writers of books about the Mediterranean, of whom there are lots, had failed to keep such a mob under control. I had no intention of trying.

'Where were you thinking of starting?' Wanda asked me one cold morning in deepest Dorset when the idea of the Mediterranean had finally taken shape.

'I was thinking of Gibraltar,' I said. 'There's a nice view from the top and I could start the book at the end, with the collapse of the British Empire, like they do in films. The Americans should like that, the bit about the collapse. Or I could start in Egypt, on top of the Great Pyramid. The only thing is you can't see the Mediterranean from the top of it.'

'I thought you said you wanted to go back to Naples,' she said.

'I do, at some stage,' I said.

'Well why don't you start in Naples and go clockwise round the Mediterranean instead of dashing off in all directions like a lunatic?' she asked.

So we did.

In the Streets of Naples

The train trundled into Naples through the happy hunting grounds of the Camorra in the suburbs of Grumo, Frattamaggiore and Casoria, past the Cimitero Monumentale up on the hill at Poggioreale and the Cimitero Nuovo, past a forgotten section of the city called the Rione Luzzatti, past the Mercato Agricola and the Prison, the Carcere Giudiziario, and past the Pasconello marshalling yards in which long lines of carriages stood shimmering in the sun like so many red-hot ingots. It was so hot that I wondered if the place might literally explode.

'There are no hotels in Pozzuoli,' a *sollecitatore*, a tout for one of the hotels, said as, carrying our luggage, we entered the foyer of the Stazione Centrale, which although built almost entirely of stainless steel and plate glass was, after the train in which we had been immured for about eight hours, a haven of coolness if not of quiet. We wanted to stay in Pozzuoli, outside the city to the west, partly because we knew it would be quieter than Naples and partly because it is on the shores of the fascinating region known as the Campi Flegrei, the Phlegraean Fields.

'*Non fare lo stupido!*' Wanda said. The very rude equivalent in

Italian of 'Don't be bloody daft!' 'There were dozens of hotels and pensions when we last stayed there.'

'Well, there aren't any now,' he said. 'They're all kaput. There are *terremoti*, earthquakes.'

'Of course there are hotels and *pensioni* at Pozzuoli,' the man at the official Tourist Information desk in the station said when we appealed to him. 'This man is lying – *va via!*' he said to the *sollecitatore*, and when he had gone off, grumbling to himself, 'There are altogether nineteen hotels and *pensioni* at Pozzuoli; but unfortunately they are all full.'

We asked him how he knew they were all full.

'Because other visitors who arrived earlier today have also asked to stay in Pozzuoli and I have telephoned every one of them. All are full.'

And with that, because we were hot and done in, we allowed him to consign us, telling us how much we would enjoy staying in it, to a *pensione* in Mergellina that might have won a prize, if the owner had wanted to enter for it, for the noisiest and worst *pensione* in its class anywhere on the Italian shores of the Mediterranean.

He, too, the man at the information desk, was lying. In fact all the hotels and *pensioni* in Pozzuoli were completely empty, which was not surprising considering that the town was being shaken by up to sixty earthquake shocks a day of an intensity between three and four on the Mercalli scale.

'The only thing the hotels at Pozzuoli are full of is *paura* (fear),' said an elderly gentleman who we found sitting on a bench at the railway station at Pozzuoli watching the trains go by, when we went there a few days later.

'And what are you doing here, then?' Wanda asked him, 'if it's so dangerous?'

'*Io*,' he said, '*Io sono di Baia. Vengo ogni giorno in treno. Sono in pensione. Mi piace un po' di stimolo.*' ('Me? I'm from Baia. I come in here every day on the train. I'm an old-age pensioner. I like a bit of excitement.')

Loaded with inaccurate information we went out through the swing doors of the station into Piazza Garibaldi which was filled with orange-coloured buses, where yet more of the local inhabitants were waiting to practise their skills on us: vendors of hard and soft drugs, contraband cigarettes and lighters, souvenirs, imitation coral necklaces; male prostitutes; juvenile and not so juvenile pimps, pickpockets and bag-snatchers, as well as large numbers of inoffensive, if not positively kindly Napoletani. In fact it was just like any other open space outside a main station anywhere.

Somewhere near the middle of the Piazza someone, presumably someone unused to Naples, had tethered a motorcycle to a lamp standard with the equivalent of a small anchor chain that would have been difficult to cut even with bolt cutters, threading it through and round the front wheel instead of through the frame, a serious error. Now, all that remained of the motorcycle was the front wheel, still chained to the lamp standard.

It was obvious that whatever had happened elsewhere in the Mediterranean in the twenty years since we had last visited it, basically Naples was one of the places that had not changed.

Six nights later we were sitting at a table in the open air in Piazza Sannazzaro, at the west end of Naples, midway between the Mergellina railway station and Porto Sannazzaro where yachts, fishing boats and the big, grey, fast patrol boats of the Guardia di Finanza, the Italian equivalent of the British and American customs, lie moored practically alongside the fast, perhaps faster, smaller boats used by the smugglers, the Contrabbandieri.

One of the entrances to this Piazza is by way of a long, fume-filled tunnel, the Galleria della Laziale, which runs down into it under Monte Posillipo from what was, until recently, the village of Fuorigrotta (Outside the Grotto), now a huge, modern suburb out towards the Phlegraean Fields to the west.

At the point where this tunnel enters the Piazza there is a set of traffic lights which are set in such a fashion that they only operate in favour of pedestrians at intervals of anything up to five minutes, and then only for something like thirty seconds, before the drivers of vehicles once again get the green, which in Naples is interpreted as a licence to kill.

But because this is Naples, when the light turns green it is still not safe for pedestrians to cross here (or anywhere else in the city for that matter), even with the lights in their favour, as motorcyclists and drivers of motor vehicles still continue to roar into the Piazza whatever colour the lights are.

This is because for Neapolitan drivers the red light has a unique significance. Here, in Naples, it is regarded as a suggestion that perhaps they might consider stopping. If however they do stop, then it is practically certain that those behind will not have considered the possibility of them doing so and there will be a multiple collision, with everybody running into the vehicle in front. Because of this possibility it is equally dangerous for Neapolitans, whether drivers or pedestrians, to proceed when the green light announces that they can do so.

At this particular set of lights there is yet another danger for pedestrians waiting on the pavement. When the lights are against the traffic emerging from the tunnel, any motorcyclist worth his salt mounts the pavement and drives through the ranks of those pedestrians who are still poised on it trying to make up their minds whether or not it is safe to step into the road and cross.

And what about the orange light? It is a reasonable question to ask.

'And what about the orange light?' Luccano de Crescenza, a Neapolitan photographer and writer, the author of a very amusing book on the habits of his fellow citizens, *La Napoli di Bellavista*, once asked an elderly inhabitant who passed the time of day at various traffic lights, presumably waiting for accidents to occur. To which he replied, *'l'Arancio? Quello non dice niente. Lo teniamo per allegria.'* ('The Orange? That doesn't mean anything. We keep it to brighten the place up.')

This tunnel, and another which also runs under Monte Posillipo, more or less parallel to it, the Galleria Quattro Giornate, replace the tunnel, a wonder of ancient engineering more than 2200 feet long, 20 feet wide and in some places 70 feet high, that linked Roman Napolis with the Phlegraean Fields.

Above the eastern portal of this tunnel, now closed, which emerged at Piedigrotta (Foot of the Grotto) next door to the Mergellina railway station, there is what is said to be a Roman columbarium, a dovecote. It stands on what is supposed to be the site of the tomb of Virgil, who was buried on Monte Posillipo after his death in Brundusium, the modern Brindisi, on his way back from Greece, in September, 19 BC and which was visited by John Evelyn on his way to the Phlegraean Fields in 1645.

Previously Virgil had lived in a villa on the hill where he composed the *Georgics* and the *Aeneid* but was so dissatisfied with the *Aeneid*, which he had written for the glorification of Rome, that he gave orders that after his death it should be destroyed, a fate which, mercifully for posterity, was avoided by the intervention of the Emperor Augustus, who forbade it.

Although it was by now after eleven o'clock in the evening and a weekday, it was August, holiday time, and the tables in Piazza Sannazzaro were as crowded as they had been two or three hours

previously. In fact the tables were so closely packed together tH
the only way in which it was possible to be sure which establishm
one was patronizing was by the different colours of the tableclo

These were very cheap places in which to eat, that is to say you
could have a meal, the principal plate of which might be risotto or
spaghetti *con vongole*, clams, which we hoped had been dredged
from some part of the Mediterranean that was not rich in mercury
and other by-products of industry, and almost unlimited wine (at
least two litres) at a cost of about 12,000 lire for two. (At this time,
August 1983, the exchange was around L2395 for £1, L1605 for
$1.) Here, you could eat an entire meal, which few of the sort of
Napoletani who brought what appeared to be their entire families
with them could afford to do, or a single dish. Or you could eat
nothing at all and simply drink Nastro Azzurro, the local beer
which, strangely enough, is better in bottles than on draught when it
is usually too gassy, or wine, or Coca Cola. Here, in the Piazza, beer
drinkers outnumbered wine drinkers.

One of the sources of drink in Piazza Sannazzaro was a dark
little hole in the wall with *VINI* inscribed over it on a stone slab,
from which this and the various other beverages were dispensed by
a rather grumpy-looking old woman in the black weeds of age or
widowhood or both, who spoke nothing but the Neapolitan dialect.
This dispensary formed in part an eating place called the Antica
Pizzeria da Pasqualino which offered four different varieties – *gusti
specialità* – of pizza: *polpo* (with octopus) *al sugo, capricciosa,
frutta di mare* and *capponato*, presumably filled with capon. These
pizzas are good. They make anything bought outside Italy, and
some pizzas made in Italy and even in Naples by those who are not
interested in making them properly – a bit of underbaked dough
smeared with *salsa di pomodoro*, tomato sauce, and adorned with a
few olives and fragments of anchovy – seem like an old tobacco
pouch with these items inside it. The sort of pizza that the English
traveller Augustus Hare was offered when in Naples in 1883, the
one he described as 'a horrible condiment made of dough baked
with garlic, rancid bacon and strong cheese . . . esteemed a feast.'

What he should have been eating is something of which the
foundation is a round of light, leavened dough which has been
endlessly and expertly kneaded, on to which have been spread, in its
simplest form, olive oil, the cheese called mozzarella, anchovies,
marjoram and *salsa di pomodoro*, and baked in a wood-fuelled
oven.

Amongst all the Napoletani there were very few foreigners to be seen. This was because there is relatively little accommodation in Mergellina – a couple of small hotels and three *pensioni* – and very few visitors to Naples, once they find out what can happen to them in the city, unless they are young and active and travelling together in a band, are at night prepared to go far from the area where they are actually sleeping.

Our evening in Piazza Sannazzaro had been almost too full of incident. Just after nine o'clock, a boy had ridden up on a Vespa and stopped outside the Trattoria Agostino, a place very similar to the one we were in and about fifty yards away on the corner of Via Mergellina, at its junction with the Salita Piedigrotta. There, at point-blank range, without dismounting, he had fired five shots in rapid succession, from what sounded to me more like a pea-shooter than a pistol, at a man sitting at a table outside the establishment, apparently trying to *gambizzare*, blow his kneecaps off, all of which missed, except one which grazed his bottom.

The man at the table was Mario dello Russo, aged thirty-four. He had a criminal record as a member of the Camorra, a fully fledged member of the Nuova Famiglia, the principal rivals of the now-ascendant Nuova Camorra Organizzata (NCO) with whom they were currently engaged in a fight to the death, or until some other satisfactory arrangement could be arrived at.

This battle, which was taking place under our eyes, was for the ultimate control of almost everything criminal: robbery, kidnapping, intimidation of shopkeepers, all sorts of smuggling including drugs, male and female prostitution and illegal property development not only in Naples and the offshore islands of Ischia and Capri but in the whole of Italy from Apulia and Calabria in the deep south as far north as Milan.

After five minutes, three cars loaded with members of the Squadra Mobile arrived, together with an ambulance, and dello Russo was carted off. The boy who actually fired the shots, was, in fact, a person of no consequence, what is known in the Camorra, an organization with unchanging, traditional ways of doing things, rather like Pop at Eton, as a Picciotto di Onore, a Lad of Honour, an unpaid apprentice to the Camorra, anxious to prove his worth and loyalty to the cause. The next step up the ladder was to become what used to be called a Picciotto di Sgarroe. This needed a far greater degree of self-sacrifice and abnegation, the postulant often being required to take the responsibility for crimes committed by fully fledged Camorristi and to accept whatever sentence was meted out to him by law, even if it meant spending years in prison.

Altogether, on that day alone, in the last week of August, those arrested in and around Naples included the uncle of Luigi Giugliano of Forcella, a high-ranking member of the Nuova Famiglia who had been instantly deported to Frosinone; three traffickers in hard drugs; two pairs of brothers, all between twelve and seventeen years of age, who between them had broken into twenty different apartments in the districts of Vomero and Colli Aminei, two of them being armed; a man who had assaulted the police while they were chasing two thieves; Vicenzo Scognamiglo, aged forty-nine, who had stolen a wallet from an Iranian; Bruno and Gennaro Pastore, for snatching a handbag from an American tourist; and Salvatore Imparata, aged fifty-six, and Giovanni Lazzaro, twenty, both of whom were found to be carrying guns.

That same night, Francesco Iannucci, otherwise known as Ciccio 800 (Ciccio being a diminutive of Francesco), a thirty-seven-year-old Camorrista of the Nuova Famiglia, succeeded in jumping from a prison train and getting away, although the following day he was sighted from a Carabinieri helicopter and recaptured, after having been shot in the knee. In 1975 he had been condemned to twenty-four years imprisonment for the murder of Andrea Gargiulo, otherwise known as 'O Curto (the Short One), head of a rival band of the Nuova Camorra Organizzata who specialized in extortion in Iannucci's native suburb of Torre Annunziata, on the shores of the Bay below the southern flanks of Vesuvius, not far from Pompeii.

But by far the biggest coup of the day had been the arrest, by Carabinieri of the Special Operations Group, Napoli I, of Carmela Provenzano, aged thirty-three, at her home in Secondigliano, on the northern outskirts of the city. She had been committed to the earthquake-ridden women's prison at Pozzuoli in which the occupants were now refusing, with some reason, to be locked in their cells. Carmela was the wife of Pasquale d' Amico, better known as 'O Cartunaro (literally the gatherer of cardboard boxes, for reconditioning), who besides being a scavenger was also one of the strategic planning staff in the upper echelons of the NCO.

Carmela had acted as principal courier for the NCO, maintaining a regular communication service between those of its members who were outside with those who were inside. One of her most important calls had been at the Supercarcere, the maximum security

prison, at Nuoro in Sardinia, itself a town in a region that is one of
the great epicentres of violent, organized crime on the island. There,
in August 1981, she delivered the death sentence, pronounced by
Raffaele Cutolo, otherwise known as Il Professore, head of the
NCO, on Francis Turatello, otherwise known as Faccia d'Angelo
(Angel Face). Turatello was one of the inmates, and, if not comman-
der-in-chief of the Nuova Famiglia, was certainly boss of all illicit
activity in the Po Valley, as far north as Milan, as well as being a
protégé of the Mafia.

Turatello died on 17 August, during the open-air exercise
period, having been stabbed sixty times. That same day, the Carabinieri of Napoli I also arrested Maria Auletta, aged eighteen, wife of
the Mafioso Salvatori Imperatrici, one of the *sicari* (cut-throats)
who had stabbed Turatello to death. She was what is known as a
fiancheggiatrice, a helper or flanker of the NCO.

Carmela Provenzano was arrested in Secondigliano, Maria
Auletta in Arzano. Both are small places adjacent to one another in
what is known as Il Triangolo della Morte, or Il Triangolo della
Camorra, both of which have the same significance for those who
have the misfortune to live in them and are not themselves members
of either the Camorra or the Mafia. Inside Il Triangolo, which is
made up of three main areas, Afragola-Casoria, Caivano-Fratta and
Acerra, live more than half a million people, a large proportion of
whom are unemployed and without any apparent hope of finding
employment. Everything within Il Triangolo is inadequate: schools,
water supply, housing and recreational facilities, which are practically non-existent.

Of the eight *comuni*, municipalities, that make up Caivano-
Fratta, five do not even have a single police or Carabinieri post
which might afford some protection to the inhabitants. Afragola-
Casoria, with 200,000 people living in it, does not even have a
hospital. In Acerra, which has the largest concentration of industry
– Aeritalia, Alfasud, Montefibre – the three *comuni* of Acerra,
Pomigliano and Casalnuovo, which together have a population of
100,000, have more than 20,000 unemployed, of whom 8000 are
what is known as *cassa integrati*, that is paid not to work.* At
Acerra large numbers of earthquake victims are accommodated in
metal containers of the sort carried on lorries. In the last week of this

---

* Under the *cassa integrazione* 70–80 per cent of what a worker would
normally earn is paid by agreement between the employer, employee and the state.

August, because of the heat, a four-year-old child died of asphyxiation inside one, the third child to die in this fashion in four months. Of the eight communes that make up Caivano-Fratta, which has about 200,000 inhabitants, the one with the largest number of unemployed is the one which has been industrialized. In fact, the setting up of industrial complexes in the Triangle has obliterated enormous tracts of agricultural land without providing alternative employment for the inhabitants.

It is not surprising that the Triangle is used as a battlefield by the warring clans of the Camorra; there were fifty murders there in the first eight months of 1983. The most dangerous area is Acerra, where, by the time we arrived in Naples, there had been twenty-two murders in eighteen months. Everywhere robbers, many of them no more than children, had organized themselves in bands anything up to twenty strong. Banks were constantly under attack. The only faint ray of hope in what was otherwise a prospect of unrelieved gloom and horror was that students and working men living in the Triangle had joined together to set up an organization of vigilantes, headed by a bishop. We decided to give Afragola-Casoria, Caivano-Fratta and Acerra a miss.

In view of all this general unpleasantness, it was therefore with a certain trepidation that we set off, as we did each night, to walk back to our macabre bedroom in the Pensione Canada on the waterfront facing Porto Sannazzaro, through streets that were now rapidly emptying of people, but not traffic, which continued to circulate until the early hours of the morning unabated. This room was twelve feet high, twelve feet square, lit by a very old circular fluorescent tube that when it was warming up resembled a crimson worm and was furnished with a bidet hidden by a tall bamboo screen, like a bidet in a jungle. It was also furnished, which was unusual for a bedroom, with an upright piano belonging to the brother of the proprietor. The only picture on the walls was a colour photograph of the Mobilificio Petti, a furniture warehouse at Nocera Sopra Camerelle (SA), with the telephone numbers – there were two lines, 723730 and 723751 – printed underneath it, in case one wanted to order up more furniture during one's stay.

Fortunately there were other things besides shootings, of which one soon tires, going on in Piazza Sannazzaro. Night after night we had sat in it watching a succession of events unfold themselves, always with the same protagonists, until we had come to realize that what we were looking at was an unvarying ritual. Even the order in which they took place and the participants appeared and disappeared was governed by immutable laws. It was only on this particular evening, when the Camorra had demonstrated its existence, coming up from the depths and showing a small part of itself, like some immense fish of which only the smallest part breaks the surface, that there had been any interruption.

First to open up, and the only one who remained on site throughout the entire evening, was a young man who sold raw tripe and pigs' trotters from a shiny, brand new, stainless steel stall with the owner's name and what he dealt in painted around the top of it – *TRIPPE OPERE E'O MUSSO* – in black letters, illuminated on a pink background.

The grey pieces of tripe were displayed on a sort of miniature stainless steel staircase which was decorated with vine leaves and lemons stuck on metal spikes, with a centrepiece which consisted of what looked like an urn made entirely of rolled tripe, with the pinkish pigs' trotters laid out attractively at the foot of it. Down this staircase tumbled an endless cascade of water, making the whole thing a sort of hanging garden of tripe and pigs' trotters; it was surprising how attractive looking it was, considering how unpromising were the basic materials.

Next to appear on the scene, after *E'O MUSSO*, was a very poor, very fragile, faintly genteel old lady, who looked as if a puff of wind might whisk her away to eternity. She moved among the tables never asking for money but nevertheless receiving it, for the Neapolitans recognize and respect true poverty. A surprising amount of what she received was in the form of 500 and even 1000 lire notes. This old lady rarely, if ever, made the circuit of all the tables. When she had collected what she presumably considered enough for her immediate needs, after taking into account whatever payments she might have to make to the Camorra in a way of *dovuti*, dues, or what she considered the market could stand each night without spoiling it, she would give up and totter off round the corner and up the hill called the Salita Piedigrotta which leads to the Mergellina railway station and the church of Santa Maria Piedigrotta. There, by day, during opening hours, she used to sit outside the main door, at the receipt of alms. Santa Maria Piedigrotta is the church which is the scene of one of the great Neapolitan religious festivals, that of the Virgin of Piedigrotta, which takes place, to the accompaniment of scenes of wild and pagan enthusiasm, on the night of 7–8 September.

The old lady was followed by an even older, even more decrepit couple, presumably husband and wife, each of whom carried a couple of very large plastic bags. They moved from table to table asking for bread, and because they didn't miss any out, they got a lot of it.

What did they do with all this bread?

One night, feeling mean about doing so, I followed them out of the Piazza, round the corner and up the Rampa Sant'Antonio a Posillipo, built in 1743 by Charles of Bourbon's Spanish Viceroy in Naples, Don Ramiro de Guzman, Duque Medina de Las Torres, which is one of the ways of reaching Virgil's tomb and a pillar indicating the whereabouts of the remains of the poet Leopardi. There, from a distance, I saw them eating bread as hard as they could. It was a harrowing sight. But what happened to the bread they couldn't eat? There was so much of it, and more arriving every evening. Did they sell it to other old people too infirm or too proud to go into the streets and beg? Or did they sell it to a pig farmer for swill? It was yet another Neapolitan mystery.

The old man and the old woman were followed by a *venditore di volanti*, literally a seller of flyings, in this case balloons, who always did good business with the owners of children who had long since got tired of sitting at the tables with their parents and were now zooming about all over the place.

Next came a poor, sickly, probably tubercular, humble-looking young man like someone out of a Victorian novel, who handed out colour prints, as pallid as he was, of Santa Lucia, the Virgin martyred by the Emperor Diocletian, shown holding a palm frond and, as patroness of the blind, a dish with a pair of eyes apparently swimming in it, all against a Neapolitan background of umbrella pines.

He was followed by a more vigorous-looking man carrying a sort of wooden framework, a bit like those that were once used to carry hawks into the hunting field, supported by straps from his shoulders but loaded with toy musical instruments, selling at 1000 lire a time, that looked like ice-cream cornets and which, when he blew into a demonstration model, produced a hideous noise. Soon the air was filled with the sounds of dozens of these instruments being blown by children and adults which mingled with the terrible howlings emitted by the sirens of the police cars and ambulances tearing through the streets, just as they do in every other city in the civilized world.

Then came another, older man, pushing an old-fashioned perambulator with a piece of board on top of it which he used as a mobile stand. He was a *torronaro*, selling *torronne*, nougat. On both sides of the pram he had painted the words QUESTO ESERCIZIO RIMANE CHIUSO IL LUNEDI (THIS ESTABLISHMENT REMAINS CLOSED ON MONDAYS), which was why we hadn't seen him on the evening we arrived. Below that he had added his telephone number, just like the owner of the furniture warehouse at Nocera Sopra Camerelle (SA) in case someone had a sudden, overwhelming desire to eat nougat.

Last of all, a four-man band came marching into the Piazza. Three of them were middle-aged with little black moustaches, wearing the sort of red caps with gold-embroidered peaks worn by Italian station masters when seeing a train off from their stations, bright green shirts and yellow knickerbockers with silver braided side seams. Two of them were beating drums, and the third one played the harmonica. They were led by a drum-major dressed in a white tunic with gold-embroidered epaulettes, bright yellow trousers the same shade as the bandsmen's knickerbockers and what looked like a colonial governor's hat decked with white plumes. He was whirling a baton with a Negro's head on top of it in one hand and, with the other, making various obscene gestures. Each night when we gave the drum-major his due – he was well over seventy years of age – which was not always easy at this late hour, as besides being breadless by this time, we were also running short of the kind of money we were prepared to give him, he used to hand Wanda a quantity of visiting cards, so that if she had stayed on for another week in Naples she would have had enough cards to play poker with. The print on them read:

BOTTONE SALVATORE
ORGANIZZATORE-PAZARIELLO
PROPAGANDA: PER NAPOLI E PROVINCIA
AFRAGOLA (NA)   TEL: 8697539
                          DALLE ORE 2 ALLE ORE 24

Then, when he had sucked everyone in the Piazza dry of lire, Signor Salvatore marched his band of *pazarielli*, signifying, in the dialect, entertainers of a surrealistic, loony kind, away up the Salita Piedigrotta in the steps of the old lady, the old man and woman collecting bread, the sickly young man with the prints of Santa Lucia, the seller of musical instruments that looked like ice-cream cornets, the *venditore di volanti* and the *torronaro*, to the place where they had parked the old, beat-up van which would take them all back to dear old Afragola in the heart of the Triangolo della Morte.

The entertainment was at an end. Suddenly the tables began to empty and the waiters began stacking them and the chairs against the walls. The evening was over.

But not quite over. There was one establishment that during the hours of darkness never closed. The proprietor was called Gennaro and he lived on the first floor over what a sign over the door described as a *Ferramenta e Hobbyistica*, an ironmonger's shop which also catered for those interested in hobbies, which stood next door to the shop where the grumpy old lady dispensed her *vini* and Nastri Azzurri.

This man Gennaro had a monopoly of contraband cigarettes in the Piazza, perhaps over an even wider area. All you had to do was to stand below the balcony and call, 'Gennaro!' and then more softly, '*Un pacco!*' and shooting down on a rope came a *panaro*, a wicker basket, into which you put 2000 lire which was immediately whisked away aloft. Then by return of post, as it were, you received a packet of genuine Marlboros, the only thing lacking being the Italian excise stamp.

But why 2000 lire a packet when the going price, bought from an official government *tabaccaio*, tobacconist, was 1800 lire including duty and tax? Because all the official establishments were shut. Gennaro made a killing with his *contrabbando* which by day would have to sell for infinitely less than 1800 lire to compete with what was a monopoly of the state.

There was nothing extraordinary about this way of doing business, with a basket on the end of a rope. In Naples, where many of the old tenements are eight storeys high, it is commonplace. The only difference is that there the trade is generally legitimate and the buyers, often elderly ladies living alone on an upper floor, are the ones who lower the *panari* to the sellers of such commodities as vegetables in the street below, who have attracted their attention by shouting at the tops of their voices in the dialect, '*Signo* (Signora)! The price of whatever it is is so-and-so a kilo. *Acalate'o panaro!*' ('Lower your basket!')

When Wanda decided to buy the only packet of Marlboros she ever bought from Gennaro and she shouted up, '*Gennaro, un pacco!*', the strangeness of these three words, in her north Italian, Parmigiano accent, made him sufficiently inquisitive to lean out over the railings to see who owned it, and for a moment we found ourselves being looked down on by a hard-looking character of sixty-odd with short white hair and eyes like Carrara marbles. What we were looking up at was the last link in an illicit industry, the one that actually dealt with the public. An industry which at the height of its prosperity, largely in the field of cigarette smuggling, which continued well into the seventies, supported, by its own admission, some 50,000 Napoletani and their families, out of a total population of some 1,200,000.

In the good old days up to about 1978 when the *contrabbandieri* used to challenge the customs officers to football matches, money would change hands in large quantities to keep them sweet – which it probably still does – and the smugglers' equivalent to the Royal Yacht Squadron bar at Cowes was the Bar Paris in Santa Lucia. But by that time the Camorra, and therefore the *contrabbandieri*, were already deeply involved with drugs and the special relationship they had enjoyed with the Guardie had come to an end, and, what had been unthinkable until then, the Guardie actually took to opening fire, if not actually at the *contrabbandieri* themselves, then on their *motoscafi*, although how it was possible to discriminate between one and the other at night it is difficult to imagine.

It was at this time that the *contrabbandieri* did something that only Neapolitans would think of doing. They formed a union which they christened Il Colletivo Autonomo Contrabbandieri, the Autonomous Collective of Smugglers, and called a public protest meeting, advertising it with posters which read more or less as follows:

SMUGGLING AT NAPLES ALLOWS 50,000 FAMILIES TO SURVIVE ALBEIT WITH DIFFICULTY. FOR ALMOST A YEAR NOW THE GOVERNMENT AND THE CUSTOMS HAVE DECLARED WAR ON US. HANDS OFF THE CONTRABAND UNTIL YOU FIND US ANOTHER WAY OF LIFE! COME TO THE MEETING OF ALL SMUGGLERS OF NAPLES ON THURSDAY NEXT IN FRONT OF THE UNIVERSITY IN VIA MEZZOCANONE 16.

A particularly appropriate venue as large numbers of students actually worked for the Paranze a Terra (an organization for distributing contraband).

Now, five or more years later, there were still 50,000 Neapolitan families involved in smuggling at Naples and more money was involved, as would be natural to keep pace with inflation even without taking account of drug smugglers.

There had been some changes in Naples since we had last taken a fairly prolonged look at it, back in the autumn of 1963, and it would have been surprising if there had not been.

Then we had been working on a guide book to the hotels, *pensioni* and restaurants in southern Italy, a task that had left us, even before we left Naples and began to tackle the rest of the Italian peninsula, in a state of near collapse. At that time the *pensione* with the piano had not existed, although there were one or two hotels and *pensioni* that ran it very close.

Some of the biggest changes that had taken place, apart from whole areas in which the original buildings had either fallen down of their own accord or had been knocked down and rebuilt, were down in the docks, all along the waterfront as far as San Giovanni a Teduccio, where the *pontili*, the landing stages, stretch out like long fingers into the filthy waters of the Bay, always a dangerous place, if only because of the long lines of freight cars propelled by tank engines that used to come stealing up behind one on their way to or from some marshalling yard. One was only saved from death by the engine drivers letting off a tremendous blast on their whistles. Altogether the place was a madhouse, what with steam engines whistling, ships, some of them big passenger liners, blasting off on their sirens announcing that they were leaving for the Hudson River and similarly distant destinations, and the appalling din made when a crane driver skilfully dropped a whole slingful of packing cases into a ship's holds, shattering them so that the *portuali*, the stevedores, could get their hands on the contents, just as crane drivers and stevedores did in every other port in the world at that time.

Now there were no more steam engines; no more *transatlantici* stealing out into the Bay in the golden light of early morning; no more crane drivers dropping packing cases making music in the ears of the *portuali*. These noises had been replaced by the ghostly whirrings of the special lifting machines, each of them worked by one man in what had become an automated wilderness, as they picked up the pilfer-proof containers and either loaded them on to a container ship with the minimum of human interference, or else on to an articulated truck.

Now, denied what for centuries they had regarded as their legitimate perquisites of office, the heart had gone out of the *portuali*, and providing that the money could be found, and it almost certainly would be, by 1985, 750 out of a total workforce of 1700 *portuali* would have voluntarily taken the sack. What to do with the remaining 950 was a problem that no one in the government or in the port authority had yet had the courage to face. What was obvious was that as far as being a place of interest to travellers such as ourselves, or to anyone but the technically minded, Naples, as a port, like Barcelona, Marseilles, Trieste, the Piraeus, Iskenderun, Beirut, Haifa, Alexandria, Tripoli, Tunis, Algiers and Tangiers, was finished.

What had gone, too, from many parts of the city in which previously it had operated at full blast, was what can only be described as the roaring street life. The change was particularly noticeable in the heart of Montecalvario, the large grid-iron of streets, alleys and flights of steps to the west of Via Toledo, that immensely long, straight street which under five different names (the others are Via Roma, Via Enrico Pessina, Via Santa Teresa degli Scalzi and Corso Amedeo di Savoia Duca d'Aosta), rather like Broadway, bisects the city from south to north, from the Royal Palace where it looks out on Piazza Trieste e Trento at the seaward southern end to the foot of Capodimonte at the top, north end where the other royal palace of Naples looks out over the city and the Bay.

These changes were not noticeable at first. It is only when you reach La Speranzella, the Street of Some Hope, which runs across Montecalvario parallel to the Toledo, and you see that many of the tall tenements are only prevented from collapsing by forests of wooden beams and metal scaffolding and that they have been abandoned by all except the most stubborn or desperate for accommodation, that you realize that the heart of Montecalvario is gone and that one single, fairly powerful earth tremor would bring the whole place crashing down in a vast mountain of rubble.

Here every different flight of steps from one level to another, every one of the sixty or more streets, every alley, has its own shrine, to Santa Lucia, San Gennaro, the patron saint of Naples, to Our

Lady of Piedigrotta and so on, tended by old ladies who charge the lamps with oil, change the candles, collect any offerings, while meanwhile, in a sort of grotto beneath the shrine, the terracotta figures of men and women, which often include a priest among them, fry in purgatory.

Now what was perhaps the most vigorous street life in Naples was to be found in and on either side of Spaccanapoli, literally the Street that splits Naples, in the same way as Via Toledo does from north to south but from west to east. A long, long street with eight different names which begins as Via Santa Lucia al Monte high up in Montecalvario below the Corso Vittorio Emanuele, coming to an end in a *vicolo cieco*, a cul-de-sac, called Borgo Tupputi, half a mile from the Stazione Centrale in Piazza Garibaldi. An astonishing, fascinating street full of medieval, renaissance, baroque and rococo churches, palaces and monuments; bookshops; repairers and vendors of second-hand dolls; and with long, narrow dangerous alleys running uphill from it in an area infested with robbers, one of which is full of makers and sellers of *presepi* (cribs) and the painted terracotta figures of the infant Christ, the Virgin, the Shepherds and the Kings and the animals which every Neapolitan family brings out in Christmas week; artificial flowers for cemeteries and religious images. The streets running down from it towards Corso Umberto, such as those around the Forcella, the home of Luigi Giugliano, whose uncle had been deported to Frosinone, were still the abode of *puttane*, tarts, some of them enormous.

Twenty years previously, sent off by Wanda to conduct this particular piece of fieldwork by myself, awe had overcome lust as I looked for the first time at these mountainous women somehow inserted into skirts so tight that it seemed that they must burst, bigger even than many of their biggest customers, who were themselves gigantic. Now, fat or thin, they were fighting an uphill battle against the thousands of male prostitutes and transvestites who, as long ago as the seventies, as everywhere else in Italy, were already beginning to outnumber them, if they had not already done so. Some, seeing their livelihood threatened by the indifference of a seemingly increasingly myopic clientele and not receiving much support from the Nuova Famiglia or the NCO, who would take a percentage of any earnings, whether they were male, female or transvestite, pinned cards on the doors of their places of business announcing that whoever was inside was a *PUTTANA VERA* – a Genuine Prostitute.

The beggars of Naples were now less numerous, less ragged than they had been twenty years previously. The poor, in fact, although they might be relatively poorer than they had been, now looked slightly more prosperous, more bourgeois. Some of the raggedest beggars were still to be found lying on the steps leading up into the enormous Galleria Umberto Primo, which has a nave 160 yards long and is 125 feet high with a dome towering 60 feet above that, a place that for at least a couple of decades after 1943 was the centre of every imaginable and unimaginable clandestine activity. It was now more difficult to see in Naples what had appeared in a photograph taken in the seventies, and used by de Crescenza to illustrate his book, of a man lying on a flight of steps apparently in the depths of winter with an empty begging bowl beside him and a notice which read, '*Ridotto in questo condizione di mio cognato*' ('Reduced to this condition by my brother-in-law').

But although there were now more bag-snatchers, more pick-pockets, more people ready to beat you up if for no better reason than to give you something to remember them by, as there were almost everywhere else in the Mediterranean lands, or Europe, or the entire world for that matter, there seemed to be slightly less *truf-feria*, petty swindling. It was now less certain that, having made some purchase in the Mercato della Duchesca, or in the street, in the Forcella, for instance, and having had it parcelled up, you would find on opening it up later that something of the same size and weight had been substituted for it, although I was sold a guide book to Pompeii, sealed in plastic, which turned out to be nothing more than the cover with blank pages inside.

On the other hand, to be more or less sure of keeping what money you had about you, it was now doubly necessary either to wear a money belt or carry it inside one's shoes and, even then, you could not be absolutely sure that someone might not knock you down and take them from you, or even cut off your feet if necessary in order to get at it. The city, too, seemed to have lost some of the skills that for so long after the war had made it one of the great world centres of the imitative arts. Perhaps whatever skill we had possessed in searching out these artefacts had deserted us, but we now experienced difficulty in locating facsimiles of Vuitton trunks, or bottles purporting to contain ten-year-old Glen Grant, Fernet

Branca* that back in 1963 had existed in almost too great abundance, considering how slow anyone's individual intake is of this particular product, Hermès' Calèche or Chanel Number 5.

Nothing was ever wasted among the Neapolitan poor and to some extent this is still true today. There used to be and perhaps still are whole families devoted to the reanimation of second-hand clothes. These *rianimatori* used to hang the garments in closed rooms in which bowls of boiling water were placed which gave off a dense steam which raised the nap of the material. If the garment had a moth hole or a cigarette burn in it, fluff was scraped from the inside of the seams with a razor blade and stuck over the hole with transparent glue.

Until recently there were *solchanelli*, mobile shoe repairers. A *solchanello* carried the tools of his trade in a basket with a board on top which he used as a seat on which he could squat down anywhere and begin work. Uttering a strange cry, '*Chià-è! Chià-è!*', to attract attention he would sometimes latch on to some unfortunate person with a hole in one of his shoes or a sole coming off and follow him, sometimes for miles, all the while reminding the victim of the defect in an insistent monotone until whoever it was, unable to stand it any more, sank down in despair on the nearest doorstep and allowed the *solchanello* to carry out the repair.

In Naples the loss of one of a pair of shoes does not necessarily mean that the other will not have a long and useful life ahead of it, even if it is not sold to some unfortunate person with only one leg. It is still possible to find what are known as *scarpe scompagnate*, unaccompanied shoes, in the great market for new and second-hand shoes which, weather permitting, takes place every Monday and Friday in Corso Malta, an interminable, dead-straight street that runs northwards from the Carcere Giudizario on Via Nuova Poggioreale to Doganella, at the foot of the hill where the cemeteries begin.

Few people, even Napoletani, buy one shoe. Some, however, can be persuaded to buy two shoes which do not match. Luccano de Crescenza recorded a conversation in dialect between a potential buyer of two odd shoes and a vendor of *scarpe scompagnate* which went more or less as follows:

'But these shoes are different, one from the other!'

---

* It is said that in one year, 1978, 500,000 bottles of imitation Fernet Branca were seized by the customs at Naples alone.

'*Nosignuri, so tale e quale* – they are exactly alike!'

'Well, they look different to me.'

'And what does it matter if they look different? That's only when you're standing still. Once you start walking they will look exactly the same – *tale e quale*. Let me tell you about shoes. What do they do, shoes? They walk. And when they walk one goes in front and the other goes behind, like this. In this way no one can know that they are not *tale e quale*.'

'But that means I can never stop walking.'

'How does it mean you can't ever stop walking? All you have to do when you stop is to rest one shoe on top of the other.'

Sometimes in Naples one felt that one was in a city on the Near Eastern or North African shores of the Mediterranean, with Castel Sant' Angelo its kasbah or Capodimonte its seraglio, because in it the makers and vendors of particular kinds of merchandise tend to come together and occupy whole reaches of streets and alleys as they do in bazaars and souks in Muslim countries, so that Via Duomo becomes the street of the wedding dresses and the appropriately named Via dell' Annunziata the one in which newly arrived Neapolitans are fitted out with cribs and baby carriages.

Uphill from Spaccanapoli there is a narrow alley which runs up alongside the church of San Gregorio Armeno, which was once a convent of Benedictine nuns and has a famous cloister which was given the rococo treatment at a time in the first part of the eighteenth century when the viceroys of Naples were no longer Spanish but Austrian – Austria having been given Naples and Sardinia in 1713 by the Treaty of Utrecht which had brought to an end the War of the Spanish Succession – viceroys who would themselves soon cease to exist, the last one being ejected by the young Charles of Bourbon in 1734.

In this alley are to be found some of the men and women who model and bake and paint and dress the miniature terracotta figures, sometimes finding and using ancient materials to do so, and painting the back-cloths, the *fondali*, for the *presepi*. At Christmas the whole of this little alley is illuminated and decorated with hundreds of these figures.

Amongst the most remarkable of the *presepi* that have survived wars and earthquakes and all the other evils to which Naples and the Neapolitans have been subjected, are those in the Certosa di San Martino, the former Carthusian Monastery on the hill below the Castel Sant'Elmo, now a museum.

Among the first to inspire the construction of these great eighteenth-century set pieces was a Dominican, Father Rocco, the famous preacher and missionary to the poor of Naples, who was afraid of no one, rich or poor, and saw this as a way to bring the mystery of the nativity to the people of the city. He was also responsible for the setting up of shrines at street corners in the city. This was in the 1750s, and until 1806 the lamps and candles lit at these shrines were the sole source of illumination in the streets of the city.

It was Father Rocco who inspired Charles to order the building of the enormous Albergo dei Poveri – it has a facade nearly 400 yards long – for the poor to live in, and it was he, too, having set up a *presepio* in a grotto in the park at Capodimonte, who imbued the King with enthusiasm for what was to become a life-long passion. From that time onwards, Charles and his family reserved a part of each afternoon when he was in residence to working on one of his great *presepi*, designing and modelling the settings, while his wife and daughters chose materials and sewed and embroidered the costumes. In doing this he set a fashion. One of these *presepi* in the Certosa, which depicts the arrival of the Magi, is made up of 180 lay figures, 42 angels, 29 animals and 330 *finimenti* – the jewellery, the musical and agricultural instruments, the ruins, the grottoes, the trees and the temples, the fruit and vegetables, the strings of sausages. The Three Kings, their gold-embroidered turbans encrusted with pearls, wearing silk pelisses lined with fur, have arrived at the scene of the Nativity with a great concourse of followers, Asiatic and African, and are looking down at the Child who is lying on a bed of straw at the foot of what remains of a temple with Corinthian columns and a ruined archway. A band of blackamoors and Turks, ringing bells, blowing into strange wind instruments, playing harps and cymbals and beating drums and blowing on trumpets, is still winding down the hill to the scene of the Nativity through a pass in the mountains, together with the pack animals. The camels which have carried the caskets containing the gifts of gold and myrrh and frankincense on their long journey have already arrived, while others are waiting to be unloaded; and there is a dwarf leading two monkeys on chains dressed in a miniature version of what the other noblemen are wearing, a coat of wild silk embroidered with precious stones and lined with fur and with a turban, like theirs, swathed in pearls, but without the *chibouques*, the tobacco pipes, some of them carry in their belts, and the *yataghans*, the curved Turkish swords.

To the right the scene is more mundane. There is a market place full of miniature facsimiles of fruit and vegetables and meat that are so lifelike that one instinctively reaches out to touch them. The modelling and painting of these fruits and vegetables was a specialized art, the work perhaps of Giuseppe di Luca, one of the great masters of it, but we shall never know.

And there is *la Taverna*, the inn with a band of musicians playing outside it, men of a sort you can see today in the streets of Forcella and Spaccanapoli or among the *contrabbandieri* of Mergellina, apparently oblivious to the great events taking place only a few yards away, above which a band of angels in swirling draperies with attendant *putti* are suspended by almost invisible cords in a pale blue heaven.

But we, with our noses pressed against the glass which separates us from these scenes, like children in a museum, can hear in the imagination as well as see everything that is going on because of the genius of those mostly unremembered men and women who constructed these scenes two hundred or more years ago: the clashing of the cymbals, the beating of the drums, the squeaking of the violin outside the tavern, the roaring of the camels, the neighing of the horses, one of which is frightened and is rearing on its hind legs, the sound of the women gossiping in the market place, the beating of the angels' wings.

Nothing much had changed either in the realms of death. It was still just as easy to lay on a horse-drawn funeral in Naples as it had been back in the early sixties. Hearses drawn by eight, ten or even twelve horses running in pairs and driven by a single *cocchiero*, coachman, were still available to convey the Neapolitans, or anyone else who fancied it, on their last journey to one of the vast cities of the dead on the eastern outskirts. In fact the same firm, Bellomunno, still had a monopoly of this sort of funeral. There are large numbers of Bellomunnos in the Naples telephone book, all devoted to what are called *Pompe Funebri*, Funeral Pomps, otherwise the undertaking business, all of them belonging to the same clan, some of them having splintered off to form their own set-ups. The only branch of Bellomunno not listed is the horse-drawn section, and its stables off the Via Don Bosco, in a not-easy-to-be-found street called the Rampe del Campo, the Ramps of the Fields, are ex-directory.

Via Don Bosco is a long, long street, straight at first, then winding and partly cobbled in its later, mountain sections, which begins in Piazza Carlo III opposite the Albergo dei Poveri, begun by Charles' architect Ferdinando Fuga in 1751 but never completed. It then runs up through Doganella under an enormous concrete fly-over which joins Via Malta, on which the shoe market is held, to the Tangenziale, the Naples Ring Road. Via Don Bosco passes on its way the Cimitero Vecchio, the Old Cemetery, at the foot of the hill, the Cimitero Santa Maria del Pianto (of the Crying), and the sad-looking Protestant Cemetery, eventually reaching the square called Largo Santa Maria del Pianto. From here one road leads to Capodichino Airport; another, the Via del Riposo, to the Cimitero della Pietà, in which the poor are buried; and a third, Via Santa Maria del Riposo, to one of the principal entrances to the two biggest cemeteries, the Cimitero Monumentale and the Cimitero Nuovo, in both of which the dead are dried out in the tufa soil for eighteen months before being filed away in niches on an upper floor.

It is a lugubrious part of Naples at any time and certainly not one in which to linger unaccompanied (you can get knocked on the nut just as easily in a Neapolitan cemetery as anywhere else in Naples), but one in which on almost any day in working hours, providing that business is normal, anyone interested in horses and/or horse-drawn funerals can see at least one horse-drawn hearse making its way up the long ascent to one or other of these resting places. Those ghouls who enjoy any sort of funeral or are simply interested in horseless carriages can see an almost endless procession of motor hearses of various degrees of melancholy splendour all on the same course.

There are few places in the world, now that the Ancient Egyptian and the Imperial Chinese dynasties are no more, apart from Bali, where death is celebrated in such a memorably conspicuous fashion.

Until long after the last war (and even now Bellomunno employees are not prepared to take an oath that such an operation could not still be organized out in the sticks) it was possible to assemble a cast of hundreds, even thousands, of professional mourners to follow the hearse, provided that those who were left alive had inherited sufficient financial clout to pay them: squads of orphans, or if not real orphans simulated ones whose parents were only too happy for them to appear as orphans for the occasion, all of them, real or simulated, dressed in deepest black. Provided there was sufficient inducement, whole bevies of nuns, as well as hosts of professional wailing women, could be made instantly available.

Up to 1914, and possibly even later, the corpse was accompanied by strangely dressed hooded members of the deceased's *Fratria*, the Brotherhood to which so many Neapolitans then belonged. At a yet earlier date, the hearse was also accompanied by a body of poor men wearing black stove-pipe hats, grey uniforms over their rags and carrying black banners with the initials of the deceased person embroidered on them, all chanting a doleful litany which began:

> *Noi sarem come voi sete . . .*
> We shall be as you are . . .

This grey company of death, as one Neapolitan described them, were the *Poveri*, the Poor of the Hospice of San Gennaro, all of them penniless, many of them ex-soldiers who had fought as mercenaries in various parts of the world. They lived, when not accompanying funerals, in the Ospizio di San Gennaro dei Poveri, now a psychiatric hospital, which was founded in the seventeenth century among the Christian catacombs, which they used to show to visitors along with the church next door, which was built on the site of a chapel in which the head of San Gennaro* was at one time preserved after his martyrdom in AD 305 at Pozzuoli.

We set off for the Bellomunno horse-drawn branch on the Rampe del Campo in rain that became progressively heavier while we waited for a bus to take us there.

Travelling up Via Don Bosco, having passed Charles's enormous workhouse, was more like being in the Mile End Road on a wet December afternoon than twelve o'clock in Naples, in August. It was not therefore surprising that we missed the whistle stop for the Rampe del Campo and found ourselves at the beginning of the long haul up to the cemetery plateau, and by the time I realized the mistake and had managed to struggle forward through the bus

---

* San Gennaro's blood is first said to have liquefied in the hands of the sainted Bishop Severus on the occasion when the body was first translated from Pozzuoli to Naples at the time of Constantine. The first documented liquefaction took place in the Abbey of Montevergine on 17 August 1389.

The miracle repeats itself three times a year: on the first Saturday in May, when the two phials are taken in procession to the great, bare convent church of Santa Chiara in Spaccanapoli, and on 19 September and 16 December in the Cappella del Tesoro of the Cathedral, on all three occasions before enormous audiences.

shouting the equivalent in Italian of 'Here, I say . . .' to the driver and had persuaded him to make an unscheduled stop, we were just coming up to the concrete fly-over.

He did stop, under the fly-over, making it abundantly clear that he thought we must be a couple of tomb robbers, wanting to get down in a place that has very little else to offer in the way of diversion, even in fine weather, except a visit to the Cimitero Vecchio.

But there, underneath the fly-over, with ten horses, and every-one else involved taking a breather before attacking the long *salita*, was one of Bellomunno's huge, jet black, baroque hearses with a jet black coffin inside behind expanses of glittering plate glass, a top-hatted, long-black-coated coachman on the box, and a pair of uniformed mutes doubling as grooms holding the two lead horses' heads with, behind them, four pairs of magnificent, jet black Dutch horses, like the leaders all tossing their heads and all steaming like mad. And behind the hearse a long line of black motor cars, containing the supporters.

'What happened to the old *cocchiero*?' Wanda asked the coach-man on the box high overhead who was about twenty-five and as wet as we were. 'He was a very kind man. The last time we came to the Rampe del Campo was in a taxi and he sent us back to Naples in one of your motor hearses to save us the fare.'

'He died in 1973,' he said. 'They gave him a fine funeral. And you, too, will soon be dead if you don't change your clothes,' looking down on us where we stood in a pair of puddles. 'At the top of the *salita*,' he went on pointing up the hill, 'in Largo Santa Maria, beyond the Cemetery of Santa Maria, there is a pizzeria called the Loggia del Paradiso (Verandah of Paradise) which overlooks it. That is the cemetery we are bound for. Go to the Loggia and tell them I sent you. They will dry your clothes by the oven and lend you some while you're eating. The hearse which will take this coffin down into the cemetery from the gates is a motor one. I can't get into it with ten horses. After the funeral the driver and his men will go to the Loggia to have their lunch, and when they go back to the city, which will be about two o'clock, I will ask them to take you with them and drop you off in Piazza Garibaldi.'

From the automobiles, which were as black as the hearse itself and crammed with mourners, the women heavily veiled, came the sounds of groans and sobbing. The *cocchiero* winked and waved his whip with a graceful gesture, comprehending everything in and out of sight: the pouring rain, the appalling, thundering traffic, the fearful landscape, the keening women and the corpse high overhead behind him.

'*Com'é bella Napoli!*' he said.

Then he shouted to the men holding the heads of the leaders; they let them go and they were off, their hooves skidding a bit on the cobbles, eventually breaking into a trot with the grooms hanging on behind the hearse, out into the pouring rain up towards the Cemetery of Santa Maria del Pianto.

Warm and dry and full of lunch on the way back to Piazza Garibaldi in the Bellomunno motor hearse, we caught up on what had been happening to the old firm in the course of our twenty years' absence.

They no longer had the white horse-drawn hearse used for children, or the small, black, two-horse one in their stables at the Rampe del Campo; but they still had two of the big ones, one of which – the twin of the one we had seen that morning – was undergoing extensive repairs and redecoration which would take many months to complete. This work of reconstruction was being carried out, part time, by a skilled body-worker from Alfa-Romeo, called Vincenzo di Luca, a man known in the horse-drawn carriage trade as 'a builder and varnisher'. His family had carried on these trades for generations, and he was one of the last, if not the last, to practise them in Naples – it was fortunate for Bellomunno that he was still a youngish man. His son, who was about eighteen or nineteen, although capable of doing this work and at present assisting his father, preferred to look after the horses in the stables at the Rampe del Campo and this was what he was now doing. To build a new hearse of this kind would take three and a half years, and it was probable that Bellomunno would eventually decide to do so. The cost of building such a vehicle would be prodigious. It would involve the use of various sorts of wood, all of which would have to be properly seasoned, iron, steel, brass, leather, cloth, glass etc., and the services of one or two craftsmen such as di Luca who would now have to carry out a wide variety of works which would previously have been carried out by a number of specialized craftsmen: body-makers who built the upper parts, carriage-makers who constructed and put together all the underparts, wheelwrights, joiners, fitters, trimmers, blacksmiths, painters and polishers. Such a hearse might be given up to twenty separate coats of paint and varnish. One of the great difficulties in the 1980s was to find suitable rubber to make the solid tyres.

In 1983 a horse-drawn funeral employing ten horses cost between 2,000,000 and 3,500,000 lire. The last twelve-horse funeral Bellomunno had organized had been that of Achille Laura, a shipowner who had also been mayor of Naples, earlier that year. He was what is known as a *pezzo grosso*, literally a big piece, an important man with various far-reaching affiliations; everyone who was anyone and almost everyone who was no one turned out for his funeral, for fear that his absence might be noted. A funeral of this sort could well have cost 7,000,000 lire.

Such funerals are particularly popular with senior members of the Camorra, just as Camorra weddings – at which diamond-studded shirts are often worn by male guests – are notable for conspicuous consumption. Whether horse-drawn or motorized, they are not very popular with those Neapolitan undertakers who are called on to organize them. The last time Bellomunno put in a bill to the family of a deceased Camorrista for a horse-drawn funeral – whose funeral they didn't say – instead of receiving a cheque through the post, they got a bomb through the counting-house window.

An Evening in Venice

During the autumn following our Neapolitan excursion we laid what plans we could for our clockwise journey round the Mediterranean, which, thanks to Wanda telling me to get on with it and plunging me into Naples instead of going off and sitting on top of the Rock of Gibraltar and feeling imperial, had started before it was intended to.

That winter we set off for Chioggia, a fishing port at the southern end of the Venetian Lagoon, about twenty miles south of Venice, a place that is picturesque enough in summer but in winter can look a bit pinched and poverty-stricken and has extremely draughty side-streets. It is also noted for having inhabitants who are extremely difficult for an outsider ever to get to know. Here, worn down by the efforts of trying to hire a boat for a private trip to Venice at a price we could afford from monoglot Chioggiotti who see quite enough of polyglot visitors such as ourselves for eight months of the year without being pestered by them during the other four, we decided to leave their austere but strangely attractive city – in which by far the jolliest place is the fish market – by public transport. In summer we could have gone the whole way by steamer, but because this was the dead season there was no direct service and we would have to travel first by boat across the Porto di Chioggia, the southernmost of the entrances to e Lagoon, to the Litorale di Pellestrina, one of the three elonga , offshore dunes which together form the Venetian Lagoon an at the same time protect it from the fury of the Adriatic, and from there take a No. 11 bus along the Litorale to Porto di Malamocco, the entrance to the Lagoon which now takes all the biggest ships, where it is driven on to a ferry and taken across to the Litorale di Lido to continue its journey to Piazzale Santa Maria Elisabetta, where one can take a No. 11 *vaporetto* across the Lagoon to Venice. Nothing to it, really.

Although we had failed in our dealings with the Chioggiotti, it would have been easier, if we had been really pushed, to do a deal with them than with the Veneziani, who have a tariff for everything and with whom there is no possibility of bargaining, something a lot of other representatives of Christendom discovered back at the time of the Fourth Crusade on their way to the Holy Land.

At the last moment before the Venetian fleet, which the Crusaders had booked in 1202 to take them to the scene of the action, was due to sail with them on board, from their assembly point on the Litorale di Lido, some of their commanders found themselves unable to meet their commitments to the *Veneziani* who, although there were fewer Crusaders than had been originally contracted for, still insisted on being paid, according to the tariff, the full passage money for those who had not turned up.

This deadlock was only resolved when the Doge Enrico Dandolo, who in spite of being nearly ninety and almost blind was leading the expedition in person, made a deal with their leaders whereby the Venetians would forgo part of the payment in exchange for help while en route in re-taking Zara, one of their ports on the Adriatic, which had gone over to the Hungarians.

But even this was not enough for the Venetians. Once they had reduced this Christian city with the aid of the Crusaders, a campaign that was punished by the Pope excommunicating all the Venetians and all the Crusaders taking part, the Doge then imposed a further condition: that the Crusaders should help the Venetians to storm yet another stronghold of Christendom, the Greek Byzantine city of Constantinople, in order, ostensibly, to restore the Emperor, who had been deposed, but in fact to revenge the death of thousands of Venetians who had been slaughtered there by the Greeks ten years previously, and to make Venice the most influential power in the eastern Mediterranean. The Doge himself led the combined forces against the city in April 1204, breaching the seaward walls and taking it by storm, virtually destroying it and gathering loot of a magnificence that was to make Venice the envy of the world. It also made her – personified by the Doge, who stayed on and eventually died and was buried there – mistress of three-eighths of what was now to become a Latinized city, as well as of Durazzo, on what are now the Albanian shores of the Adriatic, Lacedaemon, otherwise Sparta, the Greek islands of the Cyclades and Sporades, and Crete. The other five-eighths of the city became the property of Count Baldwin, who was crowned as Latin Emperor of the East in what had now become, as Santa Sofia, a Roman Catholic cathedral, as did half the Byzantine territory which lay outside the walls. The other half was given to various Crusader knights, who held it as vassals. Altogether, for the Venetians, it had been a famous victory.

By the time we sailed from Chioggia, the Lagoon, the Litorali, and the Adriatic out beyond them were shrouded in freezing fog, and when we got down at the boat terminus on the Litorale di Pellestrina, which is just opposite the cemetery, and decided to miss the bus connection and take a later one in order to see the *murazzi*, the sea walls, it was with some regret that we watched its rear lights disappearing into the fog.

The houses in Pellestrina, clustered about a big white church, were a series of rectangles painted in ox-blood, vivid blues and greens and soft greys that rendered them almost invisible in the fog. Closely shuttered against it, as they were, only the drifts of smoke from the strange, tall Venetian chimneys showed that they were inhabited.

Walking amongst them we came to the *murazzi*, on the seaward side of the Litorale. They had been conceived by a cosmographer, Father Vincenzo Coronelli, in 1716, and work was finally begun on them in 1744 under the direction of Bernardino Zendrini, a mathematician. It took thirty-eight years to complete them at a cost of forty million Venetian gold ducats, and they were the last major works undertaken by the *Magistrati delle Acque*, the Magistrates of the Waters, who were responsible for building and maintaining the defences of the Lagoon and the city against the Adriatic, before the shameful extinction of this Republic of the Sea by Napoleon in 1797. They replaced previous defences which consisted of wooden palisades that had to be renewed every six years, long groynes extending seawards and musk-smelling tamarisk planted to give stability to what was mostly sand, defences that each winter had been breached and destroyed with monotonous regularity by the sirocco storms. More than 14 feet thick at the base, two and a half miles long, and nearly 20 feet high, they are built of gleaming white blocks of marble, some of them more than 6 feet long and a yard and a half wide, all brought from Istria on the Yugoslavian side of the Adriatic in barges, the same stone used to build so many of the churches in Venice and the Lagoon. Now, ghostly in the fog, they stretched away into it on either side, the only sound the Adriatic sucking at their outer defences, an enormous breakwater of heaped-up boulders.

Although the *murazzi* are the most impressive to the eye of all the works carried out by the *Magistrati* in and around the Lagoon, equally important was what they did to the rivers. It was they who were responsible for the death of the Po di Tramontana. Until the sixteenth century the mouth of the river was directed towards the Valle dei Sette Morti, an area of the Venetian Lagoon north of Chioggia, which the river had turned into an area of *laguna morta*, dead lagoon, only inundated at high tides. They decided, with the presence of mind and self-interest which had always to their rivals been one of the Republic's least lovable characteristics, to direct the river southwards. In five years thousands of labourers cut a channel, called the Sacca di Goro, from the Po Grande into a bay of the Adriatic east of Pomposa, where the great Benedictine abbey still stands in which Guido d'Arezzo invented the musical scale. By this boldly conceived piece of hydraulic engineering the Po di Tramontana ceased to exist, Venice was preserved and the results for the Po Valley and the Delta were disastrous. The silting process was accelerated and, although the area of the Delta increased nearly three times in the space of 220 years, the inundations increased and no one, except the Venetians, was better off.

But in spite of their success in turning away from the southern part of the Lagoon and finally destroying the Po di Tramontana, they were still subject to the recurrent nightmare that the same silting-up process might happen further north in the part of the Lagoon in which the city stood and deprive it of the isolation on which it depended for at least part of its power and importance; it might also block the vital channels to the sea.

The Republic had before it the awful examples of other great ports in the Mediterranean, long since silted up and left far from the sea, all of which we were subsequently to visit in the course of our travels: Pergamum, Ephesus, Miletus, Patara, the high and dry port of Xanthus in Lycia, in western Asia Minor. And much nearer home they had the equally awful example of Ravenna, a former lagoon city, dependent for its continued existence on tidal movements, acquired by them but only long after it was high and dry, the only memorial to its former Byzantine greatness five splendid churches in the wilderness. And there was also Ferrara, founded on the right bank of the Po in AD 450 by refugees from Attila and his Huns, left equally high and dry.

In the seventeenth century the *Magistrati* re-routed a number of other rivers so that instead of flowing into their lagoon, they by-passed it completely and flowed into the sea. When the Venetians had finished this colossal work, the Brenta, which originally came out into the Lagoon behind Venice, entered the Adriatic south of Chioggia; the Sile, a very pretty little river which, nevertheless, was doing enormous damage to the Lagoon by pouring silt into it north of the city, was directed into a canal which carried it into what until then had been the bed of the Piave and into the sea near Jesolo; while the Piave itself was turned into the bed of the next river to the north of it, the Livenza.

Later that afternoon we descended from the No. 11 bus on the Litorale di Lido and groped our way through the fog to a dark, deserted waterfront behind the Casino, which faced the Lagoon. It is difficult to write feelingly about something you can't see, and the fog that shrouded the Lagoon was impenetrable. In fact we could hear more than we could see of it: the melancholy crying of gulls, the tolling of a bell mounted on a buoy moored out in one of the channels, the noise of boat engines and, occasionally, angry cries as helmsmen, set on collision courses, recorded near misses. Altogether, with the whole of the Mediterranean to choose from, it was a hell of a place to end up in on such a day. We might just as well have been on the Mersey, for all the *genius loci* I was able to sop up, and this made me think of home, a hot bath and a couple of slugs of Glenmorangie.

'You're in trouble, author,' said Wanda, my companion in life's race, near the mark as always, sensing that I felt like emigrating back to Britain, 'if you can't see what you're looking at.'

As she said this, as if to show that she wasn't always right, the fog lifted, not everywhere, not over Venice itself which remained cocooned in it, but here and there, and for a few moments that didn't even add up to minutes we found ourselves looking down long corridors of vapour illuminated by an eerie yellow light that must have been the last of the setting sun, down which one had distant prospects of mud banks uncovered by the tide, with laby-rinths of channels running through them, and one or two of the almost innumerable islands of the Lagoon which supported until quite recently – and some still support – monasteries, nunneries, forts, miniature versions of Venice, a cemetery, and the lonely enclosure to which, once every ten years when it begins to fill up, bones are taken; fishing settlements, lodges used by the wild-fowlers who in winter wait in barrels sunk in the Lagoon for the dawn and dusk flights, quarantine stations, lighthouses, hospitals, lunatic asylums, prisons, barracks, magazines that, when they were full of gunpowder, had a tendency to go up in the air, taking their custodians with them, deserted factories, old people's homes, pri-vate houses, market gardens, vineyards, and some that were just open expanses that a farmer might visit once or twice a year to cut the hay. The channels among them were marked by long lines of *bricole*, wooden piles either driven into the bottom with their heads pressed together, as if they were lovers meeting in a lagoon, or else in clusters of three or four, also with their heads pressed together as if they were conspirators discussing some dark secret. Some of the more important channels had lights on the *bricole*. Some that were only navigable by the smallest sorts of craft, such as gondolas and boats called *sandali*, were indicated by lines of saplings.

There was another, equally momentary vista of part of one of the industrial zones that had been created by filling in vast areas of the northern part of the Lagoon and its mud flats, a huge, night-mare, end-of-the-world place without houses or permanent inhabi-tants, made up of oil refineries, chemical, fertilizer, plastic, steel, light alloy, coke, gas and innumerable other plants all belching dense smoke and residual gases into the sky and effluents into the Lagoon, so various and awful that collectively they made up a brew that even to a layman sounded as if it had been devised by a crew of mad scientists intent on destroying the human race, which in effect is what they are doing. Then the fog closed in again, more impenetr-able than ever now that the sun was almost gone.

According to the tide table I had bought that morning in Chioggia it was now just after low water at Porto di Lido, what had been the principal entrance to the Lagoon and to Venice when it was commonplace to see 60,000-ton tankers wandering about in St

Mark's Basin. This was until they dredged the deep-water channel from Porto Malamocco to Marghera, using the material brought up from the bottom as infilling for the Third Industrial Zone. About now the flood would be beginning to run through Porto di Lido, Porto di Malamocco, and also through Porto di Chioggia, the three entrances that the Magistrates of the Waters had left open centuries ago, having sealed off the others after years of trial and error, by doing so preserving a delicate balance which allowed Venice to function both as a city and a great seaport. Now, for six hours, the tide would flow into the Lagoon, which is not what it appears to be – a single simple expanse of water – but is made up of three distinct basins, each separated one from the other by watersheds known as the *spartiacque*, spreading through its main arteries and myriad veins, channels so small that no chart shows them, and scouring and filling the canals of the city itself. Then, at the end of the sixth hour, when it was at the full, the tide would begin to run out, loaded with the effluent of the industrial zones, which sometimes includes dangerous quantities of ammonia and its by-products of oxidation, phenol, cyanide, sulphur, chlorine, naphtha, as well as oil from passing ships and boats, all the liquid sewage of Venice, the peculiarly filthy filth of a city entirely without drains, a large part of the solid ordure produced by its inhabitants, and at least a part of that produced by Mestre and Marghera, together with vast quantities of insoluble domestic detergent. One of the more awful sights in the Lagoon used to be a mud bank at Marghera with mountains of ordure rising from it, preserved, presumably for all eternity, or until they burst, in plastic bags. There they waited for an exceptionally high water, an *acqua alta*, to distribute them over other distant parts of the Lagoon, with thousands of gulls, apparently unable to penetrate them with their beaks, hanging frustratedly over them. All because a large incineration plant, built in the Second Industrial Zone, failed to work.

Twenty years ago the only fish of any size that was indigenous to the Lagoon and which reproduced itself in it was something called the Gò (*Gobius ophocephalus*), which nested in the mud on the edge of the deep canals. All the others were caught in the open sea and penned in the *valli* at the northern and south-western ends of the Lagoon. Mussels were also cultivated. Whether it is safe to eat any of these fish today must be questionable. There is no need any more for the Commune to display the warning against swimming on the door of the crumbling open-air swimming place on the

Zattere, the long waterfront in Venice facing the Giudecca Canal. It is only too obvious.

The Adriatic performs this operation of filling and emptying the Lagoon four times every twenty-four hours over an area that used to be roughly thirty-five miles long and up to eight miles wide, but is now much less because of infilling and the construction of new *valli*. That is except during period of what Venetians call *la Colma* or *l'acqua alta*, high water.

Even though the moon was nearly full there would be no *acqua alta* on this particular night. *Acqua alta* is not dependent on the tide itself being exceptionally high, or even high. It occurs when the barometric pressure falls sufficiently low to allow the level of the Adriatic to rise on what is a very low coastline, and when the strong, warm, south-westerly sirocco blows up it. If the barometric pressure is low enough and the sirocco is strong enough at the time when the ebb is beginning in the Lagoon, the water is penned inside it, unable to get out, and when the next tide begins to press in through the three entrances, the *Porti*, and is added to the high water already there, the natural divisions between the three basins of the Lagoon, the *spartiacque*, cease to exist and Venice and many other islands, inhabited and uninhabited, are flooded. Other factors can make the *acqua alta* even higher – heavy rain, a full moon, something called the *seiche*, the turning of the Adriatic on an imaginary pivot – but the sirocco and a low barometer are the two indispensable conditions.

This is not a new phenomenon. The records of the *acqua alta* from the thirteenth century onwards are full of entries such as 'the water rose to the height of a man in the streets' (on 23 September 1240); 'the water rose from eight o'clock until midday. Many were drowned inside their houses or died of cold' (in December 1280); 'roaring horribly the sea rose up towards the sky, causing a terrible fear . . . and with such force that it broke the Lido in several places' (in December 1600).

In 1825, the *murazzi*, neglected since the fall of the Republic in 1797, were breached during an enormous storm, but were made good again. On a day in 1967, the first year in which accurate measurements were kept, the water rose five feet above the average sea level. In the forty-seven years between 1867 and 1914, only seven exceptionally high waters, those more than three and a half feet above the normal level, submerged the city; but in the fifty years between 1917 and 1967 Venice sank beneath the waves more than forty times, an extraordinary increase, so that looking at a vertical graph of these high waters during the period from 1867 to 1967 the lines representing them appear as eight more or less isolated trees between 1867 and 1920, some thick clumps in the thirties, late forties and early fifties, and a dense, soaring forest in the late fifties and sixties. The longest line of all is the one showing the *acqua alta* of 4 November 1966.

During the night of 3–4 November, the sirocco blew Force 8, the barometer fell to around 750 mm, there was continual heavy rain and waves twelve feet high roared in over the Litorali, submerging Cavallino, the northernmost one, smashing the elegant bathing establishments on the Lido and hurling aside the outerworks of the *murazzi* on Pellestrina, the great boulders piled fifteen feet high, then breaching, in ten different places, the walls themselves, composed of huge blocks of marble six feet long, but on which no proper repair work had been done for more than thirty years. This time the water at Venice rose six and a half feet above the average sea level, and the result was spectacular.

It poured under the 450 or so bridges (scarcely any Venetians, let alone outsiders, agree about the number of bridges in the city, or any other of the following figures), overflowing the 177 – some say 150 – canals, the *rii*, 46 of which are branches off the Canalazzo, the Grand Canal, inundating the 117, or 122, or whatever number of shoals or islands on which the city is said to be built, the 15,000 houses in which large numbers of people were living on the ground floors in the six *sestieri*, or wards, into which it is divided, and the majority of the 107 churches, of which 80 were still in use. It also inundated 3000 miles of streets and alleys, the various open spaces, the *campi*, so called because they were once expanses of grass, the *campielli* and the *piazzette*, not to speak of the only Piazza, St Mark's, with an unimaginably vile compound of all the various effluents mentioned previously in connection with the Lagoon. To which was added diesel oil and gas oil which had escaped from the storage tanks, leaving the city without electric light, means of cooking or heating, or any communication with the outside world, not to speak of the awful, immense, much of it irreparable, damage done to innumerable works of art.

The *acqua alta* persisted for more than twenty hours. The most dangerous moment came at six in the evening, when the water reached the highest level ever recorded. This was the moment that the Venetians call the *acqua morta*, when it should begin to go down but doesn't. By this time the glass was down to 744 mm and if at this moment a fresh impulse had been given to the waters by the sirocco, forcing it to yet higher levels, Venice might well have collapsed. As it was, a miracle occurred. The wind changed. It began to blow from the south-west, a wind the people of Venice and the Lagoon call the *vento Garbin*, and by nine o'clock that night the waters began to fall and the city was saved, at least for the time being.

Long before we stepped ashore from the steamer on to Riva degli Schiavoni, the great expanse of marble quay off which Slavs from the Dalmatian coast used to moor their vessels in St Mark's Basin, darkness had added itself to the fog, creating the sort of conditions that even Jack the Ripper would have found a bit thick for his work down in nineteenth-century Whitechapel.

The fog dissipated what had seemed a romantic possibility when we left Chioggia but now seemed a crazy dream, that we might sweep into Venice from the Lido on the No. 11 steamer up the Canale di San Marco and see the domes and campanili of San Giorgio Maggiore and Santa Maria della Salute not as we had seen them once, coming in from the sea in the heat of the day, liquefying in the mirage, then reconstituting themselves again, something that would be impossible at this season, but sharply silhouetted, appearing larger than life, against the afterglow of what could equally well be a winter or summer sunset, with what would be equally black gondolas bobbing on the wine-coloured waters in the foreground. This was a spectacle we had enjoyed often, usually in summer, coming back after a long afternoon by the lifeless waters of the Lido with sand between our toes and stupefied with sun, our only preoccupation whether we would be able to extract enough hot water from the erratic hot water system in our equally decrepit hotel to allow us to share a shallow bath; and whether we could find another place to eat, in addition to the few we already knew, which was not infested with, although we hated to admit it, people like ourselves, fellow visitors to Venice who on any day in the high season, July and August, probably outnumber the inhabitants.

Never at the best of times a very substantial-looking city – even the largest buildings having something impermanent about them, due perhaps to the fact that they have not only risen from the water but, however imperceptibly to the human eye, are now in the process of sinking back into it – on this particular evening the fog had succeeded in doing what the mirage could only accomplish for a matter of moments – caused it, apart from its lights, to disappear from view almost completely.

Disembarking from the steamer, we turned left on Riva degli Schiavoni, passing the entrances to the narrow *calli* which lead off from it, Calle delle Rasse, where the Serbian material used for furnishing the interiors of the *felzi*, the now largely extinct cabins of the closed gondolas, used to be sold, and Calle Albanesi, the Street of the Albanians, down which some of our fellow passengers had already vanished. While walking along the Riva we just missed falling into what is, because it is spanned by the Bridge of Sighs, the best known and most photographed canal in Venice after the Grand Canal, the Rio Palazzo. This would have been a bore because besides contracting pneumonia (our luggage was already at the railway station), if we had inadvertently drunk any of it we would have had to rush off to the Ospedale Civile, San Giovanni e Paolo, in order to have pumped out of us a mixture the smallest ingredient of which was water. Then we crossed the Rio by the Ponte di Paglia, passing on our right hand the Palazzo delle Prigioni, from which the magistrates known as the *Signori di Notte al Criminale* used to look out at night for evil-doers, *malviventi*, arrest and try them, and if they were sufficiently low and common and criminal, sentence them to the *Pozzi*, otherwise the Wells, the cells at the lowest level of the *Prigioni*, which were reserved for the worst sort of common criminals.

Then on along the Molo, the furthest point pirates ever reached when attacking Venice, back in the ninth century when it was young, past the forest of piles where the gondolas were moored, now, in this weather, all covered with tarpaulins, as they would be in the Bacino Orseolo, the basin behind the Piazza San Marco where there is another big fleet of them moored. For no one on a day like this would have used a gondola, unless they were *sposi*, newly married, or were dead and being conveyed in a funeral gondola to Isola San Michele from one of the undertakers' establishments on the Fondamenta Nuove. In fact, today, scarcely anyone goes to the cemetery in one of the old funeral gondolas, which were picturesquely decorated with a pair of St Mark's lions in polished brass; now the undertakers' boats are almost all big, powered vessels.

Then we turned right into Piazzetta San Marco, with the Palazzo Ducale on one hand and the Mint and the Library designed by

Jacopo Sansovino on the other, passing between the feet of the two immense grey and red granite columns that someone had brought here from Syria or Constantinople. Somewhere overhead, invisible in the fog, the grey column supported the bronze lion, really a chimera, a fire-breathing monster with the head of a lion, the body of a goat and the tail of a serpent, whether Etruscan, Persian or Chinese no one really knows, to which some inspired innovator has added wings. The other bears a marble figure poised on a crocodile, said to be that of Theodore, the Greek saint who was the patron of the Veneto until the body of St Mark arrived in such a dramatic fashion in the city (having been hastily cleared through customs in Alexandria by Muslim officials who had been told he was a consignment of pork). In fact the statue is not one of St Theodore at all, but is made up of several pieces from the ancient world, the topmost part being a magnificent head of Mithridates, King of Pontus. The statue is a copy. The original is in the Palazzo Ducale.

We entered the Piazza, described by Napoleon, in a rare light-hearted mood, and with reason, as the 'finest open-air drawing room in the world', an immense open space, originally paved with bricks, now covered with black trachyte, a fine grained volcanic rock of rough texture, from the Euganean Hills near Padua, ornamented with narrow inserts of white Istrian marble. The design, made by Andrea Tirali in 1723, forms a pattern of interconnecting squares and rectangles, punctuated by white dots on the black background, so that from the belfry of the Campanile high overhead, the Piazza looks as if two parallel rows of black and white carpets have been laid end to end in it on top of a large, black, fitted carpet, for the reception of some distinguished personage.

Although a superficial glance gives one the impression that it is rectangular, the Piazza is a trapezoid, a quadrilateral having neither pair of sides parallel, and is more than thirty yards wider at its eastern than at its western end.

Three sides of it are occupied by what appears to be one enormous, soot-blackened palace of what are, to all but the most pernickety, irreproachable dimensions. The fourth side is occupied by what is arguably the most fantastic basilica in Christendom, San Marco, a building surmounted by Islamic domes, embellished with cupolas and gilded crosses on top of them, that look more like extra-terrestrial vehicles sent to bear the building away to another world than the work of an architect.

To the right of the Basilica, facing the square, is the smallest of the two squares that lead into the Piazza, the Piazzetta dei Leoncini, furnished with a fountain and red marble lions. At the far end of this little piazza is what was once the splendid banqueting hall which used to be linked with the Ducal Palace by a corridor; and at the point where it ceases to be the Piazzetta and becomes the Piazza, an archway leads out of it into the street of shops called the Merceria dell'Orologio under the Torre dell'Orologio, a very pretty building with two bronze giants on top of it, who together strike the hours for the clock below on a great bell. Hidden within the tower are the Magi who, in Ascension week, emerge from a little side door, preceded by an angel, and pass before the Virgin in her niche above the gilt and blue enamelled clock face to vanish through a similar door on the far side, a procession they make every hour.

To the left of St Mark's Basilica the new Campanile, surmounted by a pyramidical steeple panelled in green copper and a gilded figure of the Archangel Gabriel, soars 322 feet into the air, far above anything else in the city, even the campanile of Santa Maria Maggiore. On 14 July 1902, the 113th anniversary of the sacking of the Bastille, at ten in the morning and with scarcely any warning, the original Campanile telescoped into itself and fell into the Piazza, having previously successfully withstood being struck by lightning, shaken by earthquakes, and being insidiously undermined by the *acque alte*. In doing so it damaged the corner of the Libreria Sansoviniana, initiated by Jacopo Sansovino, completed by Vincenzo Scamozzi and described by Palladio, in the sixteenth century, as 'the richest and most decorated building ever perhaps created from ancient times until now'. It also completely destroyed Sansovino's Loggetta, which was used as a guardroom when it was built; missed his magnificent bronze statues of Minerva, Apollo, Mercury and Peace, but smashed his terracotta group of The Virgin and Child (later repaired) and the Child John the Baptist. It also wrenched from its position at the south-east corner of the Basilica the Pietra del Bando, the stump of porphyry column brought by the Venetians from Acre in 1256 and set up here at the place from which the laws of Venice were promulgated, but sparing the fabric from damage. In falling, four of its five bells were broken, but the biggest, the Marangona, so called because one of its functions was to tell the craftsmen of the *Marangoni*, the guilds of the city, when to begin and stop work, was undamaged and was found protruding from the mountain of rubble which filled the eastern end of the Piazza. Also shattered was the beaten copper figure of the Archangel Gabriel which came plummeting down from above.

And behind the Campanile in the Piazzetta di San Marco, but visible from the Piazza, part of the west front of the Palazzo Ducale can be seen, luminously beautiful, its body clad with pink and white marble in the form of Gothic arcades one above the other, a wonder of lightness and beauty. Altogether the finest enclosed spaces to be found anywhere in all the Mediterranean lands, finer than St Peter's Square in Rome. Perhaps, as Napoleon said, the finest in all the world.

All that was visible of this wonder of the world on this particular night in January were the enfilades of lights which hang in elegant glass globes under the arches of the long arcades of the *procuratie*, once the offices and residences of the Procurators of Venice, who were the most important dignitaries after the Doge, vanishing away into the fog towards the far western end of the Piazza where the wing known as the Ala Napoleonica, built to replace a church torn down by his orders, was completely invisible. Beneath the arcades there were some amorphous, will-o'-the-wispish smudges of light, which emanated from the windows of expensive shops and cafés. There were also some blurs of light from the elegant lamp standards in the Piazzetta di San Marco, where the fog was even thicker. All that could be seen of the Basilica were the outlines of a couple of bronze doors, one of them sixth-century Byzantine work: nothing at all of the great quadriga of bronze horses overhead in front of the magnificent west window, copies of those looted from the Hippodrome at Constantinople by Doge Dandolo after he had taken the city, plunging ever onwards, stripped of their bridles by the Venetians as a symbol of liberty, on their endless journey from their first known setting-off place, the Island of Chios, through what were now the ruins of the world in which they had been created.

Now the giants on top of the Torre dell'Orologio began banging away with their hammers on the big bell, as they had done ever since they were cast by a man named Ambrosio dalle Anchore in 1494, some 489 years ago, the year Columbus discovered Jamaica, a slice of the action the Venetians would like to have been in on, the year Savanarola restored popular government in Florence, something they themselves were already badly in need of. They made things to last in those days. No question of replacing the unit if something went wrong.

It was five o'clock. Soon, if it was not raining, or snowing, or there was no *acqua alta* to turn it into a paddling pool, and there was none of this damn fog, the better-off inhabitants, those who wanted to be thought better-off and those who really were badly-off but looked almost as well-dressed as the rest, which is what you aim at if you are a Venetian, having changed out of their working clothes would begin that ritual of the Christian Mediterranean lands, something that you will not see in a devout, Muslim one, the *passeggiata*, the evening promenade, in Piazza San Marco and in the Piazzetta, in pairs and groups, young and old, the old usually in pairs, the young ones often giving up promenading after a bit and congregating on the shallow steps that lead up from the Piazza into the arcades, the ones that in summer have long drapes hanging in them to keep off the sun, which gives them a dim, pleasantly mysterious air. So the Venetians add themselves to the visitors who swarm in the Piazza at every season of the year, costing one another's clothes, casting beady, impassive eyes on the often unsuitable clothes of the visitors, as their predecessors must have done on various stray Lombards and other barbarians down on a visit, and on the uncouth Slavs and Albanians who came ashore at the Riva degli Schiavoni. Those on whom they had not looked so impassively had been the Austrians who filled the Piazza in the years between 1815 and 1866, the period when, apart from a few months of brave but abortive revolution in the winter of 1848–49, the Venetian States were under the domination of Austria, to whom they had originally been sold by Napoleon in 1797. (He got them back again in 1805, only to lose them when Austria received them yet again at the Congr ,s of Vienna, a couple of months before Waterloo.) In those years the Austrian flag flew in the Piazza in place of what had been that of the Republic of St Mark, an Austrian band played, which it is said no true Venetians opened their ears to, let alone applauded, and one of the two fashionable cafés that still face one another across its width, the one which was frequented by Austrians, was left to them.

Meanwhile other, less elegant but equally ritualistic *passeggiate* would be taking place in the principal *calli*, *campi* and *salizzadi*, in other parts of the city, and there the younger ones would probably flock to some monument and drape themselves around the base of it. There would also be crowds in the Merceria dell'Orologio, *merceria* being a haberdashery, which is still, as it always was, filled with rich stuffs which the Veneziani love, a narrow street which leads from the clock tower into Merceria di San Giuliano and from that into Merceria di San Salvatore, once the shortest route from San Marco to the other most important centre of the city, the Rialto. This was the way the Procurators and other important officials used to follow on their way in procession to enter the Basilica, and the one followed by persons on their way from the Rialto to be publicly flogged.

Then, quite suddenly, after an hour or so, except at weekends or on days of festa, old and young suddenly disappear indoors, many of them having to get up what is in winter horribly early in order to get to work on the terra firma, leaving the Piazza and other places of *passeggio* to visitors and to those making a living by catering to their needs.

Tonight the *passeggiata* was definitely off. The pigeons had long since given up and gone to bed – that is if they had ever bothered to get up in the first place, and the only other people on view were a few dark figures with mufflers wrapped round their mouths, hurrying presumably homewards, some of them coughing as they went. The only people, besides ourselves, who were not on the move were a lunatic who was sitting at the feet of the Campanile gabbling away happily to himself, and a pretty young girl, dressed in a smart, bright red skiing outfit, to which even the Venetians could not have taken exception, and those après-ski boots with the hair on the outside, that make the occupants look as if they have forgotten to shave their legs. She was leaning against a pile of the duckboards the municipality puts down in various parts of the city when an *acqua alta* is expected, listening in on her earphones and reading *Fodor's Guide* with the aid of a pocket torch.

'Hi!' she said, removing her earphones and switching off, at the same time displaying a mouthful of pearly white teeth that had not been near a capper's. 'Would you mind repeating that? I didn't get it.'

'We said, "Good evening, it's a rotten night".'

'Yes, it certainly is a lousy night. This is my first time in Venice. What an introductory offer! My sister and I came down this afternoon from Cortina. The son of the guy who runs our hotel there gave us a lift but once we got out of the mountains we couldn't see a thing, not even Treviso. It was like being out in the boondocks. It's brilliant in Cortina. My sister's back where we're staying, not feeling so good. I guess we should have checked out on the weather. We've got to go back tomorrow. Maybe it'll be better tomorrow. I haven't even seen a gondola yet.'

'There are some over there,' I said, 'moored by the Molo. But you have to watch your step. We nearly fell in.'

'I'll check on the gondolas on the way back to the hotel,' she said. 'I was just boning up on the Piazza San Marco, about it being beautiful at all times of day and night and all seasons of the year, one of the only great squares which retains a feeling of animation when there are very few people in it. Personally, I don't think this Fodor person was ever here in a fog. He says bring plenty of color films. What a laugh! Personally, I think it's kinda spooky, what with that poor old guy over there hollering away to himself and that bell going on all the time. Why, it wouldn't surprise me if we saw some old Doge.'

It wouldn't have surprised me either, standing where we were in the heart of Doge-land in freezing fog listening to a bell on a buoy making a melancholy noise somewhere out in St Mark's Basin.

What is strange, if not spooky, about Venice is the feeling of impermanence brought on by the thought that not only are the waters constantly rising in it because of the general increase in the levels of the oceans brought about by the melting of the polar ice, but that the city is at the same time sinking because the re-routing of rivers has deprived it of alluvium and because of the enormous amount of water and methane gas that until recently was being drawn out of the subsoil in the Industrial Zones. So that one day, quite suddenly, without warning, just as the Campanile collapsed, so too will the wooden piles that support the buildings of the city, of which there are said to be more than a million beneath Santa Maria della Salute alone, suddenly give up supporting them and allow the city to disappear forever.

Much of the city is crumbling as well as sinking. Everywhere leprous walls and rotting brickwork proclaim the fact. Much of it is also abandoned, empty. Great palazzi on the Grand Canal – many of them built as warehouses in which the merchants lived, as it were over the shop, some of them big enough, now that there is no merchandise, to house a hundred persons – have watergates through which the merchandise used to pass which look as if they have not been opened for a hundred years. The steps leading up to them are covered with long green weed which sways in the wash of motor boats and water buses. Inside, the vast room on the *piano nobile* is lit, if at all, by a 40-watt bulb. Sometimes another, equally feeble light in a room high up under the eaves proclaims that there is a resident caretaker. This feeling of emptiness extends far beyond the confines of the Grand Canal. You can feel it up in the Quartiere Grimani, in the territory around the Arsenale, in the Ghetto with its enclave of the Venetian equivalent to skyscrapers hemmed in on all sides by water, and in the alleys of San Tomà where the cats of Venice reign supreme and there is scarcely a dog to be seen.

But then, just when you begin to experience a sense of horror at being alone in this dead city, you are treated to a series of glimpses – through windows that are invariably barred – of a family sitting around a table to eat *risotto alle vongole*, risotto with clams, which is being brought to it in a cloud of steam, of children doing their homework, of someone working late in an archive, of a man and a girl kissing, of an old couple watching television, like a series of realistic pictures hung in the open air on walls of crumbling brick and flaking stone.

Deciding that we needed a drink, we walked to Florian, which is under the arcade of the Procuratie Nuove on the south side of the square.

Florian is the oldest café in Venice, opened by someone called Floriano Francesconi in 1720, and it has a faded and beautiful elegance all of its own which if once destroyed one feels could never be repeated, but perhaps it has been restored: Venetian craftsmen are wonderfully adept at making copies of the antique and then 'distressing' them, which is the expression used in the trade for making things look older than they are.

Tonight, the rooms in Florian overlooking the Piazza, with the innumerable mirrors, the painted panelling and the alcoves barely large enough to contain one of the little cast iron tables, were empty. The Venetian dowagers, ample or emaciated and certainly rheumaticky, rheumatism being an endemic Venetian disease among the aged, who would normally be here at this hour sipping tea or hot chocolate and talking about death and money, sometimes with equally ancient male contemporaries, were all at home, being cosseted by equally ancient maids, fearing if they went out *prendere un raffredore*, to catch a cold, or worse. The majority of visitors who come to Venice in the hot weather rarely enter these rooms, preferring to sit outside in the Piazza, where there is more action.

Tonight, what action there was was in the bar, which is about as comfortable as most bars have become in Italy, which means that

there is hardly anything to sit on. In it three men and three girls were
standing at the bar drinking Louis Roederer, which is a terrible price
in a shop in Italy and an unimaginable price in such a place as
Florian, where anything, even a beer, costs at least twice as much as
it would in a more modest establishment.

The men were dressed in tweed and grey flannel. Two of them
had camel-hair coats draped over their shoulders and the third wore
a double-breasted herring-bone coat. All three of them wore Rolex
watches and beautifully polished black or brown moccasins with
tassels, one of the badges of the well-off, or those who want to be
thought well-off, everywhere. All were over forty, possibly nearer
fifty, with dark hair so uniformly and stylishly grizzled that I was
tempted to ask them if they had barbers who grizzled it for them.
They had typical Venetian faces: prominent, rather Semitic noses,
the calculating eyes of shopkeepers, which in fact was probably
what they were, shopkeepers who looked as if they might be
involved in slightly questionable activities but nothing that would
normally lead to actual prosecution, and if it did, and was successful, would only involve a fine which they could afford. Hard faces,
softened for the drinks with the girls; the faces of men not easily
amused, or much given to laughter, unless in the form of some
carefully controlled internal convulsion; the faces of men who were
by nature slightly condescending, omniscient – to put it bluntly –
know-alls, courteous, suspicious, contemptuous of outsiders, enjoying being in the position of being able to observe others, but not
enjoying being scrutinized themselves.

The girls were in their middle twenties. All three wore wedding
rings, in addition to other loot, on their fingers. What were they, we
both wondered. These men's mistresses, other men's wives? They
might, just conceivably, be their daughters, or their nieces. No one
was giving anything away, not even the barman whom they all
called by his first name. Uniformly well-formed, long-haired, long-
legged, the sort of girls who can wear flat heels and still look as if
they are wearing high heels, not particularly beautiful but so
well-groomed that most men would not notice the fact, the product
of female emancipation in post-war Italy where, until well into the
sixties, girls stayed at home with their mothers in the evening, were
chaperoned if they went out, and it was exceptional to find one who
could drive a car. These girls looked not only as if they drove cars,
but drove fast ones.

They did not look like typical Venetians, although, like the men, they interpolated whole paragraphs in Venetian dialect into their conversation, that strange amalgam which has strains of French, Arabic and Greek overlaying the Italian, blurring and contracting it. Perhaps girls do not become typical Venetians until they become older. Their mothers would look as Venetian as the men they were drinking with; their grandmothers would be the dies from which typical Venetians are pressed. These girls just looked like girls. Whether they were well-off or not, they were giving a convincing display of being so. It was difficult to imagine a band of such overtly conspicuous consumers, dressed like this and loaded with expensive ephemera, sallying out into the fog from some drinking place in SW1 and walking home without being mugged, for this is what they were going to have to do when they did leave, in a city without motor cars, that is unless they slept over the premises or had bodyguards waiting for them.

One of the girls, who was wearing a Loden cape, announced that she had just inherited an eighteenth-century villa, in the country somewhere west of Treviso, destroying, in her case, the theory that she might be either daughter or mistress – perhaps they were assistants to the shopkeepers. Apparently it was in a very bad condition, having been used as a farmhouse for more than fifty years.

'What should I do with it?' she asked. 'It could be very beautiful.'

'I would insure it for a lot of money,' one of the men said. 'Say four hundred and fifty *milioni* [about £190,000 or $266,000]. And then I would pay someone to burn it down.' It was difficult to know if he was joking.

The villa she was talking about was one of the country houses to which rich Venetians, Trevisans, Paduans and Vicenzans used to escape from the heat and stench of their cities in summer and in the autumn. They began building them in earnest in the sixteenth century, although some date from as early as the fourteenth century, and they built them in the plain between the foothills of the Alps and the lagoons. They continued to build them far into the eighteenth century, by which time they had become almost symbolic of the frivolity and lack of energy for commerce which characterized the last years of the Republic. They lined the banks of the Brenta Canal between Mestre and Padua with them, making of it a watery triumphal way. The best known is the mysterious and withdrawn Villa Malcontenta, one of the masterpieces of Palladio – together with the Villa Capra at Vicenza, the most famous Palladian villas – which stands on its right bank near Mestre under what is now almost invariably a sulphurous sky, with the plants and factories of the Industrial Zone creeping closer to it every year. They built them on the banks of the Sile, which emerges as a pond full of vegetation in the plain west of Treviso and bubbles and seethes its way through this charming little city, apparently unpolluted. And they built them along the Terraglio, now a nightmare road, Strada Statale 13, between Mestre and Treviso, where villas with the sonorous names of past and present owners – Villa Gatterburg *ora* Volpi, Villa Duodo Melicki *ora* Zoppolate (shades of Villa Newby), some in vast parks full of planes and cedars, with statues on the cornices looming against the sky – are today hemmed in by filling stations and windowless factories painted in bilious colours. And they built them in the depths of the country, miles from anywhere.

The Venetians went to their villas by gondola, or in the large rowing barges called *burchielli*, which had a sort of miniature villa on top of them in which the passengers could shield themselves from the elements and from the vulgar gaze. When there was no water-way leading to their villas, they travelled by ox-cart, which must have been pretty uncomfortable.

Their movements were as regular as those of migrant birds. The exodus from the city began on the eve of St Anthony's Day in June and they stayed in the country until the end of July, after which they went back to the city. On October the first they went to the country again and in November, at the end of St Martin's Summer, the time when the last grapes are picked which were not ripe at the *vendemmia* in October, they returned to Venice for a round of theatres and masked routs. As Venice declined, so the diversions increased in extravagance.

At night in their villas they gambled until dawn, unless there was some other diversion. They rose late, to watch other people cultivating their gardens and their vines, to visit their labyrinths, contemplate great nature, ponder further improvements and, as time went on, contemplate and ponder their diminished bank balances. For the Venetians were seldom content with one villa. It was not uncommon for a single family to own a dozen. At one time the Pisani owned fifty. More than two thousand villas are still in existence in the Veneto.

Of the great Venetian villas the grandest is the Pisani family's villa at Stra* on the Brenta Canal east of Padua, which has huge stables, a labyrinth, a fantastic gateway-cum-belvedere flanked by columns encircled by spiral staircases and crowned with statuary; and on the ceiling of the ballroom frescoes of angels blowing trumpets, *putti*, eighteenth-century gentry, one of them well placed between the thighs of a naked lady who has temporarily landed on a cloud, and what look like Red Indians, all by Giambattista Tiepolo, forever whirling across a pale blue sky. Another huge villa is the Villa Manin, at Passariano, south-west of Udine, which is so large that its outlines actually show up on the 1:200,000 Touring Club Italiano map. This was the villa built for the last Doge, Lodovico Manin, and with its immense all-embracing arcaded wings it resembles a small town rather than a habitation. The smallest of the villas is the exquisite Casa Quaglia – the Quail House – built in the fourteenth century at Paese, west of Treviso, now a shamefully neglected farmhouse, which has Venetian Gothic windows and a facade painted in the form of a tapestry with fabulous animals.

Some, however, like the one inherited by the girl in the bar at Florian's, are in decay. In a typical one of this sort, if it is big, several families of *contadini* may live in the *barchesse*, the curving wings, which spring from a central block in which most of the windows have been bricked up on the lower floor. Inside, the immense salon on the *piano nobile*, in which the ceiling may be entirely covered with seventeenth-century frescoes of gods and goddesses floating in the air, may also be half full of corn on the cob. There are great cracks in the ceiling, the door openings are covered with tattered sacking, and one day, soon, it will collapse.

'How would you like to spend the evening?' I asked, opening my favourite guide book. According to this, the *Guide Julliard de l'Europe*, there are four intelligent ways to spend an evening in Venice: the first and dearest is to hire a gondola (a closed one if one has improper thoughts and the means to gratify them); the second is to instal oneself at a table in the Piazza San Marco; the third to look for adventures in the streets and alleys; the fourth to go to bed with a good book and a bottle of Scotch. 'When one has tried all these,' the authors say, 'there are the night clubs.'

---

* Now owned by the state, which has such great difficulty in finding custodians that it is frequently closed in winter.

'I know which one you'd choose,' Wanda said, 'but you can't hire those closed gondolas any more.'

'I wouldn't choose any of them on a night like this.'

'What time's the train?'

'Eight forty-five. It's half past five now. I think we should go. I'm awfully hungry. We can have dinner at that place near the Colleoni monument. What do you call it?'

'You mean the Trattoria alle Bandierette.'

'Yes, that'll take at least twenty minutes in this weather. We'd better telephone them and see if they can feed us around six-thirty. Then, by the time we've walked to the station, or if it's going we might get the *circolare** from the Fondamente Nuove, and get the bags out of the *deposito*, we shall just make it. Lucky we booked to go by train. We'd look pretty silly with plane tickets for London on a night like this.'

'I'm glad we're going home,' Wanda said, who gets fed up when it's cold, as she had done once in Siberia. 'Just for now I've had enough of travelling and enough of the Mediterranean. I want to sleep in my own bed for a bit.'

* There are two services of water buses that circle Venice in opposite directions, Service No. 5 Circolare sinistra and destra.

II
THE ADRIATIC

On the Way to the Balkans

One of the problems about travelling round the Mediterranean under your own steam and not as part of a group is the cost of transportation. Luckily, by one of those miracles to which we fortunately are no strangers, we were offered a trip back to Venice, which we had so capriciously abandoned because it was foggy, on the inaugural run of the Venice–Simplon–Orient Express.

The scenes at Victoria before this inaugural train was hauled away by a humdrum British diesel (it had not been possible to use steam engines on any sections of the route because of lack of steam train facilities) were memorable for anyone interested in such trivia, which included us. For the first time for many a day the rich, or those making a stab at being thought to be so, like ourselves, could be seen travelling together and the station was awash with what Veblen described in his *Theory of the Leisure Class* as 'conspicuous consumption'.

It had been suggested that we come dressed in the manner of the thirties and as a result pre-1939 taxis and motor cars of the same period hired from specialist hire firms were rolling up, one of them a mauve Panther which to my untutored eye looked like an overblown Bugatti. These disgorged a merry throng: gentlemen in wing collars and Panama hats, ladies in white felt and pill-box hats, and yards of beads. Liza Minnelli arrived bowler-hatless in non-period black, which suited her. Denise, Lady Kilmarnock, a partner in the firm which was promoting all this, was splendid in a shocking pink turban and was the life and soul of the party. I had a new shirt for the occasion. My wife had a new white beret. Nigel Dempster, gossip columnist of the *Daily Mail*, also had a new shirt. Calmest of all was Jennifer, society columnist of *Harpers and Queen*. The best organized of all the recorders of this and succeeding scenes, she had done her homework on her fellow travellers. She had no need to go scurrying around finding out who was who. Meanwhile the Coldstream Guards' band played away like anything.

At 11.44 on the dot, having settled into a coach called Zena, used on the *Bournemouth Belle* from 1929 to 1946, we pulled out to the accompaniment of an enormous fanfare of trumpets. The interior was exquisite, the result of taking the whole thing to pieces and rebuilding it (in Lancashire) and the work of such people as cabinet-makers skilled in marquetry, and upholsterers.

Soon we were tucking into a delicious collation: watercress soup; salmon with tarragon cream, carrot and fennel; iceberg and mint leaf salad; tomatoes stuffed with mushrooms; and 'Henley Pudding', sort of mousse; with the glasses and cutlery, designed in France, which you can buy if you have enough of the necessary, setting up a magic tinkling.

Meanwhile, we were wondering who among this glittering throng was the Duchess of Westminster, Princess Esra Jah of Hyderabad, Rod Stewart, Sir Peter and Lady Parker (head of British Rail and designated 'Folkestone only'), the grandson of George Mortimer, inventor of the Pullman Car, and Mrs Wheeler and son, the second people to book for this trip, back in 1978, all of whom were reputed to be on the train. As a result, although I had a pre-1914 Baedeker which would have given us a blow by blow account of the route to Folkestone, there was not much chance to use it or glimpse anything more than an occasional oast-house from the window.

At 14.00 we left Folkestone (and the Parkers, who had been given a good old grilling by the press as to why Sir Peter's British Rail trains weren't like this one) on a Sealink ferry, preserved from the common herd in the Verandah Deck Saloon which was reserved for VSOE passengers, but not protected from the media, who had been totally pre-empted by teams of Japanese television cameramen who had recorded the journey, travelling with the train all the way to Venice on a trial run and also following it with a fleet of helicopters.

Ninety minutes later, at Boulogne, we had our first sight of the European section of the train, seventeen coaches in the dark blue and gold livery of the Compagnie Internationale des Wagon-Lits et des Grands Express Européens decorated with bronze cyphers, drawn up on the quay side. There were greetings from the Mayor, or was it the President of the Chamber of Commerce?

Eleven sleepers, each with sixteen or eighteen compartments, restaurant cars, a bar car with a grand piano in it, staff and baggage cars, had all been restored at Bremen and Slyke near Ostend with what must have been a goodly slice of the £11,000,000 it had cost to get the two trains on the rails. These sleepers were Lx, L denoting luxury, the cars associated in people's minds with the old Simplon–Orient. They had been everywhere, on the Rome Express, the Berlin–Naples, the Aegean Express and Taurus, the Nord Express to Riga before the war. We were in Wagon-Lit 3525, built at La Rochelle in 1929, decorated by René Prou, master of wagon-lit design, stored at Lourdes during the Second World War, last used on the Simplon–Orient and Rome Expresses between 1949 and 1961. Our luggage, which we hadn't seen since Victoria, was already in the compartment. At 17.44, to the accompaniment of a band of serenading musicians, the train pulled out for Paris.

Changing for dinner in Lx 3525 — the decree was that ladies would dress and dinner jackets would be worn — was a feat of acrobatics, like the Marx Brothers in the cabin scene on the Atlantic liner (some of these compartments got smaller during conversion) and I got the bottom fly button of my trousers done up through the top buttonhole.

Down in the bar car it was like an Arabian night; everyone was dressed to the nines, with feathers and bandeaux. The champagne was flowing from those expensive Indian-club-shaped bottles. There we met an American husband and wife who owned their own parlour and sleeping cars back home in California where they hitched them on to trains and rode out to Kentucky or wherever the spirit moved them.

Dinner, which cost £20 ($28) a head (lunch and drinks on the train in England were included in the fare), was served while we were in the outskirts of Paris. It was cooked and presented by the chef, Michel Ranvier, late of the three-stars-in-*Michelin* Troisgros restaurant at Roanne. Memorable was the *Foie Gras de Canard Entier Cuit Tout Naturelle*, the little lobsters served *à la Vinaigrette d'Huile d'Olive*, and the *Jambonnette de Poulette au Vin Jaune et Morilles*.

It took hours, due to one of the gas stoves in a kitchen going wrong, but who cared, we were not going on anywhere afterwards.

There was a red carpet down at the Gare d'Austerlitz, but no nobs to see us off, the present administrators of the country disapproving of conspicuous consumption and no one else wanting to be associated with the venture.

Then on through the night with a pianist, Monsieur Dars, at the grand piano in the bar, belting Scott Joplin and such as we roared down the line to Switzerland. The piano was such an impediment to navigation that sometimes I wished we'd brought a chain saw with us.

At 04.22 we arrived at Vallorbe, 266 miles from Paris, a station in the strange no-man's-land between France and Switzerland, where as always a man plodded past groaning 'VALLORBE . . . VALLORBE', while another tapped the axles with a hammer, as in *Anna Karenina*.

I was asleep when they put the croissants on the train at Lausanne at 05.21, all the way along the shores of Lake Geneva and all the way up the Rhone Valley; waking in the entrance to the Simplon tunnel for the 12½-mile run under the Lepontine Alps, between Monte Leone and the Helsenhorn, where the previous week one of the Japanese camera crew had been nearly decapitated, putting his head out of the window in the middle of it.

We ate the croissants and drank coffee running along the shores of Lago Maggiore. Cork and cedar trees rose above the early mist on the Borromean Islands and the place names on the map – Stresa and Locarno – were those of long-forgotten treaties made before the war. It was going to be a lovely day. At Milan, at 10.00, the papers came on board with pictures of a frigate burning in the Falkland Islands.

Lunch on the train, £15 ($21) a head if you had to pay for it, was tagliatelle with butter, small chickens in a delicious sauce, smoked salmon, Parma ham, strawberry tart, the most delicious lemon cake and more of the Laurent-Perrier champagne on which everyone had been over-indulging themselves. Then, three hours out of Milan, we rumbled through the hideous environs of Mestre and out along the causeway to the beautiful, sinking, stinking city in the Lagoon.

We arrived at Santa Lucia Station at 14.44 to be greeted on the platform when we descended by the stationmaster, the massed concierges of the Cipriani, the Gritti and the Danieli, the assembled staff of the Venice–Simplon–Orient Express and the Gondolieri Chorus.

Miss Minnelli left in another little black number decorated with bugle beads. She told me she had enjoyed the trip. We never saw her again. Boats took us away up the Grand Canal, a vision in the sunshine, to stay at the Cipriani for free. It was all over.

Leaving Venice some considerable time later, this time in a van by the causeway across the Lagoon, turning right at Mestre on the old main road to Trieste, we crossed the plains of the Veneto and Venezia Giulia. For much of the way the road, as are most of the other main roads in northern Italy, is lined with developments, factories and furniture showrooms mostly, whose owners now choose what were previously remote rural locations for them, so that for long periods of time it is impossible to see the country on either side at all.

It is country which when one can see it is of endless flatness, through which the irrigation ditches stretch away to what seems like infinity between the high embankments, just as they do in the Po Delta. In summer, in the heat of the day, when the mirage is operating, this country sometimes looks more like a jelly than terra firma. In it, in summer, the farmhouses and villages stand like islands isolated in seas of ripening corn and grapes. (In winter they stand in seas of freezing mud.) In autumn, in late September or October, the *contadini* in their wide-brimmed straw hats, at this season engaged in the *vendemmia*, take shelter beneath the vines, around half past nine or so, by which time it is already hot, to eat their *merenda*, just as we do in the vineyards around I Castagni.

The rivers that flow down through the plain from the Alps into the lagoons and marshes that fringe the coast are the Piave, the Tagliamento and the Isonzo, which first sees the light of day as the Soča, bubbling up over clean sand in a deep cleft in the rock in the Julian Alps in Yugoslavia, each of them in full, sometimes dangerous, flood in spring when the mountain snows melt. In the hot weather long reaches of them are often nothing more than arid wildernesses of shingle with a few livid green stagnant pools among them. Rivers that were practically unheard-of in the outside world until the First World War when hundreds of thousands of Italians and Austro-Hungarians died fighting one another on their banks.

Having crossed the Isonzo, the most eastward of these rivers, we arrived in the late afternoon in Monfalcone, a rather sad shipbuilding and industrial town on the shores of the Gulf of Panzano, an inlet at the head of the Gulf of Trieste, sad-looking because it was more or less destroyed in the First World War and then rebuilt in the early twenties at a time when domestic as well as public architecture was rather sad anyway.

The only old building of note is the castle, and even that is not exciting as castles go, although the view from it is magnificent, over what is actually only a small part of the vast plain which extends uninterruptedly for some 300 miles from the Julian Alps to the Maritime and the Cottian Alps in which the Po rises on the French frontier beyond Turin, with the shining lagoons reaching into it from the sea and with towers and campanili rising into the air above it, of which that of the cathedral of Aquileia, the Roman city sacked by Attila, is the most easily identifiable.

The castle stands on the very edge of what the Italians call Il Carso, the Yugoslavs call the Kras and German-speakers the Karst, a wilderness of limestone here rising in a steep escarpment abruptly above the town and the plain, like a whale surfacing from the depths of the ocean, scarred by quarrying, utterly bare except for a few plantations of conifers and innumerable electric pylons which protrude from it like harpoons. Having fought and negotiated so ferociously either to obtain or retain it, it would be comical, if it was not tragic, to see how the Italians have treated what they are always going on about as their patrimony.

Much of the Carso is bare rock, but parts of it are covered with ash, rowan, hawthorn shrubs and holm oaks, the last vestigial remains of the primeval forest that provided some of the wooden piles on which, miraculously, Venice still stands, although now plantations of conifers are rapidly changing its appearance.

Here, among what in some places look like torrents of rock, the making of the fields, before the coming of the bulldozer, was the back-breaking work of generations of men and women and their children. Here, you can still see piles of pale, rain-washed stones, as much as ten feet high and sixty feet long, like great burial cairns, all hand-picked from this wilderness to make a field of red earth perhaps three feet deep and thirty yards long in which vines, corn, turnips or potatoes could be grown.

It is a place of extremes. In winter the fearful wind called by the Slovenes the *Kraška Burja*, by the Italians the *Bora*, sweeps over the plateau from the north-east, sometimes attaining a velocity of up to 130 mph and in the past upsetting heavily laden ox-carts and even halting trains on the railway line from Trieste to Ljubljana, although it now rarely blows with such ferocity, possibly because the plateau is being protected by the reafforestation.

The early part of the year is particularly beautiful. The grass is fresh and green and carpeted with snowdrops, daffodils and lilies of the valley, and the hillsides are covered with narcissus.

In summer a huge, brooding silence envelops the Carso, a silence accentuated by the endless shrilling of cicadas that seems eventually to become part of the silence itself. The woods have a sinister, claustrophobic feeling about them and one has the sensation of being watched, and one *is* being watched anywhere close to the Yugoslav–Italian frontier, across which, walking in the woods, it is easy to stray.

Here in the Carso, ten minutes after the most violent rainstorm, there is no water to be seen; it has all gurgled away through fissures in the rock. For the Kras is hollow. Beneath it there is a whole subterranean world, only a minute part of it explored, of vast caverns, dark, secret rivers and black, icy lakes. From the air it looks as if it has been subjected to intense artillery bombardment, as it was when it was a major battlefield in the First World War. Its entire surface is pitted with craters but these are natural phenomena. The largest are called, in Slovene, *kolisevke*, basins with vertical sides as much as 300 feet deep and a quarter of a mile wide, huge caves whose roofs have collapsed. A smaller variety, *doline*, are blocked-up swallow holes that once led underground, funnel-shaped depressions anything from six to sixty feet deep and up to three hundred feet in diameter which contain the best earth and are cultivated as sunken fields.

One of the principal rivers is the Reka, which, as the Timavo, by which name it is still known to Italians, was as famous in classical antiquity as the Nile or the Euphrates and was written about by Virgil, Martial, Ausonius, and Strabo, who said that it contained specks of gold.

At Škocjan, a village that stands on a natural bridge of rock between two precipices, the Timavo plunges beneath one of them into a cave as high as a twenty-storey building, and emerges on the other side of the village in a *dolina*, five hundred feet deep and a third of a mile wide, eventually to disappear from view in the Lake of the Dead, four miles under a mountain.

It has been established, by someone who dropped fluorescein into it, of which one part can be detected in up to twenty million times its volume in water, that the Timavo then flows into the subterranean Lake of Trebiciano, which is at the bottom of a thousand-foot shaft in what is a sort of no-man's-land beyond the municipal rubbish tips of Trieste, on its way to enter the Adriatic near Monfalcone twelve miles away in Italy at San Giovanni Timavo. There it emerges from the base of a cliff in an arcadian place which remains arcadian only because it is the property of the Trieste waterworks, beside a church built on the site of a Roman temple itself built to hallow the spot. After its twenty-mile journey underground, it bubbles up in a series of pools, partly hidden from view by the willows that bend over them, before flowing over a series of weirs into the sea in the Gulf of Panzano, where its mouth is now disfigured by an enormous marina. Here, the Argonauts are supposed to have landed. Here, though strictly forbidden, because it belongs to the waterworks, we had a lovely picnic on the grass.

Down below in the caverns of the Carso there are strange creatures: *Troglocaris Schmidti*, a cave crab with a round belly which swims canted over to one side as though its ballast has shifted, and which sometimes, if it takes a wrong turning, gets sucked up into the Yugoslav drinking-water system; and, most remarkable of all, *Proteus anguineus*, a weird, stick-like member of the salamander family with four legs, that somehow survived the ice age in the temperate cavern air. Amphibious, breathing either through lungs or gills, according to which element it is in, quite blind, although born with embryonic eyes that later disappear, in its native habitat it lives for fifty years, and in captivity enjoys a diet of worms and mince meat. There is also a variety of blind spiders, scorpions and centipedes, all said to be either light brown or to have no colour at all.

The plateau of the eastern Kras through which the Timavo flows, mostly underground, was and is still the birthplace of some of the finest horses the world has ever seen. The rough ground and the excellent grass which grows on it combine to produce a race of horses of exceptional strength and speed with thick shanks, supple knees and particularly well-formed, strong hoofs.

Here, the ancient Greeks, and later the Romans, bred their horses for war and the great chariot races. In the oak woods near

Škocjan the Thracians erected a temple to Dionysus, protector of horses. At Lipiča, among the same sort of oak woods only a few miles away, there is a mews and stud founded in 1580 by the Archduke Charles, brother of the Emperor Maximilian II. He introduced the Spanish horse into Austria and for 339 years, until the end of the Empire in 1919, horses from Lipiča were supplied to the Imperial Spanish Riding School at Vienna, the only great riding school to survive both the French Revolution and the Napoleonic Wars: and for more than 240 years this breed of white horses, sired by Arab-Berbers brought from Andalucia, horses from Polesine in the Po Valley and, in the eighteenth century, from Germany and Denmark, performed the evolutions of the *haute école* in the great white baroque Winter Riding School in the Josefs-Platz, more like a ballroom than a *manége*, that is the masterpiece of the architect Fischer von Erlach.

These are the horses, Lipizzas, or Lippizaners, white as marble when grown, compact, broad-chested, with thick necks, long backs, thick, long manes, and with protuberant and intelligent eyes – fully grown they are between fifteen and sixteen hands – that when you see them moving with a high knee action in a natural, spirited trot, which at Vienna would be later schooled into what is known as the Spanish Walk, remind you of the horses on a Greek urn, or else of Verrochio's statue of the horse being ridden by the condottiere Bartolomeo Colleoni in Campo SS Giovanni e Paolo in Venice, next door to the little restaurant, the Bandierette, where we had our dinner before leaving for London on the Simplon Express.

The stallions at Lipiča are descended from one of six hereditary branches of the male line: Pluto, descended from the Danish stallion born in 1765; Conversano, from the brown Napolitan born in 1767; Napolitano, from a bay of that name born in 1790; Favory, a dun Lipiča born at Kladrub, another imperial stud between Prague and Brunn, in 1779; Maestoso, a grey born in 1819 at Mezohëgyes in Hungary of a Spanish dam sired by a Lipiča; and Siglavy, a grey Arab born in 1810, also at Mezohëgyes. Originally there were eighteen dynasties of dams at Lipiča. Several are now extinct. At Lipiča a horse takes its name from his forefather, followed by that of its dam – Siglavy-Almerina, Pluto-Theodorasta, and so on.

Lipiča no longer supplies horses to the Spanish Riding School. The Austrian horses now all come from Piber, near Graz in Styria, and the stud at Lipiča has become a sort of tourist attraction, although it still supplies horses to the state stables and they are exported all over the world as circus and saddle horses. In the Balkans, at least until recently, they were much used for heavy agricultural work.

Some years ago there were rumours that the stud was to be closed down and that all the horses were to be sold to a sausage factory which has its premises conveniently close by, but nothing came of it.

'You have been here before,' any reader who has got this far may well say. It is true I have been, many times, in this part of the world, in the Carso. This is the country, part of Slovenia, itself one of the republics that make up Yugoslavia, in which my wife was born; its inhabitants proud, prickly people with long memories, some of them endowed with second sight, musical, very fond of singing, passionate lovers of flowers, part of a tiny nation conquered by Charlemagne in the seventh century, which, although it struggled successfully to preserve its language, never attained independence. Many of them are now scattered to the far ends of the earth, principally in Australia and South America.

This was the place she meant when, tried beyond endurance by some domestic row, she used to cry, majestically, 'I shall return to my country and my people!'

Actually, she never did carry out this threat. Instead we returned there together year after year, usually with our children, to stay in her parents' house.

Over this disputed territory – about twenty miles deep and altogether about the size of Long Island – which has always been one of the principal ways of access for the people of Middle Europe to the Mediterranean, have flown, among others, the flags of Bonaparte's Illyria, of Austria-Hungary and, more recently, those of both Italy and Yugoslavia, which now have it divided unequally and uneasily between them.

To Italians, the Carso is, as it always has been, the frontier between Latin civilization and what they regard as Slavonic barbarism. It is a very old habit for them to think of it as such. This was the region held by the Tenth Legion and called by the Roman Senate 'The Impassable Confine'. In their brief modern tenure of it, which lasted about twenty-five years, they succeeded in extending their hold over it, but at great cost. Between 1915 and 1917, fighting against the Austro-Hungarians, in the twelve battles of the Isonzo, in the small area between Monte Michele north of Monfalcone and the Adriatic, they lost 175,000 men, a quarter of their losses in the entire war.

To the Austrians it was Der Karst, or Das Küstenland, now not much more than a nostalgic memory of a time when Trieste was the Austro-Hungarian Empire's principal port on the Mediterranean. To the Yugoslav nation it is the Kras, what they failed by a hair's-breadth to seize at the end of the Second World War, which would have given them a prestigious outlet on the Mediterranean, and which became a danger point in their relationship with the West. To the Slovenes it is also the Kras, but to them a place where for some 1300 years they have wrested a hard-earned living from its inhospitable terrain.

After 1918 it was annexed by Italy, and Slovene villages began to have their names printed together with their Italian equivalents on signposts and on Italian maps, as they still do on Italian maps even though many of them are now in Yugoslavia. Under Mussolini, the teaching of Slovene was forbidden and Slovene school-teachers were replaced by Italians, the Slovene teachers being sent to Italy. There, those who spoke no Italian – most spoke German as a second language (the Slovenes, as members of the Empire, fought in the Austrian army in the First War) – experienced the same difficulty in communicating with their pupils, until they had learned the language, as did monoglot Neapolitans sent to teach Italian to Slovene children, which was what happened to my Slovene father-in-law.

That afternoon we crossed out of Italy at the frontier post at the hamlet near Trieste called Fernetti and into Yugoslavia at Fernetič, which is the name for the same place on the Yugoslav side.

Although it is fairly easy to find frontier officials equally disagreeable to deal with as the Yugoslavian officials on the shores of the Mediterranean, it is difficult to find any more disagreeable to deal with. If nothing else, they make one realize the difference in the tempo of life in Yugoslavia and Italy, now the length of a cricket pitch away. To watch a Yugoslav frontier official examining your passport is like watching one of those fascinating slow motion films, taken over a period of weeks, which shows a plant breaking through the earth, burgeoning and gradually flowering before one's eyes. Wriggling among the contents of our luggage, the fingers of the customs official were like pale grubs. Thus we entered for the umpteenth time the country in which my wife was born, and to which she had so often threatened to return for ever.

As her mother was now very recently dead – her father had died some years previously – we had decided that this time, before going to stay with other members of her family, we would vary what had been for some thirty-five years an immutable itinerary, and visit first of all a distant kinswoman of hers who had invited us to spend the night in the village in which she lived in the eastern part of the Kras. Here, as in other places in the Mediterranean lands, kinsmen, and kinswomen particularly, recognize kinship to a point at which, in England – but not perhaps in Wales or Scotland – they would long since have ceased to be acknowledged as still existent. Here, everywhere you turn, are to be found kinsmen and kinswomen extending outwards in ever-increasing circles, like ripples on a pond when you throw a stone into it until, in the end, rather like the family of Queen Victoria which covers over two pages of small print in *Whitaker's Almanack*, almost everyone is your kin.

This village could have been the prototype of any village in the Kras. Its stone houses, huddled together as if for mutual protection, had walls feet thick, most of them hidden away in walled courtyards behind heavy oak doors under high, carved stone archways. These courtyards, havens in which the owners and their animals shelter from the rigours of the climate and modern Yugoslavia outside, are full of flowers in summer, something about which Slovenes are quite dotty. (My mother-in-law once, at the age of eighty, brazenly took cuttings inside one of the temperate houses in the Royal Botanical Gardens at Kew which did very well in her garden in the Kras.) Overlooking the courtyard, at the upper storey, a wooden balcony runs the whole length of the front of the house with an outside staircase leading up to it, and this balcony and the staircase leading up to it are also full of flowers – asters, dahlias, pansies and geraniums, mostly displayed, as are the ones in the courtyard, in old tin cans with their lids cut off.

The bedrooms look out on to the balcony. The old-fashioned ones are furnished with big dark wooden or iron beds some of which weigh up to three or four hundred pounds. They stand on scrubbed wooden floors and the walls are hung with photographs of immediate ancestors that look as if they have been taken as well as framed by the local undertakers. Younger married people now have flashier furniture, wardrobes and beds with veneer and lots of mirrors, but the women, young or old, unless they are Party members, will have hung a print of the Virgin above the bed as an insurance against misfortune and, perhaps, excessive high jinks.

In the centre of the village is the church, with a white bell tower rising above it to one side and sometimes with the bell rope swinging in the breeze under an arch at the foot of it.

Nothing that the Government or the Party could do after the war, when Yugoslavia became officially communist, to stop the people, particularly the women, in these villages from going to church, was even remotely successful. In the years from 1945 onwards, when priests were forbidden to wear vestments and say mass, they went to the church just the same and simply stood inside it in a silent gesture of defiance and disapproval. When transport to distant places of pilgrimage to which they were accustomed to go was denied them, they set off for them on foot.

Wanda's kinswoman worked as a waitress in a *gostilna*, a village inn. Its courtyard was shielded from the sun by a trellis of vines so thick that those sitting beneath it were in perpetual twilight. Under it men were playing cards, slapping them down on the tables and making a great deal of noise. One of the characteristics of the Slovene language, at least up here on the Kras, is that those who speak it often sound as if they are engaged in a violent quarrel when, in fact, they are thoroughly enjoying themselves. Also under the vines there was a bowling alley made of rolled earth. In such a place the only woman on view is usually the waitress. The *gostilna* is like a London club, a man's world.

From the terrace of the inn, long, stone-walled expanses of rock with a bit of earth in them masquerading as fields, and interspersed with windbreaks of young trees, swept up to the foot of the mountains, the Nanos, and the Javornik. The Nanos with its bare, high summit covered, as it often is, with what looked like a wig of white cloud; the Javornik, to the south of the gap through which the road and railway run eastwards to Ljubljana, covered with dense forest which still harbours within its fastnesses red deer, wild boar, wolves and what are some of the last European brown bear.

Marija, Wanda's *soi-disante* kinswoman, was a widow of indeterminate age, good-looking, if not positively sexy, in a black, widow's-weedy sort of way. She took us into the building and sat us down at a table in a pale, austere room of which the only other occupants were four fierce-looking young men in blue overalls, who looked as if they might be off duty from a filling station and were playing the same game that was being played on the terrace, a form of whist, slamming the cards down on the table as if they were practising to cut it in quarters with a karate chop, making the rafters ring with cries of what was either rage or triumph.

In one corner there was a big white-tiled wood-burning stove with a long, silver-painted metal pipe extending up from it and across the width of the room and then out into the open air through a hole in the outer wall, which would ensure that the room was always stiflingly hot in winter, however cold it was outside. Old-fashioned lace curtains effectively obstructed what would have been the same view from the windows that one could enjoy outside on the terrace, and the walls, which had been stencilled with a pale apple-green pattern on a white background, rollers being used for this purpose, were hung with the stuffed heads of various sorts of small game, game that were now completely extinct a few miles away over the border in Italy. (It is a paradox that the enthusiasm of the communist apparat for the chase organized on capitalist lines, to the exclusion of the *hoi polloi*, has led in many communist countries to a positive proliferation of species that in many capitalist countries in Europe have long since become extinct.)

There was also an astonishing profusion of what can only be described as Victorian potted plants, aspidistras, castor oil plants and such, all standing on rather wobbly whatnots. It was all terribly melancholy and over everything hung a faint but palpable, slightly acid smell, compounded of Slavonic cooking, cigarettes, drainage and other elements, difficult to identify, let alone describe, but once inhaled never forgotten. It was a room that was the prototype of a room in a village inn anywhere between the one in which we were now sitting near the eastern shores of the Adriatic, and the Volga.

Here in the Kras, in spite of the heat and the vines heavy with black grapes, not more than twenty miles from its shores, one felt the Mediterranean world receding, could sense that people were no longer looking to it either for sustenance or inspiration, but to Middle Europe.

Having seated us at the table Marija hurried away and after a bit returned carrying a tray on which there was a litre bottle of red wine, a plate of the local ham called *pršut*, so thinly sliced that it was almost transparent, and a kind of flat, crusty bread called *pogača*, which she proceeded to cut up, meanwhile making pantomime gestures of eating and drinking to me, reinforcing them with little cries in Italian, which she had somehow got it into her head I was unfamiliar with, of '*Bere! Mangiare!*', using an infinitive form commonly reserved for cretins, monoglot soldiers of invading armies and infants still at the breast. The *pogača* was hot from the wood oven, which was outside in the back yard. The *pršut* was delicious, a rare delicacy. The smoking of this sort of ham is usually carried out in late autumn or in winter and the process of preparing it is only commenced at the time of the full moon. At any other time an inferior product will result. Like many other peasant communities around the Mediterranean, and also elsewhere, the inhabitants of the Kras are still to a great extent governed by the moon in their everyday life. No one used to be surprised, for instance, when one of the apparently robust wooden bedsteads, bought by a newly married couple, disintegrated if it was purchased at the time of the new moon. No other fate could be expected for it. But that was in the past. Now, in the 1980s, bedsteads disintegrated whatever phase the moon was in.

To prepare this ham it was first kept in salt for a week, then it was put in what looked a bit like an old-fashioned letter press for another week, the pressure being increased daily. It was then hung in a chimney to smoke over a fire of ash wood and after that it was hung for anything from seven months to a year in a dry place, having been previously sprinkled with pepper as a protection against flies which, together with dampness, were its principal enemies. By the time a *pršut* reached Trieste, a good one was about as expensive as smoked salmon.

The wine was Teran, the product of a close circle of about a dozen villages north of the main road from Trieste to Ljubljana, between the Nanos range and the present frontier with Italy. It is a deep purple colour, almost black, with a taste that some people, when they first try it, compare to that of rusty old nuts and bolts. It is best either with hot food, or else with the *pršut* and the *pogača*. It is not a wine to drink by itself. It improves on acquaintanceship.

Meanwhile, we ate and drank, while Marija constantly refilled the glasses, particularly my glass, which somehow became empty quicker than Wanda's, all the time going on and on to Wanda in Slovene about births and deaths and marriages and who had emigrated where, only pausing to go out and get another bottle.

'Marija says we must drink,' Wanda said, I thought illogically. Usually she spends her time telling me not to.

'I *am* drinking. It's you who's not drinking. Anyway, why doesn't *she* drink?'

'Here, it is not the custom for widows . . .'

'It's not the custom for anyone to drink like this, even where I come from. You'd think she wanted to keep me here in pickle.'

'*Bere! Bere!*' ('Drink! Drink!') said Marija, who was already refilling my glass. From the yard outside came the sounds of what later proved to be a free-range chicken being slaughtered.

'That's our dinner,' Wanda said. 'Now they're going to pluck it, draw it, truss it, put it in a pot on top of the stove with butter and rosemary. It's going to be hours before we eat dinner.'

'How many hours?'

'Three hours.'

'It's only seven o'clock now. It'll be ten. By then I'll be dead at this rate. Why didn't you tell her we'd be happy with something simpler? An omelette or just more *pršut*, more *pogača*.'

'I did but she wouldn't listen. Now she wants to give you some *žganje* to keep you going.'

'Why don't you stop her? What's come over you?'

'She will be very upset if you don't drink. She will say that you do not like her drinks. Tonight you *must* drink. It is the custom.'

'*Bere! Bere!*' cried Marija, this by-now-to-me-terrible woman, bringing a clean glass and more than half filling it with *žganje*, then waving her arms as if she was performing a conjuring trick or conducting some vast alcoholic orchestra. What Wanda said was true. The more I drank the more she seemed to warm to me.

Žganje is the equivalent of Italian *grappa* or French *marc*, spirit distilled from the skins, pips and stalks left over after the grapes have been pressed and the wine made, but here, in the sticks, home-made and much stronger than what is normally sold commercially because it has been distilled more often. On top of what I had already drunk it was murderous.

'Look,' I said, 'I've either got to go to bed until it's time for dinner, or go for a walk or something. I just can't go on like this.'

'You can't, we're going to sit with the deads.'

'You mean a wake? What they had for your mother?'

'I don't know what you call it in English. In Italian it's *veglia*. You sit with the deads.'

'I know you sit with the deads,' I said. 'We did it with your mother.'

'Yes, that's right, wake for the deads. A very old lady, ninety-three, called Nunča Pahorča, Marija's aunt, died this morning. She was very nice. She's being buried tomorrow.'

'Listen,' I said. 'I'm half tight. If you think I'm going to sit by some dead dear old lady for three hours until dinner's ready you've got it all wrong. Besides, we had enough of this funeral thing in Naples.'

'It's better than sitting here getting dronker,' she said. 'And I was only joking about the chicken. It was being killed for someone else. Ours is nearly ready. And you know it doesn't matter about being a bit dronk, others will be dronk also. We shall only stay a few minutes.'

'OK,' I said. 'Let's go, before she brings any more *žganje*. Otherwise it'll be a double funeral and I don't fancy sharing a vault with a nice old lady of ninety-three.'

The house in which the remains of Nunča Pahorča were on exhibition was very small, for she had been a widow for twenty years and had moved to it when her husband died when she herself was well over seventy. Nunča means 'aunt' in the dialect spoken nearer the Adriatic, where she had once lived, but where she now lived she would have been known as Teta Pahorča.

The heavy old bed, in which she had died only a few hours before had been taken to pieces and removed temporarily to a shed in her vegetable garden, where it now stood together with a bedside table on which there were a number of bottles containing various liniments that were sovereign remedies against aches and pains, the sort that have labels with gloomy likenesses of their moustached and bearded inventors and their scrawly, illegible signatures printed on them. Now, washed and changed by a couple of the women of the village who knew how to do these things, she lay dressed from head to foot in her best black, from the black lace mantilla which covered the snow-white hair of which she had been so proud to her black felt boots, on her best linen sheets which were part of her marriage trousseau and which she had kept for more than seventy years for this purpose, in a plastic coffin with simulated metal handles, lined with pink ruched nylon, her now waxen features decently composed but no longer with any human attributes, her hands crossed and holding a candle and a rosary that had been placed in them. The walls of the room had been hung with black cloth by the undertaker's men; a tall candle burned at each of the four corners of the coffin, and at the foot of it, on a table, there were sprigs of box and a receptacle containing holy water.

The room was full of people. Most had come to pay their respects, take a sprig of the box, dip it in the holy water, sprinkle it over the corpse, stay a little while to pray or talk to relatives and friends about the virtues of the deceased, and have a drink, after which they left to get back to their televisions, and be replaced by other mourners. Some of the men, of whom I was one, were, as Wanda had forecast, a bit 'dronk'.

The remainder, women mostly, old and young, although there were one or two elderly men among them, sat on hard upright chairs round the coffin, dressed in their best clothes, the women reciting the rosary, counting the decades of the Aves, the Ave Marias, on their beads, sometimes at the conclusion of a whole fifteen of them stopping to recount some edifying anecdotes about Nunča Pahorča who had always been very devout, sometimes to the distraction of her husband. They talked about how she had never missed going to mass and benediction and how she used to tick off the acolytes for picking their noses or otherwise misbehaving themselves during the celebration while the priest's back was turned. And once they sang a Slovene song, which was one of her favourites, and which began:

Tam cěz jezero	There, over the lake,
dol na gmajničo	Down in the meadows
je prelepi dom	Is the most beautiful place
moje zibelke . . .	Where my cradle was . . .

After which they wept a bit, had another little drink and began reciting the rosary once more. Long after midnight, by which time we had finished dinner, we went back with Marija for a second visit, and found that they were still at it and showed no signs of giving up.

The dinner was memorable, although like a relieving force for a beleaguered garrison it only arrived in the nick of time to save me. The chicken, which had spent its life scratching among the grit in the back yard, was flavoured with rosemary and full of delicious natural juices. With it we had *ajdova polenta*, like Italian *polenta* but grey not yellow, made from the seeds of a white flower which grows all over the Kras in summertime, and really meant to be eaten with *golaž*, goulash, which was also on the menu that evening. Many of the dishes served in this part of the world have Austro-Hungarian origins. With it we ate *radič*, a bitter, delicious green salad, and *fižol*, cooked, dried red haricot beans, with olive oil and vinegar. Last of all, as a great treat, we were given *cespljevi cmoki*, dumplings made with flour, potatoes and egg, like Italian *gnocchi*, each dumpling stuffed with a plum, sprinkled with sugar and then eaten with a sauce of melted butter and fried breadcrumbs. After all this, and more Teran, and more *žganje*, we went to bed.

The next morning, after having attended the funeral of Nunča Pahorča, following the coffin to the cemetery on foot, feeling decidedly unwell, in a procession which included almost all those inhabitants of the village able to walk, and seeing the red earth thud down on it as it lay alongside her husband's in the grave, we went away, crossing the ridge of the Javornik mountains which here formed the pre-1939 frontier between Yugoslavia and Italy, where the now empty casemates of the two not very friendly nations still face one another across vestiges of what had once been fields of barbed wire.

Then we drove along the far shore of the Cerkniško Jezero, which was staging one of its customary disappearing acts – hay was being harvested from the bottom of it – to Planina, a village in the pass between the Nanos and the Javornik which carries the main road from Trieste to Ljubljana.

A rather unusual lake, the Cerkniško Jezero, normally a sheet of water seven miles long and six feet deep, at certain seasons, of which this was one, disappears without warning, together with its inhabitants which include fish with horns and a freshwater jellyfish. Besides these fishy inhabitants, and in winter enormous numbers of waterfowl, it also has a ghostly population of skeleton warriors armed with lances and axes and mounted on skeleton horses. From time to time they rise from beneath the surface and, preceded by flocks of skeletal birds, circuit the lake making the night hideous with the clattering of their bones and weapons.

At Planina, the Pivka, another underground river, emerges in a deep valley, having been joined, also underground, by the Rak, a river which has its origins beneath the Cerkniško Jezero. In the valley at Planina the now-augmented Pivka is joined by a third river which also emerges from underground at this point, the Malenska, after which, still called the Pivka, it flows through watermeadows of extraordinary beauty until, eventually, it sinks for what is the last time in its career beneath the Ljubljanski Mountain near Ljubljana, beyond which it joins the Sava and eventually the Danube, flowing with it into the Black Sea.

Across the river from Planina, standing on the edge of the forest from which the red deer come down into the park from the Javornik, is the Haasberg, a castle, a country house really, of the Princes of Windisch-Graetz, a family reputed to have owned ninety-nine castles in Austria-Hungary before 1914, a figure that makes one suspect that this is legend because anyone having ninety-nine castles could surely not have resisted the temptation to acquire one more and make it a round hundred. Nevertheless, when the Italians annexed a large slice of what had been until 1918 Slovene territory in Austria-Hungary, the Windisch-Graetz still had sufficient influence to have the new frontier moved sufficiently far to the east, a matter of yards, for the house itself to be on Italian soil. The stones marking the boundaries can still be seen in the park behind the house.

The Haasberg was burned by the Yugoslav partisans in 1944 when it was an Italian headquarters. Now it is an empty shell. The watermills that stand one above the other in the valley of the Malenska are ruined; the church in the park unused, occupied by thirteen members of the family lying in stone sarcophagi. (The fourteenth sarcophagus lies empty with its lid drawn to one side, waiting for an occupant who will now, presumably, never come.) Very old retainers, one of whom was pottering about the dilapidated barns and outbuildings in a battered green hat, recall what to them was a happier age before the Second World War.

Whatever the Carso or the Kras may be, this sad and beautiful place has nothing at all to do with the Mediterranean and never has done. Here, if anywhere, you can say that the Mediterranean world ends and that of Middle Europe begins.

A Night in Montenegro

South of Rijeka the Adriatic Highway with its sometimes amazing views of off-shore islands that appear to be swimming one behind the other, like a shoal of sea monsters, extends almost to the Albanian frontier. Now, in late summer, the roadside and the cliffs below it on what had been until recently one of the most beautiful coasts in the entire Mediterranean were littered with the detritus of snacks and picnics and with the shattered and burnt-out shells of motor cars whose occupants, down here on holiday from the Nordic north, had departed this life for what one hopes is a better world.

Along this road, one of the most perilous in the world in high summer, were the official camp sites, surrounded by high wire fences which effectively separated the campers from the local inhabitants, keeping the former in, the latter out. Some of the larger camps were guarded by armed soldiers and spending the night in one of these places I really felt that once more I was in a concentration camp. As on the shores of most other Mediterranean countries it was forbidden to camp anywhere other than in an organized camp site. Given the state of the roadsides it was difficult to see what else the authorities could do. But for the existence of these camps, some of which after months of continuous occupation were themselves in a repulsive condition, there would probably have been large scale outbreaks of typhoid.

Now the season was nearly over. Soon the Highway would be largely deserted, except by long-distance lorries, and the cleaning-up squads would emerge to haul away the wrecks of automobiles, clear away the beer cans, burn the plastic, unblock the drains in the camp sites and replace the shattered lavatories and wash basins. We kept our spirits up by reminding one another that we were on our way to Cetinje in Montenegro where we were going to stay in the Grand Hotel.

The road to Cetinje, the former capital of Montenegro, begins near Kotor, a seaport at the head of the Gulf of the same name, an astonishing inlet of the Adriatic, with the Crna Gora, the Black Mountain from which the country takes its name, rising above it.

The town stands at the foot of the Lovčen, a summit which rises more than 5700 feet above it, and appears to be still intact behind the fortifications built by the Venetians which zigzag up the mountainside from it.

It was only necessary to go into it through the main gate down by the harbour, as we did, to realize that something was seriously wrong with Kotor. Inside the walls, the city was moribund. A great earthquake which had convulsed large portions of the Balkan Peninsula in 1979, had rendered it uninhabitable, doing to Kotor what a succession of invading Saracens, Serbians, Tartars, Hungarians, Bosnians, Venetians, Austrians, French, British, Russians, Austrians again, Montenegrins, Turks (who had unsuccessfully besieged it in 1538 and 1667), other earthquakes, in 1563 and 1667, and an outbreak of plague in 1572, had all failed to do, except temporarily.

Yet in spite of this latest misfortune Kotor, although more than half-dead, was not completely so. A few stubborn inhabitants still lived within its walls, either in deep, dark, labyrinthine streets, from most of which the afternoon sun had long since gone by the time we arrived in them, that is if it ever shone into them at all, or in little squares, some of them still sunlit, in which children played happily, streets and squares in which the houses and palaces, most of them long since converted into tenements, were often either shorn up with balks of timber or else had already been gutted and were shells empty of everything except rubble. Its fate, or only hope, perhaps, depending on how one regarded such things, was to become a museum city, although even that seemed improbable, for it gave the impression that even one minor tremor might be enough to demolish it completely. Meanwhile, the bulk of its former inhabitants, hoiked into the twentieth century in this unpleasant fashion, now either lived in caravans or in lightly built, more unattractive but less dangerous modern houses out beyond the walls.

Because of all this it was no longer possible to visit what other travellers describe as the amazing treasury of the twelfth-century cathedral of St Tryphon and see the head of the city's patron saint, also the patron saint of gardeners, who was born in Phrygia, the son of a gooseherd, and was put to death in Nicaea in about AD 250, a relic which the citizens of Kotor are said to have acquired out of a ship bound for Europe from Asia Minor, together with other assorted relics of other saints, arms, legs, etc., for 300 gold pieces. Nor was it possible to see the great wooden crucifix, with its tormented Christ nailed to it, said to have been given by Baldwin II, the last Latin Emperor of Constantinople, to the widow of a thirteenth-century Serbian king. Perennially hard-up, he also, at about the same time, disposed of the Crown of Thorns, a portion of the True Cross, the baby linen of Jesus, the Lance, the Sponge and the Chain of the Passion, the Rod of Moses and part of the skull of St John the Baptist – to St Louis, Louis IX of France, the most Christian king.

By the time we left Kotor the sun had already gone from the town completely, as it does quite early, leaving it in cold, dark shadow, and dense black clouds hung threateningly over the tops of the surrounding mountains, although, out beyond the inlet on which the city itself is built, the Gulf was still bathed in sunlight.

The main road to Cetinje by way of the Lovčen Pass was a wild one even by Montenegrin standards. It climbed the steep side of the Lovčen, on the summit of which the remains of Petar II Petrović Njegoš, Prince-Bishop of Montenegro, last of a line of prince-bishops who began to reign in 1516 when the previous ruler retired to Venice, are entombed in a remarkable mausoleum designed by the Serbo-Croat sculptor Ivan Mestrović, who died in 1962.

The road to the Pass, lined with ruined forts, climbed through plantations of oak and pine ravaged by fires that had only recently swept the mountainside. It was loosely metalled, full of pot-holes, had twenty-four major hairpin bends on it and was only one vehicle wide, with lay-bys. Its outside edge frequently overhung precipices and at some places gaps in the masonry, as they did in so many places on the Adriatic Highway, showed where vehicles had been driven clean through the protecting walls taking the occupants on what had been, presumably, a spectacular exit to eternity.

Our ascent of it was made more difficult by a large caravan of picturesquely-clad gypsies who were descending it from the Pass in horse-drawn carts, on foot and with numbers of animals running loose along with them; but finally, having emerged from a tunnel that had been driven through one of the outlying spurs of the massif, we reached the Pass, which was literally white with sheep. Here the sky was threatening and a few drops of icy rain fell. Already old women in long, rusty black skirts and white-moustached men wearing little round black pill-box hats and waistcoats and what looked like baggy jodphur breeches of heavy, brown homespun were urging the flocks and the cattle that had been grazing around the head of the Pass down to the little village of Njeguši in anticipation of the coming storm.

The village was disposed along one side of what Slavs call a *polje*, a big green meadow that had once formed the bottom of a lake, with dark woods extended down to the edge of it on the far side. Above it loomed the Lovčen, its limestone rocks now a steely grey in the rapidly gathering darkness. This wild spot was the birthplace of Petar II Petrović Njegoš, the future ruler of Montenegro, sometime between 1811 and 1813.

From the village the road wound up past abandoned and roofless houses to another pass, the Krivačko Ždrjelo, at around 4300 feet, on the rim of another enormous *polje* in which Cetinje stands more than 2000 feet below.

Just below this pass there was an inn, a *gostiona*, which is the Montenegrin way of spelling *gostilna*, where we stopped for a drink.

Inside it four men, one of them the proprietor who was in his shirt-sleeves, were drinking the Albanian brandy called XTRA. All were drunk and beginning to be acrimonious. It was not a place to linger. The three customers had their vehicles parked outside, one of which was a large petrol tanker, and when we got up to go one of them, who turned out to be the driver of the tanker, easily identifiable by his overalls, got up, too, clutched one of the lapels of my coat in order to keep himself in an upright position and, swaying backwards and forwards on his feet like some Cornish rocking-stone, announced that he was about to drive his tanker down to

Kotor by the road we had just climbed to the Lovčen Pass. How he was proposing to do this and remain alive was a mystery.

By the time we emerged from the *gostiona* the storm was directly overhead and for an instant a single, blinding flash of lightning turned the grey limestone of the mountain a dazzling white. It was followed by a single, deafening roll of thunder which reverberated among the rocks. Then an apocalyptical wind blew, bending the trees as if they were reeds. Then the heavens opened.

Thanking our lucky stars that tonight we would sleep in a Grand Hotel instead of in the back of a van unconverted for this purpose, which was what we had now been doing on and off for months, we set off downhill through the downpour into what, insofar as we could see anything at all, resembled a crater filled with twisted rocks, narrowly missing a head-on collision with a bus that was groaning up through the hairpin bends on its way to Njeguši, loaded with what we later discovered was part of the day shift of the 'Obod' factory in Cetinje which made refrigerators and other electrical appliances, the 'Košuta' footwear factory and the 'Galenika' factory for processing pharmaceutical preparations, all of whom would have been a serious loss to the economy.

By the time we reached the city it was completely dark and the rain that had been clouting down had given place to a monotonous drizzle; so dark that in a dimly-lit boulevard opposite what had once been the building occupied by the Italian diplomatic mission I ran over and killed a black cat which darted across the road in front of us. However, even this melancholy incident failed to dampen our spirits completely. For we were looking forward to staying the night at the hotel, which was not just any old hotel but the Grand Hotel of Vuko Vuketič, as it used to be known, otherwise known as the Lokanda, one of the last hotels of its kind in the Balkans: the Balkans strictly speaking being the mountains in Bulgaria that extend across the country from the Yugoslav border to the Black Sea: but in the sense in which I interpret it, the one in which it is commonly used, of the Balkan Peninsula, the lands between the Adriatic and the Black Seas.

I had last stayed in it in the 1960s. I remembered it as a rather splendid cream- and yellow-coloured building with a sort of semicircular foyer that was a bit like a Victorian greenhouse. Originally built in 1864, it was the first hotel to be constructed in Cetinje and to it were sent the official and honoured guests of what was then the Montenegrin capital, which even in its heyday never had more than

5000 inhabitants. (Now it had more than 10,000 inhabitants and had several large factories producing, as well as electrical appliances, shoes, pharmaceutical products and white bauxite.) At one time the hotel housed the United States diplomatic mission. Reconstructed in 1900, and enlarged in 1929, it had two restaurants and forty bedrooms. In its remarkable foyer and in other public rooms, all rather dingy when I was last there, tall old men in national costumes with huge white moustaches, some, almost unbelievably, still with Lugers and Mausers and other weapons stuck in their cummerbunds, sat sipping away at their *rakijas*, their Albanian XTRA brandies and various other strong drinks for hours on end while remembering old blood feuds, an activity which in Montenegro had been raised to an art form. In fact one visitor, the author of the excellent *Companion Guide to Jugoslavia*, J. A. Cuddon, records one of these Montenegrin mountaineers taking out his pistol and shooting a mad dog in one of the dining rooms.

The hotel stood in what had been a windswept square when I was last there, for although it was already spring down on the Adriatic, 2100 or so feet below, up here at Cetinje, which is invariably snowed up for five months of the year from October until the end of February, there was still snow on the ground.

Now, on this really foul, wet night, we looked forward to the hot baths which could usually be had in it, sometimes to the accompaniment of alarming clanking noises from the plumbing system; to the big drinks, the scalding hot lamb soup we planned on ordering, and the great gobbets of Montenegrin pork, all brought to the table by ancient servitors; and after that to retiring to bed in one of the large and shabby but clean bedrooms. All things I remembered about the hotel with pleasure from my previous visit and of which I had spoken enthusiastically and perhaps too frequently to my fellow traveller. I could even remember the way to it, through little streets lined with lime and black locust trees, the latter a form of acacia.

By the time we reached the square in the centre of the town in which the hotel stood a thick mist had descended on it and as it was ill-lit I got down and set off on foot to look for it, leaving Wanda in the vehicle.

There, at the southern end of the square in which I remembered it as standing, I was confronted with what looked like an enormous pancake but on closer inspection turned out to be a mound of yellowish rubble. There was no sign of the hotel.

'Excuse me,' I said to a passer-by who had halted, curious at my interest in a heap of rubble, speaking in Italian, which sometimes serves in these parts of the world. 'Do you happen to speak Italian?'

'Yes,' he said.

'Can you please tell me the way to the Grand Hotel?'

'Grand Hotel,' he said. 'That is the Grand Hotel,' pointing at the mound of bricks and plaster.

'But what happened?' I asked.

'It was the earthquake,' he said. 'The great earthquake of 1979. It destroyed not only the Grand Hotel. It also damaged and destroyed a large part of the city.'

'Is there another hotel?' I asked him, remembering that back in the sixties although the Grand Hotel had been the only one of any consequence in Cetinje, there had been some talk of another hotel, although whether it was built or about to be built I could no longer recall.

'No,' he said, 'there is no other hotel. The Grand Hotel was the only one. Tourists are no longer allowed to stay in the town. In fact there is no longer even a Tourist Office.'

I told Wanda. At first she thought it was funny about the hotel, especially as there had been no loss of life when it collapsed, although there had been elsewhere in the city. Then when she realized that it meant another night in the van and, if the police found us, probably a long drive all the way back to the coast at Budva, where the nearest hotels and camp sites were, her vocabulary was immense.

In spite of the drizzle and the fog it was the hour of the *passeggiata* in the main street, which although many of its buildings had been badly damaged was either being rebuilt or had already been built in their original, old-fashioned form.

Young, tall, dark and incredibly handsome men, moustache-less and pistol-less, and equally beautiful girls wearing jeans and as upright as if they had been brought up to carry pots and heavy weights on their heads, as they probably had, walked up and down in little bands past the lighted shop fronts of the pleasant, pale-coloured buildings I remembered, talking animatedly, smoking cigarettes like chimneys and eyeing one another. Apart from the two of us there was not a tourist in sight and the Tourist Office, as my informant had already told me, was closed, with a notice in the window to that effect.

We dined well on the sort of huge pieces of pork we would have been offered at the Grand Hotel if only it had remained standing, quantities of bread – there were no vegetables of any kind on offer – a delicious pastry stuffed with figs, a sort of baklava, but softer than the Greek variety, and drank copiously of a robust red wine of the region called Vranač Plavka in an effort to banish the thought of another night in the open, in a restaurant which resembled a brick-lined *bier-keller*, except that it was on the ground floor. The waiters, who were all well over six feet tall, wore white shirts and black trousers and black waistcoats. Male guests drank oceans of beer straight out of the bottles, spurning glasses; and old men of the sort I remembered with moustaches like racing bicycle handlebars kissed one another before settling down, as I had remembered them doing, to speak nostalgically, according to Wanda who could understand some of what they said, of what had been until quite recently an almost unbelievably violent past.

'He who revenges himself is blessed,' was one of the dicta of family life in a country where male children used to have loaded firearms placed in their hands before they could even stand on their two feet, let alone fire them, in order to prepare them to be good Montenegrins, worthy members of the only Balkan State that was never subdued by the Turks. For Montenegro, until the Second World War, was a man's country in which a woman's lot was to perform menial tasks such as agriculture, beget as many male children as possible to make up for the constant death roll among the men, and attend the funerals of their lords and masters when they failed to survive a *ceta*, one of the predatory raids they spent so much of their time either planning or taking part in. The results of such expeditions were subsequently recorded for posterity by *gus-lari*, minstrels, many of them blind, who used to accompany their recitals of these bloody doings on the *guslar*, a one-stringed instru-ment rather like a lute, made of wood, or clay, or copper, sometimes even of stone. Some of the ballads, which the *guslari* knew by heart, were anything up to seventy thousand words long and are still recited today in some parts of what is the smallest Yugoslavian republic. Now these feudal practices were ostensibly no more in Cetinje.

After dinner, having ascertained that there was no official camp site in Cetinje and therefore no camping, which put us in a rather difficult position, we drove hurriedly away and hid the van and ourselves with it behind one of the walls of what had been the royal park, outside the Crnojević Monastery, otherwise the Monastery of the Virgin, so named after Ivan Crnojević who built it in 1484. This original monastery, which he surrounded with a moat and heavily fortified, was razed to the ground by the Turks in 1692, again in 1712 and again in 1785. Above it on a hill, when I had last been in Cetinje, there had been a round tower called the Tablja which the Montenegrins used to decorate with the skulls of Turks, emulating by so doing the Turks who built the Celé Kula, the Tower of Skulls, at Niš in Serbia which they decorated with a thousand Serbian skulls, a few of which are still in position. Whether the Tablja was still standing or whether it had fallen a victim to the earthquake it was impossible to say because it was dark, and the following day, with the fog still persisting, we forgot to ask.

What with earthquakes, the Turks who had set fire to it and destroyed it three times, and the Austrians, Italians and Germans, who had each consigned it twice to the flames, it was a wonder that there was anything left of Cetinje at all. One of its proudest possessions, now in the Treasury of the Monastery, is the skull of the Vizier Mahmut-Pasha Busatlija of Shkodër in Albania, one of Montenegro's greatest enemies and the last Turkish leader to fight his way into Cetinje and destroy it and the Monastery, in 1785, who was killed in a great battle with Petar I Njegoš in 1796.

There, behind the wall, we spent, as we anticipated we would, an awful night, which not even the good red wine of Vranač Plavka we had drunk alleviated. Soon after we arrived some policemen drove up in a car to the Monastery, obviously in search of us, and we only narrowly escaped discovery.

Meanwhile the rain, which had become torrential again, drummed on the tinny roof of the van making sleep impossible. Finally, in the early hours of the morning, when the rain had finally ceased and we had at last succeeded in dropping off, we were besieged by a pack of savage dogs, one of a number of such packs that infested the park and which had already made the night hideous with their barking and fighting. Why they chose to surround our van was a mystery. Perhaps they could smell a salami that we had hanging up in it.

There were still several royal palaces at Cetinje. The Old Palace, otherwise known as the Biljarda, was a long, low single-storey stone building with strongpoints at each of its angles, more like a fort than a palace, built as his residence by Petar II Petrović Njegoš, who reigned from 1830 to 1851 and was six feet eight inches in his socks. Previously he had lived in the Monastery. Besides being a prince and bishop of this country half the size of Wales, and before that having been a monk, he was also a warrior who led his people in resisting Austrians and Turks, a traveller, crack shot, player of the *guslar* and author of an epic poem, the '*Gorski Vijenac*', otherwise 'The Mountain Wreath'. As a result of being all these things, he was naturally also the hero of the Montenegrins, and is to this day. The Palace was called the Biljarda because it was to it that the Prince, in the face of what might have appeared to anyone else something of insuperable difficulty, had a very large slate-bedded billiard table from England manhandled three thousand feet up the mule track from Kotor to the Lovčen Pass – at that time the road did not exist – then downhill to his birthplace, up again to the Krivačko Ždrelo Pass and then 2000 feet down through a chaos of limestone to the Palace, where it was installed without the slate being broken.

Not much more than a bomb's toss away from the Biljarda was an elegant palace, painted in *sangue-de-boeuf* picked out in white, the residence of King Nikola I Petrović, the first and last King of Montenegro, a cultured, ruthless despot of a sort the Montenegrins were perfectly prepared to put up with providing they were allowed to destroy Muslims and one another. He ruled for fifty-eight years, from 1860 to 1918, having assumed the title of king in 1910. Forced to flee the country in 1916, when it was occupied by the armies of Austria-Hungary, Montenegro having entered the war against them in 1914 on the side of Serbia, he never returned, dying in exile in Antibes in 1921. After the war, in 1919, as a result of a Balkan version of a free vote, Montenegro became part of Yugoslavia and remained part of it until 1941 when the Italians occupied it and proclaimed a new kingdom. In 1945 it again became part of Yugoslavia.

Now the Palace of King Nikola, which had been seriously shaken by the earthquake, stood swathed in plastic sheeting, a hollow shell, awaiting restoration. Outside it was the tree under which the King used to sit, dispensing Montenegrin justice.

At the Art Gallery of the Socialist Republic of Montenegro, which is housed in the former Government House, the Vladin Dom, the largest building in Montenegro, we were kindly received by the Director, a cultivated man who was very upset about the siting of the 'Obod' electrical appliance factory, which had been plonked down in a prominent position in the town and had done nothing to improve its appearance. He himself, as director of the gallery, had suffered an almost worse aesthetic misfortune in the form of an enormous inheritance of paintings known as the Milica Sarić-

Vukmanović Bequest which, although it did contain a number of good paintings, including works by foreign artists, was largely made up of post-war kitsch of a particularly awful sort which he had not only been forced to accept but put on permanent display, completely swamping what was otherwise an interesting and representative collection of Montenegrin art from the seventeenth century to the present.

Then, having admired the outsides of various buildings, some of which had once housed the Russian, Austro-Hungarian, Turkish, French, English and Italian diplomatic missions, some of them wonderfully eccentric buildings, and having failed to find the Girls' Institute, one of the first girls' schools in the Balkans, founded in 1869 by the Empress Maria Alexandrovna of Russia, with which Montenegro had a close relationship before the First World War, we left Cetinje with genuine regret, and took the road to Albania.

Albania Stern and Wild

From Cetinje we travelled down to Virpasar on the shores of Lake Shkodër by a very minor road through the Kremenica Mountains. There we waited for Tour Group ALB 81/6, the group with which we were to visit Albania, group travel being the only permitted form of travel in the country, to arrive in a bus from the airport at Titograd, which they did at a quarter to eleven at night. We now numbered thirty-four people – English, Scottish, Welsh, Irish from both sides of the border who didn't mix with one another, three Canadians, a New Zealand lady and a German boy with a fine, full beard, apparently anxious to try out the Albanian barbering facilities. No Americans were allowed into Albania, no Russians, no Chinese, no Yugoslavs, nobody with 'writer' or 'journalist' inscribed in his or her passport, no males with long hair or beards, unless 'with a large shaven area between sideboards and start of beard . . . should authorities not be satisfied in this respect beards will be cut by the barber on arrival'. No mini-skirts, maxis, flared trousers, no bright colours ('People may be asked to change,' although a couple of girls defiantly flaunting forbidden, folklorique maxi-skirts were not). No Bibles, since a bold band of Evangelists, having pondered the possibility of dropping Bibles on the by-that-time officially Godless Albanians in a free fall from a chartered aircraft, had decided to join a tour and deliver them in person. No Korans, either.

While eating dinner – soup with what looked like weeds in it from the lake and the worst sort of Balkan rissoles – we observed our new companions, wondering, as they were too presumably, who among us were revisionists, anti-revisionists, who was representing MI6, the CIA and similar organizations, and which ones were writers and journalists in disguise.

Meanwhile, the Tour Leader went over all the other things we weren't to do in addition to wearing beards and skirts of forbidden lengths while in Albania. There seemed an awful lot.

'What happens if I die in Albania?' asked a fragile septuagenarian with her mouth full of rissole.

'There's a hot line to the French Ambassador in Tirana (Tirana is the capital of Albania). He takes over. It shouldn't hold us up much.'

Next morning the sun rose out of the mist over the lake, looking like a large tangerine, silhouetting the rugged peaks of Albania the Mysterious, away on the far side of it.

It was market day at Virpasar and the market was taking place under the trees at the end of a causeway which crossed a little arm of the lake. Every moment more and more people were arriving with their mules and donkeys, driving or riding them along the causeway, the women wearing white head-dresses, and white skirts with white pantaloons under them. Others, fishermen and their wives, all dressed in black, were arriving by water in narrow, pointed boats with their outboards roaring. There were also a number of young Albanian men with the same razor sharp noses with moustaches to match that had made the late King Zog of Albania such a memorable figure. With their white felt skull caps they looked rather like bald-headed eagles. Two of these young men were being subjected to a prolonged interrogation by a couple of grim-looking Yugoslav policemen. There are large numbers of expatriate Albanians living in Yugoslavia on the periphery of Albania and at this particular time most of these areas were in a state of ferment. In fact much of Kosovo-Metohija, an autonomous region in south-west Serbia, abutting on northern Albania, with a population of about a million Albanians, was in a state of revolt, under martial law, and foreigners were forbidden to enter it.

Within a matter of minutes I, too, found myself being subjected to an equally severe interrogation, having been arrested for photographing the naval base when in fact I had been photographing a rather jolly-looking lady who was crossing a bridge on a donkey on the way to the market.

We set off for Albania in a Yugoslav tourist bus, crossing the lake by a causeway which carries the main road and the railway from Bar, the port on the Adriatic coast, to Titograd, the present capital of Montenegro. Then after a bit we turned off on to a lesser road, which leads to the frontier between Yugoslavia and Albania. It ran through a wide plain at the foot of bare limestone mountains in which sheep were being shepherded by women wearing the same white outfits the women had worn in the market at Virpasar, and there were a lot of market gardens. We sat in front next to the driver and he said that most of these people were Albanian Catholics and very hard-working.

The road crossed a saddle and an inlet of Shkodër Lake was revealed. Green watermeadows extended to the water's edge, in which willows were growing in the shallows. The water was greenish-blue, choked with aquatic lotus, and beds of reeds inhabited by egrets and white herons extended far out into it. Men were fishing in the channels between them and women were working from their narrow boats, gathering water chestnuts. There are carp in the lake which weigh forty pounds or more and which, when smoked, are regarded as a great delicacy. According to the driver, sardines enter it to spawn by way of a river from the Adriatic, of which it was once an inlet. Beyond the lake, to the south-west, were the ragged tops of the Krajina Rumija mountains. Along the roadside scarlet-flowering pomegranates grew. It was a cloudless day. The atmosphere was already incandescent with heat. The lake shimmered in the haze. To the left bare hills rose steeply, shutting off the view of the mountains further inland. There was not a house to be seen. Rich Italians came here in winter to shoot wildfowl. It was an eerie place, as almost all places close to frontiers seem to be, perhaps by association of ideas. The coach radio emitted blasts of outlandish music which the driver said was Albanian.

The Yugoslav customs house was on another, longer, deeper inlet of the lake, called the Humsko Blato, which was about as wide as the Thames at Westminster. White buoys down the middle of it marked the frontier.

Forty yards or so down the road beyond the Yugoslav customs house was the Albanian one, near a hamlet called Han-i-Hotit where, in the time of the Ottomans, there was a *han*, a caravanserai.

Here, while we waited on the Yugoslav side, the Tour Leader told us that the Albanians would take from us any literature of an even faintly political character and all newspapers if we tried to take them into Albania and that the Yugoslavs would do the same if we tried to do the same with any Albanian literature when leaving. Here, a lady who was a member of the group asked if she could use the lavatory in the Yugoslav customs house, the door of which stood invitingly open, revealing a pastel-coloured suite, and was told brusquely by an official that she couldn't, and must wait until she got to Albania.

Also waiting to cross was the Albanian football team, on its way back to Tirana from Vienna, after having been defeated in the European Championships. We felt sorry for them. They looked so woebegone in their shabby, variegated clothes, nothing like bouncy international footballers usually do. One of them had bought a bicycle tyre and inner tube in Vienna. One of our party, a Welsh football enthusiast, asked them for their autographs and this cheered them up a bit.

We were now joined by two Italian gentlemen intent on entering Albania who arrived in a motor car, having driven from Rome.

'You cannot enter Albania without a visa,' one of the Yugoslavs said in Italian.

'But where do we get these visas?' one of them asked.

'At Rome!'

'*Va bene, torniamo a Roma,*' the driver said, without hesitation, and turning the car round headed back for Bar, where they had disembarked from the ferry from Italy the previous day. When they had gone, it suddenly occurred to me that the official had not told them that they would not be allowed into Albania unless they were with a group, and I asked him why.

'Because they did not ask me,' he said. And he seemed to think it a good joke.

Now we lugged our luggage, the young aiding the aged and infirm, along the sizzling expanse of road which constituted the no-man's-land between the two countries, looking a bit like survivors of some disaster, to the very border of Albania, where we were halted at a barrier by a savage-looking soldier in shiny green fatigues, armed with a machine pistol. To the right was the inlet in which fast little motor boats were kept ready in the shallows, where orangey-yellow water fuschia were growing. To the left was the steep hillside and, running along the foot of it, an electric fence with white porcelain insulators supporting the wires, about eight feet high with overhangs, which would have made it impossible to scale even if the current was off. It looked as if it was no longer in use and I wondered if it had been the sort that frizzles you to a cinder or the kind that rings bells, or indeed the type that does both, and whether it actually encircled Albania.

The barrier was surmounted by a sign bearing an imperialistic-looking double-headed black eagle and a red star on a yellow background which announced that this was the *Republika Popullore e Shqiperise*, Shqiperia being 'The Land of the Eagles'. Knowing that I would have difficulty in remembering how to spell this later on, I began to write it down in a notebook, but the sentry made such threatening gestures that I desisted.

Here, with us all still standing on the Yugoslav side of the barrier, Nanny, our Tour Leader, handed over a multiple visa, procured from the Albanian consulate in Paris, with photographs of all thirty-four of us attached to it, most of them taken in those smelly little booths that can be found in amusement arcades or on railway stations. It made the visa look like an illustrated catalogue for a chamber of horrors and it took the official, to whom he now presented it, some time to convince himself that what he was looking at were real people, although one would have thought that he must have had plenty of experience of looking at similar documents.

It was during the inspection of these credentials, in the course of which we were called forward to be identified one by one, that he discovered that the numbers printed on our two passports did not tally with those on the multiple visa. This was because our old passports had expired when we applied to join the tour and the new ones had not yet been issued to us when the visa was applied for by the tour company because of a strike by British passport officials. Eventually we were admitted, probably because the coach that had brought us to the Yugoslav frontier had already driven away and we would have been a problem to dispose of.

Now, in the customs house, one of the antechambers to Albania, we were ordered to fill in customs declarations, and a wave of collective panic seized the group when it was discovered that the only two languages in which the questions were posed were French and Albanian.

Possèdez-vous les objets suivants Poste émetteur et récepteur, appareil photographique, magnétophone, téléviseur, refrigerateur, machine à laver et d'autres equipements domestiques, montres, narcotiques, imprimés comme lettres, revue du matérial explosif?

As a result of not knowing what a lot of this meant, normally law-abiding members of the group imported radios, tape recorders, copies of English national newspapers, the *New Statesman*, *Spectator*, *New Scientist* and a pictorial souvenir of the Royal Wedding, although one timid girl, asked by a hopeful official if she had any pornography about her, blushingly handed over a copy of *Over 21*.

Here, in these otherwise bare rooms, we had our first close-up of Enver Hoxha (pronounced Hoja), founder of the Albanian Communist Party in 1941, First Secretary since 1954 of the Central Committee of the Party, and the Leader, apparently for life (he was born 1908), photographed with survivors of the 1979 earthquake, below a placard with an injunction from him that read: EVEN IF WE HAVE TO GO WITHOUT BREAD WE ALBANIANS DO NOT VIOLATE PRINCIPLES. WE DO NOT BETRAY MARXISM-LENINISM.

From then on we were confronted everywhere by his smiling, cherubic-mouthed, well-nourished – no sign that he was forgoing the staff of life – slightly epicene image. It was Evelyn Waugh who, while on a war-time mission to Tito, suggested that Tito was a woman and he could with equal propriety, or rather lack of propriety, in both cases belied by their records, have said the same about Hoxha. We saw him on enormous hoardings, sometimes marooned in the middle of fields, usually wearing a silvery-looking suit with matching trilby and carrying a bunch of flowers, like a prodigal son, who has made it successfully into the ranks of the bourgeoisie, returning to visit an aged mother in a hut. Sometimes he was depicted, but usually only in more sophisticated surroundings such as the foyers of tourist hotels, straining to his bosom pampered little girls, of the sort popular with his hero and mentor, Stalin, some of whom were wrapped in equally silvery furs.

'Shall we be able to see him in Tirana?' was the first question we asked the Albanian interpreter who would be accompanying us on our tour and who was about thirty-five with streaks of black hair plastered down over a brainy-looking noddle, like a baddie in a Tintin book. He looked at us as if we were a couple of loonies.

*

The first Albanian I ever met, and the last for some twenty-five years, was Zog, the King of Albania.

It was in Egypt in 1942, and I was spending my leave from the Western Desert in a rather grand house in Alexandria. While I was breakfasting with my hostess, the chef appeared, as he always did at this time of the morning, in order to receive his instructions for the day.

'There will be twenty to luncheon,' she said as she did more often than not, at least whenever I was staying in the house, addressing him in French, and the chef inclined his head without batting an eyelid. And to me, 'I do hope you will come. I am sure the King will enjoy talking to you.' They then went on to consider the menu in detail.

The King was then forty-nine years old, very tall and very thin and dark with a razor-sharp moustache of the sort I later learned was much affected by Albanians. His Queen, Geraldine Apponyi, a Hungarian countess, was extremely good-looking, if not downright saucy-looking.

The King spoke French with his host and hostess and the various other guests of high rank who were present. From what I could hear he appeared, rather like Edward VIII, to be interested in trivia; but he looked a tough customer. I never spoke to the King or the Queen, being a very junior officer of no consequence. Instead, I got a rocket from a general who was also present for wearing a flannel suit instead of uniform. I told him that my uniform was in a bad state of repair and that it was being mended by an upstairs maid, which impressed him. 'I don't have an upstairs maid,' he said, with unconcealed regret. He also asked me what I was doing and I told him that I wasn't allowed to tell him as it was supposed to be secret, which was true but didn't go down very well either. Altogether, it was not a luncheon easily forgotten.

The King, together with Queen Geraldine, had left his kingdom when it was invaded by the Italians in April 1939. With him were ten chests said to contain the entire Albanian gold reserves, and twelve Ghegs, supposedly loyal members of his tribe, whose job it was to guard them, as well as act as bodyguards. The King and Queen had travelled extensively since their departure from Albania, I was told by a woman sitting on my left who appeared to be exceptionally well informed about them.

Eventually they had arrived in France in 1940, just in time to see it fall, having previously been in Greece, Turkey, Rumania, Poland,

Sweden and Norway. From France, with the Queen and his four sisters, the King departed for England in some haste, in a specially chartered steamer from St Jean-de-Luz, near the Spanish border, in order to avoid being taken by the Germans. He and his family were already on board when he saw some of his bodyguard making off in a boat, in the direction of Spain, together with the royal treasure. There was just time to set off in pursuit, take the treasure on board and liquidate these henchmen before setting sail. On arrival in London, he put up at the Ritz before going north for the grouse shooting in August 1940, an odd time to be shooting grouse, with the Germans practically on the threshold, by which time, so my neighbour said, the Gheg bodyguard had been reduced to a point bordering on the non-existent. Now, apparently bodyguardless – at least he appeared to be at this luncheon – the King had arrived in Egypt. The son of a Muslim tribal chief, he was originally called Achmed Zogu, and had risen to the position of President of the Albanian Republic before being proclaimed King in 1928. He was now apparently poised for further travel – '*son deuxième piste*' was how my informant described it – but without any immediate hope of returning to his native land, and in fact he never did.

For eight years after the first war Albania was a constitutional republic. During the last war, the War of National Liberation against the Axis, the Left, having successfully liquidated the Centre and Right with the unacknowledged and perhaps unintentional aid of the Allies, founded a National Independence Front which in October 1944 became what was surprisingly known as 'The First Democratic Government of Albania'. At the end of the following year the Communist Party, the only permitted party, won the first general election.

After the war the country became even more remote than it had been previously, a sort of communist Tibet. In 1946 the Albanians displayed their independence by mining the Corfu Channel which resulted in the sinking of two British destroyers with the loss of fifty-four lives, but, when accused of doing so, claimed that another country, probably Yugoslavia, had laid the mines. The International Court awarded Britain £900,000 in damages but Albania refused to pay. The British, who had in the vaults of the Bank of England what is now estimated to be about $30 million of Albanian gold which had been seized from the Germans at the end of the war, refused to return it, on the grounds that the United States and Italy had previous claims on it. And so they do, because Albania had nationalized US and Italian property in the country without offering compensation. (Albania is still demanding the return of this gold, plus interest, as a pre-condition of reopening diplomatic relations with Britain, which ceased in 1939 when the Italians invaded the country and the King left it. Whether this gold includes any residue of whatever the King made off with is not clear. Well, it isn't clear to me.)

In 1946 the United States broke off relations with Albania (having together with Britain and Russia recognized the Provisional Government in November 1945), at the same time vetoing Albania's admission to the UN, with Britain's support, and Albania did not become a member of it until 1955. To this day no Americans are allowed to enter Albania on any pretext. In 1948 the Russians quarrelled with the Yugoslavs and, as a result, the Albanians broke with the Yugoslavs, who had given them considerable financial aid and had sent them 4000 technicians and numerous youth cadres, all of which they could ill afford, in order to help the Albanians build their first railway line and also to reconstruct the port of Durrës. The Albanians accused the Yugoslavs of practising 'Tito-ite Capitalism' and, not altogether without reason, of 'Colonialism'. They still continued to be very friendly with Stalinist Russia.

In 1961, the year after Stalin's death, the Albanians broke with the Russians, partly because they themselves were becoming increasingly pro-Chinese, partly because Khruschev was cultivating relations with the USA and also because he was denigrating what was in Albania the revered memory of Stalin. In spite of this they still continued to have trade relations with some Eastern Bloc countries, notably Rumania and East Germany. The Russians had given the Albanians really massive assistance, totalling some 500,000,000 roubles, and had helped them through their First and Second Five-Year Plans and with the initiation of the Third Plan, which began in 1961. They had also lent them 15,000 technicians who led the way in building factories, equipping towns and harbours, building themselves a secret base on Sazan Island in the Adriatic, and in re-equipping the Albanian army.

Next to come, and eventually depart, were the Chinese. Between 1961 and 1978, as interested in securing a base in the Mediterranean as the Russians had been before them, according to themselves they injected the equivalent of $5 billion into the Albanian economy (other sources say $200 million) and sent in 4000 Chinese technicians who worked on the construction of a large oil refinery near

Elbasan, the Mao Tse-tung Textile Factory in Berat (now known as the Organizatës së Rinisëtë Filaturës të Kombinatet të Texstilëve Berat) and the Mao Tse-tung Metallurgical Complex at Elbasan, which had its name changed, when they left, to the Steel of the Party Metallurgical Combine.

By the time the Chinese left in 1978, after the death of Mao, accused of sabotaging the Sixth Five-Year Plan and betraying Marxism-Leninism by doing business with the capitalist powers, Albania was self-sufficient in natural gas and had an exportable oil surplus, although by 1980 production had sunk from 2.5 million tons in the mid-1970s to 1.5 million tons. By 1981 production of high grade steel had come to a temporary halt because of lack of skilled workers; on the other hand, by that year Albania had become the world's second largest exporter of chrome. By now it also had a surplus of hydroelectric power and was able to export electricity to Yugoslavia.

Among other things the Albanian leaders are said to have objected to in their special relationship with China was the future role envisaged for their country by Chou En-lai, one strikingly similar to that thought up for it by Khruschev – '*Un jardin fleuri du socialisme*', a puppet state consecrated to agriculture. Now they were alone, officially isolated from East and West, but still with some clandestine links, admitting to no friends anywhere.*

My first attempt to visit Albania was back in 1962. The nearest Albanian Consulate was in Paris and it was there I went from London in pursuit of an Albanian visa.

It was a cold, wet, wintry morning in Paris when I eventually located the consulate after a rough crossing from Dover to Dunkirk by the now defunct Night Ferry. A plaque on the front gate which announced that this was the Albanian Consulate could have done with a bit of Brasso. The facade of the building was covered with some sort of dense vegetation.

I rang the door bell. Instantly, as if I was expected, a metal shutter opened in it.

'*Qu'est que vous voulez?*' a disembodied voice asked in French even more execrable than my own.

'*Je desire aller en Albanie.*'

'*Pourquoi?*'

'*Pour faire des vacances.*'

---

* The Chinese are now, in 1983, said to be back in Albania.

'*D'où venez-vous?*'

'*Je suis Anglais.*'

'*NON!*' said the voice, definitely and violently. The shutter slammed shut and after an early lunch I went back to London.

Years were to pass before I finally succeeded in getting an Albanian visa.

We set off for Shkodër, the principal city of northern Albania, in an Italian-built Albturist bus fitted with almost new tyres with Chinese characters impressed on them. Either the Chinese had left behind enormous quantities of tyres when they departed, or else they left the moulds. They were to be seen everywhere in Albania, fitted to trucks and jeeps and buses.

The driver was about fifty-five. He spoke good Italian – his parents were Italian – and proved to be a mine of misleading information, as well as of sinister Italian proverbs that would have had the Camorra in stitches. When he found that we, too, spoke Italian he made us sit up front in the seats with the best view, which made some of the other members of the group, with what they considered inferior seats, jealous. We wondered why they envied us, stuck up front with him and the interpreter, who, as soon as the bus got going, began to deluge us with statistics about percentages, kilowatt hours and similar stuff. When not doing this he played interminable patriotic music and the songs of wartime partisans, still very much in demand apparently, on tape. It was difficult to take a shine to either of them.

Beyond the hamlet of Han-i-Hotit the road wound round the head of the inlet and through wild, serrated limestone country before entering a wide plain which extends from the foot of the mountains to the lake shore.

These particular mountains conceal within them what are to foreigners, and have been for fifty years, perhaps the most unknown and inaccessible regions of Albania. This is, or was, the land of the Ghegs, Roman Catholics renowned for their wildness (King Zog was a Gheg, although apparently a Muslim Gheg; his sister married a son of the Turkish Sultan Abd ul-Hamid II), their huge noses and scythe-like moustaches, of the sort still worn to proclaim their identity by some expatriate Yugoslav Albanians, of whom there are some millions.

The southern part of the country is the home of the Tosks who, like the Ghegs, have their own dialect – Albanian is a beautiful language of Indo-European origin, a dialect of ancient Illyrian with Greek and Latin affinities – but no noses to speak of, and no moustaches of any consequence either.

What was extraordinary, on the road to Shkodër, and everywhere else we went subsequently in Albania, was the extent of the defences. On either side of the road what looked like countless thousands of concrete mushrooms sprang from the ground. Every part of the plain, every valley, had line after line of them drawn across it. Every village, every town and city, had concentrations of these blockhouses in and around them. And back on the hillsides there were bigger blockhouses and casemates for the heavy guns. None of this was a relic of some past emergency. They were still being pre-fabricated at a furious rate, although only the bigger ones, with guns mounted inside them, were actually manned.

These until recently utterly barren, limestone foothills grazed by goats now burgeoned with fruit trees. Further south and near the shores of Lake Ochrid, which forms part of Albania's eastern border with Yugoslavia, such plantations were on a vast scale, and followed the configuration of the hillsides, one above the other, like contour lines. And there were enormous olive groves and vineyards, many of them so recently planted that neither had yet yielded a crop. Such works, many of them in very inaccessible situations and in a country in which mechanization was still in its infancy, suggested the employment of very large numbers of workers, perhaps the employment of forced labour.

Mile after mile the road to Shkodër, like most other main roads in Albania, was planted with avenues of black poplars which formed tunnels of shadow beneath which the workers in the fields were now taking refuge from the awful noontime heat. Most of them were women, wearing white head-dresses, black skirts and thick brown stockings, and they looked whacked; nothing like the heroic, uniformed women – advancing out of the dawn waving rifles with fixed bayonets and announcing the imminent demise of Imperialism and Revisionism – on the poster-hoardings at the roadside and in the fields, sites which they shared with the First Secretary. Here, they were harvesting maize, tobacco and sunflowers. All of them were old enough to be mothers. Some of them were old enough to be grandmothers.

'What happens if they have babies?' Wanda said in English to the interpreter, who was having one of his brief rest periods from giving us the percentage and kilowatt treatment.

'The mother is allowed six months' leave, during which she gets 80 per cent of her wages. When they start work again the babies are kept in day nurseries.' It was the driver who answered, the one who said he spoke no English but certainly understood it, butting in, speaking in Italian, using the word *nidi*, literally 'nests', for nurseries. 'Here,' taking the opportunity of which all good communists avail themselves whenever it presents itself to come up with some good news about the regime, 'we have no contraception, no abortion and no living together before marriage as you have in England. Here, we have very big birthrate, more men than women, the biggest in Europe. Here, when they had the last census, in 1975, they found that the population had tripled in fifty-two years. Here, agriculture is very important. Here, one worker in every five is in agriculture.'

'Well, where are all the men?' she asked. There were few men to be seen, and most of those were driving tractors, hauling produce or workers behind them in trailers.

'The men are in industry.'

It was the same further south, where the workers in the rice and cotton fields in what had been, before the war, the malaria-ridden, poverty-stricken coastal plain, were almost all women.

'But what do you want all these extra people for? In a few years you'll have so much machinery you won't know what to do with them.'

'We shall need them to fight the forces of Capitalist Imperialism and Revisionism,' he replied.

I would have liked to have asked him what about the forces of Communist Imperialism, which also seemed currently to be having a good run for its money, but didn't have the energy.

Great changes had taken place on the road to Shkodër since my last visit in 1968. Then the road had been a rough metalled track full of pot-holes and the bridges over the then dry torrent beds were the trunks of trees laid one beside the other. Now it was asphalted and the tree trunks had been replaced by concrete bridges. On the forty-mile journey to Shkodër we only saw one car, a brand new yellow Polski, a Polish-made Fiat, which had been in collision with a lorry loaded with workers and was no longer looking so good – neither was the driver of this government-owned vehicle, who, although unscathed, was probably for the high jump. There are no privately owned cars in Albania and we saw only about two or three dozen cars during our entire stay in the country. Petrol was only one lek a litre (there were fourteen point something leks to the pound at that time or about twenty to the dollar) but there was nothing for the man-in-the-street to put it in, even if he could buy it.

We saw in the back of an open lorry a bride dressed in white on her way to be married; bullock-carts, perhaps the only vehicles apart from tractors that would be capable of negotiating, as they are in India, the deeply rutted earth tracks that led off the main road to distant hamlets when the winter rains would turn them into what would be a morass; and we saw Russian and Chinese jeeps, some of the Russian ones in a state of near-collapse, which was not surprising as the last shipments probably took place around 1960, although there was still a factory making spare parts. Otherwise the most common vehicle was what looked like a covered motor delivery van of the 1920s, except that it was motorless and was horse-drawn.

Also on the road, often all over it, there were cattle, flocks of sheep, goats, foals, independent-minded pigs and, keeping to the verges, the morning shift of black-smocked school-children on their way home – there are two shifts a day, from six o'clock to midday, and from one o'clock to seven – all uttering loud 'Oorays!' and waving. The grown-ups were not so wavy. In the course of these forty miles I saw one dog and no cats. Altogether I saw six dogs and no cats in ten days, although other members of the group claimed to have seen one or two rather mangy cats. Was this dearth a legacy of the Chinese, to whom both cats and dogs are still delicacies? Through these crowds of animals and humans the driver wove his way at high speed with the indifference to lesser breeds which is generally a sign of membership of the Party anywhere, horn blaring, bucketing the passengers in the back seats over the axle who were trying to take surreptitious photographs through the side windows at 1/1000 second and ending up with reflections of the inside of an Albturist coach. The rear window was deliberately left covered with dust throughout the tour to make photography from it impossible. We passed collective farms with long, single-storey barns and the small town of Kopliku, which looked as dejected as it had done on my last visit, except that then it had been market day and the place had been full of people from the mountains dressed in picturesque costumes. To the right, the trees near the lake shivered like jellies in the mirage. The heat was immense.

We arrived in Shkodër at the southern end of the lake.

The earthquake of 1979 had also done terrible damage in Albania, rendering a hundred thousand Albanians homeless. In Shkodër, it had killed about eighty people and injured another three hundred. Now, rebuilt, Shkodër was a city rather than a town. Apartment blocks, many of them built of rough, unrendered brick which made it difficult to know whether they had been completed or were still waiting to be rendered, now dwarfed the old red-tiled houses and shops that survived. Broad boulevards had been built, one of which led to a Palace of Culture, and a lot of buildings that hadn't fallen down had been torn down to make a triumphal square, as they had in other places in Albania, and what had been clocks with Chinese numerals on their faces had been taken down but not always replaced by European ones, as a clockless clock tower testified.

Like all other places in Albania at this time Shkodër appeared to be *en fête*. Hoardings in the principal squares announced the opening of the Eightieth Party Congress, which coincided with the Fortieth Anniversary of the foundation of the Albanian Communist Party, and the streets were spanned by innumerable red banners bearing such slogans as RROFTE PARTIA YNE POPYLLON – Long Live the Party and the People. Big colour blow-ups of photographs of the bosses, which must have been taken anything up to thirty years back, testified to their capacity for survival.

We were put up in a newish, tall hotel, overlooking the principal square, which was more or less typical of all the hotels we were to stay in in Albania. Some had lifts that worked, or didn't work, or had none at all, which could mean humping one's luggage up five floors or so, unless some kindly member of the staff, and many were kind, offered to help you or you could get a transfer to a lower level. All were insanely honest, rushing out from the foyer on departure mornings brandishing disposable razors, moulting old tooth-brushes and items of a more intimate nature that their owners had left in the waste bins, hoping never to see again.

Most hotels had long, long corridors carpeted with hand-woven runners. These runners were never quite straight and walking on them gave one the impression that one was slightly tight. As everywhere in the Balkans, there was a profusion of potted plants. In one hotel they proliferated to such an extent that they hung down the well of the staircase twenty feet or more from an upper floor, making contact with the staff behind the reception desk difficult.

The rooms were very clean. Everything worked, except in one hotel where nothing worked above the ground floor and some madman had pinched all the lavatory seats in the communal bathrooms, and all the door locks. As in Russia there was not a wash plug to be seen anywhere.

In the hotel shops the same goods were on sale, presided over by what looked like the same po-faced girls I remembered from thirteen years before – hand-woven mats in rather crude colours, embroidered blouses, cigarette and pipe tobacco, both made in Shkodër, the lethal Albanian cognac, felt slippers and round mud-coloured felt skull caps.

At Shkodër we ate, as we would from now on, in the Tourist Restaurant, cheek by jowl with French, Italian, German and Austrian groups attended by waitresses in old-fashioned waitress uniforms and little lace caps, and a head waiter wearing a black tie. Albanians were excluded. They had their own, more animated eating places. More imporant foreign guests – including some North Vietnamese who were making the rounds – dined in private suites.

These first two meals at Shkodër, lunch and dinner, were more or less prototypes of all the meals we were to eat, good and bad, everywhere. Lunch was the good prototype; rice soup, calves' tongues, stuffed aubergines, a tomato salad made with olive oil of a quality difficult to come by even in Mediterranean lands, cream caramel and a bottle of a local red wine called Kallmet, which only cost six leks and, in a shop round the corner, even less, only four leks.

After this meal, ignoring the interpreter's order, given in the form of a mandatory suggestion, that we should rest for an hour or so in our rooms, the two of us rushed out of the hotel before he could stop us to see what we could of the town, unaccompanied.

At the entrance there was a band of rather dirty, furtive looking little boys, one or two of them with untreated impetigo, nothing like the well-scrubbed school-children, all of them members of the Young Pioneers, membership of which was obligatory from the age of seven, who were later displayed to us, or even those more rural but equally wholesome ones who had hailed us with loud 'Oorays' from the roadside. One had the impression that these children were minor delinquents, playing truant from school and the Young Pioneers. They asked us for chewing gum and ball-point pens, but we had none to offer. They were afraid of no one. Cuffed or even frog-marched by Albturist coach drivers or the chauffeurs of the heavily-curtained Mercedes and Volvos of visiting VIPs, they always came back. Most hotels in Albania had a similar band waiting outside them.

Out in the square, where five roads and boulevards met, an unbelievable quiet reigned. Apart from one or two jeeps whining past, an occasional Czechoslovakian bus with a trailer loaded to the gunwales and some people sedately pedalling old Chinese bicycles, there was scarcely any traffic in what was now the centre of the city. In the midst of this expanse a policeman who looked worn out by the responsibilities of office – he should have taken a trip to the Place de la Concorde to realize how lucky he was to be here – was blowing his whistle at careless pedestrians. He blew it at us, too, when we tried to cross a segment of it, and it was a good thing he did, otherwise we would have been mown down by a cyclist, which would have been pretty silly on our first afternoon in Albania.

Then we went 'round the corner', which for us – there was of course no hope of evading the dreaded Sigurimi, the secret police, who had eyes and ears everywhere – came to mean putting as much distance as possible, even for a few minutes, between ourselves and interpreters, trusted, upper echelon members of the Party masquerading as coach drivers, the Tour Leader and any members of the group who might be expected to shop us. In this case 'round the corner' took us to a street of pre-1914 shops, dark and cavernous, in many of which the floors had been freshly watered, as had the streets outside.

One of these shops was a bookshop and, as in almost all Albanian bookshops, the customer was separated from the merchandise by a wooden barrier, which meant that every time I wanted to look at a book I had to ask the assistant, who was the sort who purses her lips when asked anything. Fed up, I leapt the barrier and got a severe ticking-off. There were lots of children's books, some of them showing the little darlings brandishing rifles with bayonets just like Mummy on the hoardings in the country.

Apart from the assistant in the bookshop, we were well received by shopkeepers and shoppers alike, especially by those who spoke Italian. But only inside the shop, and then only if they thought the other shoppers could be trusted. Some even allowed us to take their photographs. Outside in the street it was as if we had ceased to exist. Basic commodities, including food, were relatively cheap, but salaries were low in relation to them, if what the driver told us later was to be believed. In this way it was exactly like any other communist country in which the miracle is that, given what most people earn, they can afford to buy anything at all. Judging by the forests of television aerials, large numbers of people in the towns seemed to have television, but a set cost 4500 leks (£325 or $455), nine months' salary at the lower end of the wage scale, and there appeared to be no facilities for hiring, or hire purchase.

According to the driver, whose home was in Tirana, whom it was difficult to believe even when discussing the most mundane matters but subsequently proved to be right, wages ranged from a minimum 500 leks (about £36 or $50) a month to 900–1000 leks, the price of a radio, which might, he said, be a junior minister's portion, although as such he would have massive perquisites – 600 leks being about the average (£50 or $70). In 1977 the maximum/minimum ratio was reduced from 2 to 1 to 1.8 to 1 to discourage undue ambition. He himself, so he said, got 650 leks.

Food was relatively cheap. The good dark bread was very cheap. Butter was 20 leks a kilo, the excellent olive oil 13 leks a litre, a pot of jam 6 leks, a bottle of beer 4 leks, the same price as a bottle of decent wine, a melon, relatively expensive, 2 leks. Fresh vegetables – it was summer – were abundant. Butchers' shops were nearly always shut when we turned up, but what one could see through the windows seemed to be of rather poor quality. Certainly there were no calves' tongues of the sort we had been served in the hotel in Shkodër. There was no rationing, but there were shortages of some commodities. The fat people we saw in Albania either had something wrong with them or were members of foreign groups.

Good cigarettes – there were lots of brands to choose from, the Albanians smoke like chimneys (no warnings about it being dangerous to health) – were 2.5 leks for twenty. The worst, which were called Partisani, burned like a slow fuse.

A pair of quite elegant women's leather sandals cost 126 leks, a baby's soft leather boots only 7 leks. Nylon stockings – there were no tights on display – were 23 leks and huge bunches of suspenders were exhibited to keep them up. A poor quality plastic handbag was 215 leks. A full-sized pram 950 leks. A new, Albanian-built bicycle 1000 leks. A small fridge, made at the 'Obod' factory in Cetinje, was 4000 leks.

There was no litter in Albania, partly because the Albanians had not yet learned to package merchandise for home consumption, other than screw it up in a bit of brown paper, and because chucking it about was a serious, anti-social offence. There was no dogs' mess, either, because there were no dogs; and no graffiti, only partly because of a lack of suitable writing instruments. On the other hand pollution was a terrible problem, the sort of smog that hung over Elbasan, south-east of Tirana, resembling that over the Black Country between the wars – the Chinese-built steelworks at Elbasan looked as if it was undergoing a gas attack and the waters of the Shkumbin River, on the banks of which the city stands, resembled black treacle.

Back at the hotel we were given a whole series of rockets by the interpreter, by the driver and by the Tour Leader, for going off without permission. We had also been reported by the unidentifiable but omnipresent Sigurimi for taking photographs of people.

'You were taking pictures of peoples in shops without permission,' the interpreter said. 'It is forbidden.'

'But look,' I said, 'the tour brochure says you can take pictures of people if you first ask their permission. We did ask, and they said, yes, we could.'

'If they did give permission, they are wrong,' he said. 'You can ask permission to take photographs of Albanian peoples but Albanian peoples cannot give it.'

After our ticking-off for going round the corner, we were taken up to see the Fortress of Rozafat on the rock above the town, built by the Venetians in 1396 and heroically defended by them against the Turks under Suleiman Pasha in 1473, who lost 14,000 men attempting to take it, only to lose it to Mehmet Pasha in 1479, who is said to have lost 30,000 before the garrison surrendered.

It was here in the fortress that Edward Lear, while at Shkodër on his sketching trip through Albania in October 1848, was entertained by the governor of the fortress, a Turkish Pasha of Bosnian extraction, who treated him to a dinner of fifty courses. 'Nothing,' that most entertaining of travel writers wrote

> was so surprising as the strange jumble of irrelevant food offered: lamb, honey, fish, fruit; baked, boiled, stewed, fried; vegetable, animal; fresh, salt, pickled; solid; oil, pepper; fluid; sweet, sour; hot, cold . . . the richest pastry came immediately after dressed fish and was succeeded by beef, honey, and cakes; pears and peaches; crabs, ham, boiled mutton, chocolate cakes, garlic, and fowl; cheese, rice, soup, strawberries, salmon-trout, and cauliflowers – it was a very chaos of a dinner!

From the rock on which it stood, a lot of the vast panorama was much as it had been when Lear was sketching it. On the shores of the lake shepherds were tending their flocks in the watermeadows. Below the rock the Bojana River flowed south out of the lake and then westwards by a navigable channel into the Adriatic, forming for part of its course the frontier with Yugoslavia. Down at the foot of it there was a mosque that Lear had sketched, now vandalized and with its minaret destroyed, and in the rock itself there were casemates housing the guns covering the approaches to the bridge which carries the only road to central and southern Albania. Soon they would also cover a railway bridge which would carry the new line that was being pushed up from the Durrës to Shkodër, which one day perhaps would extend as far as Han-i-Hotit on the frontier, and eventually be linked with a Yugoslav line from Titograd and the rest of the European railway system.

Back in the city what appeared to be the entire population, now all cleaned up after their eight hours' labour, were engaged in the *passeggiata*, strolling up and down under the trees in the gloaming engaged in animated conversation, a custom the Albanians probably learned from the Italians between the wars when the two countries were on friendly terms, for it is certainly not something they would ever have learned as subjects of the Turks.

Long after we had finished eating the worst sort of dinner – rissoles like big toes that had gone to sleep, followed by sickly cream cake – some sad musicians began to play; sad because they had been waiting ages to play for us and no one told us they were waiting to do so. To their accompaniment the driver and the interpreter, displaying the softer sides of their natures, danced an Albanian equivalent to the Yugoslav *kolo*, with handkerchiefs.

Later, two members of our group, a pair of women's liberators, began to attack them about the place of Albanian women in society and in bed, which, after some ten hours in the country, was not beginning to sound or look all that rosy to them, and the evening ended on an acrimonious note. In fact a lot of evenings ended on an acrimonious note on account of there being nothing to do, a lot to drink, and the driver and interpreter hanging about, outstaying their welcome. Television programmes were primitive. Endless, lingering shots of industrial plants and interminable political harangues and discourses which could scarcely have appealed to an Albanian worker after an eight-hour working day. Newspapers were equally indigestible and we never saw anyone carrying, let alone reading one. Football results were written up on boards displayed in the street. By 8 p.m. on weekdays most people had gone home to bed. By ten the streets were as quiet as the grave. 'God, what an evening!' we said to each other at the end of this, and each succeeding one.

Dawn came about 6 a.m., by which time the municipal water-carts were well advanced with their work of dampening the streets. Old ladies, who in Britain would have long since been consigned to a home, were already on the go, wielding their besoms as they do in communist countries everywhere, overlooked by a very unavuncular bust of Stalin. (Albania is the only place in the communist world where you can still contemplate a bust of Stalin.) The square below our window resembled an enormous enlargement of a Lowry painting, filled with the matchstick figures of what might be described without offence as the dirty workers, en route either to fight their way on to the buses or else board lorries which groaned away with them into the industrial areas, or even further into the unimaginable interior. The next wave, the school-children, some of them wearing red, Young Pioneer scarves, took off at 6.45 a.m., to be followed, at 7.15 a.m., by bureaucrats strolling to their offices with briefcases. Last of all came shop assistants.

After breakfast, we were escorted to the Muzeu Ateist, the Museum of Atheism, Albania being officially Godless since 1967, a promised treat which our hosts perversely showed signs of withholding from us when they saw how enthusiastic we were.

It was housed in a pleasant nineteenth-century villa that must have belonged to what Russian communists call 'the former people', across the square from the hotel. Like its much larger counterpart, the Museum of the History of Religion and Atheism in the former Cathedral of Our Lady of Kazan in Leningrad, where they used to have a very funny nineteenth-century engraving of a gloomy-looking Roman Catholic monk carting a peasant girl into his monastery camouflaged as a sheaf of wheat in a sack, some of its exhibits were slightly lubricious. The Roman Catholic Cathedral at Shkodër was now a sports hall.

Downstairs in the main hall, where a placard announced predictably that 'Religion is the Opium of the People' and photography was permitted, *Then* and *Now* maps showed the past and present state of religion in Albania. The *Then* maps showed Albania before religion was officially abolished, full of mosques and churches, when 73 per cent of the population were Muslims, 17 per cent were Orthodox and 10 per cent were Roman Catholic (in 1938 there were said to have been 144 religious institutions, 48 schools and one hospital). The *Now* maps showed Albania in 1973 with 307 schools, 371 hospitals and clinics and no mosques or churches.

The actual process of destruction began after 1967, during Albania's equivalent to the Chinese Cultural Revolution, when the students were given the task of blowing up or otherwise obliterating religious buildings, destroying graveyards and publicly ridiculing anyone who still continued his religious observances. Only a few mosques were spared, some, presumably, because of their architectural significance. Those priests and members of the laity who, in spite of everything, persisted in practising their religion were either done away with or sent to forced labour camps. The only sect to have survived, semi-clandestinely, are the Bektashi, an order of Shia dervishes who unite Islamic, pre-Islamic, Christian and pagan beliefs. That they have succeeded in doing so is itself a near miracle.

Later on the tour, emerging from a gorge in the Shkumbin River, east of Elbasan, we passed four of these forced labour camps in quick succession, which we had been told to look out for by someone who knew their whereabouts. Behind them in the mountainside were large stone quarries, and one of the abiding memories of the trip to Albania was the sight of a shaven-headed party of unfortunates being marched back to their huts in the last of the light by their armed guards.*

Upstairs in the Museum, where for some obscure reason photography was forbidden, the visit became endless. The Director, the first director of an atheists' museum most of us had ever seen, laboriously described every item in detail in Albanian which the interpreter, who must have committed some serious crime to have been given his job in the first place, equally laboriously turned into English. We saw confessional boxes, photostats of letters from an Albanian bishop to his superiors in Rome reporting on priests who

---

* Albanians in exile said that in 1981 there were 40,000 prisoners in forced labour camps. The Albanians themselves admitted to 5000. They were engaged in quarrying, land drainage, tree planting and other heavy works, including railway construction. One of the worst of these camps is or was at Burrel, some twenty miles north of Tirana, where a sign over the entrance gate reads: 'This is Burrel Where People Enter But Never Leave'.

had been engaging in unseemly practices, or had contracted clap, engravings of Spanish Inquisitors sending heretics up in smoke, photographs of mad-looking mullahs, priests welcoming Fascist invaders or engaging in what the caption described as 'rock and roli' with female parishioners, and a hollowed-out Bible with a pistol secreted in it.

'But it isn't a real gun,' someone said. 'It's plastic.'

'The Director says he hasn't noticed that the gun was plastic,' the interpreter said, 'but he says that at one time it must have been a real one.'

As we were leaving we were invited to sign the visitors' book. One entry was by a member of the Franco-Albanian Friendship Society, who wrote in it, '*La groupe a été ravie de la visite dans ce musée de l'Athéisme*'. One could only suppose that in order to be ravished they must have been tight. And one of our group wrote that she had been thrilled by it too.

On the way south after leaving Shkodër we met a number of boy and girl student volunteers from Tirana University who were working on the construction of a railway line, rather listlessly shovelling ballast on the permanent way in the midst of a treeless plain, while flat cars loaded with rails made by Krupp in West Germany, hauled by Czechoslovak diesel engines, were run up and down the line in an attempt to flatten it, apparently without much success.

'It'll never be right, whatever they do to it,' an English engineer who was a member of our group said gloomily. 'It's just hopelessly badly built.'

These students, who were studying French and were in their last year at the university, were asked by a French Canadian, a member of the group masquerading as a university professor but actually a journalist, which French authors they had read or heard about. He was told Zola, Stendhal, Voltaire, Rousseau and some other eighteenth- and nineteenth-century writers. None of them could name a single French writer of the twentieth century, just as a similar group, further up the line, who were studying English, could not name a single twentieth-century author of any work in the English language, including Americans.

During this time, twice and thrice daily admonitions of the more inquisitively minded members of the group, of whom we were numbered, became part of our lives, either for taking photographs of what were mostly completely innocuous subjects, or else for wandering off to look at whatever was outside the hotel instead of sitting meekly in the lounge waiting for the coach to leave.

Eventually, things came to an ugly head at Apollonia, a ruined Graeco-Roman city on a hill above the sea near Fieri, which flourished between the third and first centuries BC, where the remains of a temple of Artemis and of an exquisite small theatre were to be seen. There was also what had been an Orthodox monastery, built, according to Lear, who spent a very uncomfortable night in it in October 1848, by the Albanian despot, Ali Pasha of Tepelenë, in order to encourage the local Greek Christians, who were scared stiff of him, to remain where they were and cultivate the surrounding country which they would otherwise have fled, leaving it to what the Pasha would have described as his more lackadaisical, shiftless co-religionists. It was a charming place, very little changed since Lear wrote his description of it.

Behind the monastery and the church, which had a number of very beautiful but very badly neglected ikons propped up in the narthex, exposed to every extreme of heat and damp, was something now extremely rare in Albania, a partly undesecrated Christian cemetery. Up to that time any cemeteries we had seen fleetingly from the bus were new ones with standard, undenominational tombstones. In this one there still remained the tombs of eight members of the same family, the last of whom had been buried as late as 1980. What influence, I wondered, could this family have had, sufficient to enable their tombs to remain undesecrated and to allow for the burial of one of its members to take place so recently?

The view from the cemetery, which stood on a bare, windswept hillock, was extensive, across fields to the sea and further inland to some low hills with perhaps the most heavily fortified defence system we had seen anywhere in Albania, the *pièce de résistance* of which was a battery of twenty-four heavy guns.

When we returned from visiting the cemetery the driver took us to one side and revealed himself for what he was. We had long since realized that he was important, far senior to the interpeter, but not quite how important. It was impressive to think that the Albanian administration could afford to squander the ability of such a man in such a mundane job. Perhaps, like the Chinese, they often have to squander able people in mundane jobs because there is simply no one else with sufficient ability to perform them. Perhaps it was punishment for wrong-doing or some kind of deviation, of a sort that I had envisaged as being the fate of the interpreter, doomed to translate the observations made by the Director of the Museum of Atheism, possibly for the rest of his life.

'What did you see behind the church?' he said.

'I saw some old stones lying about.'

'What sort of old stones?'

'I don't know. We couldn't see very well. We left our glasses in the coach. They looked like tombstones.'

'What else did you see? What about the view? What did you see in the view?'

'There were a lot of those concrete fortifications.'

'Now, be careful how you answer. Did you take photographs?'

'No. You can have the film if you want to. In fact you can have the whole lot if you want them.'

'Now listen to me,' he said. His eyes were like marbles. He was a little terror, this commissar, and he was certainly putting the wind up me. 'I can do anything I like with you, or anyone else in this group. I know who you are. I know what the girl is who is supposed to be painting flowers. She is from the BBC. I know what the Canadian professor is. You think I am just a little lorry driver who has travelled abroad, taking frogs' legs to France (which was one of the jobs he had admitted to doing as a long-distance lorry driver), only speaks Italian and laughs at your jokes.'

'Well, what do you think I am?' I said.

'I think you are from British Intelligence.'

'I'm not in British Intelligence or any other Intelligence,' I said. 'I'm not intelligent enough, or mad enough, and if I was I wouldn't be in Albania for all the tea in China,' not intending to make what sounded like another poor attempt at a joke. 'Surely you can see that. As for laughing at my jokes, that's something you never did.'

'You just be careful, Mr and Mrs Newby,' he said, 'just be careful. You are in danger. You always have been in danger, ever since you crossed the frontier.'

'One last thing,' I said. 'If you were all that worried by us going behind the church, why didn't you stop us? You saw us going. And, anyway, if you don't want anyone to go there, why not simply put up a notice telling them not to? I think you wanted us to go there, so that you could frighten us to death. Well, you've succeeded.'

'All the time I wonder what you're doing with a group like this,' he said.

'I wonder what you're doing with a group like this,' I said.

'One of my jobs,' he said, 'the one I like least, is to prevent you, and people like you, being sent to prison.'*

What was most disagreeable about Albania, apart from the prying and repressions to which the proletariat of all communist countries are subjected, was the gross inequality which one has learned to take for granted in all those so-called revisionist communist states which flirt with capitalism but which seemed here, in a country where a purer, more primitive, communism was still ostensibly being practised, doubly grotesque, the leaders, in spite of this, living a life of luxury hidden in their seaside villas at Durrës and in the official enclave in the capital, Tirana.

At Sarandë and Butrint, resorts on the Adriatic coast, across the channel from Corfu, wives or girl friends of Party officials described to us by the interpreter as being 'workers on a day's holiday' wore beautifully cut, simple dresses that looked as if they had emanated from couture workrooms, pearl necklaces, gold-rimmed sunglasses, elegant shoes and carried handbags of soft leather, none of which were available in the shops in Tirana, or anywhere else in Albania. When they went swimming at a place called Ksamil, on the coast between Sarandë and Butrint, well out of sight of the real workers, it was in foreign-made bathing costumes, and one only had to look at their long, painted fingernails to see that not only had they not participated in a month's obligatory agriculture within living memory, but that they had probably never worked what here in Albania is an official eight-hour day. Their swains, equally elegant, carried Japanese transistors, items also not found in Albanian shops. Under the circumstances, it was not an agreeable sight.

On our last afternoon in Albania en route for the Yugoslav frontier, between Shkodër and Han-i-Hotit, our coach was brought to a halt on the outskirts of a village by a funeral procession of men wearing suits and the brown-stockinged women we had seen working in the fields, which appeared to comprise the entire population. The coffin was carried on the back of an open lorry and was covered by a fine old carpet, which gave the impression that the dead person may have been born a Muslim. Looking at the inscrutable faces of the mourners at this atheistic comrades' funeral, who resolutely refused to break ranks in the face of the driver's impatience to pass them, it was difficult to imagine what they felt about the complete

* According to the interpreter, among other penalties in Albania handed out by a People's Court, theft is punished with seven years' imprisonment, and murder by twenty-five years', followed by more hard labour; traitors and spies are shot.

extirpation of their religion, or anything else of a spiritual kind. Was it imagination that led one to detect an air of profound gloom among them rather than of grief for the dead person? Not having been allowed to speak to them about such matters we shall never know. All that one could be sure of was that the spectacle would have brought joy to the heart of the Director of the Museum of Atheism and would have ravished the member of the Franco-Albanian Friendship Society who had signed his visitors' book.

III

GREECE

Grecian Shores

After Albania we took the night ferry from Bar on the coast of
Montenegro to Igoumenitsa in Epirus, that part of Greece that
somehow seems remote from it, between the Pindus Mountains and
the Ionian Sea that was Albanian under the Turkish empire, and is
still in many ways more Albanian than Greek. We slept on deck in a
fierce, north-west *maestrale* under a big moon, with the big mountains of Albania appearing to rise sheer out of the water to port,
seeing at first light places we had visited on that same coast a week
previously on our trip through Albania, all of which now looked,
seen from the deck of a Yugoslav ship, as inaccessible as Tibet. Then
we came into the harbour at Corfu below the citadels the Turks
never succeeded in taking from the Venetians, with the sun already
up and all the coast down to Cape Aspokávos at the southern end in
a mist of spindrift.

Although it was September, the end of the season of mass travel,
the dusty quayside at Bar had been crowded with boys and girls,
most of them from Germany, the Netherlands and Scandinavia,
with a sprinkling of French and Australians, but for some inscrutable reason hardly any English, on their way to Corfu, Delphi, the
Parthenon and the Cyclades to bathe in the last, now fast weakening

rays of the summer sun – some of them wearing plastic nose guards against it – before returning to do whatever boys and girls with student cards do in winter, even if they are not students, in such places as Düsseldorf, Amsterdam, Oslo, Stockholm and Copenhagen. With their hair done up in bandeaux, they resembled a pow-wow of Red Indians in a dust bowl.

And by the time we reached the passenger decks of this Yugoslav ship with its uncouth purser and its equally uncouth reception staff, having paid the equivalent of £100 ($140) for the pleasure of travelling on it for one night, together with our van, these Wander-vögel had already shuffled aboard, bowed under the weight of their enormous packs that towered high above their heads, and had invested not only the 300 seats, which were all that were provided to seat 600 passengers, but had taken over every foot of deck inside and outside, with the exception of those parts of the open deck which were exposed to the full force of the *maestrale*.

'Gentleman! Lady! You want ticket for Bar, for this evening,' were the words with which we were greeted by the touts for the rival ticket agencies whose offices line the waterfront when we came ashore at Igoumenitsa, a place which although it has obviously been there a long time has an air of transience, not surprisingly as it caters almost exclusively for those in transit. To which we answered, having had enough of the Yugoslavs, their shipping line, and their not-so-good ship *Slavija*, 'GRR! Buzz off!'

We fled Igoumenitsa and spent the rest of the morning recovering from Albania and the MV *Slavija* on the shore of a wide bay to the south of Plataria of which we were the only occupants, swimming, sunbathing, eating grilled sardines in a little restaurant facing the sea and drinking a bottle of retsina for which the proprietress, in what must have been a moment of insanity, charged us a monstrous 220 drachmas (the drachma being currently 121 to the pound, 170 to the dollar), then rapidly reduced it to the going rate, 25 drachmas. Later, we drove on to Parga, once a small Venetian seaport, on a dangerous, precipitous coast, reminiscent of Amalfi, with a citadel embellished with the lion of St Mark set on top of a conical hill, above a labyrinth of narrow streets. In one of these, under an arch which led from the harbour into the town, we bought thick, green olive oil from an old man in a dark room, the best we had yet discovered in the Mediterranean outside Albania, pressed from olives harvested the previous winter in the great groves of ancient trees which surrounded the town. And from another old man we bought a strange, sweet, orange-coloured liqueur that was not made from oranges, in a pretty, old-fashioned shop lined with bottles of various other liqueurs, all of which he had concocted himself.

Late in the afternoon we arrived at Préveza, a small port at the entrance to the Gulf of Arta, an inlet from the Ionian Sea about twenty-five miles long and ten miles wide, in winter the abode of wildfowl. Although the waterfront was a bit arid, Préveza was not as unprepossessing as our guide book said it was. In fact, some of its back streets were both picturesque and interesting and were full of useful shops. In one which sold religious articles we bought a couple of church candles to illuminate our dinner, which we were unable to eat in the open air owing to the enormous numbers of mosquitoes which infest the region. As late as 1956, the Admiralty *Pilot Guide to the Mediterranean* said that the inhabitants suffered from what it quaintly described as 'ague', presumably meaning malaria.

In another, a knife grinder's establishment, we had a terrific edge put on our carving knife and also on one of those lethal French knives called la Main Couronnée, made by the firm of Chopinel, which Wanda always carries with her, ostensibly to peel potatoes. In a wine shop full of barrels, presided over by two bearded, white-moustached gentlemen, we drank a glass of the rare but somewhat sickly red wine of Andípaxoi, a little island which lies south of Paxoi. Then, after we had brought some hot, freshly baked bread from an old-fashioned baker's shop and had a couple of glasses of excellent retsina from an equally old-fashioned café to take away the taste of the wine of Andípaxoi, we felt that Préveza was not as bad as it was made out to be.

In addition it exported, if the Admiralty *Pilot Guide* was to be believed, olive oil – there were certainly large olive groves every-where – wool, butter, cheese and *valonia* (which are the acorn cups and unripe acorns of the Eurasian oak, *Quercus aegilops*, used in tanning, dyeing and making ink), receiving by way of imports cotton and woollen goods, petroleum, and wine, which apparently does not flourish to any great extent here on the shores of the Gulf of Arta.

We crossed the Strait, Stenón Prévezis, here only a quarter of a mile wide, by a car ferry, for this is the way to Levkás, and to another road which runs along the southern shores of the Gulf to join the main road to Missolonghi, and climbed on to the top of the fort on the southern side, built by the Venetians who occupied Préveza from 1499 to 1699, when they were forced to cede it to the

Turks by the Treaty of Carlowitz. They got it back by force of arms in 1717, then in 1797 lost it, this time for ever, to the French, who themselves had it taken from them in 1798 by Ali Pasha. The Turks then kept it until it fell to the Greek army in 1912. From 1881 to 1912 the frontier between Turkey and Greece ran through the middle of the Strait. This was the scene not only of the battle of Actium but of another even more shameful action in which a Christian fleet, led by the Genoese admiral Andrea Doria, failed to join battle with the Turkish fleet commanded by Barbarossa (Hayrettin Paşa), allowing one Venetian ship, the Galleon of Venice, to take the brunt of a series of attacks by dozens of Turkish ships.

It was a delightful situation. Behind the fort a grove of black poplars sighed in the south-westerly breeze which was bringing a German yacht in under sail over the bar in a glittering sea to spend the night at Préveza.

Apart from this view of the sea and of the wooded promontory on the north side of the Strait, the immediate environs of what had been the Actium of the ancient world were not all that inspiring.

Down by the ferry landing there was a kiosk selling cigarettes and a rather revolting-looking café. Beyond them was the road to the south, running through a treeless plain in which, bounded by a desolate shore, there was a military aerodrome.

'With the whole of Greece to choose from you certainly made a wonderful choice,' Wanda said, with that logic which even after nearly four decades of marriage never fails to infuriate me. Still infuriated with one another, we walked along the shore – I myself saying, 'You would spoil it all. You always do!', implying that this was the chance to write the mood-piece of a lifetime about Actium and the great sea battle which in 31 BC decided the future of the Roman world, walking along a foreshore loaded with plastic bottles and black oil, backed by a grove of eucalyptus, out towards a curving, whiteish sand spit with a beacon on the end of it and a large inlet on the far side which I, rightly or wrongly, identified as Actium.

It was beyond this spit, in an inlet of the Gulf of Arta, that all through the winter of 32–31 BC, and throughout the following spring and summer, Mark Antony kept his fleet at safe anchor, or drawn up on the shore, in what was to be the last of the civil wars following upon the murder of Julius Caesar in 44 BC. There, in the late summer of 31 BC, Antony, governor-general of the territories east of the Adriatic, found himself bottled up by the fleet of Octavian, ruler of the west. And on the morning of 2 September, after five days on which the wind had blown strongly and steadily from the south-west, making it impossible for his ships to clear the Straits, short of food and deciding that some decisive action was imperative, he ordered his fleet to break out of the Gulf and engage the enemy. It now emerged, under a cloudless sky, consisting of 500 ships, led by what were some of the biggest vessels in the Roman world, quinquiremes, galleys with five banks of oars on either side, triremes, and merchant vessels converted to be ships of war. The largest of these ships were fitted with high superstructures or turrets manned by Eastern archers and equipped with *ballistae* which hurled stones and with machines for discharging darts. The sides of these huge ships were reinforced with balks of timber to prevent them being rammed, and this made them slow and unwieldly to manoeuvre. These giants were followed by the ships of the Phoenicians and the Egyptians, which had gaily-painted upperworks, gilded bows, and streamed with flags and pennants. Extraordinarily conspicuous among all these was the floating palace of Cleopatra, a galley furnished with silken sails dyed with Tyrian purple, propelled by oars sheathed in silver.

Awaiting them in the open sea were the 250 vessels of Octavian's fleet, under the command of Agrippa, assembled in two divisions. Much lighter vessels, much more manoeuvrable than those of Mark Antony, and crewed by some of the finest sailors of the ancient world, they were more than a match for Mark Antony's crews, who were demoralized by inactivity and so depleted that men who had never been to sea, mule drivers and labourers, had had to be conscripted to bring the ships' companies up to strength.

The action began about noon with Agrippa's triremes running in close, shearing off the oars of Mark Antony's quinquiremes, which were so enormously heavy that it was impossible for the rowers to ship them, in doing so suffering surprisingly little damage from the archers and the *ballistae* in their towering turrets. And almost before it had begun, although no one either in the ships or watching from the land realized it, the battle was lost. Quite suddenly, what had been up to this moment a calm sea became an agitated one when a north-east breeze off the land sprang up. As it did so, the crews of the Egyptian squadron of 60 ships could be seen making sail, the first ship to do so being Cleopatra's galley, which was already setting course for Alexandria.

It is said that this was part of a pre-arranged plan; that

Cleopatra, on board whose galley a large amount of treasure had been loaded just before the fleet sailed, was on her way to Egypt, there to rally those of Mark Antony's legions that still remained there, and with the means to pay them. Certainly, she was not the sort of woman whom anyone would accuse of cowardice. Ruthless, scheming, evil she might be, but certainly not frightened of anyone.

What was ignoble was the behaviour of Mark Antony, who abandoned his flagship for a swifter vessel and had himself conveyed aboard Cleopatra's galley, narrowly escaping capture on the way to it, there to be welcomed by his mistress and, surrounded by every sort of luxury, to sit in the bows with his back to the ship's company, contemplating his utter disgrace as the galley sailed southwards. This was the end of him as a ruler and commander.

When Antony and Cleopatra were seen to be fleeing the scene of action, some of their captains drove their ships ashore and became anonymous spectators, joining those hundreds of thousands who were already watching the battle. Others continued the struggle, gallantly lashing their huge vessels together, turning them into huge, oarless fortresses, better to resist Agrippa's men, who by this time were setting them on fire with burning arrows and jamming rafts loaded with inflammable substances against their sides. By four o'clock the battle was over. Twelve thousand of Antony's men had perished and those ships that were not either destroyed or taken that afternoon were later burned at their anchorages inside the point.

The spectators of this battle, one of the decisive battles of the ancient world, were the 200,000 men of the opposing armies who were stationed on either side of the Gulf, inside the Straits, but who could do nothing to influence it; Octavian's 80,000 infantry and 12,000 cavalry, whom he had ferried across the Adriatic from Brundisium and marched through Albania to this remote spot in order to frustrate Mark Antony's plan to invade Italy and bring the horrors of civil war to the peninsula; and Mark Antony's army of 100,000 infantry and 12,000 cavalrymen which included Egyptians and barbarians supplied by those eastern Asian rulers who had been forced to recognize his authority (many of whom had already deserted to Octavian). So perished Antony's nearly realized dream of becoming Emperor of the East and West, with the capital of the Empire not at Rome but at Alexandria, which would have had consequences difficult, if not impossible, to envisage.

On this day, 2 September 31 BC, the civil wars that had plagued the Roman world finally ended, as did the Republic. Octavian became Caesar, appropriating to himself the name of his great-uncle, and also called himself Augustus, as such becoming the first Emperor of Rome. By the autumn of the following year he was master of Egypt and of its treasure, and Antony and Cleopatra, who found herself unable to work her will on this new ruler of the world, were both dead.

In what was the fast gathering dusk, having crossed the Strait, we stood at the foot of the great crumbling theatre, one of the once splendid buildings with which Octavian had adorned the city of Nikopolis, which he built more or less on the site of the encampment from which he and his army had watched Agrippa's great victory. Bats flitted through the arcades of the auditorium and from the marshes on the shores of an inlet in the Gulf of Arta which are said to be infested with snakes and reptiles, some of them venomous, and undoubtedly are infested with billions of mosquitoes, malarial or otherwise, came the reassuring din created by thousands, if not millions, of frogs.

Then we followed a track past the remains of the stadium for about 500 yards, to see the place where Octavian pitched his tent before the action, on which a monument was raised, dedicated to Neptune; all that remained of this monument was a large plinth with holes cut in the side of it which were used to display the prows of ships captured in the action. To populate Nikopolis, Octavian (now Augustus) arbitrarily moved to it the populations of Aetolia and Akarnania, more humble places in the neighbouring parts of western Greece, in much the same way that so many of the inhabitants of post-war Britain were hi-jacked from their homely environments and settled in what was ostensibly better accommodation to satisfy the whim of some local authority. Whether or not the *hoi polloi* enjoyed living on the shores of what was later to become a malarial marsh, the city flourished. St Paul wrote the Epistle to Titus here in the winter of AD 64, and later a school of philosophy was founded here by Epictetus. It was also said to have been the birthplace of the thirteenth Pope, St Eleutherus, who was elected in AD 177 at a time when the language of the Church of Rome was still Greek. Plundered by the Visigoths, rebuilt by Justinian, it endured until it was finally destroyed by the Bulgarians in the eleventh century. So disappeared one more of the cities of the ancient world.

From Préveza we drove north again, crossing the Acheron (the River of Grief), one of the rivers of Hades, the unseen Lord of the Lower World, the Acheron here flowing through a wide plain on the last part of its journey from its source in Mount Tomaros, a mountain south-west of Ioannina, to the Ionian Sea.

It was such a new road that whoever had just finished coating it with liquid tar half an hour previously had been so anxious to get home to their tellys that they had forgotten to put up any warning notices. As a result we ran through this lake of hot bitumen at about 50 mph and emerged from it with a van that was not spotted with tar but was completely black, as was the white Mercedes (and the white caravan it was towing) of a wretched German who was travelling in the opposite direction.

Nearly weeping with vexation we drove at top speed to a hamlet on the coast called Limenískos Fanári, known to the ancients as the 'sweet harbour'. It was a pretty place at the mouth of the Acheron, now called the Mavropotamos, with two or three cafés down by the water's edge and fishing boats tied up alongside among the reeds that lined the estuary; but for the moment, with the tar hardening on what was virtually a new vehicle, we had no eyes for it. Hoping that we might enlist some help, we stopped opposite one of the cafés, which had four men sitting outside it at a table playing cards, and began to try and clean the van, using petrol from a spare can and cotton wool from a first-aid set. When that ran out we tore up one of my shirts which I had always rather liked.

It took one and a half hours to get most but not all of it off (it was even on the roof), and another twenty minutes to get it off ourselves and our clothes; and it would have taken even longer if a small, kindly, fat schoolboy had not appeared and offered to help. During this entire period the men at the table playing cards did not cast a single glance in our direction.

Then, having rewarded the little boy, who seemed sorry that it was all over, we drove to a down-at-heel-looking café further along the estuary which had a camp site, and there, fed up and exhausted, had a somewhat limited but profitable conversation with a very dark young man, while what proved to be his father sat in a corner drinking ouzo and saying nothing.

'How much is the camp site a night?'

'Hundred drachma. Not so much, isn't it?'

'How much is the retsina?'

'One bottle, twenty-nine drachmas. Not so much, isn't it?'

'That's too much. No one pays twenty-nine.'

'OK. Too much. How much you want to pay?'

'Twenty-five.'

'OK. Twenty-five drachmas. Not so much, isn't it?'

Then his mother, who was even darker than he was and surprisingly resembled a beautiful Hindu, cooked us a delicious dinner of pork chops with rosemary. It is said that some of the inhabitants of this piece of coast of what is now Greece but was once Albania are the descendants of Negro slaves brought here when it was part of the Turkish empire.

All night I had terrible dreams about being in a German bomber that was crashing over Southampton but never actually hit the ground, just kept on going down.

We woke in the morning to find that chance had brought us to one of the more beautiful shores of the Mediterranean.

Beyond the fence that hemmed the camp site in, which was so full of holes that it could not keep anything either in or out, there was a beach of fine sand on which the sea fell ceaselessly, not with the long sighing sound that the Atlantic makes even on the calmest days, but – with a north wind blowing – a restless, pattering sound. The beach curved between two headlands, the nearest one, above the mouth of the river, covered with holly trees and small holm oaks and with a chapel with a red-tiled roof, built of whitewashed stone near the headland, which was more like a big white barn than a chapel. It had a cross on top of it that was used as a leading mark by the fishermen. The other, more distant headland was covered with scrub.

Into this bay, close under the headland with the chapel on it, the Acheron/Mavropotamos, the antithesis of a river of Hades, a sand bar partially blocking its mouth, flowed slow and deep into the Ionian Sea.

Here, on this point, where the river entered the sea, stood the café where we had eaten the previous night, a deplorable construction built partly of tin sheeting, partly with whitewashed breeze-blocks which were embellished with crude drawings of fish, crayfish and a mermaid, and roofed with lethal asbestos. Built only a year previously, it could easily have been forty years old, for it was already both aged and ageless, somehow contriving, by one of those miracles which can only be performed on the shores of the

Mediterranean, to look, if not beautiful, right. It stood in a grove of eucalyptus trees which were growing in what, until they were planted there and had become established, were sand dunes, and there one could sit outside it under a shelter of reeds listening to music of a strange, distinctly non-European sort that the son had put on tape.

The lavatory arrangements were almost indescribable. Here, as in so many non-Muslim places on the shores of the Mediterranean (Muslims use water for this purpose), you did not put the used paper down the hole but in a cardboard box, in order not to block up the primitive drainage arrangements. Some day perhaps, when the season was finally deemed to have ended, or when we went away, for we were the last guests, it would be emptied. The only wash basin in the entire camp site, which in the height of the season accommodated more than 150 campers, had no waste pipe. On the site, water was pumped to the showers which worked and to the lavatories which didn't. The refuse bins, which had never been emptied of the ordure left by the last intake of campers, were scarcely visible beneath mounds of overflow.

At the far end of the beach, at the foot of the scrub-covered point, another, smaller, river, in which the cattle grazing in the plain congregated in the heat of the day, entered the bay.

Behind the waterfront, where the men had played cards, a completely new town had arisen and was still arising, for some of the houses were nothing more than empty brick and concrete frames. The fisherman who owned our café, whatever he may have been previously, was now distinctly indolent. He did not need to be anything else as he also owned one of the cafés on the waterfront as well as the whole waterfront here, so one day, if he laid off the ouzo a bit, he might wake up to find himself a millionaire, for it is inconceivable that such a beautiful place could be left more or less unscathed much longer.

We spent three days here, soaking up the sun, trying but failing to summon up the energy to visit a ruin called the Necromanteion of Ephyra, the Oracle of the Dead and of Hades, which was somewhere hidden in the Plain of Fanári. In the heat of the afternoon, covered in fly repellent, we slept in the shade of the eucalyptus trees. The outer world from which we had come, stepping out of it, as though through a looking glass, receded. We lived on fish, pork chops, eggs, peppers, tomatoes, cooked in various ways by the enigmatic Hindu. We only ate food that had been cooked. With the lavatories and the dustbins in mind, this was not the sort of place to indulge a passion for anything in its raw, native state, such as green salads. In the evening we used to cross the river at the bar, up to our necks in water, and walk out into the marshy plain which stretches away westwards to the sea, a strange and beautiful place, like the Indian plain on the banks of the Ganges, full of clumps of tall pampas grass that looked as though tigers might be lurking in them, reeds, wild sage and trees with fern-like fronds, an abode of cows and their herdsmen, and shepherds with their sheep, rather than tigers.

Once we climbed up among the dwarf holly and the ilex to the white chapel, which once a year became a place of pilgrimage, to find it shut; then continued on up to the top of the headland, to where it fell away in a sheer cliff as if someone had cut it with a knife, and there looked down into green shimmering depths in which one imagined the Nereids might live.*

On the way back we met a shepherd with his sheep, moving them along the bank, who spoke English. We had just at that moment seen a snake in the marsh and we asked him what sort it was, and if it was dangerous. He was an old man and had, he said, spent many years working as a janitor in Pittsburg, although it was difficult to imagine it.

'There are snakes,' he said, looking at it where it was wriggling aimlessly – we could see now that it was not really a snake at all, but some sort of slow worm, 'that are blind. It used to be said that they see only once a year, on the Saturday before Easter Sunday, and that God had made them blind because they might harm people. This is such a snake.'

At seven o'clock each evening the fishermen went out, taking their boats over the bar to shoot their nets which they would haul in at dawn, and for a while all was excitement and activity. Around seven-thirty clouds of swifts, having swooped continuously over the river, settled in the trees, making an astonishing noise like hundreds of miniature alarm clocks going off. Upstream now the river was greengage green, downstream, towards the sunset and the bar, it was the colour of the lees of wine, the same colour as the sky and the sea beyond. By eight-thirty it was quite dark.

We left early the following morning to go to Suli. The fisherman

---

* The daughters of the sea god Nereus, but also female spirits, nymphs, sometimes malevolent, who, with other spirits known under the generic name of Exotica, inhabit the Greek countryside.

gave us one of his bottles of ouzo. We both knew we would never go back. It would be better not to. One can rarely duplicate moments of happiness. The summer was ended.

In the Steps of Ali Pasha

The way to Suli used to be up through the gorges of the Acheron River where it emerges into the Plain of Fanári, at a small place called Glyki. We travelled to it by a road so densely crowded with tortoises, all on the march across it apparently bound for some pre-determined destination, that we felt obliged to get down and remove them from it, many of them having already been squashed by passing vehicles whose drivers could easily have avoided doing so if they had wished. Glyki was a rather ruinous place with a pleasant café on the tree-shaded bank of the Acheron near the mouth of the gorge. It looked a suitable subject for one of Edward Lear's sketches or paintings, and in fact he may have sketched or painted it while visiting Suli in the course of a journey in the spring and summer of 1849 which took him from Préveza to Parga, eastwards through the mountains of Epirus to Ioannina, over the Pindus range to the monasteries of the Meteora in Thessaly and through the Vale of Tempe.

When we visited Suli its isolation was about to be destroyed by a motor road, full of hair-pin bends, amazingly wide in places and with an appalling surface because it was still unfinished, which had been bulldozed through a wild, mountain region, covered with dense growths of oak, ilex and pines for a distance of some ten miles and one in which there were scarcely any habitations apart from herdsmen's bothies and the rude habitations built by charcoal burners.

On the way to it we passed a large encampment of these charcoal burners who, they told us, would remain here in the mountains until the weather broke, which they said would be quite soon.

It was a scene of extraordinary activity. Long lines of mules laden with timber were being brought down from the heights above by savage-looking muleteers and their handsome but equally wild-looking womenfolk. The quantity of wood collected in this way was enormous and huge piles of it lay about in what appeared to be the utmost confusion. To burn the charcoal they set up the timber on end in conical piles up to twelve feet high and anything up to twenty feet in diameter at the base. They then covered them with earth and charcoal dust, leaving a vertical chimney in the middle, open to the air. These piles were now smoking away through their chimneys, rather like wigwams with fires burning inside them.

The carbonization began at the top and worked downwards, and from the outside towards the centre. The highly skilled work of controlling the combustion was carried out by men whose clothes and skin were almost jet black. Their job was to open and close various holes around the base of the pile and half-way up the sides, which controlled the combustion, a process that could take any-thing up to three weeks and would produce a quantity of charcoal equivalent to about a quarter of the weight and about 60 per cent of the bulk of the original timber. The heat generated by these slowly combusting piles of wood combined with that of the hot sun overhead was appalling.

Wild-looking though these charcoal burners and muleteers might be, they were kindly, hospitable people, both men and women, taking us to their camp fire, plying us with delicious, sweet, slightly smoky tea which had some unidentifiable herb in it, and happily posing for group photographs. How long these people would continue to earn their living in these particular mountains once the road was completed was uncertain. 'The wood,' as one of them (who spoke Italian and acted as interpreter) said, 'will still have to be cut and will still have to be lashed to the pack-saddles and brought down to the road. But now there is a road it seems likely that the timber will be loaded on to lorries and taken to some modern plant where the charcoal will be made, using kilns and retorts fitted with condensers which is a less wasteful method. If this happens not only shall we charcoal burners lose our jobs but there will no longer be any need, as there has been up to now, for mules to carry the charcoal down to the plain in sacks as there was previously when there was nothing but a mule track.' He spoke with a complete absence of rancour, almost with resignation, as – in the course of this long journey in the Mediterranean lands – I had noticed simple people often do when they find their way of life threatened, in this case one which their forebears, he said, had practised since time immemorial.

Suli, the one-time capital of the Suliots, now consisted of a few houses scattered about a sort of pass or plateau, with a chapel standing on a height above it. On the far side of this plateau, where there were a number of older houses on the mountainside, the road descended steeply before climbing again to the foot of the great Turkish fortress perched on the Trypa, the Hill of the Thunderbolts, from which sheer precipices fell away to the gorges of the Acheron, 1200 feet below.

We left the vehicle and climbed up to what was a second pass at the foot of the fortress rock under a hot sun. It was an enchanting place, with a couple of wells, a shrine of the sort common at passes anywhere in southern Europe, shaded by two big plane trees that the Turks may have planted there 180 years previously when they took Suli, beneath which a youthful shepherd of about twelve years of age was reclining, surrounded by goats and sheep. Just below it, in the full heat of the sun, an old man and his wife were building what looked as if it was going to be some sort of ticket office, using breeze-blocks. When it was finished they would then sit in it, issuing tickets to the tourists who would be disgorged from the coaches that had ground up to this astonishing place.

Having asked the miniature shepherd to call off his fearfully savage dogs, which had come bounding down the mountainside in order to tear us to pieces, I left Wanda, who had decided to help the ancient couple in the construction of their ticket office and was now busy handling breeze-blocks, and set off up a steep path, the way being marked by black rags which someone had stuck on the bushes which covered the hillside. The walls of the castle were still standing, all except those on the face where the main gate was, where they had collapsed. Above them, in what had been the principal court-yard of the Albanian-Turkish governor, another fine plane tree rose, looking rather like an immense green umbrella. High overhead a pair of eagles hung almost motionless on the air currents. The only sounds in the ruinous courts were those made by cicadas and the droning of bees and other insects. An adder was asleep in the sun, curled up on a stone.

This, and the lower town, were the sites of the former mountain capital of the Suliots: wild, independent warriors, Greek-speaking Albanians, Christians who, like the Pargiots, the inhabitants of Parga, had never been converted to Islam by the Turks and had never been conquered by them, even centuries after Murad II had taken Ioannina, the principal city of Epirus, in 1430.

Towards the end of the eighteenth century the Suliots began to be a nuisance to the Turks in the person of Ali Pasha, the cruel, ruthless and disobedient representative of the Sultan in Epirus. They harassed his protegés, the Muslim farmers in the coastal plain, and carried on an interminable sort of predatory warfare with their immediate neighbours, this being the principal justification for existence of all Epirots and Albanians, whether Christian or Muslim.

It proved extremely difficult to put down the Suliots. From the end of the 1780s until the first years of the new century, Ali Pasha, rendered doubly barbarous by being thwarted, made innumerable attempts to capture Suli, all except one (when some 500 Albanian Muslims were led into a part of their territory by two treacherous Suliots, Pilios Gousis and Karanikas, using secret paths known only to the Suliots) being unsuccessful, and even this only yielded him a relatively small part of their territory. The Suliots, men and women alike, contested literally every inch of the way. Even the final attempt to take Suli after a siege led by Ali's son, Veliz, at the head of 18,000 men, proved unsuccessful. Veliz was forced to raise the siege and grant the Suliots a safe conduct out of their fortress on the Trypa, where they had suffered the agonies of thirst and famine, which would allow them to retreat to Parga, Zalonga, Vourgareli and other places of their choice with their honour unblemished.

As soon as they quitted the safety of their fortress, however, Veliz, like all the members of his family a master of perfidy, attacked them, and the end of the Suliots was a terrible one. Some were massacred, some blew themselves to smithereens with gunpowder, taking their opponents to eternity with them, some, including unmarried girls and married women, hurled themselves from the precipices, the latter with their offspring clutched in their arms, all of them to avoid the dishonour of being taken, the men to avoid the horrible tortures that certainly awaited them, the women to avoid slavery. At the Rock of Zalonga, sixty Suliot women dashed their children on to the rocks below, then hand in hand danced to the edge of the precipice, one by one throwing themselves down at each recurring round of the dance until none remained. Those who succeeded in reaching the coast at Parga fled, as did the Pargiots, to Corfu and other of the Ionian Islands. Later, many of these survivors, some of whom took service in Corfu under the French and Russians, fought against the Turks in Greece in the War of Independence, though not particularly distinguishing themselves at the siege of Missolonghi, where their intolerable demands for money may have accelerated the demise of Byron. Eventually they mutinied, and had to be sent away.

Now, only a few ancient houses, and perhaps these were of Turkish origin, and the castle called the Kiáfa, or Suli-Kastro, and that was Turkish, built by Ali Pasha on the site of their own fortress to obliterate their memory (in which Lear had spent a thoroughly uncomfortable night as the unwanted guest of the Muslim governor), remained of what had been sixty-six Suliot villages. It was as if the Suliots had never been.

Back on the road from Igoumenitsa, on the way to Ioannina, what used to be a twenty-hour ride on horseback, we visited a small monastery. It was half hidden from the road in a little dell. The open space in front of it was an arcadian place, shaded by planes, with a little spring of clear water bubbling down into a stone basin, and very quiet except for the humming of the monks' bees, busily at work on behalf of their masters. What must have been at least a couple of coach parties had just left, having picnicked under the trees, leaving behind them 346 empty German beer cans, an even larger number of paper cups, quantities of unconsumed food already thick with bluebottles, and masses of soiled and sticky plastic. A lot of this muck had been thrown into the spring. The place was a disaster area.

Feeling rather self-conscious, as one does when casting oneself in a do-gooder role, we began to clear up the mess, watched from one of the upper windows of the monastery by a young, bearded monk who must have thought we were out of our minds. Then a shepherd arrived to graze his sheep on the green grass under the trees. Seeing that all they would have if things were left as they were would be a diet of plastic, he also began to help us. As none of us had any matches to get a fire going, I knocked on the door of the monastery and asked the monk who answered it if he could let me have some. He did so, instantly, but showed no signs either of displeasure at the filthy mess the coach party had left behind or of pleasure at what the three of us were now doing to clean it up. Perhaps the monks quite enjoyed having coach parties picnicking on their doorstep, welcoming any kind of diversion in such a quiet spot.

Ioannina, so-named after St John the Baptist, stands on the shore of a lake in a hollow plain. Beyond it rises Mount Mitsikeli, an impressive limestone mountain nearly 6000 feet high, and the peaks of the Pindus range. It is a singularly beautiful situation; the lake edged with green reeds and watermeadows in which sheep are pastured, and behind them vineyards, green fields in which the harvest had long since taken place, fields of tobacco, and apparently floating in it offshore, a wooded island, the site of several monasteries, the earliest of them, Nikolaos Dilios, built in the eleventh century.*

The city is noted for its fur and tanning industries and for the gold and silver embroidery and filigree work which is still carried on here by its inhabitants – Greeks, Albanians, Vlachs from what was known as Great Wallachia, otherwise Thessaly, and Jews – and their artefacts can be found in what, when we were there, were the hot, noisy, narrow streets of the bazaar which still have a distinctly Turkish air. Above all this, within the walls of the old city, was Litharítsa (otherwise known as the Demi-Kule, or Iron Fortress), the dismantled fortress of Ali Pasha, and a couple of mosques, all that remain of fourteen, one of them, the Mosque of Aslan Aga, now a museum embellished with some extremely eccentric pictures illustrating some of the more discreditable acts perpetuated by Ali Pasha. What Lear, who enjoyed himself here, described as 'the strange gilded tomb where lies the body of the man who for so long a time made thousands tremble' was not accessible when we were there, as it was in a military area.

We were at the end of a long journey in the company of Ali

---

* The other monasteries are Prodromos, dedicated to John the Baptist, Panteleimon, Ayios Nikolaos Spanos and Ayios Elouses. All of these were built originally in the thirteenth century and are adorned with frescoes.

Pasha. We had first felt his cold shadow at his birthplace at Tepelenë in what is now southern Albania, where the great fortress he built stands in strange proximity to apartment blocks, at the foot of the Klissoura Mountains in a region that now produced coal, then at Parga, at Préveza, at Suli and now at Ioannina, where he came to a not untimely end.

He was born in 1744, surnamed Arslan, the Lion. He was a Tosk, the tribe or clan which inhabited, as they still do, the southern part of Albania. His father, who was a bey, a provincial governor, died when he was fourteen and it is said that the family was subsequently dispossessed of part of its patrimony by predatory neighbours, and that his mother and sister were violated by peasants during a riot against excessive taxation. Whether this is true or not, his mother, a remarkable woman, deliberately brought him up to be both cruel and cunning and with a remarkable capacity for biding his time until the opportunity presented itself for taking what was usually a hideous revenge on those whom he considered to have wronged him or obstructed his designs. It is said that his mother murdered his half-brothers in order to have more to settle on him and that in order to make sure that there should be no impediment, he himself murdered his surviving brother. It is also said that he then imprisoned his mother for attempting to poison him and that she died while still incarcerated. Whatever the truth of these allegations, it was Hamke, his mother, who gave him command of his first robber band. Thereafter, his advancement was rapid. He married the daughter of the Pasha of Dhelvinákion, a place now in northern Greece on the southern borders of Albania, then brought about his death, as he did that of his successor. He also brought about the downfall of the rebellious Pasha of Scutari, now Shkodër in northern Albania, for which the Sublime Porte at Constantinople rewarded him not only by appointing him bey of his father's old territory, but also by giving him the job of assistant to the Derwend-Pasha of Roumelia, a Turkish province composed of central Albania and western Macedonia, with the task of putting down brigandage. He deliberately allowed the brigands to continue unchecked and this resulted in the Derwend-Pasha being executed and Ali, thanks to his foresight in distributing bribes to the appropriate ministers in Constantinople, getting his job, being appointed not only Derwend-Pasha of Roumelia but also Pasha of Trikkala in Thessaly.

The following year, 1788, with what was a by-now-greatly-enlarged robber band, which he had enlisted for the purpose, thus depriving these regions of their own autonomous robber bands, he took Ioannina, thereafter, as its Vizier, conferring on it, and all the other regions of which he was the overlord, a degree of law-abiding stability that had been rare up to this time, and which found great favour with his masters at Constantinople.

In about 1790 he began the first of his campaigns against the Suliots, the results of which we have already seen, and in 1797, after the collapse of the Venetian Republic, which Napoleon had brought about, he succeeded in persuading him to send a number of French military engineers to oversee the fortification of his capital. He was less successful in his attempt to persuade Napoleon to let him have Parga and Préveza, which by this time were garrisoned by French troops, but when the news arrived of Napoleon's débacle in Egypt Ali Pasha had the audacity to attack Préveza, forcing the French garrison to surrender and making it his principal port.

It was at about this time, having characteristically waited the best part of forty years for a congenial opportunity to present itself, that he revenged himself on those who had allegedly so ill-used his mother and sister by locking the entire population of Gardiki, a town in the Pindus range, in a monastery, then having them butchered by 400 of his Albanian guards, reserving a more lingering fate for the two principal protagonists, one of whom he had spitted and then roasted alive over a fire, the other flayed alive and then minced.

In 1807 he had hopes that Napoleon might have obtained Parga for him at the Peace of Tilsit, but not unnaturally the Emperor did not exert himself on his behalf and Parga remained French until 1814, when it was given to the British who, rather disgracefully, handed it over to the Sultan Mahmud II, which meant that it fell into the hands of Ali Pasha, who was now master of all Albania, Epirus and parts of Thessaly in eastern central Greece, while his son, Mouktar Pasha, was appointed ruler of the Morea, the Peloponnese.

In November 1809, Byron arrived at Ioannina, hoping to find this prodigious ruler, whose notoriety if not fame had by now spread far and wide, in residence, only to be told that the Vizier was away besieging the castle of Berat, north of Tepelenë, but had left instructions that a house was to be put at the English lord's disposal and that all his wishes were to be gratified. After riding out into the city and visiting the splendid palaces of Ali and his grandsons, which Byron found too ornamented for his taste, he set off on a nine-day journey on horseback to Tepelenë. The following day Ali Pasha appeared, and Byron's description of him is more or less as his pictures show him at this stage of his life, when he was about sixty years old: very short, very fat, with a full white beard and with an imperious eye. The meeting was a great success. Ali Pasha detected signs of good breeding in the smallness of the poet's ears and hands, which were also of an acceptable degree of whiteness. While Byron was there, as he wrote to his mother from Préveza, Ali Pasha looked on him as his son, and treated him as a child, sending him sweet-meats, but also begging him to visit him and smoke a pipe with him at night, when he had more leisure for entertaining his noble guest.

In 1800 the Vizier became enamoured of a Mme Frossini, the wife of an important merchant of Ioannina, who was already carrying on an affair with Ali's son, Mouktar Pasha, while her husband was away on one of his frequent business trips. She had been brought to Ali's notice by Mouktar's wife, who had not taken kindly to seeing her own jewellery being lavished on Mme Frossini by her husband.

When Ali set eyes on his son's mistress he was so enamoured of her that he immediately sent his son away on a campaign and then asked her to transfer her affections to himself. When she refused, he accused her of being a spy and had her drowned from a boat in the Lake of Ioannina, together with seventeen other ladies of what was alleged to be easy virtue who had been chosen to keep her company.

Four years later, in 1805, Ali Pasha became enamoured of a Mme Vassiliki and, after having his own wife put to death, he made her his mistress. She was a more serious lady who belonged to a secret society which was working for the independence of Greece and, as a Christian, she was to be instrumental in saving the lives of many of Ali Pasha's Christian subjects, who up to this time had often been in some danger of losing their lives simply because they were Christians. Thanks to Mme Vassiliki, from this time onward his reputation in this particular field showed a marked improvement.

For the next fifteen years he enjoyed unbridled power, but in 1820, when he was seventy-six years of age, he was unwise enough to have one of his ex-officials, who had moved to Constantinople, murdered there while in the service of Sultan Mahmud II. In July 1820, the Sultan declared Ali Pasha to be a rebel and a traitor, and the Pashas of Turkey-in-Europe were ordered to close in on him with their forces. None were happier than the Suliots, some of whom had returned to the mainland from Corfu and now saw an opportunity to take revenge on the author of their misfortunes.

The following year saw him closely besieged in Ioannina, with not only his officers deserting him to take service with the forces of the Sultan but also his own sons. Meanwhile, the Turkish fleet had taken his principal port, Préveza, and was now blockading the entire coast of Epirus.

By this time, partly because these events were engaging the attention of the Turks, the Greeks had commenced their War of Independence, so it was now doubly necessary for the Turks to bring the siege to a rapid conclusion.

The siege was commanded by Khourschid Pasha and lasted fifteen months. The operations of the attackers were limited by the fact that the Vizier had immured himself on an upper floor of his citadel, together with his harem, having packed the ground floor with sufficient barrels of gunpowder to blow up the citadel and a large part of the city if the faithful retainer he had installed there obeyed his instructions to light the fuses and detonate them, should what looked like becoming a successful attack take place.

Under the pretence of offering him a free pardon from the Sultan, Khourschid, who seems to have been every bit as guileful as his opponent, told him that he should leave the citadel and cross to the monastery of Panteleimon, on the island in the lake, there to await the arrival of the document. This Ali Pasha rather surprisingly agreed to do; but when Khourschid returned, it was with a warrant for his execution, and in an exchange of fire – the bullet holes can be seen to this day – the brave old ruffian was killed.

Meanwhile the faithful guardian still waited in the citadel with a smouldering match for his master's order to touch off the gunpowder, which could only be countermanded by sending him a broken ring, which was now delivered to him.

As soon as he was dead Ali Pasha was decapitated and his head, suitably embalmed, was placed on a silver salver, tastefully wrapped in red silk tissue, and then displayed to the populace of the city, who apparently were greatly cheered by this spectacle, before being sent to the Sultan in Constantinople as a proof that he was finally dead.

Mme Vassiliki was more fortunate, or rather she was cleverer, or more cunning. It was she who betrayed the secret of the broken ring to Khourschid Pasha, or one of his officers, having prudently taken shelter in another cell. Carried to Constantinople, a prisoner with the remainder of Ali Pasha's harem, she was spared by Sultan Mahmud who, rather unfairly, perhaps because they were Muslims and therefore less than the dust, had all the others hanged. She died in Greece, poor and forgotten, but not necessarily any more unhappy than when she had catered for the needs of the Vizier, in 1835.

At a pleasant café shaded by plane trees on the shores of the lake, we talked to a waiter who had emigrated to Australia a few years previously with his wife and children, had grown tired of it, returned to his birthplace and was now, once again, planning to re-emigrate. 'I came back here to Ioannina with the equivalent of £20,000 ($28,000) in Australian dollars,' he said. 'That was two years ago. Since then we have consumed a large part of it. I was a croupier in a casino in Sydney. It was a fine job. In four minutes, working in the casino as a croupier, I could earn the price of a bottle of the retsina you are now drinking in this café which, as you know, is much more expensive than if you buy it in a shop. Here, working in this restaurant, it takes me thirty minutes to earn the same amount of money. Now we are going back to Sydney before we are left with no money at all, and I shall be a croupier again and my wife will once more be happy. But I shall not be happy.'

We left him among the empty tables, a small, sad figure who hated Sydney, hated Australia, loved his native city Ioannina but couldn't afford to live in it, the familiar dilemma of those born and bred in the Mediterranean lands.

Monasteries of the Air

Reluctantly leaving Ioannina, passing the cave in which in 1611 Dionisos Skylosophos, Bishop of Trikkala, was skinned alive for leading a revolt against the Turks, we took what, when all this wild region was part of the Turkish Empire in Europe, was the road to Constantinople.*

After skirting the north shore of Lake Pambotis, the road climbed above it along the flanks of Mount Mitsikeli, from which, looking back, there was a magnificent view of the city and of its promontory and the island on which Ali Pasha came to a sticky end, on which there is now a taverna famous for eels and crayfish. Then, at the Mázia Pass, another panorama opened up, this one of the great forests and peaks of the Pindus range and, far below, of the upper waters of the Arachthes River, which flows into the Gulf of Arta, to which the road now descended.

From the valley of the Arachthes the road climbed up through a wilderness of sandstone in the Pindus range, with Peristeri, a 7500-foot peak, looming out of the forests to the south of it, high

* By way of Trikkala, Larissa, which the Turks called Yenisher (New Town), Salonika and Thrace.

above one of its tributaries which, like so many of the rivers of Epirus, flowing to the Ionian Sea, has its source near the village of Métsovo. This was a long, rambling, very pleasant village on a mountainside covered with beech, box and ilex trees and divided into two parts, the 'Prosilio' (facing the sun) and the 'Anilio' (away from the sun), by the enormous chasm of the Metsovitikos River, one of the rivers of the Pindus that have their sources here. Its inhabitants are Vlachs (Vlakhi or Vlakhiots), Christians of Wallachian origin, who took refuge in this wild region during the Turkish occupation. They used to travel as far afield as Hungary, Russia and Germany to work as labourers and artisans. They were also and still are principally itinerant shepherds, making the transhumance with their flocks from the plains of Thessaly in summer to the High Pindus.

Some became millionaires. One, Giorgios Averoff, emigrated to Egypt where he became a merchant, accumulated a vast fortune and built hospitals and schools in Alexandria, Athens and his native village. He also provided the Greek government with the wherewithal, about £300,000 ($420,000), to buy a second-hand Italian armoured crusier, which originally cost £950,000 or $1,330,000 to build, which was named after him. Such a man, who benefits Greece and the Greeks, is known to his compatriots as an 'Evergheti'.

Now in the 1980s the descendants of this egregious band of shepherds, labourers, artisans, millionaires and destroyers of Turks and robbers, were to be seen sitting under one of the enormous plane trees in the little square from which the main street stretched away uphill flanked by picturesque buildings housing little shops selling wooden artefacts, embroidered textiles and good hand-woven carpets, imbibing the wine-like air, amiable, dignified, old and not-so-old – some of them in their mid twenties – most of them moustached, all wearing the uniform of the Vlachs of Métsovo: black pill-box hats, short black homespun jackets, black and white homespun breeches, pleated linen shirts and shoes with black pom-poms on them. Lively-looking heirs to another age, they gave the impression that they only needed a word from some chief among them to bring out their weapons from wherever they had cached them and take up their positions with their full-skirted womenfolk on the mountainside, ready to consign the Muslim infidel to perdition.

We were about to leave this place, though we had a strong disposition to linger indefinitely, feeling perhaps mistakenly that in spite of its inhabitants having come to terms with tourism to the extent that they admitted its existence, they had not allowed their ancient pattern of life to be even slightly disturbed by it, when, as if to prove this contention, one of the younger men rose to his feet, greeted us warmly and insisted on taking us to a taverna for a drink.

From Métsovo we climbed through forests of beech and pine, some of them immense trees, to the Katára Pass, on the way seeing muleteers unloading timber from their animals at the roadside and in the meadows hooded shepherds, for it was suddenly cold here, watching their sheep and goats.

Here, 5600 feet up at the Pass, from where the snow clad mountains of the Pindus could be seen rising behind Métsovo, the weather changed. As if by magic huge masses of black, swirling cloud appeared overhead and it began to rain, at first heavily, then torrentially. It was only surprising that it did not fall in the form of snow, the pass being frequently snowbound between October and May.

Now we left Epirus for what in summer can usually be described as the sun-baked plains of Thessaly, descending towards them – they were still a long way off – by a road full of hairpin bends with the rain clouting down. At first it ran through the same sort of beech and pine forests we had climbed through to the Pass, then amongst holm oaks and finally through a region of scrub and red earth which had turned to liquid mud, all the water running not to the Ionian Sea as it had previously, but, now that we had crossed the watershed, to the Aegean. In what was now the last of the light we started looking anxiously for a place where we could camp for the night with a sufficiently solid foundation for the vehicle. At the same time we wanted to be out of sight, not that there would be many evil-doers about on such a night in this, still one of the loneliest and wildest parts of mainland Greece, still in the high Pindus, the abode of the brown bear, wolves, wild boar, lynx, Egyptian and griffon vultures and even the golden eagle.

Eventually, by which time it was pitch dark as well as pouring, we found just such a place by a lonely crossroads.

There, inhabited by one poor, bedraggled, lonely donkey, who was tethered to a stake outside it and roaring away as donkeys do when they feel themselves lonely and abandoned, we found the concrete shell of what promised to be a pretty hideous building. In it Wanda cooked delicious lamb chops, bought in a butcher's shop in Métsovo, by the light of a pressure lantern, while the donkey, bribed with sugar to stop making such an appalling noise, happily munched away at our mattresses, unseen in the darkness. Here, with a sufficiency of red wine that had not been mucked about with, we experienced what for travellers are those only too rare moments of peace and contentment when they actually succeed in finding a good place in which to pass the night.

In fact it was not all that good. The only place on such a night was either indoors, or with one's van under cover. The rain that was hissing down soothingly enough while we were eating and drinking our dinner also drummed with incredible violence on the roof of our van, making sleep impossible; to this were added the dreadful noises made by the donkey who, having experienced the pleasures of sugar for what was certainly the first time in his life, was drawing attention to the fact that he wished to continue with the treatment.

The rain ceased at dawn, by which time the donkey had fallen into a sort of semi-coma, and when we emerged stiffly from the van it was to find ourselves in a grey, dripping world, looking down into a valley the upper slopes of which were covered with squalid-looking tin huts housing sheep and goats, the modern equivalent of bothies, up to which their owners were already climbing from a village that lay below them half hidden in mist.

Of all the strange, exotic and outlandish sights to be seen in any of the lands bordering on the Mediterranean few have created a greater impression on travellers than the astonishing rock formations of various shapes and sizes that soar into the air in closely massed clumps above the valley of the River Peneus near the place where it emerges into the Thessalian Plain from the gorges of the Pindus in what is still the territory of the Vlachs.

The majority of these columns, pilasters, stalagmites, giant mushrooms, needles, pinnacles, islands, spikes, cylinders, drums, stacks, obelisks and tusks, which are just a few of the similes that have been attributed to them, were made more remarkable by the fact that the largest number of them, and the most inaccessible, had monasteries built on them, to which there was no access except by rope, drawbridge or ladder and, in the earliest times, by scaffolding pegged to the rock.

'Twelve sheets would not contain all the wonders of Meteora, nor convey to you an idea of the surprise and pleasure which I felt in beholding these curious monasteries planted like eagles' nests, on the summits of high and pointed rocks,' wrote the architect, traveller and explorer of remote and wild places, Charles Robert Cockerell, on a journey which off and on kept him in the Mediterranean lands for seven years, in the course of which, among other notable works of ancient art, he discovered the reliefs forming the frieze of the temple of Apollo in Arcadia, which was bought by the British Government and now forms one of the more spectacular adornments of the British Museum.

The best description of the Meteora is that of Robert Curzon, later 14th Baron de la Zouche, who travelled extensively in Egypt, the Holy Land, Albania and Greece in the years from 1833 to 1837. In his book *Visits to the Monasteries of the Levant*, one of the classics of Near Eastern travel, he gives an amusing account of visiting these and other monasteries in search of manuscripts. Curzon had travelled from Ioannina to Meteora in 1834 by the same route that Edward Lear followed fifteen years later and the one that we had also followed (scarcely a coincidence as that was and is the only route to it from Ioannina).

At that time the region had been so infested with *klephti*, robbers, that Curzon had been constrained to furnish himself with a *firman* signed by the then Vizier of Ioannina, Mahmud Pasha, which would, he hoped, act as a safe conduct and also enable him to obtain an escort if he wished to do so. The law of the Vizier in fact scarcely extended as far as Métsovo, as Curzon discovered when he reached it and found himself provided with a so-called escort by the headman of the village. They instantly conducted him to a lonely spot where they began to rob him and it was only by exercising great presence of mind that he was able to persuade them to conduct him to the lair of the band of which they were members and of which the headman of Métsovo was in fact the chief, where he eventually persuaded the second-in-command to provide him with five of his Wallachian ruffians to accompany him on his way.

Even today it is still possible to understand the fascination that the Monasteries of the Air exerted on these and much later travellers, although for the most part visitors, since the 1920s and 30s, have no longer been swung aloft in nets, steps having been cut in the rock. Only supplies are still taken into some of the remaining monasteries by this method.

From the moment the visitor stood at the foot of one or other of the great pinnacles looking up at one of the seven monasteries (there are now only six) from amongst the lush jungle of vegetation that grew at the foot of them, and saw these buildings, some of them literally cantilevered out over the void in the hair-raising, and one suspects not always necessary fashion beloved by the builders of orthodox monasteries on cliffs and rocks everywhere, and sometimes hearing the sound of bells tolling hundreds of feet overhead, he knew that he was about to enter a strange and different world.

There was a ritual attached to visiting a monastery in the Meteora. To attract the attention of the monks it was customary to fire a gun, the equivalent, as Curzon remarked, of knocking on the front door in less dangerous parts. Then, if the party looked more or less acceptable from such a height, which in the case of Curzon's party was at first in doubt as it included the ruffians he had been given to escort him to Meteora from the robbers' lair, a thin cord would be let down to which the visitor, very much in the role of a suppliant, could attach, that is if he had any, whatever credentials or letters of recommendation he had had the foresight to provide himself with. They were then whisked aloft where they were subjected to a searching and sometimes protracted scrutiny by the Agoumenos, the Abbot, or whoever was in charge at that particular moment who could read.

If it was then agreed that the visitor should be admitted a net was lowered, hooked to a rope which was invariably very old, monks living on rock pinnacles being necessarily of a frugal nature, and if it was agreed that he could stay the night, sufficient of his personal entourage to cater for his bodily comfort but not enough to take the monastery by force, two usually were deemed enough, were windlassed aloft, unarmed, in the net by ten to a dozen monks, which might be almost the entire complement of the monastery, heaving away on the capstan bars, with the net spinning like a top, wearing out the rope even more than it was already, as it rose with infinite slowness into the air, an operation that at Barlaam for instance, which was 222 feet above the embarkation point at the base of the rock, entailed winding up 37 fathoms of rope and could take anything up to half an hour.

If the visitor, as was the case with Curzon, was reluctant to entrust his life to this device, there was sometimes the alternative, which existed at Barlaam, of climbing a series of rickety wooden ladders, which were attached to the vertical rock face by wooden pegs, some of which had broken loose from the cliff at their lower ends, so that the ladders hung away from it over the void, making the transfer from one set of ladders to the next extremely hazardous, an alternative to the net so horrible that very few were bold enough to attempt it, or if they did, refused to descend by the same means. Even Curzon elected to leave Barlaam in the net.

Once he had been drawn into the monastery by the monks, in whom simplicity sometimes bordering on gormlessness, stubbornness and lack of any kind of aesthetic feeling seemed equally compounded, he found himself in a community which had been functioning in much the same way ever since a hermit, named Barnabas, founded what was called the *Skete* of the Holy Ghost between AD 950 and 970, a *skete* being a small monastery. Previous to this presumed foundation the hermits had lived in holes in the rock faces, some of which can be seen to this day with wooden platforms in the mouths of them on which the hermits could take the air, reached by crazy wooden ladders. Some of these pigeon holes in the rock were later used as places of banishment for recalcitrant monks.

At its greatest the Meteora consisted of thirteen monasteries and twenty smaller communities, and after the Turkish conquest they became places of refuge as well as places of prayer.

The treasures which the monks could sometimes be persuaded to expose to view were extraordinary and varied, and still are: silver reliquaries containing the heads of founders, saintly relics, the gold-embroidered mitre of a founder, vestments, including a chasuble embroidered with gold and pearls belonging to the Palaeologi, a gold cup belonging to the Cantacuzene, former patrons of one of the monasteries, a crucifix carved with scenes from the Old and New Testaments so small that they can only be viewed through a magnifying glass which took a monk named Daniel twelve years to make.

There was also an extraordinary wealth of frescoes and ikons not really acceptable to the nineteenth-century taste. They depicted what looked to the uninitiated like identical bands of saints, wearing, for example, identical, fluted, casque-like hats on their heads and with beards, combed, parted and done in ringlets, which made them look as if they were the finalists in some beard-dressing competition, all gazing calmly, unworried, untouched by grief, thinking of other things, at some point beyond the beholder in a far distance, while below them the Virgin, attended by St Ephraim, one of their number, passes away (a seventeenth-century Dormition in the Monastery of Barlaam). There were also innumerable scenes of martyrdom: future candidates for canonization being boiled alive, chopped in half, impaled, burned, broken on an agonizing wheel, both martyrs and those who are martyring them showing no emotion of any kind – the torturers might equally well be tending a garden as impaling a saint; the saints already mentally with God – so that looking at them, and at such great masterpieces of the fourteenth century as the Virgin in Lamentation and Christ in Piety, one begins to understand that one is not looking at people, human beings with human attributes, as one would find in a picture painted, say, in fourteenth-century Italy, but at symbols, painted to remind one to remember them and what they represent.

But what distinguished the Meteora monasteries, and other Orthodox and Coptic monasteries in the Mediterranean lands – on Mount Athos, in Jerusalem, in Egypt on the Nile, and in the sandy wastes of Sinai – was the accumulated wealth of priceless manuscripts and printed books which, to put it mildly, were treated in a pretty offhand manner by their custodians, most of whom were not *au fait* with either Ancient or Hellenic Greek, the Copts being equally negligent and equally unable to read their amazing books, so that what Curzon, the cultivated bibliophile, saw in the course of his monastic visits was the equivalent of a massacre. In the Monastery of Pantocrator on Mount Athos more than a hundred ancient manuscripts, all that was left of the library, many of them fine large folios, were lying amongst rubble. They had been either washed clean by rainwater or else had become stuck together in a solid, brittle mass like a huge biscuit. In the Monastery of Barlaam in the Meteora, the Agoumenos, on being asked by Curzon if he would sell a folio Bulgarian manuscript and an eleventh-century copy of the Gospels in quarto, chucked them into the dusty corner from which he had plucked them as a sign that he did not wish to do so. What went on at the Monastery of St Katharine in 1844 is told by Constantin von Tischendorf, who was on his first visit to the library in which he was to discover, twelve years later, the Codex Sinaiticus, 347 leaves of a fourth-century manuscript of the New Testament in Greek and parts of the Old Testament, later sold by the Bolsheviks to the British Government and now in the British Museum.

In the middle of the library, however, there also stood a large basket with the remains of damaged manuscripts. When I went to examine it, the Librarian, Cyril, remarked that its contents had twice already been emptied into the fire. What was there now was the third filling, which by all appearances was destined for the same fate. Judge of my astonishment when I pulled out of it a number of parchment leaves covered with Greek writing, which from their palaeographic characteristics could be judged to be of the highest antiquity . . . I had seen nothing that could be judged to be older than the leaves I saw at Sinai. Their contents proved to be Old Testament matter . . . the total number of leaves was 129. The basket being destined for destruction, I was able to secure that the smaller number of leaves, 43, which were lying loose nearby, was withdrawn at my request. When I asked later to have those that remained, difficulties arose from the side of the Superior, although he himself betrayed no knowledge of the affair. I merely noted the bare contents of the remaining 86 leaves . . . But I recommended Cyril, the Librarian, . . . most urgently to guard these precious leaves well. I added – and everything else at all similar to this that may be found.*

This was the Codex Friderico-Augustanus, still preserved to this day in the University Library at Leipzig.

By the time we reached the Meteora we had left it too late, at least twenty years too late. There was a huge coach park outside the Monastery of the Transfiguration, the Great Meteoron, full of coaches from the cold European north, and lined with stalls selling junk. St Barlaam, that had been so difficult to enter, now had a bridge thrown across the chasm and the interior was like that of a railway station, full of oracular guides, and the refectory had been converted into a museum, admission 3 drachmas, closed 1 p.m.–3 p.m. It was almost impossible to enter the beautiful church of the Katholikon, built by Nektarios and Theophanes Asparas of Ioannina, between 1542–44, to see its noble frescoes, because of the huge numbers of people. Now only two monks lived in the Monastery of the Transfiguration, which was almost entirely given up to mass tourism. Only one monk lived in Ayia Triadha, the Monastery of the Holy Trinity; but nuns had re-occupied Rousanou.

Phalanxes of motorcyclists roared around what was now a panoramic road that had done its bit to help destroy the unique feeling of silence and solitude that had once reigned here, broken only by the sound of bells and the *semantra*, the flat beam which was beaten with a mallet, summoning the monks to prayer.

---

* From Heinz Skrobucha, *Sinai*, Oxford University Press, 1966, quoting, in translation, Tischendorf's *Die Sinaibibel: Ihre Entdeckung und Erwerberung* (Leipzig, 1871).

What had not changed were the inaccessible places: the pigeon holes in the cliffs, homes of the earliest anchorites, the cleft rock of the Prodromos with the ruins of its monastery, abandoned in 1745; the rock on which the Hypselotera, highest of all the monasteries, originally reached by vertical ladders, dedicated to the Highest in the Heavens, was built in 1390, only to be abandoned in the seventeenth century because of the horrors of the ascent; the Hypapanti, still visitable, set in a huge cavern and adorned with frescoes; and the completely inaccessible Ayia Moni on what is more like a needle than a rock, built in 1614 and destroyed by an earthquake in 1858; Ayios Dimitrios, destroyed in 1809 when it was bombarded by Turkish artillery, having become the lair of a band of *klephtis*. All these, except the Hypapanti, were still left to the nesting vultures, as they had been for centuries.

The Ascent of Mount Olympus

Still in a state of shock at the thought of the Monasteries of the Air, where we had planned to spend some days, rising from chasms full of motor coaches and monks frenziedly selling picture postcards to fulfil their day's quota, I decided to realize the ambition of a lifetime, which was to climb to the summit of Mount Olympus and look out, god-like, over the wide Aegean.

'How big is this Olympus?' Wanda asked when I announced my intention and when I told her, after looking it up, that there were ten summits, none of them less than 8,800 feet, and that seven of them were over 9000 feet but that there was no need to climb the whole lot on the same day, she said she would 'tink about it', which meant that she would probably stay at the base camp.

We set off through the Plain of Thessaly under a lowering sky in a light drizzle which made the fields of stubble on either side of the road look particularly uninteresting. Even the River Peneus at Trikkala, compressed between concrete embankments and spanned by hideous bridges, contrived to look awful.

Soon we arrived at Larissa, which is famous for its ice-cream, its storks – but they had already left – halva and, something rather rare in Greece where they don't exactly grow on trees, bicycles, what looked like 72,300 of them (which was the number of its inhabitants at the last count, or whatever the current number was), all being ridden at once. There were also approximately twice that number of cars and trucks. The noise was indescribable. In Larissa we waited for hours while some panel-beaters extruded our van which I had driven backwards into a tree, under the impression that I was driving a tram, in and out of the rain which sometimes drizzled, sometimes came down in torrents, as if it was bath night for Olympian Zeus, who was now only a few miles and some 9000 vertical feet away, and he had turned on the tap with his big toe and let it overflow. We waited in patisseries, cafés, under orange and lime trees, even for a few brief moments in a cinema, all of which were conveniently situated in the main square which apparently had so many different names that even the Larissans were not sure what to call it. We also took refuge from the rain in the Archaeological Museum, in what the guide book said was the unfinished cathedral and among the vestiges of a classical temple almost next door to it, which was not much good for keeping the rain out. We ordered roast lamb in a modest-looking restaurant, countermanding the order when we found that it was going to cost 800 drachmas a portion, paying for the bread we had eaten and skedaddling. How can one really say that one likes any place under such circumstances, even Larissa?

What had we learned about the Greeks in our brief sojourn in their country? We seemed to have spent most of our time up to now consorting with Albanians, Pargiots, Suliots, Vlachs and what were said to be the descendants of Negro slaves, one of whom looked like a Hindu. They were certainly inquisitive, hyperactive mentally, thirsty for knowledge, believing whole-heartedly in the benefits of education, as were the benefactors of Métsovo (but they were Vlachs), tactful, astute, cunning (dishonesty is not, as in most other Mediterranean countries, or anywhere else for that matter, a national characteristic), courteous to strangers who might appear unheralded in their midst, temperate and chaste, at least amongst themselves, reserving – like most other dwellers on the shores of the Mediterranean – unchastity for visitors, extremely patriotic, extremely democratic, convinced of their superiority over other nations, particularly intellectual, ambitious, thrifty, loving money, brave.

Then we left Larissa for the Vale of Tempe by what the indispensable *Blue Guide to Greece* called 'the usual route', that is past the Museum which, considering that it was a mosque and therefore only had one room in it, had seemed to devote a disproportionate amount of space to a single menhir, through the area – and there is one in every town – devoted to the crushing of defunct motor cars, then following the road past the sugar refineries, which ran parallel to the railway line to Thessaloniki, otherwise Salonika, a place to be avoided at any cost.

Ahead, on one hand we should now have been looking at the peaks of the Olympus range, on the other at Ossa, rising above its stony foothills. This was the mountain that had the misfortune to have Pelion, a mountain in Magnesian Thessaly, stuck on top of it by the Giants who were intent on using it as a mounting block from which to reach the summit of Olympus in their war with the Gods, known as the Gigantomachia, which they lost. All we could actually see were some of the stony foothills. Everything else was covered with ten-tenths cloud. It might have been Balmoral.

We entered the Vale of Tempe, which separates Olympus from Ossa and, through which the Peneus flows on its last five miles or so to the Aegean Sea, one of the wonders of antiquity, said to be the work of Poseidon, the god of earthquakes and water. This defile, although it was easily defended against invaders attempting to reach the interior of Greece, could easily be turned, as Xerxes discovered in 480 BC when he took his army over mountain roads causing the Greeks to abandon their position and fall back on Thermopylae, as did the Germans in 1941. Older guide books praise the beauties and virtues of the Vale of Tempe, the wonderfully fresh air in the verdant gorge, the grandeur of its almost vertical cliffs, partly clothed in ivy and other climbing plants, the abundant waters of the Peneus, no longer compressed between concrete embankments as they are at Trikkala, flowing in the shade of willows, terebinths, lentisks, oleanders, wild fig, *agnus castus* and laurel, laurel which Apollo, having killed the serpent Python, the dragon that guarded Delphi, and having purified himself in the waters of the river, carried to Delphi, where he replanted it by the spring known as the Castalian Fountain, initiating a cult. In memory of this act, a band of young men were sent at intervals of eight years from Delphi to Tempe, where they took cuttings of the now sacred laurel which they carried back to their native city.

What most guide books fail to say is that the Peneus, flowing deep in its midst, has to share the Vale not only with a railway line but with a multi-lane highway decorated with concrete lampposts, the main road from Salonika to Athens and the Piraeus, that winter and summer it is jam-packed with juggernaut lorries, and that to stop at a lay-by when travelling eastwards, as we were doing, involves turning across the path of oncoming traffic travelling westwards, something which requires more courage than many people possess.

Eventually emerging from this spectacular mess on to the shores of the Aegean, we left Thessaly behind and at what would have been sunset if there had been any sun, arrived at the little town of Litochoron, one of the setting-off places for Olympus which is situated in a plain at the foot of the eastern outriders of the mountain, a wasteland of sand, scrub and stone brought down from the mountain and until well into the 1920s a place infested with bandits, which slopes away gently to the shores of what is known as the Thermaic Gulf, at the head of which lies the city of Salonika.

Described by climbers who visited it in the early twenties as being a miserable village, Litochoron had suddenly found favour as a health resort, especially for those suffering from tuberculosis, and now it was a pleasant little place, if not one in which most people would want to linger very long, any more than they would want to stay in the Cheddar Gorge indefinitely, with about 6000 inhabitants, most of whom invaded the square each evening for the Greek equivalent of the *passeggiata* and also to witness the ceremonial hauling down of the national flag by soldiers of the Greek army, who have a ski school on the mountain. They were a friendly lot, the people of Litochoron, and we had a number of interesting conversations in the cafés with well-dressed gentlemen who had spent most of their lives in such far off places as Pittsburg, Darwin and West Hartlepool but had never climbed Mount Olympus or even thought of doing so.

Until a motor road was built up through the Mavrolongos valley, one of the principal ways into the heart of the massif, Litochoron was the place where pack animals and a guide were usually engaged by those intending to make the twelve-mile trek to the top of the mountain, which normally took two days. But now one could start from Prionia, where there was a restaurant, water, which was difficult to find higher up, and where the pack animals were now kept. It was possible, although a rather arduous exercise, to reach the top and come down again to Prionia in a single day; and after listening to an expert in the Greek Alpine Club office in Litochoron, who said that the black cloud that was currently blanketing the entire massif down to a height of around 6–7000 feet might well remain on it for a week or more, I decided to climb it the following morning.

We spent the night in Litochoron at the New Youth Hostel, Director Demetrios Irantos, whom we never saw, the whole place being run by what looked like a small boy, we ourselves being probably the most ancient youths who had ever stayed in it. Mr Irantos' brochure assured us that while we were on the premises we would enjoy 'the breezing of the Aegean Sea' and 'perfect neatness'. It was a friendly, if somewhat crowded place, filled when we arrived to claim the last two bunks with keen young British back-packers, nothing like the ones with earrings we had encountered on the quay at Bar and Igoumenitsa. These were all male and wore great boots and practical but inelegant clothes; hill walkers with a distinctly aggressive approach to their chosen pastime, and far into the night they droned on about how many hours or days it had taken them to do the Yorkshire North Moors walk or sections of the Pennine Way which apparently were now almost as crowded with walkers as a motorway with vehicles.

The only thing seriously wrong with Mr Irantos' Hostel was the shower compartment, which he had somehow succeeded in hewing out of the corner of what was already a ridiculously small room. It was so small that it was impossible to take a shower without the water actually playing on the live electric light which illuminated it and which, whether it was switched on or not, constituted such a hazard to life that some waggish guest had stuck a label on the door with the announcement 'Frying Tonight' printed on it.

Having set the alarm for five o'clock the following morning, which woke the other guests, I got up, looked out of several windows but could see nothing of Mount Olympus or anything else, even though the economically-minded municipality had switched off the street lamps which was a help rather than a hindrance. On my way back to bed I found a notice board to which Mr Irantos, or one of his aides, had pinned a short list of edicts and helpful suggestions, two of which I copied down, being unsure whether or not I might pass this way again. One read: 'At bed at 11 o'clock at night the outdoor is after this time closed. These are not about the people who have private room', which showed that even here, on the slopes of Mount Olympus, just as there was for the Gods on the summit, there was one law for the privileged and another for those who couldn't afford, or didn't want, a private room.

The other, a more kindly one, read: 'You can eat and wet clothes in the playground of the Youth hostel.' Funny? Well, I thought it was funny, but it made me wonder how good I would be at writing the same thing in Greek and pinning it on the notice board if I happened to be the warden of an English Youth Hostel catering for Greeks.

It was just as dark at six, by which time some of the conquerors of Olympus and the Pennine Way were beginning to complain about my alarm clock going off all the time, and so at seven I woke by natural means. Wanda had never slept at all since my first morning call, being a light sleeper.

At eight o'clock we arrived at Prionia, on the way having stopped in the bottom of the Mavrolongos Gorge, where it was almost as dark as night under the trees, to look at all that remained of the monastery of Ayios Dionisos. Built at the beginning of the 16th century, blown up by the Turks in 1828, rebuilt some twenty-five or thirty years later, it was finally destroyed in 1943 by the Germans, who might be pardoned for suspecting that such a remote building might be being used as a base for clandestine activities.

At Prionia, where there was nothing apart from the small eating place and the wooden building used to stable the mules, there were a number of vehicles, all of them with German registrations, most of them Volkswagen caravan conversions with their occupants asleep inside them. The weather was incredibly gloomy. Black cloud pressed down into the gorge so heavily that the weight of it could actually be felt, and I developed a violent headache. I left at eight-thirty, after a large breakfast, passing a beautiful waterfall which fell into a crystal clear pool, the last source, I had been told, before the summit, where I emptied my waterbottles of the tap water from the hostel and refilled them, then followed the red markings painted on the rocks, the going very steep now, through thick forest of pine and beech and other deciduous trees, some of them big specimens, rounding the heads of numerous side valleys.

At nine o'clock I crossed the dry bed of a torrent into which an enormous avalanche, which had stripped the mountainside clean of them in a swathe a hundred yards wide, had pitched what must have been thousands of tons of shattered tree trunks to form what before the forest guards had cut a way through it, using dynamite, was an impassable barrier. This was more or less the limit of deciduous trees, apart from a few scattered walnuts, and now the mist became even thicker than it had been.

It began to rain heavily. The atmosphere was incredibly humid. Having to choose between being soaked to the skin by rain or wearing a waterproof jacket and being soaked with perspiration, it was difficult to know what to do. I chose to be wet with rain. At nine-thirty I passed a sign which read 'Spilios Agapitos Hut – 1 Hour', and as it was officially 2½ hours from Prionia to the hut and I had only been climbing for an hour, I decided to go for a strictly private record attempt to reach the hut in 1¾ hours as there was nothing to see en route except the trunks of trees looming in the mist, and I was so wet that the sooner I got there the better. At quarter past ten, having passed through a belt of enormous conifers with trunks between four and five feet thick that must have been anything up to a thousand years old, I reached the hut, the Katafiyo Spilios Agapitos, the property of the Greek Alpine Club, at 6890 feet.

It had been a very stiff climb and the only other people I had seen were an expensively-dressed couple whom I would have identified as English except that they carried alpenstocks and answered my 'Good morning. Rotten weather!' with '*Guten tag. Ja, schrecklich wetter.*' The hut was filled to bursting point with something like sixty people, all either French or German. I was the only English person present. There was a huge fire, but it was difficult to get at (I would have liked to dry my wet shirt which I had changed for a dry one), being hemmed in by people sitting with their backs to it, reading old copies of the *Reader's Digest*. The noise and the heat were unbelievable. Presiding over this throng was the custodian and guide, Costas Zolotas, and his wife, who was cooking the midday meal, a good-looking, friendly couple. I drank a brandy and felt better. Whether all these people had already climbed the mountain, were about to climb it, or had no intention of climbing it, was not clear.

I left for the summit at 10.40. The fog was still thick. Sparrow-like birds flew about aimlessly, close to the ground, as if afraid of getting lost. The trees were thinning rapidly now and soon there were none at all. After about half an hour the track became very steep, making long zigzags up what was now bare mountainside, over screes. By now I was beginning to be very tired and I realized how silly I had been to establish my private record between Prionia and the hut. During this time I met three people, all on their way down, two of them a young Swiss man and his wife, both carrying neatly rolled umbrellas, with a very lively little girl of about eight dancing down ahead of them in the mist telling them to hurry up. It was now that I made a serious mistake. In order to cut out the interminable zigzagging I tried to climb the mountain vertically, and in doing so found myself slipping and stumbling and sometimes falling flat on my face on piles of loose scree brought down by people who had taken the same sort of short cut descending the mountain that I was trying to take while going up. What was worse, when I tried to find the main track again I was unable to do so and had to continue climbing on the loose stuff. I felt terrible. Every few hundred yards or so my legs gave way and I had to sit down with my heart pounding away, wondering if I was going to die, not caring much, shamed by the small birds that, completely unafraid, were energetically hopping about me, no doubt hoping that I represented some form of sustenance, or would jettison something edible. If I was going to die, presumably of heart failure, there were worse places to give up the ghost than on the upper slopes of Olympus at what must have been around 8500 feet.

At around 12.15, while taking one of these obligatory rests and wondering whether or not I was going to make it to the top, I was overtaken by a young German who looked almost as done-in as I felt, and whose only luggage was a plastic bag with a loaf of bread in it. As he had no water and I had no food, we decided to pool our resources and go to the summit together. It was really no place to be alone anyway, visibility being down to twenty yards. It turned out that he was a physicist at Göttingen University. The last graduate of Göttingen University I had met on a mountainside had been a professor of entomology with only one lung who was chasing butterflies, but that was a long time ago, in the Apennines in 1943. Climbing with a companion gave me fresh heart, and in a few minutes we reached the ridge, which the inadequate map kindly provided free by the Alpine Club of Litochoron showed to be the ridge leading to the foot of the Skala summit at 9400 feet. The ridge, over which a bitter wind was blowing, overhung a void full of what looked like dirty cotton wool in what was called the Louki Cirque.

In another quarter of an hour we reached the foot of the Skala summit, which was invisible in the clouds, and began to make what, in the circumstances, unroped, I considered to be an extremely hazardous traverse under the buttresses of the main arête. This was an enormous wedge-shaped monolith, now invisible, from which rose the three main peaks of Skala, Mytikas and Stefani. Hazardous because the whole of this east face of the mountain consisted of either loose slabs or crumbling limestone full of limestone chippings, now covered with a glaze of ice on which it was only too easy to slip and fall into the depths of the Louki Cirque. It seemed extraordinary that no warning of any kind was given to climbers, most of whom had no mountaineering experience and were not properly equipped, that they might have to traverse a thoroughly unstable, ice-covered rock face.

Now the red-painted rocks led upwards into a sort of couloir and at one o'clock we emerged on to the narrow summit of Mytikas, otherwise the Needle, the Pantheon of the Gods, the highest point of Olympus, from which to the east, from where we had come, it fell away into the Cirque, immediately below us, as did Skala and Stefani, the Throne of Zeus. And there we crouched with flurries of snow whirling about us in the screaming wind, unable even to see the Throne of Zeus or anything else, nibbling bread, sipping cold water and becoming colder every minute but reluctant to leave, having done better than Sultan Mehmed IV who is said to have made an unsuccessful attempt to climb it in 1669.

Squatting up there, enveloped in freezing cloud, with a Force 7 wind blowing, 9570 feet above the Aegean, it was a bit difficult to understand how Homer had been able to write, without having tried it out for himself (rather like a house agent who can write a convincing description of a house without actually seeing it) that 'never is it swept by the winds nor touched by snow; a purer air surrounds it, a white clarity envelops it and the Gods there taste of a happiness which lasts as long as their eternal lives'. But perhaps they were there still, the Gods, invisible to our profane gaze, rendered indifferent to bad weather by the *ichor* that flowed in their veins, the substitute for blood that rendered them imperishable and incorruptible, sitting there in their hierarchies, the twelve great gods – Zeus, Poseidon, Hephaestus, Hermes, Ares, Apollo, Hera, Athene, Artemis, Hestia, Aphrodite and Demeter; Helios, Selene, Leto, Dione, Dionysus, Themis and Eos, and their courtiers – the Horae, the Moirae (The Fates), Nemesis, the Graces, the Muses, Iris, Hebe and Ganymede. All of them presided over by Zeus, ruling with an iron hand concealed in a silken glove, robust, grave, in the fullness of maturity, bearded, with thick waving hair, dressed in a long mantle which left his chest and right arm free, on official occasions holding in his left hand a sceptre, in his right a thunderbolt, and with an eagle at his feet. Here they passed the long days in feasting and happy conversation, sitting at their golden tables drinking nectar from golden cups constantly topped up by Hebe and passed from hand to hand, being entertained by Apollo playing on his lyre, sung to by the Muses, eating the sweet-smelling ambrosia that if a mortal ate of it would make him, too, immortal, and that if it arrived too late would at least preserve his corpse from decay. Here they sat appreciatively inhaling the smell of burnt offerings that drifted up to them from the fires lit in their honour by mortal men and women in the other world thousands of feet below, at the day's end returning each one to the detached accommodation built for them by Hephaestus, the lame craftsman god, there to rest or, in the case of Zeus perhaps, and others so inclined, to perform what for him was one of his multitudinous acts of creation. How one envied them all.

'I suppose that you will write about meeting a funny little German physicist from Göttingen on top of Olympus when you get back to England,' the young man said, who had himself lived in Cambridge for a year, after we had taken ritual photographs of one another which when mine was developed looked as if it had been processed in mud.

'If I get off this mountain alive I will write that I met you and that without you I wouldn't be standing here,' I said, and I really meant it. And together we went down to make the traverse once more above the Louki Cirque to the Skala ridge, up which, unknown to me, Wanda was doggedly plodding to rescue me.

By 5.30 p.m. that evening we were back at Prionia drinking delicious hot sweet tea looking up the Mavrolongos Gorge towards the three summits which were now swimming in a cloudless sky, bathed in the golden light of the setting sun.

IV

TURKEY

A View of the Hellespont

In what was something between winter and very early spring we travelled in a taxi through eastern Thrace, where there was no sign of spring at all, and down to Cape Helles on the Gallipoli peninsula at the mouth of the Dardanelles. The vehicle was a black Bel-Air, still as immaculate as it must have been when it came off the production line around 1965. Seeing it for the first time as we emerged from our hotel in Istanbul was rather like encountering a living dinosaur, or a mammoth just emerged from a block of Siberian ice, and, in fact, it turned out to have been a mistake to have chartered such a museum piece and its driver.

At the lighthouse at Cape Helles the driver stopped, there being no more road, this being the extreme south-western point of Turkey-in-Europe with beyond it a free fall to the Aegean Sea, and began doing what he had done on every other occasion when we got out of his taxi: he produced a cloth and began removing the dust that started to settle on it each time we got going. In this case it was the thick red dust of the Gallipoli peninsula, dust that only now very old soldiers and sailors still remember from 1915.

As he performed this ritual he did what he always had done, sucked his teeth in a disapproving, audible way, at the same time giving us reproachful looks, as if to imply that we were responsible for the countryside, in this case the peninsula, being in such a state, and therefore for the state of his taxi which, in a sense, I suppose we were, being the only two of the three of us who actually wanted to visit Gallipoli, the Dardanelles and the Troad (the part of north-west Asia Minor surrounding the city of Troy), which was why we had hired him in the first place.

He was an Armenian and gloomy. I had always had a soft spot for Armenians, a race who have spent more time being massacred than any other people in the Mediterranean regions in the last eighty years or so, more than 600,000 in 1915–16 alone. At first we tried to cheer him up by telling him that things might have been worse. For instance it might have been raining, in which case his taxi inside and out would have been covered in mud, not just half an inch or so of dust that would come off with the flick or two of the wrist, but it was no good. So we let him be gloomy. We weren't feeling all that cheerful ourselves. Battlefields, especially comparatively modern ones, such as the one we were on, are hardly ever jolly.

In 1915 the Allies, in order to create a diversion and break the deadlock on the western front, mounted an expedition against the Turks, who had joined the Germans the previous October, hoping that an eastern campaign would turn the German flank. It was an original concept but doomed to failure by half-heartedness and inadequate planning, and opened badly when, on 18 March, the Turks inflicted what proved to be a decisive defeat on the combined Allied fleets, which were attempting to force the Dardanelles, sinking three battleships, admittedly not very modern ones, seriously damaging three others and killing 700 men with the loss of only 40 of their own side, an action which the Allies broke off and never resumed, having failed to clear the minefields. The High Command therefore decided to force the Straits by landing on the Gallipoli peninsula. British, Australian, New Zealand and French divisions were landed in April and August but the casualties were appalling and the expedition was abandoned at the end of the year.

We walked uphill from the lighthouse to the Cape Helles Memorial, a tall obelisk nearly one hundred feet high. Beyond it the peninsula stretched away, also uphill, in the general direction of Constantinople, as it still then was (it only became Istanbul in 1930), the ultimate goal of all those men whose names are recorded on its walls, and of so many others, none of whom ever reached it, through stony fields, dry-looking country without a perennial stream of even the smallest description running through it, with olive groves, scrub oaks, little groups of cypresses and mulberry trees, with the fruit already ripening, providing what in summer would be the only shade.

The great majority of the men whose names are recorded on the Memorial, and those who are buried in the six Cape Helles cemeteries and the majority of the French who are buried or otherwise remembered in their cemetery above Morto Bay, died in attempts to take Krithia village on the forward slopes of Achi Baba, a big, bare 700-foot-high top above the Narrows which the Allies believed to be one of the key points of the peninsula. There are 20,763 names carved on the walls of the Helles Memorial, 14,617 more on the four other memorials, at Chunuk Bair, Hill 60, Lone Pine and Twelve Tree Copse, none of whom have known graves; and in addition, there are the names of 9503 men who are buried in one or other of the thirty-one Commonwealth cemeteries close to the beaches of Anzac and Suvla Bay and on the wild and lonely hills. Of the 34,000 British and Commonwealth dead, 27,000 were buried in unidentified graves.

Of the 9000 French and colonial dead, 6000 were either never identified or never found. The Turks who died (more than 60,000 and something less than 90,000) are commemorated by the enormous monument above the entrance to the Straits on the site of the ancient city of Elaeus. There are no Turkish cemeteries. The Turks did not bury their dead or record their names, so in a sense they are all unknown soldiers.

Of the 489,000 Allied troops engaged, 252,000 became casualties; of the approximately 500,000 Turks, 251,309 were casualties.

Reading these seemingly endless columns of names on the Allied Memorials, so neatly inscribed on panel after panel, I had the feeling that I had first experienced long ago as a cadet in the Chapel of the Royal Military College at Sandhurst on Sunday morning church parades in another war, when bored by those militant devotions, I had read off the names of the Officer Cadets, inscribed on the Carrara marble columns, who had died in that First World War – that I was working my way down a column of entries in a set of enormous ledgers dealing exclusively with death, ledgers in which there were no credit entries, only debits.

Immediately to the left of the lighthouse were the ruins of a coastal battery in which a pair of guns installed here by German technicians before the First World War to command the western approaches to the Dardanelles had been thrown down from their mountings. And beyond and below this battery there was a small bay, about the size of a Cornish cove, with a gently sloping amphitheatre of ground ascending from a crescent-shaped beach to a village of white-washed houses with a minaret rising above it.

At the far end of this beach there was a white castle on a height above it, Sedd-el-Bahr, the Barrier of the Sea, from which the village with the minaret took its name. The beach was V Beach and just above it there was a grove of wild olive trees and Judas trees, already in flower in this hollow, which also sheltered spring roses and santolina bushes from the cruel northern winds, as it did a British war cemetery in which lie buried what remained of 696 men who tried to take this little beach and died in the face of concentrated Turkish machine-gun fire in April 1915, in what was one of the most spectacular massacres of the Gallipoli campaign.

Out beyond all this were the Dardanelles, dark blue and flecked with white, brilliant in the late afternoon sunshine, with a big Soviet tanker punching up into the western entrance against a Force 7 north-easter, probably on its way to Constanta or Batum.

On such a day, with such a wind from the north-east increasing the pressure on the surface of the Aegean, and with the winter snows melting in the 900,000-square-mile basin of the Black Sea, the west-going stream would be pouring out through the Dardanelles at about three knots, perhaps more up at the Narrows, twelve miles inside them.

While this was happening on the surface, anything up to fifty fathoms below the heavier, saltier waters of the Aegean would be flowing eastwards through it into the Sea of Marmara and up the Bosphorus into the Black Sea, maintaining its salinity in spite of the enormous amount of fresh water that flows into it from the rivers of central Europe, Russia and Asia Minor. With a strong south-westerly wind the process is reversed. With a wind just sufficiently strong to check the surface outflow without actually reversing it, the current comes to a standstill.

Some 4000 yards away across the mouth of the Straits to the south from Sedd-el-Bahr, there was another castle, Kum Kale, the Sand Castle. Both castles were built by the Grand Vizir Muhammad Kiuprili in about 1659, a man 'whose integrity and strength of character', in the words of C. A. Fyffe, a distinguished nineteenth-century historian, 'did much to counteract the pernicious influence of degenerate sultans and to prop up for a season the declining empire'.

Kum Kale stands on a low promontory where Homer's River Scamander, otherwise the Menderes, enters the Hellespont, having wound its way down into it from its source on the slopes of Mount Ida and through the Plain of Troy. This river is not to be confused with another Menderes, the Büyuk, Great Menderes, the ancient Maeander, from which derives the term 'meander', which enters the Aegean south of Izmir by way of a plain in which stand the ruins of ancient Miletus.

The Plain and its Hellespontine and Aegean shores are a depository of the fabulous dead of the ancient world. In this part of the world, where the relics of antiquity protrude above the surface of the earth at innumerable points but not always in very recognizable form, nothing is very certain. Near where we were standing on Cape Helles, trying to handle a map that was behaving like an out-of-control spinnaker, there was supposed to be a tumulus containing the remains of Protesilaus, the first man of Agamemnon's army to set foot on the soil of Asia and the first Greek casualty of the Trojan War. Both the Admiralty *Mediterranean Pilot* and Murray's *Guide to Constantinople and the Troad*, admittedly published a long time ago (the *Mediterranean Pilot*, the more modern of the two, after the First World War), said it was there but we were not able to find it. Perhaps it was at Elaeus, the now vanished city which stood on the heights above Morto Bay, beyond Sedd-el-Bahr.

It was on this tomb of Protesilaus that Alexander the Great offered a sacrifice to the Gods before setting off to Asia in 334 BC in the hope that they might favour his expedition and allow him to lead it to a triumphant conclusion. As an additional insurance against possible disaster he erected there a temple to Zeus, in his guise as the Lord of Happy Landings, to Heracles and to Athena, who besides being the virgin goddess of wisdom and practical skills was also an authority on prudent warfare. Then, as if all this was not enough, having embarked on the waters of the Hellespont, in mid-stream he sacrificed a bull to Poseidon, and poured a libation of wine into the water from a golden cup in order to propitiate the Nereids, the daughter of Nereus, whose wife's name was Doris.

Out of sight from where we stood, high above the Aegean shore between Kum Kale and the ancient promontory of Sigeum, now Cape Yenisehir, which is the north-easternmost point of Asia Minor, are the mounds believed to cover the ashes of Achilles and his friend Patroclus. Achilles, one of the foremost of the Greeks at the Siege of Troy, had taken to his tent and skulked there while Patroclus, borrowing his armour, led the Myrmidons into battle. Patroclus was killed by Hector, son of King Priam of Troy, and Achilles swore to avenge his death. It was the loss of his devoted companion that brought him back into the battle, during which he killed Hector and dragged his body round Patroclus' tomb for twelve consecutive days. Achilles in his turn was then killed by another of Priam's sons, Paris, with an arrow which penetrated his only weak spot – the Achilles tendon.

The mound of Achilles is riddled with the burrowings of innumerable archaeologists and other inquisitive persons; that of Patroclus, the smaller of the two earthworks, is in better shape in spite of having been used as the foundation for a Turkish gun emplacement in the First World War. In fact it may not be the tomb of Patroclus at all. It could be the tomb of Antilochus, the great runner who brought to Achilles the news of the death of Patroclus. If this is so then the ashes of Achilles and Patroclus are, as Homer said they were, in the same tomb.

The mound containing the tomb of Ajax, the gigantic, rather slow-witted leader of the Salamis contingent, who recovered Achilles' dead body, then killed himself in a fit of pique when Achilles' armour, retrieved from the Trojans after Patroclus' death, was given to Odysseus and not to him, is conspicuous on the high, bare ground overlooking the Hellespont east of the mouth of the Scamander and between it and the more than ruined city of Rhoetum: more than ruined because the only evidence of its existence, like so many other cities in this part of the world, are some fragments of pottery, some bricks and some splinters of sculptured white marble and the like.

Unfortunately, savants have now proved, beyond reasonable doubt, that the present tumulus, which has a broken vault within it, dates from the first century AD, and was therefore constructed about 1300 years after Ajax's death. What a bore they are, taking away all the pleasures of the imagination, which is almost invariably better than the reality. It was here, too, off Elaeus, in AD 323, that the fleet of Constantine the Great, Emperor of the West, engaged with the fleet of Licinus, Emperor of the East, which had been anchored off the Tomb of Ajax, defeating it and leaving Constantine master of the world.

And there were innumerable others, illustrious and not so illustrious, who died in the great naval actions of the Hellespont, whose remains are either between thirty and fifty fathoms deep down on the bottom of the Straits, or out in the Aegean, or else, more likely, carried away eastwards by the submarine current, either into the Sea of Marmara, or, even further still, through the Bosphorus into the Black Sea.

Inside the 4000-yard western entrance, the Straits begin to widen out until, five miles inside, between Erenkeui Bay, which lies below the beautiful wooded hills on the Asian side, and the much more barren, steep-sided, scrub-covered hills on the Gallipoli peninsula, four and a half miles of water separates the two. Then they begin to contract again until at the Narrows, thirteen miles inside, only 1600 yards separate Europe from Asia. It was here that the Greeks under Alcibiades defeated the Spartans off Cynossema on the European side, the place where Hecuba, wife of King Priam, is buried. She was turned into a dog for blinding the murderer of her son, Polydorus, and also for killing his three sons. She was also the mother of Hector and eighteen other of Priam's sons, including Paris.

Here at the Narrows, in 1452, the year before he took Constantinople, Mehmed II, the Conqueror, built the two castles of the Dardanelles, the Boghaz-hisarlari, on the European side close to Hecuba's tomb, and on the Asian side the Chanak-kilesi, which took its name from Chanak, now Cannakale, a town a little upstream which was originally founded by the Genoese and where, until comparatively recently, a very attractive rough sort of pottery was made.

It was these two inner forts, with heavy German guns mounted in them, that on 18 March 1915, in spite of being continuously shelled by battleships of the British and French fleets with shells of up to 15-inch calibre, were, although severely damaged, never put completely out of action.

Further up the Hellespont from Cannakale, in May 480 BC, Xerxes, the Persian, looked down from the heights above the Narrows at Abydos on the Asian side on his army crossing over to the European shore between Sestos and Madyos by a bridge of boats, reflecting gloomily as they did so on the transience of human life.

Here, too, a century and a half later, in 334 BC, while Alexander was offering sacrifices and libations at the mouth of the Hellespont, his army under Parmenio crossed it into Asia from Sestos to Abydos, using merchant ships and 160 triremes. What a sight these two crossings of the Straits must have been. Here, too, at some unknown date, Leander drowned while swimming to a rendezvous with his lover, Hero, whose temple of Aphrodite of which she was the high priestess was in the wooded groves above Sestos, woods that are there still; a difficult feat which Byron, on his way to Constantinople and wind-bound at the Narrows in a frigate, performed without coming to grief. He crossed in the opposite direction, from Europe to Asia, as did a number of officers of the Royal Navy and a Jewish gentleman.

Further in still, at the mouth of the Aegospotamos, a now unimportant rivulet on the European shore, Lysander and the Spartans destroyed the Athenian fleet of Conon and Pericles, after which Athens capitulated, thus ending, in 405 BC, the Peloponnesian War which lasted twenty-seven years, the one which Thucydides, its historian, described as 'a disturbance'.

And all along the wooded Asian shore of the Straits, between its mouth and the Narrows, there are yet more of the ancient dead, soldiers and sailors less well known than Achilles or Patroclus, as well as the more peaceable inhabitants of cities of which the largest visible remains are often those fragments of marble and pot sherds lying in a field, long-lost cities of the ancient plain, Rhoetum, Ophrynium, on the brow of a hill, where a grove to Hector once stood, Dardanos on the heights near Point Kepez where the Narrows begin, and where, in the 1870s, the Turks, a people who make things last, mounted a forty-ton Krupp gun to replace the muzzle loaders, cast in brass and bronze and firing stone projectiles, that had defended the Straits since the fifteenth century.

And beyond this Asian shore of the Hellespont, now at this hour of the afternoon with a dusty, golden haze hanging over it, was the Plain itself in which from 1871 to 1873 Heinrich Schliemann, together with his young Greek wife, Sofia Engastromanos, whom he had married for her supposed resemblance to Helen of Troy – she was certainly strikingly beautiful – laboured in often atrocious conditions on the mound of Hisarlik with their work force in search of Homer's Troy, and where together they discovered in astonishing if not downright mysterious circumstances the wonderful gold hoard of the third millennium, deep down in what he thought was the city of King Priam.

The sun was setting now beyond Imbros, bathing the Cape and the peninsula in a brilliant light, accentuating the redness of the earth from which the spring rains of 1916 had washed away the last traces of the blood which for eight and a half months it had soaked up like some gigantic sponge.

In the whole of this extensive landscape the only living things besides ourselves, some seabirds hanging on the wind and the driver, who had long since finished polishing his taxi and had fallen asleep inside it, exasperated by these foreigners who stood for hours studying books and maps, some of which blew away, sending them chasing after them through the fields, was a large, unmartial-looking Turk swathed in what appeared to be a number of kilim rugs and mounted on a small donkey which he was urging from west to east across the tip of the peninsula over what had been a battlefield.

He was so large and the donkey was so small that beneath him and his kilims the donkey's body was completely invisible and one was left with the impression of a Turk with four legs trotting across country from the Aegean Sea to the Dardanelles and urging himself onwards by beating himself with a stick.

We woke the driver and without a word he drove us away towards Istanbul through the sheltered lanes of what had been the village of Krithia, which was now called Alcitepe, where in the gloaming children played happily together outside the whitewashed houses in the dust: leaving the young men of 1915–16 to be remembered by memorials or else in their noble, lovingly-tended cemeteries under the friendly trees, in which the sighing of the wind, apart from the sea murmuring upon the beaches, is often the only sound to be heard on this now otherwise almost forgotten peninsula; leaving them among the wild anemones, the carpets of pale pink cistus, the rosemary, the pink oleanders, the yellow flowering santolina, the irises and the purple heather. Soon it was quite dark.

Baths and Bazaars

What would they have found, the young men of 1915 who wrote 'To Constantinople and the Harems' and 'Turkish Delight' on the sides of the troop ships in Mudros Bay on Lemnos before sailing for Gallipoli, if by good fortune Colonel Mustafa Kemal and his Nineteenth Division had failed to hold the heights at Chunuk Bair on that April Sunday morning, and they had actually entered the city?

They would have found themselves in the capital of a decrepit, dying empire, still, perhaps, apart from Peking, the most interesting and mysterious of the great cities of the world and one from which, although still incomparable as a distant prospect, as it is to this day, much of the beauty had already long since melted away.

What they would have wanted to see and do, the young men of 1915, was what every visitor wanted to see and do, not only soldiers and sailors (and some did get there when Turkey capitulated and the Allied fleet anchored in the Bosphorus in the autumn of 1918): to see a harem on a grand scale and the bazaars, and to have a Turkish bath.

A Turkish bath is something that is becoming increasingly difficult to find in Britain, most of them having been knocked down and replaced by the sauna, which is about as much fun as being buried alive in a red-hot cigar box. In London you can still have a Turkish bath if you are a member of the Royal Automobile Club in Pall Mall, which is not the same thing as being a motorist member of the RAC. If you are a woman, or look sufficiently like one, you can use the sumptuous ladies' bath at the Dorchester.

No one, not even the proprietors, who presumably have some kind of trade association, seem quite sure how many *hamams* there are in Istanbul, but according to the proprietor of the beautiful Çinili Hamami, the Tiled Bath near the Aqueduct of Valens, there are more than a hundred old Ottoman baths, of which something like eighty are in use. Only the wealthiest ever had their own *hamams*. Often they were and still are adjacent to mosques, and because the great majority of the inhabitants are without showers in their houses, dislike bathing in standing water and are a cleanly people, the *hamam* is an institution that is unlikely to die out. As the Reverend Robert Walsh, Chaplain to the British Embassy at the Sublime Porte, the slightly risqué Irish author of *Constantinople and the Seven Churches of Asia*, wrote of the Turks in the 1930s, quoting an unnamed authority, 'they hold impurity of the body in greater detestation than impurity of the mind, ablution being so essential that without it prayer will be of no value in the eyes of God'. 'The Law enumerates *eleven occurrences*', he went on, failing to enumerate them, 'after which a person must wash, some of which are exceedingly curious but not fit for the public eye'. At the time when he was writing, and long after it, marriage contracts included a provision that the husband had to give his wife bath-money. If he failed to do so, all she had to do was to go before a *cadi*, a Muslim judge, and turn her slipper upside down. If the husband still failed to produce the necessary admittance money, it was a ground for divorce.

Let us enter a *hamam*. In this case the Çinili Hamami, built for the famous Turkish corsair Barbarossa Hayrettin Paşa by the great mosque architect Sinan around 1545. It stands in a street high above Atatürk Bulvari, a sort of super highway that cuts through the old city from the Atatürk Bridge over the Golden Horn, goes under the Aqueduct of Valens and, if you continue along it until it becomes Mustafa Kemal Caddesi, and you don't put your brakes on, deposits you in the Sea of Marmara.

The form of Çinili Hamami and most other *hamams* is based on that of a Roman bath, but as comparatively few readers have probably ever had a Roman bath it may perhaps be permitted to describe it. Going in through the swing doors one finds oneself in the *camekân*, a large, square, very lofty, domed, rather dim reception room, partly surrounded by a raised platform on which bathers leave their clothes and rest after the bath and with galleries with private rest rooms leading off them. In the middle of the room there is a beautiful marble fountain with, when I was there, goldfish swimming around it. Here, too, are piles of towels (the consumption of towels is prodigious), the reception desk where you deposit your valuables with the custodian, the tariff displayed over it, apparatus for tea-making, soft drinks and a band of attendants, *tellahs*, none of whom speak a word of English, all of whom are hoping that you are going to have something which most Turks don't have because of the cost, a nice expensive *masaj* at about 300 Turkish lira which is really a gift to foreigners with the pound sterling ($1.40) at around this figure. The prices are more or less the same in the majority of *hamams* off the tourist route, such as this one. The bath (the *banyo*), costs 175 TL, soap is sometimes an extra, some people bring their own. What is called *kese*, a rub down with a rough mitten which peels off layers of old skin which looks like grey dough, costs 40 TL, is well worth having and follows the *masaj* if you have it. If you have the lot you would be expected to give a collective tip amounting to about 200 TL.

Now the *tellah*, when he judges you to be in a dangerously near state of complete undress, hands you two thin, striped towels called *pestemal*, in one of which you gird your loins. The trick is to do this without exposing yourself. You are not in the bath house of a rugger club on a Saturday afternoon, and Turkish gentlemen are not only not interested in what you have brought from the West, they are actively interested in not seeing it.

You are then given a pair of *nalin*, wooden pattens on which it is very easy to skid, and propelled through a door into what is called the *soğukluk*, which is little more than a corridor with a little dome at either end, the equivalent of a Roman *tepidarium*, the purpose of which is to keep out the cold air in the *camekân* and keep the hot air in the steam room which leads off it. In most *hamams*, the lavatories lead off the *soğukluk* and as most of them were installed back in the sixteenth century this is no place to linger. In the worst sort of *hamam* their presence can make itself known throughout the entire edifice.

The next and final door leads into the *hararat*, the steam room, vast and cruciform, lined with pale grey marble in this case decorated with panels of tiles, with a central dome supported by columns and other smaller domes in the side chambers and niches in the walls, each of which is furnished with a beautiful marble basin filled with elegant brass hot and cold water taps. The domes have perforations in them filled with inverted hemispheres of glass to admit the light, and when the sun is overhead this steam-filled chamber is illuminated by long parallel shafts of light which reach down into it and produce an unearthly and pleasing radiance.

In the middle of it is the *göbek taşi*, the navel or belly stone, the hottest part, a raised marble slab with the furnace beneath it. On it, according to the time of day – business is brisk in the evenings and on holidays – ten to a dozen Turkish gentlemen may be lying, one or two of whom may speak some German, some of whom may be discussing *futbol* with as much animation as anyone can muster in an atmosphere with the consistency of hot porridge. Others will be reclining, semi-comatose. Those covered with a curious mixture intended to remove superfluous hair should be given a wide berth. Singing is forbidden.

After half an hour you will begin to sweat prodigiously. After an hour you will probably have had enough and if you have contracted for a *masaj* will be approached by an attendant who will seize you, pin you to the ground and begin to knead you and twist your limbs with a variety of excruciating and crafty locks. This is followed by the *kese* and by soaping and washing, the attendant using a bowl called a *hamam taşi* to scoop the water out of the basins. All the time the bather is covered, but if he is washing himself and wants to reach the parts the attendant doesn't want to, he hangs the other towel with which he was provided over the entrance to the sluicing place as a sign that he is engaged in attending to himself. The ceremony is over. Swathed in fluffy towels from Bursa in places of the better sort, the bather is led away to recover in the *camekân*, either on the public benches or else in one of the *cabinets privés*.

The entrance to the ladies' bath, if there is one, is always separate, usually round the corner. In the Çinili Hamami the facilities are identical. In some *hamams* they are smaller. In others ladies have access to the gentlemen's baths at certain hours. Some have no facilities for ladies at all. The penalty for a man straying, even by mistake, into a ladies' bath used to be death.

According to her, the ladies' baths visited by Wanda, an indefatigable investigator (four baths in three days and a rigorous inspection of the rest), were much more jolly than the gentlemen's, a female version of White's Club without the booze, as opposed to the ones I bathed in, which were more like the Athenaeum without the bishops. Everyone was kind to her, both attendants and bathing ladies being fascinated by her pallor, taking her for a Circassian slave escaped from a harem. There was a lot of singing and laughter and scurrilous gossip in the women's baths and in all of them small children raced around naked like miniature streakers. Everyone else wore briefs – ladies should take a pair with them – but there seemed to be far less *pudeur* than in the men's department; and in one bath she was massaged by a lady with wildly swinging bosoms, but much less violently than I was by her male counterparts. She gave her masseuse 700 TL for the whole treatment which included the tip, and as the masseuse constituted the entire staff she was delighted.

Outside the snow that had been falling turned to rain, cold, hard winter rain, streaming down over the city from the direction of the Black Sea, and what had been snow turned into a hideous slush underfoot. The proprietors of the stalls in the Sahaflar Çarşisi, the Market of the Second-hand Booksellers, hastily covered their stocks of germ-laden paperbacks and the more sumptuous books of Islamic devotion with plastic sheets and took themselves off through the Gate of the Spoon-makers to the nearest tea house, which until quite recently sheltered under an enormous plane tree, known as the Tree of Idleness, close to the Beyazit Mosque.

This market occupies a very attractive courtyard full of vines and trees, nicer still in summer, and it is one of the oldest markets in the city. It stands on the site of the Chartoprateia, the Book and Paper Market, which flourished when the city was Byzantium.

One of the best places to be in Istanbul in winter when it rains, apart from being in a Turkish bath, is inside the Kapali Çarşisi, the Great Covered Bazaar. The easiest way to get to it from the Book and Paper Market is to leave it by the Hakkakalar Kapisi, the Gate of the Engravers, and cross Cadirçilar Caddesi, the Street of the Tent-makers, which is lined with booths occupied by tin- and copper-smiths and is perpetually blocked by people and vehicles loading and unloading. This is a very interesting street. No one makes tents there any more but any one of the owners of the booths in it will sell you old brass and iron objects, or make you a fine tin stove or an oven for your house, or run you up a copper finial for a minaret in rather less time than it takes to get a plumber to call back home. You cross this street and go through the Gate of the Fez-makers, Fesçilar Kapisi, into the shallow, uphill end of the Kapali Çarşisi.

The difficulty that most travellers experience when visiting the bazaar is the absence of a plan of it which gives any idea of its layout or the orientation of its streets, except an excellent guide book, *Strolling Through Istanbul*, by Hilary Sumner-Boyd and John Freely; but, unfortunately, this doesn't give the names of the streets in Turkish and their English equivalents, which would be a god-send. There *is* the Bazaar Committee's own plan, *Der Amtlicher Plan Des Grossen Basars in Istanbul*, but this is in German. It is also a security document and unless you have special permission to study it, you might well find yourself with half a dozen of the bazaar police dogs at your throat. Even Karl Baedeker, King of Plan-Providers, failed his readers when it came to the Covered Bazaar. Having funked this vital task, he gave them some pretty feeble advice in what was to be the first and last edition of his *Konstantinopel und das Westliche Kleinasien*, published in 1914, which was either to hire themselves a dragoman or else to furnish themselves with magnetic compasses for use in the maze of lanes, 'das Gewirr von Gassen'.

The whole Covered Bazaar is contained in a rectangle measuring 1280 feet from north to south and 1760 feet from east to west, an area of 51.7 acres. However, this area includes a number of *hans*, caravanserais for the reception of caravans, their goods and animals, some of which have doors opening into the Bazaar, some of them extremely picturesque although in an extremity of decay. If these parts are deducted, there can be no precise figure, the total area reduces itself to about 48 acres, with which Hachette's agreeably austere *Guide Bleu Turquie* concurs.

Today the number of shops is around 2875 and they employ some 30,000 people, 4000 shops if those in the surrounding *hans*, which no longer serve as *hans*, are included. Altogether there are sixty-six named streets and lesser ways (*sokaks*) in the Bazaar, although I myself have not been able to identify more than forty-seven. Their total length amounts to about 5 miles. All this information is kindly furnished by the Çarşi Esnaf Dernegi, the Bazaar Management Committee, with whom anyone is welcome to argue if they feel so inclined. This was back in 1975, when I began carrying out these investigations.

With the exception of a few narrow streets at the western end of the Bazaar, which run from north-west to south-east downhill from Yorgançilar Caddesi, the Street of the Quilt-makers, and the Street of the Fez-makers, Fesçilar Caddesi, which runs north-east/south-west, the remainder are aligned almost at right angles to one another on a simple north/south east/west grid. The main street is the Kalpakçilar Caddesi, the Street of the Calpac-makers (a *calpac* being a sort of felt or fur cap), which runs downhill the length of the south side of the Bazaar from the Beyazit Mosque to the Nuruosmaniye Mosque. Taking this street as a base line, everything in the Bazaar, with the exception of the Furrier's Bazaar in the south-east corner, the principal street of which is Kurkçuler çarşisi, where the best sheepskins and furs are to be found, lies to the north of it.

The Gate of the Fez-makers, the Fesçilar Kapisi, is at the south-west, top corner of the Bazaar, next to the western portal, the Kalpakçilar Kapisi, near the Beyazit Mosque. From it and several adjacent gates — altogether there are eighteen iron doors to the Bazaar, all of them closed at night — its streets and alleys cascade away in the direction of the Golden Horn, like tributaries on a vast map of some continental river system.

I set off, travelling north-eastwards down the Street of the Fez-makers. Apertures in the high, vaulted roof, which are covered with iron bars, admitted a subdued light, 'much in favour of the sellers of soiled or inferior goods', as Murray's *Handbook for Travellers in Constantinople*, 1908, puts it.

It so happens that this part of the Bazaar, especially around Puskülcüler Sokak, the now tassel-less Alley of the Tassel-makers, is one in which more inferior and second-hand garments are sold than any other and now they are seen to even less advantage with the aid of the new-fangled electric light. This is probably one of the reasons why a lot of this gear is hove aloft on halliards, high up under the roof and out of sight.

Nevertheless, however discussable the quality of the merchandise, the Great Bazaar provides a splendidly oriental setting for it (although the Spice Bazaar down by the Yeni Mosque at the Galata Bridge is architecturally far more distinguished), whether it is an Afghan-type sheepskin jacket which has fallen off its halliard several times and been trampled underfoot; an artificial silk prayer carpet made in Belgium, which will always remain as worthless as the day it was bought; a set of plated toothpicks imported from Solingen or a trove of old coins still warm from some local mint.

In such a setting, however, what is good is irresistible, such as the embroidered silk harem clothes which an elderly Greek used to sell in a tiny booth on the periphery of the Bazaar, for between £10 and £50 ($14–70), many of them made in the eighteenth century. 'Used to sell' because his booth is now, alas, no more and neither, I suspect, is he. But there are still multi-coloured gloves from Erzurum, socks knitted by nomads that one day soon will be museum pieces, long-haired Angora goat-hair rugs, exotic velvets from Bursa and the tough materials worn by shepherds in Anatolia, as well as carpets and kilim rugs, to name a few of the articles that are worthwhile acquiring, that is if anything is worth burdening oneself with while travelling.

I grew fond of the Bazaar during the week I spent in it. In spite of the sometimes really appalling noise it is highly organized, the confusion only in the eye of the superficial observer. Above all it is, undoubtedly, mysterious.

'I have lived eighty years in Istanbul and I do not know the city,' one venerable carpet-seller in Sahaflar Caddesi, the Street of the Booksellers in the middle of the Bazaar, not to be confused with the Book Market outside, told me. 'I have spent seventy-three of them in the Bazaar and I do not know it either.'

I like the merchants, living in a perpetual gloaming and thinking about nothing else but money, in spite of their gad-fly characteristics, with their perennial optimism and simple view of the world – that all will be well with it if only the rest of us continue to buy things we didn't know we needed.

Then and there, in the Street of the Fez-makers, all fifty-two of the shop-owners gave me a great welcome, although it was now noon and those who were Muslims should have been at prayer, either on the floors of their shops or in one of the little oratories in which the Bazaar abounds. They emerged from their shops, most of which are about the size of a normal wardrobe, to draw my attention to the merits of their radios, shiny black leather jackets of the sort worn by Balkan assassins working outside the Balkans, suedes and sheepskins and plastic shoes. There was not a Fez-maker in sight.

'Sir, Sir! How are you? Are you well?'

This is one of the things I like about the Bazaar. No tradesman on Oxford Street or Broadway would ever ask me such a question, even if I'd just had a leg off. In 1908, according to Murray's guide, the merchants used to address all male visitors, irrespective of nationality, as 'Captain'.

'I'm hungry.'

'Sir, you want leather?'

'No, I want kebabs.'

'Sir, for you we have leather kebabs.'

And he handed me an over-size visiting card on which was printed 'Leather and Sued germente for Ladies and Gentlemen', having first inscribed a cross on the back of it with his ballpoint pen.

'Why do you make a cross on the back of the card?' I asked him. 'Everyone in the Bazaar does it.'

'Sir, you know some hippie guys before we gave some cards like that. They went to their country and at border write something on wrong price. We do it for you. Now nobody can try anything.'

The dreaded Alley of the Tassel-makers is as full of fur as a surrealist tea-cup; but mercifully it is only about fifty yards long and it leads into Keseçilar Caddesi, the now sheathless Street of the Sheath-makers, which is full of settees upholstered in liverish-looking velvet and sideboards that look as if they have been sprayed with chocolate mousse. Not even the most optimistic merchant offered me one of those; but one of them tried to interest me in a bearskin from the earthquake-ridden Palandoken Mountains in the John Buchan-Greenmantle country above Erzurum, starting to bargain at around 30,000 TL.

I cantered on down the Street of the Sheath-makers, past a beautiful marble fountain with a crescent on top of it. It stands at the junction with Takkeçilar Caddesi, the Street of the Prayer Cap (or Linen Cap)-makers, which is solid with carpet-sellers, and as I flashed past one of them shouted 'You want flying carpet?'

An American store buyer was having a working lunch with her agent at a table outside one of the three best eating places in the Bazaar, since closed. I knew he was an agent just as I knew she was a store buyer because she had a gold-plated Cross pencil, a diary from Hermès and a sort of mini-Gladstone bag from Louis Vuitton, and because I have been a store buyer myself; but this is the first time I have ever seen a big store buyer eating *paça*, sheep's feet soup, which is delicious, while manipulating a Hewlett Packard calculator with the other hand.

The history of the Covered Bazaar has been one of almost unparalleled disaster. Together with the rest of the city, it has been burned down innumerable times, besides being shattered by an earthquake in 1894. In the sixty-eight years between 1633 and 1701 there were twenty-two major conflagrations. These were largely due to the Turkish habit of smoking in bed, neglecting to snuff candles, carrying hot coals with pincers from one room to another in their wooden houses, scattering them all over the place, drying their washing over the flames on wooden frames, engaging in huge fry-ups with oil during what is known as the Egg-Plant Summer (the equivalent of our Indian Summer) and engaging in plain, simple arson.

At least three of these major outbreaks destroyed large parts of the Eski Bedesten and the Sandal Bedesten, the latter, until the middle of the last century when European competition wiped it out, being the centre of the trade in rare silks which was conducted there by the Armenians. Like its namesake, the Eski Bedesten, it was originally built of wood in the reign of Mehmed II, the Conqueror, not long after he took the city in 1453. Rebuilt in stone, as was the Eski Bedesten after 1701, it is a huge vaulted building of almost Piranesian grandeur used for auctions of carpets and other valuables at 1.00 p.m. on Mondays and Thursdays. Here, sitting on one of the curved wooden benches, you can pit yourself against Turkish and Armenian dealers, starting to buy carpets from around £100 ($140) a throw. The last great fire, which destroyed practically the whole Bazaar, except the two Bedestens, was in 1954. It raged for nearly three days.

Gloria Falkenheim left. She had a label on her bag giving her name and address way out in the far west and her zip code – this is not her real name, as she might not want other buyers to know she was there, but it is very similar. All through lunch men had been passing bent double under the appalling weight of dozens of carpets, huge wooden chests that look as if they might contain Volkswagens, newly painted sofas, things like that.

These men are the *hamals*, porters, by origin most of them shepherds from the wilds of Anatolia. There are about two hundred of them. With the aid of a *semer*, a sort of back pad, they can carry up to 220 lbs. They live long, men of eighty being seen carrying weights between 130 and 150 lbs, and they are paid very well by Turkish standards, whether they are carrying anything or not. When it snows they wrap rags around their shoes to avoid slipping on the steep cobbled streets of the city.

On the way to the Eski Bedesten I visited the police station. According to one of the officers there, and what he says is corroborated by the merchants, there is very little crime in the Bazaar. At the most two or three cases of pocket picking a year. Here, in the

Bazaar, the merchants are extremely sharp-eyed. As one said, 'If there are people about with money, it is we who want it.'

Most of the crime, again according to the police, is fabricated. What they and the merchants still refer to, for want of a more modern epithet, as 'hippies' report the theft of tape recorders and cameras, having sold them at a good price, and then ask for a certificate declaring that they have been stolen. When they are back home they collect the insurance. Hippie-type tourists, collectively, are not popular in the Bazaar, principally because they never release any money if they can help it. In revenge, when they do decide to buy a sheepskin coat, for instance, the merchants try to sell them bum sheepskin coats at the highest prices they can extract from them.

The Eski Bedesten is a fantastic concentration of shops selling gold, precious stones, silver, copper and brass, carpets, antiques and onyx in an area approximately 160 feet by 230, sealed off from the rest of the Bazaar by four gates. Over one of them is a stone slab with a bas-relief of a single-headed Byzantine eagle on it. Inside I spent some time with Albert Sirazi, a young man in onyx ornaments. The raw material comes from Asia Minor. His grandfather was Persian, his mother Syrian Orthodox. He described himself as '100 per cent Turk'. His father, a watchmaker, paid the equivalent of £200 ($280) for the premises, virtually a small box plus show-cases which would fit four people comfortably around the hips. Now it is worth a lot of money, perhaps between a hundred and a hundred and fifty times as much, but it is not for sale, though business is terrible this winter, he says, the worst ever, and the worst of all, as it always is when things are bad, is onyx.

I can believe it. Onyx is horribly heavy and even more unrewarding to look at after it has been worked on than in its natural state.

'Jewellery is good business,' Albert said. 'Small stuff. Women can pass it through the custom. Leather? Things are bad in leather. Leather is good buy but no profit for seller. In all the world there is leather. You don't have to come to Istanbul for leather. Sheepskin coats 500 lira say and no business. Five people to keep and *hamals*, etc. Rents very high in the Bazaar. Business never so bad . . .'

'What about carpets?'

'Carpets are OK. Make good money. Antiques, too, pretty OK. Both have winter customers. Serious customers only come in winter. In onyx we wait for summer. In summer I make good business. Then I don't have time to eat.'

A few doors up there is an antique dealer with whom I have already passed the time of day, on this and many other occasions. He sells beautiful, plaited silver belts – old Ottoman work – and Armenian and Russian silver cigarette cases, decorated with what is called *savat*. They look as if the black embellishments, pictures of mosques, sometimes replicas of envelopes franked 'Van, 1914', are printed on them. Kitsch really, they are still good buys out in Anatolia at around £70–80 ($98–112). Here in the Bazaar a first-class one (many of them are damaged and have been clumsily repaired) costs £150 ($210). Back in 1975 the £150 ones were around £50 ($70). In 1964 the ones that were £50 in 1975 were £5 or less.

'How do you get your merchandise?' I asked him.

'We send buyers into Anatolia and they stop in the villages and shout and the peasants come out and trade whatever they have to sell, old silver, or copper, or carpets, for wheat, or money, or new things.'

'How's business? Any customers?'

'Only one today; but I made a good export. You want a glass of tea?'

A small boy appears swinging a circular tray with two glasses of scalding hot tea on it, brought from one of the nearby tea houses which are often no more than a hole in the wall.

This man had a number of ikons, most of them nineteenth century – 'OK for covering walls'. He had one good example from the end of the seventeenth century for which he wanted £1000 ($1400) as a rock-bottom price. It had an official certificate on the back authorizing its export.

'The museums have too many ikons like this,' he said, 'and much, much better. They're not really interested in anything later than the fifteenth century any more.'

I also talked with a rug and carpet dealer who has premises in the Street of the Prayer Hats. On the way there another dealer offered me 'Fifty Years Credit'.

'You want information, or you want shopping? I can give you information; but shopping is shopping,' said the carpet dealer who was young.

'Information.'

'Kilims are good at the moment. Italians like wery faded, old-looking kilims. This can be done with chemicals here, in Istanbul; but they do it better in London. English like faded, but less faded than Italians. Americans like wigourous colours. It doesn't necessarily mean they're new, providing they're wegetable not chemical dyes. You can find wegetable dye kilims ninety years old as fresh as when they were made because the owners kept them in boxes.

'For me there are three sorts of customers. Summer customers who come and go in two weeks maximum. They don't get good bargains because all the guides and travel agencies tell them they must pay half price of what we ask and no more. If we tell them real price they don't believe us. They never learn nothing about rugs and carpets because they don't believe nothing we tell them.

'Then there are what I call domestic foreigners. They are here in Istanbul for three, four years and want to learn. We never see them in summer, only winter. We give them a good price and they spend, say, about £60–70 ($84–98) a month. Then there are locals. Locals we treat the same.

'I don't like Germans, but Germans and French like to spend money and don't waste time trying to make stupid bargains.

'The most difficult are Americans. Last summer two Americans came, husband and wife. They said they were painters. They wanted to see kilims and from two o'clock until five I showed them kilims, all my stock – big stock. You can see how big. They didn't like any of them, and were rude about them, and I was tired because in summer the air in the Bazaar is wery bad.

'Then I showed them an awful, damaged one, a real rubbish, not worth nothing, to throw away. They asked the price, as they had done all the others, and I told them this one wasn't for amateurs, but for professionals who really know, and the lady said, "I never bargain. I offer you $2000 for it. Is that OK or not OK? Just tell me!" So I said it was OK.'

Finally, I visited a couple of jewellers at the lower end of Kalpakçilar Caddesi, the principal street of the Bazaar, who sold what one of them described on his trade card as 'Antiker und Moderner Schmuck'. Of the 147 shops in this street 77 belonged to jewellers.

The first jeweller weighed a thin gold chain for me with lots of clanking. Chains are popular because you are not paying for a lot of work. All gold objects must have an official hallmark.

'Is this your best price?' I asked him. 'Twenty-seven thousand lira?'

'Listen, Sir, this is 18-carat; 14-carat and the links go black. If you think this expensive I give you better price.'

'What is your best price?'

'Twenty-two thousand lira, because you are English and not American. That is my best price.'

The second shop had better stuff. Mr Ferit, I think his name was, showed me a really beautiful bracelet woven from very fine gold wire by a Greek woman who works at Trabzon on the shore of the Black Sea. Apart from the clasp, which was rough, it was good enough for Cartier or Boucheron or Van Cleef and Arpels. As I wasn't buying I told him so.

'Listen,' said Mr Ferit. 'You know how much this costs? 120,000 Turkish lira, that's about £400 ($560). You know how much time it takes for this woman to make this bracelet?. One and a half months. You think it is cheap price? You are right. And why? Because if customers find shop next door selling cheaper they will go there. That's business, isn't it?'

The parts of the Bazaar I like best because they are the least changed are those lonely reaches in the northern part, rarely visited by tourists because the shops there only sell skins and plastic foam. By 6.15 p.m. on a cold night such as this one most of them were already closed. In the remainder the shutters were crashing down and some of the street lights were already extinguished. Now the *bekjis*, the night watchmen, fifty of them, and the cats were taking over, dozens of them, and the last *hamal* went past, practically airborne under an almost weightless load of foam. Then, with the last shutter down, it was so quiet you could hear the sirens on the ships and ferry boats in the Bosphorus moaning and whistling at one another, just as one could up in the now long-abandoned harem at Topkapi.

The Harem at Topkapi

The harem – any other paled into insignificance – was the Imperial Harem at the Yeni Saray, otherwise Topkapi Saray,* the New or Cannon Gate Palace, known to foreigners for centuries as the Grand Seraglio, which had remained unused for the purpose for which it was built since 1853, when the last sultan to maintain a harem there had moved to the Dolmabahçe Palace further up the Bosphorus.

What is a harem? What is a seraglio? The best description, the easiest to assimilate, is that written by N. M. Penzer, the author of *The Ḥarēm*, published in 1936, of which what follows is a précis.

Ḥarēm is derived from the Arabic *ḥarām*, 'that which is unlawful', as opposed to *ḥalal*, 'that which is lawful'. The correct word in Turkish for the women's part of a house is *ḥarēmlik*, *ḥarēm* strictly being the occupants. The part of the house where guests are received

---

* Topkapi, the Cannon Gate, was a gate which opened on to the Sea of Marmara from the Summer Harem, south-east of Seraglio Point where there were extensive gun batteries. How the whole palace came to be known as Topkapi is not clear. In summer, two imperial caïques were always stationed there to take the sultan wherever he wished to go.

is the *selāmlik*, but this is never shortened, as *selām* alone simply means 'salutation' or greeting.

Relations with European powers gave rise to the coining of a word that would embrace not only the *harēmlik* and the *selāmlik* but the royal palace as a whole, which became known as the Grand Serail or Seraglio, seraglio being derived from the Italian *serraglio*, 'a cage for wild animals', and was adopted owing to its chance similarity with the Persian words *sarā* and *sarāi*, 'a building' and particularly 'a palace'; and this name for it was accepted both by Europeans and Turks.

The building of what was eventually to become one of the more complex and labyrinthine of royal palaces was begun by Mehmed the Conqueror in 1459, six years after he had captured the city. He chose for it what must be one of the most magnificent situations for a palace anywhere, the First Hill of the Seven Hills of the city which are now so difficult for the visitor to identify, on the promontory which stretches out from what must have always been a rather un-European shore of Europe into the Bosphorus and which shelters the inlet known as the Golden Horn from the winds off the Sea of Marmara. Previously it had been the site of the acropolis of what was originally the ancient city of Byzantium. Mehmed enclosed it within a wall three miles long and successive sultans continued to add to the palace, demolish parts of it and build them again to a different pattern, a process that was still continuing when the last sultan to live in it finally abandoned it nearly 400 years after its foundation.

Of this great palace, which housed between two and five thousand people, the harem was only a part, although a very important one, for the Grand Seraglio was not only the imperial residence of the sultan, but also the Sublime Porte, the High Gate, in Turkish the Bab-i-Humayun, the Imperial Gate, regarded, figuratively, as the seat of government and the administrative centre of the Ottoman world, on which the heads of those who had been decapitated in the Court of the Janissaries, the first court of the palace, were displayed in niches, that is if they were considered sufficiently important to warrant such a display.

The real centre of government was in the second courtyard, the Court of the Divan, beyond the Bab-el-Selām, the Gate of Salutation, in which the Chief Executioner, who was also the Head Gardener, the *Bostanji-bashi*, resided, where there was a fountain in which he could wash the blood from his sword and his hands.

There, until the middle of the sixteenth century, when it was at the height of its greatness, the sultan, the grand vizier, a handful of viziers, the lord of the admiralty, a couple of military judges and a few secretaries and accountants, meeting four times a week, ran an empire which extended from the Atlas mountains to the Caucasus and from the Adriatic to the Persian Gulf from the Kubbealti, the Hall of the Divan, two domed, now rather bleak rooms, each only thirty feet square, with a grilled window high up in one of its walls. And it is strange that it was Suleiman the Magnificent (who ruled from 1520 to 1566), himself so able a ruler, who made the decision that in future the sultan should not be present at these deliberations in the Kubbealti. In doing so he initiated what was known as the *Kadinlar Sultanati*, the Reign of Women, and from then onwards successive sultans, if they could be bothered to do so, would look down and listen unseen through the grilled window from the interior of the harem, but have no direct influence on affairs of state, which meant that only too often they became little more than puppets. Failing the sultan, the sultan validé, the queen-mother, who from now on assumed a position of disproportionate import- ance, or if they were ambitious for themselves and their offspring the *Kadinefendis*, favourite sultanas who had born the sultan a son, might listen in to the proceedings being conducted below.

The Seraglio also housed the Military School of State. In it between five and eight hundred specially selected Christian boys who had been enslaved and forcibly converted to Islam were trained as *Iç-oghlans*, 'Inside Youths', for what was known as the Inner Service, in which they acted either as pages within the palace (but not of course within the harem), or in the higher services of the sultan. The *Iç-oghlans* formed only a small part of the intake of young Christians – Austrians, Hungarians, Russians, Greeks, Italians, Bosnians, Bohemians, Germans, Swiss, Georgians, Circas- sians, Armenians and Persians. The rest either became *Spahi- oghlans*, recruits to the sultan's personal cavalry, or *Ajem-oghlans*, aspirants to the Outer Service, most of whom were engaged in manual work, *Baltajilers*, Halberdiers, or else were recruited into the Janissaries, the *corps d'élite* of the Turkish standing army, which was entirely composed of apostatized Christians. No Turks were ever admitted to any of these services.

Also in the Seraglio were two treasuries, numerous libraries, more than a dozen mosques. There was also the Pavilion of the Holy Mantle, the Hirkai Serif Dairesi, still one of the most venerated places in the Muslim world. And there were ten enormous kitchens, each of which provided for a different hierarchy of persons from the sultan downwards, which together still form the largest single building in the entire seraglio. And there were bakeries, laundries, stables, baths and waterworks and, a world within a world, there was the harem itself.

What life was really like in the Imperial Harem will never be known, because it *was* the Imperial Harem and the penalty for anyone who showed undue curiosity about it, even to the extent of pointing a telescope in its direction, could be death. In *Voyage au Levant*, published in Paris in 1725, a French traveller, Corneille Le Bruyn, wrote of an unfortunate Venetian interpreter, a Signor Grellot, who, in about 1680, was hanged from his window, which overlooked the gardens of the Grand Seraglio, for daring to gaze at Sultan Mehmed IV and his ladies through a telescope. Almost everything that has been written about it is either hearsay or conjecture, based on what had been learned about other more modest, more domestic, less sternly administered, slightly more accessible harems. Or they are the fleeting impressions gained by male artisans, clock regulators and such, or those entering in the guise of their assistants, while a black eunuch rushed them through some bit of the harem to the place where they were to perform their mundane tasks at a time when the flesh and blood occupants had either been temporarily evacuated from these particular corridors or rooms or else were down at the Summer Harem at Seraglio Point, or up at the Old Palace, the Edirne Saray, on an island in the River Tunca at Edirne in northern Thrace, which Murad II began to build in 1450, three years before the fall of Constantinople, and was destroyed in 1877 without trace. Their somewhat sparse observations – no fault of theirs – are what one might expect from a plumber's mate en route through Buckingham Palace to clear an obstructed drain while the royal family and the court are at Sandringham. What a pity it is that some literate laundress or female dressmaker, the sort of people who were allowed inside, or even a black or white eunuch, left no record of what they saw.

One more educated writer and traveller, Aubry de La Motraye, described by his French biographers as a 'veracious traveller but a superficial observer', who spent nearly fifteen years in Constantinople, from 1699 to 1714, persuaded one of the French or Swiss clockmakers who had a monopoly of clock adjustment in the Grand Seraglio, to take him into the harem in the guise of an assistant, 'dressed after the *Turkish* manner', while the occupants were elsewhere, which can scarcely have fooled even the most gormless of black eunuchs, and the record of what he saw is pretty limited, also.

> In the middle of the Hall, directly under the *Cupola*, was an Artificial fountain, the Bason of which was of the precious Green Marble, which seem'd to me to be either Serpentine or Jasper; it did not play on account of the Womens being absent . . . They had also little *Sofa's*, which had some Pieces of painted Callico flung over them to preserve them from dust, &c. Upon these *Sofa's* the Ladies sit to breathe the fresh Air, and recreate their Eyes thro' the Lattice. After the Clock in the Hall (The Throne Room Within) was put in order, the Eunuch made us pass by several little Chambers with Doors shut, like the Cells of Monks or Nuns, as far as I cou'd judge by one that another Eunuch open'd, which was the only one I saw, and by the Outside of the others . . .
>
> NB In comparing the Chambers of the *Grand Seignior's* Women to the Cells of Nuns, we must except the Richness of the Furniture, as well as the Use they are put to; the difference of which is easy enough to be imagin'd without Explication.*

There was a foot of snow in the outer courts, and more drifting down into it when we set off on a Tuesday, when the whole palace is closed to the public, with an old, rather shaky, distinctly grumpy custodian armed with several large bunches of keys, whom the director of Topkapi had kindly deputed for this purpose, to explore those parts of the Winter Harem still not shown to anyone without special permission, permission which is not easy to obtain.

The principal way into the Winter Harem, one that was never used by the sultan, is the Araba Kapisi, the Carriage Gate, a very modest affair through which the more fortunate odalisques were taken for an airing in the *arrhubas*, the spooky-looking canopied carriages with oval windows, drawn by hennaed oxen. It leads in to the Dolapli Kubbe, the Domed Anteroom lined with cupboards, in which tradesmen used to deposit goods that were to be conveyed into the harem.

To the left of this gate is another, which the custodian now opened up for us, that leads to a pavilion as idiosyncratic as the occupants for whom it was built some four hundred years ago.

* *Travels through Europe, Asia and into Part of Africa*, 1723.

This extraordinary body of men, the *Zülüfli Baltajilers*, the Halberdiers-with-Tresses, were recruited from the ranks of the *Ajem-oghlans*, and they all slept together in the room to which the custodian now took us, a galleried dormitory, the roof of which is supported by wooden pillars, painted bright red. Beneath their dormitory is a sort of clubroom lined with tall cupboards with drawers beneath them in which each Halberdier kept his own coffee-making apparatus. In the middle of this room there is a *mangal*, a charcoal brazier, used for heating a room, which like the rest of the harem was now as cold as the tomb. Beneath this room there is what was a prison.

The *Zülüfli Baltajilers* acted as guards and porters and were latterly unmutilated, although at one period they were recruited from the ranks of the White Eunuchs, most of whom were themselves imported from the Caucasus, or India, or were Hungarians, Slavonians or Germans who had been made prisoner. The White Eunuchs' sphere of influence was not in the harem, where the Black Eunuchs held sway, but in the *selāmlik*, those parts of the palace beyond the harem in which outsiders were received. Only the *Zülüfli Baltajilers* had regular access to the harem. Once a month, wearing their extraordinary uniforms, a feature of which was an immensely high collar which allowed them to see nothing to left or right, and each wearing a pair of *zülüf*, wool tresses on either side of their faces wrapped around gilded wire, an arrangement that made it practically impossible for them to see anything at all, they were marched into the harem between a double file of Black Eunuchs, bowed down under a huge weight of firewood from a store round the corner which held five hundred shiploads.

Nothing in the entire harem, apart from the Kafes, the Prison of the Princes, is more weird and redolent of horror than the three-storeyed quarters of the Black Eunuchs,* the Karagalar Tasligi, beyond the Anteroom of the Cupboards, more like a deep ditch than a human habitation; its only ornaments are a great gaping fireplace on the ground floor, the drum used in Ramadan to announce the beginning and end of the hours of fast and the sticks with which newcomers were beaten on the soles of the feet as a form of initiation, for all the world as if they were new boys at some expensive school. It was apparently not enough that these wretches

---

* According to N. M. Penzer, one of the authorities on the harem, in the reign of Murad III (1574–1595) there were between six and eight hundred Black Eunuchs in the Harem.

had had their parts swept off with a single stroke of the razor, either here in Constantinople or else in Africa for example, far up the Nile where, near Assiut, in the early part of the nineteenth century, two Coptic Christian monks had what amounted to a monopoly of this business, castrating about a hundred and fifty young Negro boys a year, after which, as a post-operative treatment, they buried them up to their haunches in warm manure. No wonder the Black Eunuchs were cruel, arrogant, jealous and petulant. At least the White Eunuchs, who administered the harem in its early years before being supplanted by the Black Eunuchs, were asked if they wished the operation to be performed before submitting to it.

Here, too, in the Courtyard of the Eunuchs, is, or was until recently, the tiny, conical sentry box manned by one of the palace dwarfs when the sultan passed by.

Among the few unmutilated men allowed to enter the harem were musicians (although the Chief Musician, and probably the others also, had to wear the curls of chastity, the *Hoca*), the Princes' Tutor, and the Chief Physician, who was so particularly suspect that he too was only allowed into the harem between two files of Black Eunuchs. (The only parts of his patients' anatomies he was allowed to inspect were their hands.)

Even cucumbers and other vegetables of inflammatory shape and size were cut into slices before being allowed in, for fear of misuse. In this harem nothing was left to chance; and it is therefore not surprising that those odalisques who were not occupying the sultan's bed, and might never do so, sometimes took an interest in one another.

The harem was unimaginably cold. No wonder old engravings show women swathed in furs huddled round the *mangals* that, together with the big, open fireplaces with their tall, exquisite chimneypieces of bronze and marble and gypsum, were the only means of heating it. With our aged custodian, who like ourselves was positively trembling with cold, we travelled through endless corridors and courtyards and sets of rooms, each one an individual labyrinth, built on what are at least six different levels, on the side of what is a quite steep hill, the result of more than twenty sultans adding to and subtracting from what Mehmed the Conqueror originally built, tearing down whole suites of rooms constructed by their predecessors to gratify some whim and building new ones to house their favourites. Because of this it was quite easy, as we found, to ascend some gaily-painted staircase which was on the verge of collapse and bang one's head on a ceiling that was now, due to some subsequent rebuilding scheme, within three inches of the floor.

Some rooms had seals on the doors because they contained treasures, or had large, rusty padlocks for which our guide could find no keys, or else found that he had brought the wrong ones. A list had been drawn up in Turkish of what he was to attempt to show us and the only way of communicating with him was by pointing to it. There were some quarters for which it proved impossible to find the entrance, let alone a key, such as those of the *Cariyeler Dairesi*, the rank-and-file of the harem women, which lay somewhere on the side of the hill above the hospital.

With him we saw one of the sets of rooms used by the *Kadinefendis*, the four favourites who had each given birth to a male heir, in which their rotting beds, shrouded in impenetrable curtains of cobwebs, were more evocative of the past, in this nightmare state of ruin, than if they had been restored. Next we inspected the suites of the Chief Laundress, the Harem Mistress and the Chief Nurse, which had balconies with a view over the rooftops to the Bosphorus on which the royal babies were given an airing, and we saw what was said to be the hospital, which was very large and built round a hidden courtyard, and the laundry, one of the few places in the entire harem, being at the bottom of the hill, where what must have been miles of washing could be hung out to dry without affecting the aesthetic sensibilities of some member of the upper echelons. We saw the Gate of the Dead, the Meyyit Kapisi, by which bodies were removed from the harem, beyond the room in the hospital in which they were laid out. There was a separate gate, in the Wall of the Second Court of the Selāmlik, the palace outside the harem, through which the dead were taken away for burial, but it is now blocked up; and we saw the Way of the Shawls, a melancholy, grass-grown passage, open to the sky, more like a moat than anything else, which runs down to a gate of the same name. This was the way by which the sultan used to set off on horseback, riding over the beautiful shawls with which it had been lined, which were then distributed amongst the most favoured women, on his way to the Girding of the Sword, the equivalent of his coronation at the mosque at Eyup, at the head of the Golden Horn. High above this passage is the Meskane, the Conservatory of Selim III where he enjoyed playing the *ney*, a sort of flute, and where he composed songs which are still sung to this day.

At the opposite end of the harem, a hundred yards or so away at the far end of the Altinyol, the Golden Road which traverses it from one end to the other, is the gate through which the sultan used to pass out of the harem on his way to the Pavilion of the Holy Mantle. Just before it is what is called the Place of Consultation of the Jinn (what one distinguished American female professor, Dr Barnette Miller, author of one of the two best books in the English language on the harem, called the 'Place Where the Fairies Deliberate'). Above it, cantilevered out above the Golden Road, is a set of eight rooms, in one of which a *gözde*, a girl who had caught the eye of the sultan, suitably embellished and with her pubic hairs removed, waited for the signal to enter the imperial bedchamber in whatever part of the harem it might happen to be at that particular moment in history. Then she would kiss the imperial coverlet before working her way up under it from the bottom end of the bed by this well blazed route into the Imperial Presence. No Turkish woman, so far as is known, ever had this honour. Their place was taken by thousands upon thousands of Circassians from beyond the Caucasus, Georgians and Armenians, a fewer number of Western Europeans, although Rumanians were very active, and possibly one French Créole from Martinique – Aimée Dubucq de Rivery, who is said to have both become *kadinefendi* and Sultan Validé. Many of them fought for the honour of being enslaved and ravished.

This act of burrowing was not simply a demonstration of male chauvinism. Any man who subsequently married a *kadinefendi* of a deceased sultan, which he could do once she had been retired from the harem to the Old Palace, the Eski Saray, built by Mehmed II, the Conqueror, on one of the other seven hills of the city, the one on which the University now stands, however elevated in rank he might be, also had to reach the summit in this fashion.

Some of these rooms had enormous gilded nineteenth-century beds in them, huge mirrors and other equally out-of-scale furniture for what are really bed-sitters with little gilded balconies above them to which there could have been no means of access unless each *gözde* was issued with a ladder. Another room, on the ground floor, had a secret staircase of incredible steepness, up which the *gözde* was required to climb, which linked it with the strange and isolated apartments of Abd ul-Hamid I, who reigned from 1774 to 1788 and was so terrified of being stalked and strangled with the silken bowstring, which was the customary method of disposing of unwanted royalty – what would seem to most people a perfectly natural reaction to living in this harem – that he had the walls lined with mirrors.

Also on the ground floor, at the junction of the Golden Way and the Meeting Place of the Jinn, are the apartments of the *haseki*. If a *gözde* was called more than once to the sultan's bed she might become an *ikbal*. If as an *ikbal*, she gave birth to a child, she became a *haseki*.

Above these rooms, reached by the same staircase that leads to the apartments of the *gözdeler*, is the Kafes, the Cage, a dozen or so rooms on two storeys – there may be more – hidden away in perpetual shadow, those overlooking the Courtyard of the Girls-in-the-Eye with heavy iron grilles over the windows. The only other window in the Kafes is in a room on the upper storey which gives a view of the sky and of part of the roof of the harem. The only reasonably comprehensive view of the outside of the harem is from the Tower of Justice which rises above the Hall of the Divan, a remarkable panorama of leaded roofs, chimneys masquerading as miniature minarets, domes and small, claustrophobically-barred windows. Beyond can be seen the Selāmlik, the Bosphorus and the Golden Horn.

To stand in the semi-darkness of these rooms, all of them now in an advanced state of decay, even for a few minutes, hearing the mice scratching away in the wainscoting and the sirens of the ships, was to have the sensation of being buried alive. Yet here, and in what remains of an earlier Kafes, a building with barred windows that still stands in what is called the Boxwood Court, which lies below the Court of the Gözdeler, beyond the now grass-grown remains of what was once a large pool, the crown prince, the *sehzade*, was imprisoned, in what was a form of living death, by whoever was the ruling sultan, probably his brother, until he in his turn became sultan, that is if he had not already been strangled with the bowstring.

Murad III, who reigned from 1574 to 1595, had 103 children by his harem women, of whom there were 1200. Of these, twenty sons and twenty-seven daughters survived him. His eldest son, who succeeded him as Mehmed III, had all his nineteen brothers put to death and seven of his father's pregnant concubines drowned.

A far greater slaughter of harem women took place in the reign of the mad Sultan Ibrahim, who reigned from 1640 to 1649. In order to clear the way for a fresh collection of women, he had 280 of his odalisques, who would normally have remained in the harem until pensioned off and sent to the Old Palace, what was said at that time to be his entire stock, put in weighted sacks and drowned off Seraglio Point. It was to prevent such consumption of the life blood of the sultanate that the Kafes was invented.

Of Ibrahim, Demetrius Cantemir wrote, in his *History of the Growth and Decay of the Othoman Empire*, published in 1734:

> As Murat [Ibrahim's brother, Murad IV] was wholly addicted to wine so was Ibrahim to lust. They say he spent all his time in sensual pleasure and when nature was exhausted with the frequent repetition of venereal delights he endeavoured to restore it with potions or commanded a beautiful virgin richly habited to be brought to him by his mother [Kosem, the Sultan Validé, who was eventually murdered in the Harem], the Grand Vezir, or some other great man. He covered the walls of his chamber with looking-glass so that his love battles might be seen to be enacted at several places at once. He ordered his pillows to be stuffed with rich furs, so that the bed designed for the Imperial pleasure might be the more precious. Nay, he put whole sable skins under him in a notion that his lust would be inflamed if his love toil were rendered more difficult by the glowing of his knees. In the palace gardens, he frequently assembled all the virgins, made them strip themselves naked, and neighing like a stallion ran among them and . . . ravished one or the other, kicking or struggling by his order.

Ibrahim was kept prisoner in the Kafes from the age of two until he became sultan at the age of twenty-four. No wonder he was as mad as a hatter. At the end of his reign he was returned to it to be murdered by the deaf-mutes with slit tongues and punctured eardrums which enabled them to resist any cries for mercy.

If a prince had the strength of mind to ask for them, he might be given teachers to fortify his mind in addition to the customary supply of some two dozen barren *ikbals* he was normally allowed. Suleiman II spent his thirty-nine years in the Kafes, before succeeding to the throne in 1687, practising calligraphy and reading the Koran. Osman III was fifty years in the Kafes and when he succeeded as sultan in 1754 – he only lived for two years after his release – he had the wall lowered which hid it from view in the Boxwood Courtyard.

The last to die in the Kafes was Sultan Selim III, strangled with the bowstring in 1807 but only after a desperate resistance which belied his gentle reputation.

There are said to be four hundred rooms in the harem. Perhaps the number depends on what one means by rooms. There are stone cupboards and secret cupboards and mouldering corridors that might qualify as rooms if one was setting out to count them. Altogether, we saw about a hundred and fifty of which a couple of dozen are normally shown to the public.

Although the Chief White Eunuch, the *Kapi Agha*, was Head of the Inner Service of the Selāmlik, the outer palace, and of the Palace School, the Infirmary, and was also Head Gate-Keeper and Master of Ceremonies (one of his subordinates, the *Hasinedar-bashi*, was also in charge of the Treasury), his power was as nothing compared with that of the Chief Black Eunuch, the *Kislar Agha*, who administered the harem in consultation with the Sultan Validé, the Queen-Mother.

The Chief Black Eunuch was also Director of the Princes' School, in which, up to the age of ten or eleven, before possibly being consigned to the Kafes or suffering a worse fate, they were educated in the exquisite tiled and panelled schoolroom above his own gloomy quarters, which overlook the Courtyard of the Black Eunuchs. He was also a pasha with his own extensive entourage and when the sultan ceased to attend meetings in the divan became the link between the sultan and the grand vizier.

The Queen-Mother was the Ruler of the Harem, the Chief Black Eunuch the link between her and the women of the harem, and between the sultan and the rest of the outside world.

The administrators of the harem were women, all of them slaves. The name by which all the harem women were known, from the Sultan Validé to the Head Housekeeper, the Head Treasurer to the Lower Lesser Laundresses, was *Cariye*, those who serve.

The financial administration was extraordinarily complex and costly. It included the payment of pocket money to the various girls on a carefully graduated scale, according to the degree of favour they basked in, and pensions to those who had retired to the Eski Saray. There were Keepers of the Baths, of the Jewels, of the Readers of the Koran, of the Scribes, of the Store Rooms, of the Table Service, all women who had exchanged the remote possibility of becoming *kadinefendis* for other positions of eminence and power.

This took no account of the women of the Sultan Validé: her Treasurer, First Secretary, First Seal-Bearer, Water Pourer, Coffee-

Maker, Confectioner, Mistress of the Robes, of the Sherbets and so on. There were twelve of them, each of whom had – they were called *kalfa* (mistress) – an *oda*, or company of women working for them, consisting of six *hayaliks*, Lesser Women, drawn from the most junior in terms of age and position in the harem. So that there were hordes of Lesser Treasurers, Lesser Confectioners, Lesser Sherbet Mistresses, etc. And there were yet other entourages, those of the *kadinefendis*, of the *sehzade*, the crown prince, and of the Chief Black Eunuch, half a dozen or more households, worlds within worlds, each with perhaps a hundred members, all spinning away like tops, independent of one another much of the time. And there was the Head Nurse, the *Dada Usta*, and her entourage, and the Midwives.

It is unfortunate that there are now no inhabitants of the harem of the Grand Seraglio still in the land of the living to tell us anything about what it was really like to live in it.

The best written accounts we have are of life in the Summer Harem; but only two men make any real pretence of having actually seen any of the girls at all. The most convincing witness – the other one writes from hearsay – is Master Thomas Dallam, a Cockney organ-maker, sent to Constantinople in 1599 to erect in the Selāmlik, not the harem, an hydraulic organ he had built, which was a gift from Queen Elizabeth I to Sultan Mohammed III, who reigned from 1595 to 1603. He wrote:

> When he [a black eunuch] had showed me many other thinges which I wondered at, then crossinge throughe a litle squar courte paved with marble, he poynted me to goo to a graite in a wale, but made me a sine that he myghte not goo thether him selfe. When I came to the grait the wale was verrie thicke, and graited on bothe the sides with iron verrie strongly; but through that graite I did se thirtie of the Grand Sinyor's Concobines that weare playinge with a bale in another courte. At the firste sighte of them I thoughte they had bene yonge men, but when I saw the hare of their heades hange doone on their backes, platted together with a tasle of smale pearle hanginge in the lower end of it, and by other plaine tokens, I did know them to be women, and verrie prettie ones in deede . . . I stood so longe loukinge upon them that he which had showed me all this kindnes began to be verrie angrie with me. He made a wrye mouthe, and stamped with his foute to make me give over looking; the

which I was verrie lothe to dow, for that sighte did please me wondrous well.

So rare in fact is a report of a genuine sighting of female members of the harem that it may be excusable to print an account of the other, although rather more second-hand one.

The man who witnessed it was the secretary and chaplain to the Swedish Embassy in Constantinople and he described it to the English traveller and scientist Edward Clarke who was in Constantinople in March 1801. What the chaplain saw were the four principal Sultanas and the Queen-Mother, Mihrisāh Sultan. This was perhaps the Créole girl, Aimée Dubucq de Rivery, a cousin, neighbour and childhood friend in Martinique of Joséphine Rose Tascher de la Pagerie, who later became wife of Napoleon Bonaparte and Empress of France. She was captured by Barbary corsairs while travelling from her convent school in Nantes to Martinique, and is said to have been presented by the Dey of Algiers to Sultan Abd ul-Hamid I later becoming, as *Naksh*, the Beautiful One, his favourite, and presenting him with a son, Mahmud II, the Reformer, on whom she is said to have had a great and liberalizing influence.

Three of the four were *Georgians*, having dark complexions, and very long dark hair; but the fourth was remarkably fair and her hair, also of singular length and thickness, was of a flaxen colour: neither were their teeth dyed black, as those of *Turkish* females generally are. The Swedish gentleman said, he was almost sure that these women suspected they were seen from the address they manifested in displaying their charms, and in loitering at the gate. This gave him and his friend no small degree of terror; as they would have paid for their curiosity with their lives, if any such suspicion had entered into the minds of the black eunuchs . . .

Their dresses [the Chaplain said, who seems to have as good an eye for detail as any fashion editress,] were long spangled robes, open in front, with pantaloons embroidered in gold and silver, and covered with a profusion of pearls and precious stones which displayed their persons to great advantage; . . . their hair hung in loose and very thick tresses on each side of their cheeks, falling down to the waist, and entirely covering their shoulders. Those tresses were quite powdered with diamonds, not displayed according to any studied arrangement, but as if carelessly scattered, by hand-fuls, among their flowing locks. On top of their heads, and rather leaning to one side, they wore, each of them, a small circular patch or diadem. Their faces, necks, and even breasts, were quite exposed; not one of them having a veil.

Clarke, together with a young Englishman to whom he was acting as a tutor on what had already proved to be a very adventurous and unconventional Grand Tour, and a M. Preaux, a French landscape artist, succeeded in entering the Summer Harem at Seraglio Point at a time of year when the occupants were still in the Winter Harem up on the hill, with the connivance of Herr Ensle, an Austrian gardener who had been responsible for laying out a garden for the sultan in the manner of that at Schönbrunn. The 'Charem', as Clarke called it, from the outside reminded him of one of the smaller Cambridge colleges – he was at that time both a fellow and Bursar of Jesus College – enclosing the same sort of cloistered court.

They were then taken to the New Kiosk, built by Selim III at his summer residence. 'There', he wrote,

> . . . We were pleased with observing a few things they [the women of the Seraglio] had carelessly left upon their sofas, and which characterised their mode of life. Among these was an *English* writing box, of black varnished wood, with a sliding cover, and drawers; the drawers containing coloured writing paper, reed pens, perfumed wax, and little bags made of embroidered satin, in which their billets-doux are sent, by negro slaves . . . That liqueurs are drunk in these secluded chambers is evident; for we found labels for bottles, neatly cut out with scissars, bearing *Turkish* inscriptions, with the words 'Rosoglio', 'Golden Water', and 'Water of Life'. These we carried off as trophies of our visit to the place.

With a wealth of material to record in the Kiosk and in the Summer Harem building in which harem women slept in tiers, one above the other, in a long corridor, it was unfortunate that M. Preaux, the French artist, whose extraordinary dexterity with pen or pencil enabled him to make lightning sketches of anything he saw, was so weighed down by feelings of guilt and apprehension that he either lost the few drawings that he had dared to make, or else threw them away, which was a great loss to posterity as no accurate representations of the interior of the Summer Harem are known to exist. Just as the Summer Harem itself, what was an enchanting collection of wooden buildings, no longer exists. It was burned down in 1863, in the reign of Sultan Abd ul-Aziz. It was never rebuilt, and when the railway finally wormed its way into the city, following the line of the sea walls round Seraglio Point in 1870, all communication between the Palace on the Hill and the Point was cut off. Today much of what was the site of the Summer Harem has been buried by the coastal highway.

To return to the Winter Harem at Topkapi, the last sultan to maintain a harem there was Abd ul-Medjid I who became sultan in 1839 at the age of sixteen. Enfeebled early in his reign, which lasted until 1861, by excessive indulgence in the pleasures which its occupants offered, he became extremely depressed by living in it – in spite of having built himself the Kiosk with an entrancing view of the approaches to the Bosphorus, now a restaurant which bears his name.

In 1843 he commissioned Karabat Balian, a Turkish-Armenian architect, to build him on the European shore of the Bosphorus the amazing rococo-style, white marble palace of Dolmabahçe, the Palace of the Filled-in Garden, on a site reclaimed from the Bosphorus by the labours of 16,000 Christian slaves three centuries previously, and before this new development a vegetable garden producing the finest cabbages in the entire Ottoman Empire. And there, when it was finished, richly embellished with chimney pieces of malachite and crimson Bohemian crystal and with a *hamam* with walls of Egyptian alabaster two feet thick, he went to live with his vast court and harem.

To pay for it he raised the money from European moneylenders, ostensibly to re-equip the Turkish Army. This was the first time that a sultan had borrowed money from the West and it was one more nail in the coffin of the Ottoman Empire.

The only survivors of an imperial harem alive today, if any such exist, would be members of the harem of Abd ul-Hamid II, who came to the throne in 1876, was deposed in April 1909, and died, after a period of exile in Salonika, in the Beylerbey Summer Palace on the Asian shore of the Bosphorus in January 1918. Or perhaps they would be survivors of the much smaller harems maintained by his successors, Mehmed V, Mehmed VI and Abd ul-Medjid II, who reigned as caliph only, from 1922 to 1924, when he was sent to exile with the other remaining members of the house of Osman.

Abd ul-Hamid immured himself in various fortified hideaways, some of them subterranean, for more than thirty years, from 1877 to 1909, in the Yildiz Park on the European shore of the Bosphorus. He was the possessor of the last really imperial harem. It numbered three hundred and seventy concubines, the youngest of whom was fifteen years old, and a hundred and twenty-seven eunuchs. The Sultan made modest use of its facilities, preferring the more lively company of a Flora Cordier, a Belgian *modiste* with a shop in Pera, a 'fair-haired girl with laughing eyes' who, when the Sultan asked her to marry him, did so, but of whom he soon tired.

Of these members of his harem, when the time came for him to board the special train taking him to exile in Salonika, he was only allowed to choose to accompany him three *kadins*, four ordinary concubines, four eunuchs and fourteen slaves and other servants, although later, when he became bored with his original selection of concubines, he was allowed to send for reinforcements, as well as for a couple of cows, some angora cats, a collection of fowls and a giant St Bernard dog. At the same time as the Sultan went into exile, thirty-one carriages conveyed the remainder of Abd ul-Hamid's women to the Harem of the Grand Seraglio at Topkapi.

There, that same year, 1909, an extraordinary spectacle was enacted. The Young Turks, who had deposed him, appalled at the cost of maintaining an entire harem in idleness, caused circulars to be sent out to various parts of the empire, particularly to the Circassian villages in Anatolia, telling their parents to come and reclaim their offspring. As a result, large numbers of Circassian peasants arrived in the capital where they were taken to the Topkapi Palace for what was virtually an identification parade, well de-scribed by the writer Francis McCullagh in his book *The Fall of Abd-ul-Hamid*:

> There, in the presence of a Turkish Commission, they were taken into a long hall filled with the ex-Sultan's concubines, cadines and odalisques, all of whom were then allowed to unveil themselves for the occasion. The scene that followed was very touching . . . The contrast between the delicate complexions and costly attire of the women and the rough, weather-beaten appearance of the ill-clad mountaineers who had come to fetch them home was not the least striking feature of the extraordinary scene . . . The number of female slaves thus liberated was two hundred and thirteen . . . Clad

in Circassian peasant dress, they are now in all probability milking cows and doing farm work in Anatolia.

This was the end of the last of the great imperial harems. Those whom no one came to claim were sent to other residences, and only a few eunuchs continued to live on at Topkapi until they, too, were evicted in 1924, when parts of the palace became a museum.

For years no proper plan of the entire palace existed, or if it did it was never published, and it was not until 1918 that two Americans, Dr Barnette Miller and Professor Lucius Scipio, an engineer, began a survey of it, assisted by Izzat Bey, a palace functionary, an *Iç-oghlan* who had been educated in the Military School of State which was abolished, together with the Sultanate, in 1922. They were not allowed to use surveying instruments because the custodians – Mehmed VI, the last sultan, was still on the throne – regarded them as sacrilegious, and they were therefore forced to pace out all their measurements.

The survey was only completed in October 1918, by which time the Turkish armies were crumbling on every front and Constantinople was being constantly attacked by huge British bombers. How strange it must have been, pacing out the dimensions of an empty harem, in a twilight world that was already no more, with an entire empire collapsing outside the walls.

It was not until 1971 that a number of rooms in the Winter Harem were opened, wonderfully restored by a Turkish architect, Madame Emine Mualla Eyuboglu, a task that had taken, working with four or five master craftsmen and some twenty assistants, eleven years. The work is still continuing.

But wherever one finds oneself in the Winter Harem, whether in a part of it that has been restored, or in a room the windows of which have not been opened for perhaps a hundred and thirty years, it is difficult, even with the aid of the most vivid imagination, to populate it with anything except a few isolated ghosts. It is as if all those inhabitants who made up the great hierarchical pyramid, of which the Sultan and the Sultan Valide, and the Chief Black Eunuch, were the apex, had not only gone for ever, but had never existed, in this, the last great extant palace where Europe ends and Asia begins.

The Plain of Troy

In wanting to revisit the plain of Troy we were only following countless others whose imagination had been excited by the stirring and often dreadful deeds that were done at Homer's Troy. Indeed at one time, when the memories of what had occurred must have been comparatively fresh, it became almost obligatory for the illustrious great to make the pilgrimage, though for all but them and their attendants, the Troad was too remote and difficult of access. This has remained true throughout the ages so that even far into the nineteenth century only the most determined travellers went there. More historians and geographers wrote of it than ever visited it, although Herodotus, 'the Father of History', in the fifth century BC, Scylax of Caryanda in the fourth century BC and Strabo, who was still writing in AD 21, had probably all been there.

The first of these illustrious persons known to have paid his respects to the Homeric dead was Xerxes, in the fifth century BC. Having seen his army safely across the Hellespont, he journeyed to Troy, where he sacrificed 1000 oxen and offered a great quantity of wine, of which large amounts were probably being produced on the Asian shore of the Hellespont even at this early date, just as they are to this day.

Some hundred years later, Alexander, first of his army to set foot in Asia, lost no time in continuing his propitiatory observances. No sooner was he safely ashore than he caused yet another altar to Zeus, Athena and also this time to Heracles, to be erected above the Hellespont, before proceeding inland to Troy. There, he made further offerings: to Athena, as patron goddess of the city; to King Priam on the altar of Zeus in one of his other roles as Patron of Households. At the temple of Athena he exchanged his weapons and armour for similar equipment reputed to be left over from the Trojan War, and which still hung there in the city. Thereafter these trophies are said to have preceded him wherever he advanced into battle, borne by his household troops. At Troy, too, he was crowned with gold by his sailing master, Menoetius, as well as by Chares, an Athenian inhabitant of Sigeum, a city only a mile or two south-wards along the Aegean shore from the tombs of Achilles and Patroclus.

But what caught the imagination of the classical world more than this was Alexander's gesture in laying a wreath on the tomb of Achilles itself, naming him a lucky man to have Homer as chronicler of his deeds, then running a course round the tumulus without clothes on, while at the same time his favourite, Hephaestion, performed similar obsequies at the tomb of Patroclus, which seems to suggest that even then those already long-dead heroes were thought to have been buried separately.

More than five centuries after Alexander had paid what proved to be his last respects to Achilles, the beastly Roman emperor Caracalla, who reigned from AD 211–17, emulated his disting-uished predecessor, while en route with his army from the Danube to Antioch, but in a more extravagant, less dignified fashion. Imagining himself to be Achilles reborn, presumably in some sort of frenzy, for he was apparently convinced that it was Patroclus's funeral he was attending, he bedecked the tomb of Patroclus with floral tributes and then, having ordered a hecatomb of animals as a burnt offering, added as an afterthought, to provide a visible substitute, the body of his favourite, the freed slave, Festus, who, it is said, he ordered to be slaughtered for this purpose. As a final gesture of extravagance, when the sacrificial fire was drawing nicely, Caracalla threw in, to the amusement of the onlookers, which they no doubt prudently kept under control, a lock of his own hair (with which he was already ill-provided, although he was only twenty-seven). He, too, then ran round the tumulus with nothing on, followed by his suite. His last act in the Troad was to erect a bronze statue of Achilles on Cape Sigeum. Two years later he was assassinated in northern Mesopotamia.

With such a comparative wealth of information available, it is strange that Schliemann should have identified the tomb of Festus as being within the tumulus of Uvecik, the biggest of all the Trojan tumuli, which lies some six miles south of those of Achilles and Patroclus, although when he excavated it he found nothing to support this belief; but perhaps it was no more random than its previous identification as the tomb of Aesyetes, whoever he may have been, by Jean-Baptiste Lechevalier, author of *Voyage de la Troade*, published in 1802, the first man, having begun his researches in 1785, to engage in archaeological exploration in the modern sense, as opposed to mere delving, in the Troad. It was he who constructed an attractively acceptable theory concerning the whereabouts of Homeric Troy, perching it on an eminence known as the Balli Dag, a much more impressive situation in many ways than the one that is now generally accepted. Certainly it cannot have caused greater surprise than that felt by Julius Caesar when, chasing Pompey through Asia Minor, he found himself high above the plain on the Balli Dag – the Hill of Honey, near the village of Pinabarsi, so called because bees live in a crack in the rock there – and, wading through the long grass that covered it, received a rebuke from one of the local inhabitants to the effect that did he not know that he was treading on the ghost of Hector. He was lucky not to have disturbed that of Priam as well. What was sometimes alleged to be Priam's tumulus is next to it, and that of another of his sons, Troilus, is some way off to the north, on a hill called the Khana Tepe.

We set out again from Istanbul and travelled to the mound of Hisarlik, which all but the most niggling consider to conceal the site of ancient Troy, in the same taxi and with the same driver who had made such a fuss about Gallipoli. Nearby is the village of Hisarlik, which did not exist until about 1865 when some Circassians built a few miserable habitations in what was largely a fever-ridden swamp, using stones taken from Schliemann's excavations. Now it is a place with a large mosque.

It was so early when we got there that the site was still locked up – no custodians in view, no savage dogs, the curse of the Mediterranean lands and everywhere else.

Knowing that we would be unlikely to pass this way again we scaled a wire fence with the aid of an old packing case that was lying about and fell into a compound in which the principal feature was a wooden horse even larger than I had imagined the original to be. It looked as if it would be more at home in some dim, northern forest than down here only about three and a half miles from the place where Agamemnon's Greeks had landed, and it had portholes cut in its flanks so that visitors could be photographed waving from its entrails. And down below it, outside what was called the *Casino Helen and Paris*, there was a genuine replica of a Trojan chariot in which, before being snapped inside the horse, one could be taken holding aloft a shield and brandishing a sword.

The *Casino* was not really a casino in the Mediterranean sense of the word, that is to say it was neither a gambling joint nor a brothel. Instead it sold souvenirs and picture postcards and offered refreshments including 'Trojan Wine' which, after something like 3200 years in bottle, might have been expected to have gone off a bit. In fact, this wine comes from the vineyards on the Asiatic side of the Dardanelles around Canakkale.

But in spite of all this tripe Troy and its environs was worth coming to see. Up on the mound, myriads of dark poppies, gladioli and other wild flowers flourished, and the wind that set the tall grass waving and bowing and sighed among the branches of the evergreen oaks and olives was of a less ferocious temper than that which was currently droning over eastern Thrace. Here, in the Troad, spring was already well-established.

Below the mound the Trojan plain stretched away to the Aegean. In it there were fields of maize, wheat that was already golden, and what would later be crops of cotton, in which women with their heads done up in white cloths were bent double weeding; and on the banks of the Scamander, where black poplars and willows grew, and along the edges of the irrigation ditches, shepherds trailed behind their flocks that were nibbling their way so slowly that watching them advance was like watching the hour hand of a clock on the move. It was a timeless scene, one that might have been enacted, apart perhaps from the cultivation of the cotton, a thousand, two thousand, years previously.

It had to be Troy. Even if the mound was not much more than a pimple on the plain compared with the other contender for the honour of concealing within it Homer's Troy, which is Balli Dag, even though Homer described the hill of Troy as 'beetling', 'lofty' and 'windy'; and even though the Balli Dag is twice the height of the mound at Hisarlik and *is* beetling and windy. But it is also seven miles from the sea, and there is no suitable ground for the chariot racing that Homer wrote about anywhere near it.

It had to be Troy because, as Edward Daniel Clarke wrote, while visiting the Troad in 1801 after his adventures in the Summer Harem, 'we stand with Strabo upon the very spot whence he deduced his observations concerning other objects in the district, looking down upon the *Simoïsian Plain* and viewing in front of the *city* [he is as free with his italics as Queen Victoria with her underlinings], one flowing towards Sigeum, the other towards Rhoeteum, precisely as he described them.'

Unfortunately, when Schliemann appeared on the scene in the 1880s, he came to the conclusion that Clarke had had the audacity to identify the site as that of Homeric Troy, whereas in fact all Clarke had done was identify Novum Ilium, founded in the seventh century BC on the site of it. As a result Clarke was landed, albeit in the tomb, with an erroneous attribution for which Schliemann never made amends, in spite of he himself having been proved wrong in thinking that what he had discovered was Homeric Troy. It was all very unpleasant but no more than one expects of savants once they have tasted one another's blood.

It *had* to be Troy, I felt, knowing nothing about it, completely ignorant but swayed by instinct, looking down into the mound through level after unexplained level – there are said to be forty-six different strata, excavated and cut through by innumerable archaeologists – unexplained because, mercifully, there was no one to do any explaining. I wondered vaguely whether the particular one we were looking at, which contained what looked like mussel shells, was the one that also contained the remains of Priam's bronze age city.

If only I had had with me a copy of *The American Journal of Archaeology*, XXXIX (1935), II, required reading on this subject, I would perhaps have been able to find the answer, which was more than I could armed with photostats of the relevant pages of four useful guide books I had consulted before leaving home.

Reading these extracts on site I felt my mind reeling. Fodor's *Turkey* said that Troy I, the oldest and deepest down, was 'a vestige of some 3500 years ago'; the *Guide Bleu, Turquie*, that it was founded in 3500 BC, but gave no indication as to when it might have gone into disuse; *Turkey, The Traveller's Guide* said it flourished from 3000–2500 BC; and *The Companion Guide to Turkey* that it flourished from 3000–1800 BC.

For Troy VI, which some identified as Priam's Troy, all gave 1800 BC, except Fodor, which gave 1900 BC, as the opening date. In Troy VII things became really difficult. The *Guide Bleu* didn't mention it at all. Fodor said 1300–900, BC, *The Traveller's Guide* gave 1275–1100 BC, *The Companion Guide*, 1300–1100 BC, *The Traveller's Guide* also said that Troy VII was destroyed by fire in 1240 BC.

There was also Troy VIIA, which, according to a Professor Blegen of the University of Cincinatti, was the city of Priam, destroyed by an earthquake about 1260 BC, perhaps the same earthquake which, according to *The Traveller's Guide*, destroyed Troy VI in 1275 BC and, according to Fodor, destroyed Troy VIIA in 1200 BC. There was no mention of VIIA in any of the other three guides, but *The Companion Guide* came up with a cunning post-script to the effect that Turkish archaeologists disagree with most of the foregoing and have consigned Priam's Troy to somewhere in the sub-basement of Troy VI, and that all the signposts on site are labelled accordingly, whether you like it or not. By which time I was beginning to feel like throwing myself down a Trojan elevator shaft.

After this it was a relief to go off and look at parts of Troy, or whatever it was, that were still more or less standing, as *The Companion Guide*, the most palatable work, advised one to do: to the House of Pillars to pretend that it was Priam's Palace, and to the South Gate to pretend that this was the Scaean Gate, to which Helen rushed down to watch Paris, who came off worst, fight a duel with her husband Menelaus.

Seeing us up on the mound, silhouetted against the rising sun, some of the country people working in the neighbouring fields began to converge on the base of it. where the wire fence makes further advances difficult, crying '*Kainz! Kainz!*' and, as they had for Clarke, 180 years or so previously, produced from recesses in their everyday, ragged working garments rather more worn and indistinct examples of the medals that had given him the necessary boost to identify the site of Novum Ilium. Soon we were doing a brisk, illicit business through the fence, confident that no modern copies could possibly be manufactured at the prices that were being asked. It looked like visiting day at a prison.

By the time we were ready to leave the site it was officially open, and at the *Casino* we bought a copy of *Greek Coins in Canakkale*, by Tayan Sevil, Archaeologist, in the hope of identifying our newly acquired loot, most of which looked as if it had been left on a railroad track and run over by a series of trains. This book, which cost 30 Turkish lira, was translated by a Mr Hasan Ediz.

'I am grateful to Hasan Ediz for his helps of translation into Enlglish,' Mr Sevil wrote in his introduction. 'What is coin: it is a kind of metallic money, using easily, that is guaranteed preciously by the government's official coinage.'

We were grateful to discover that one of our coins might, with a great stretching of the imagination, have had a representation of Dionysos on one side of it.

'Dionysos,' said a footnote to Mr Sevil's book, 'was the son of Semele who was daughter of Zeus and Kadmo, king of Thebai. According to legend of birth, Semele copulated with Zeus but she didn't believe the strength of that god whom made love and so, she was smitten by thunderbold and died. Zeus took the seven-months baby from her womb and pit his calf until the second birth.' Which last, like so much of Greek mythology, was enough to obliterate thoughts of breakfast.

After this we dismissed our taximan and sent him, and his too-much-loved taxi, back to Istanbul, and continued our journey through the Troad by bus.

The bus, painted to resemble some rare and exotic insect, was packed with country people returning to their villages from the market at Canakkale. All were heavily laden with shopping and one or two had wicker baskets containing chickens that had failed to get sold. The birds looked despondent, as if they knew they had let their owners down.

All the ladies on board were dressed in their best for this outing but their clothes were a bit disappointing for romantic travellers with their feet only recently planted on the shores of Asia: pale, drab, factory-made gabardine topcoats that looked as if they had all come off the same production line, long, baggy Muslim bloomers made of nylon, or else frumpy skirts worn with grey lisle stockings and clumpy shoes, which, apart from the bloomers, was until recently the sort of uniform English nannies used to be dressed in. A few of the young ones used make-up but they could all have done with a bit. The matrons were mostly pear-shaped, and when one of them got off at a request stop she backed down the aisle in order to save her shopping from being squashed, sweeping everything, hens and baskets and any people who happened to be in the way before her with a rock-hard, corseted bottom. When writers describe, as some do, a town as being 'bustling', what now springs to mind is a village in the Troad with pear-shaped ladies backing into one another and rebounding like dodgem cars in a fun-fair.

The men, who were mostly slimmer, not having been subjected to yearly pregnancies, all wore the shiny black suits and peaked caps, decreed by Kemal Atatürk, the great soldier, hero of Gallipoli and founder of the Turkish Republic in 1923, as part of his programme of westernization, a uniform still worn by the majority of the male working population in rural areas of Turkey.

Everyone was very friendly. Porcelain faces, which Genghiz Khan would have found unremarkable, cracked into smiles when we boarded the vehicle at Troy. There was none of the hurried veiling and twittering among the ladies which always puts the male, non-Muslim traveller in Muslim countries in the difficult-to-refute position of being thought to be excited by ladies dressed in grey gabardine topcoats, lisle stockings and clumpy shoes.

Instead they asked shyly but eagerly after our health and where we came from, and when we answered, '*Ben Ingilizce, Londonen,*' which was as near as we could get with our midget phrase book to 'I am English, from London,' those nearest answered, '*Allah razi olah!*' ('Praise be to God!') and budged up a bit to give us more room on the seat we were sitting on and were lucky to get, which was the worst one, over the back axle.

Soon this piece of intelligence worked its way up the bus and some sixty heads swivelled round to get a look at these outlandish beings. In spite of being the centre of interest it was more fun than being locked up in the back of a Bel-Air taxi in solitary splendour with a house-proud driver in charge.

It was when we were asked where we were going and said, 'Alexandria Troas, *Inshallah!*' ('if God wills!') that we ran into difficulty, as none of them had apparently ever heard of it, that is with the exception of the driver up front who had already sold us tickets to go there (and he was keeping the information about its whereabouts to himself), and one old man wearing what looked like a sawn-off fez with the remains of what had once been a green chiffon turban wrapped around it, giving him a holy air. 'What they mean,' the old man said eventually to the rest of the passengers in a loud voice, for by this time the bus was in an uproar with conflicting theories about our ultimate destination being bandied about, 'is Harabeler, Eski Stambul, not this Greek-sounding place at all.' 'Aha! *Harabeler! Eski Stambul!*' they said, nodding their heads; and from now on they looked at us with the slightly incredulous air with which country people everywhere who live surrounded by ruins, which to them are nothing more than stone-ridden obstacles in the way of cultivation, or at the best afford temporary shelter to themselves and their animals from rain and sun, tend to regard those who have made what to them are unimaginably long, pointless and costly journeys in order to view them. In other words, they thought we were barmy.

After this painless inquisition we were allowed to relax and look out of one of the open windows of the bus – open because there was no longer any glass in it – as it roared down the winding road through the varied landscapes of the Troad, scrubby wilderness with pines growing in it, fields interspersed with valonia oaks in which the same sort of people as those on the bus, who had been working in them since first light, had taken refuge for a rest beneath their carts or in the inkpots of shadow beneath the trees. For by now it was a fine, warm morning without a cloud in the sky. Then we crossed the River Scamander, in which a number of saucy-looking laundresses were walloping clothes on stones under the willow trees and shouting to one another with cheerful, coarse voices, just as the Trojan women must have done.

All the other passengers with the exception of ourselves got down at a small place called Geyikli with cries of '*Allahah ismarladik!*' ('Goodbye!') and '*Selam aleikum!*' ('Prosperity and Peace attend you!') to which we replied correctly, as the persons staying on the bus, not getting down from it, forewarned by our phrase book, '*Güle, Güle!*' ('Goodbye!') and '*Aleikum selam!*' We too would have liked to disembark. We were hungry and thirsty.

Finally, the bus ground to a halt at a place called Odunluk Iskelesi, stopped sufficiently long for us to get down, then vanished in the direction of Geyikli. This was the end of the road. Beyond it was a jetty, jutting into Besika Bay in the Aegean, and a few miles beyond that was Tenedos, a boring-looking island even from a distance (which often lends enchantment to the view of otherwise boring-looking islands).

Odunluk Iskelesi was not exactly a feast for the eye, either. Apart from the jetty, from which the ferry, presumably disregarding the bus connection, had just left for Tenedos, it consisted of some dusty-looking trees, a couple of tea houses, neither of which apparently served tea or anything else at this particular time of day, except bottled water which, in Turkey, often means water bottled by an old man sitting in the middle of nowhere by a tap. Outside tourist resorts there was no coffee to be had in Turkey at this time because of a lack of foreign currency with which to buy it.

The only other source of refreshment was down on the shore in the direction of what had been the port of Alexandria Troas, a decrepit restaurant with an unshaven owner and nothing to eat in it except a long dead fish in a fridge.

Topped up with bottled water, still breakfastless apart from some stale bread and slightly queasy from what we had seen in the refrigerator – we had been looking forward to a degustation of freshly landed fish, not a visit to a fish mortuary – we set off inland for the city of Alexandria Troas.

Soon we found ourselves imbrangled and lost, as had innumerable travellers before us, in what had once been a dense forest of valonia oaks and was now a series of groves so extensive, without being particularly lofty, that although the city was said to have walls six miles long and itself covered 1000 acres it was perfectly possible, as we now demonstrated, to walk into it through one of the now enormous gaps in the walls and walk out through a similar gap on the far side, without, apart from tripping over some low-lying remains or else bumping into something shrouded in vegetation which loomed unidentifiable overhead, seeing much of Alexandria Troas at all.

It was Antigonus the One-Eyed, one of Alexander's commanders, who named it Antigonia. He became Satrap, governor, of Phrygia and, after Alexander's death in 323 BC, commander of the army in Asia. A very able general and ruler, he was eventually defeated by a coalition of what had been his fellow generals, consisting of Cassander in Macedonia, Ptolemy in Egypt, Lysimachus in Thrace and Seleucus in Babylonia, at the battle of Ipsus in Phrygia in 301 BC. In 299 BC, twenty-four years after his death, to honour the memory of Alexander, Lysimachus, his former companion in arms and successor, re-named Antigonia Alexandria Troas.

It was not always so impenetrable. Seventeenth- and early eighteenth-century visitors record that they found themselves perambulating on a relatively open site, one that rose gently inland from the shore of Besika Bay, where the remains of the ancient harbour walls could be seen, interspersed with cornfields, vineyards, olive groves and orchards of fruit trees, above which rose the still colossal ruins, all soon to be more or less hidden by the all-embracing vegetation and the oak woods: the walls with turrets disposed at intervals along them, the innumerable temples, the great aqueduct which terminated at the Baths of Herodes Atticus, and the theatre which overlooked the sea and Tenedos, so that at evening the spectators seated in it would have been bathed in the rays of the setting sun.

But even as these intrepid visitors looked out over this magnificent, if melancholy, spectacle, braving the robbers who infested it and the feverish agues of the plain of the Troad, every hour of daylight, every day, at the same time as it was disappearing from view, it was also diminishing, however imperceptibly, in size.

Of all the cities of classical times on the shores of Turkey, Alexandria Troas, because of its convenient situation – an easy journey by sea to Constantinople – was perhaps the most pillaged. All the others were ruined and thrown down by barbarians and natural cataclysms, but in most of them the stones remained more or less where they fell, principally because, apart from those precious objects removed by discerning individuals such as Clarke himself (who sent the lower part of a marble pillar with an inscription in Greek to England from the vicinity of Callifat in much the same way as today one would send a picture postcard), the distances that separated these sites from the great cities of the Mediterranean that were still, as it were, on their feet, made it impractical to transport them thither.

If only it could have been so at Alexandria Troas! If only it had never had to merit its nickname, Eski (Old) Stambul. Early in the seventeenth century the English travellers George Sandys* and the wonderfully eccentric Thomas Coryate,* on his way to India, both witnessed the wholesale plundering of the city for stone.

This shipping away of marble to Constantinople, some of the columns and pillars to be incorporated more or less intact in the fabric of mosques, themselves often noble works of art, was not the only traffic. At the same time as it was going on, the complete destruction of these great, some of them enormous, pieces of marble had also been taking place in order to turn them into cannon-balls, an industry brought to a fine art in the latter half of the eighteenth

---

* George Sandys, *A Relation of a Iorney begun An. Dom. 1610*, 4th edn, 1647.
* Thomas Coryate, *Purchas his Pilgrimes*, 1625.

century by Kaptan Paşa Hasan, whose cannon-ball manufactory, using stone and marble columns for the larger projectiles, sarcophagi for the smaller bores, accelerated the consumption of these artefacts. They had been used for this purpose for centuries, probably since the siege and fall of Constantinople.

Lady Mary Wortley Montagu saw enormous cannon-balls being cut at Alexandria Troas in 1718, and they were still being made there as late as 1833, by which time only very few columns remained intact, and then only because of their great size or the remoteness of their situation.

One such projectile, fired across the Narrows of the Dardanelles in 1769, weighed 1100 pounds, while the prototype made in Edirne in January 1453 for the siege of Constantinople by the Hungarian gunsmith Urban weighed 600 pounds and was fired a distance of a mile from a bronze cannon with a barrel twenty-six feet long, at which point it buried itself six feet in the ground.

The last of the great edifices still to be seen in Alexandria Troas at the beginning of the nineteenth century, the Baths of Herodes Atticus – still to this day the only structure of really imposing proportions remaining – was badly damaged by an earthquake in the winter of 1809–10. The Great Aqueduct of Herodes fell or was otherwise destroyed before 1812, probably by the same earthquake.

Before this earthquake the truly enormous wreckage of the Baths was used as a seamark by unnumbered generations of seafaring men who referred to it as the Palace of Priam. 'Vulgarly termed it *The Palace of Priam*,' Clarke wrote severely, 'from an erroneous notion, prevalent in the writings of early travellers . . . [taking the opportunity to name a number of these offenders] that *Alexandria Troas* was the *Ilium* of Homer.'

One who fell into this grievous, almost unforgivable error, another eccentric of similar stamp to Thomas Coryate, was William Lithgow, who had himself recorded by an artist back at home in England for the frontispiece of his splendid book *The Totall Discourse, of the Rare Adventures, and painfull Peregrinations of long nineteene yeares travayles, from Scotland to the most famous kingdomes in Europe, Asia and Africa etc.* (1632), and for posterity, standing in the midst of the ruins of Alexandria Troas, as imagined by the artist, and calling them 'The Ruins of Ilium with the Tombs of Priam and Hecuba'. This was in 1610 or 1611.

Even Robert Wood, a very learned traveller indeed, who visited the city in 1750 and left a delightful record of this haunting, haunted place in his *Diaries* and in an essay identified it with Troy, was, as an unfriendly critic wrote, '. . . quite bewildered with Troy; converting the whole into a mass of confusion'.

As a result Wood got a terrible ticking off from Gibbon, who described him in a memorable footnote to Chapter XVII of *The Decline and Fall of the Roman Empire*, as 'an author who in general seems to have disappointed the expectation of the public as a critic, and still more as a traveller. He had visited the banks of the Hellespont; he had read Strabo; he ought to have consulted the Roman itineraries; how was it possible for him to confound Ilium and Alexandria Troas, two cities which were sixteen miles distant from one another?'*

All that warm afternoon, assailed by hunger, but with no means of satisfying it, we wandered beneath the trees among what was left of Alexandria Troas, much of it hidden by long, dry grass. It was an eerie place. Not a bird sang and there was no sound apart from the droning of what would become in a few weeks a hell of superabundant insect life. We met no one except a young man herding goats who gave us a drink of water from a greasy-looking bottle, but was disinclined for conversation, as well he might be, apparently doomed to herd goats for the rest of his life in the shadow of the valonia oaks.

Fortunately, there were none of the savage dogs which Richard Chandler, in his *Travels in Asia Minor*, described as attacking his guides when he visited the place in August 1765; no wandering Turcomans with their black tents pitched among the ruins; no foxes, no partridges, no bats in the vaults below the Baths (a vignette of which adorns Edward Clarke's *Travels*) because there were no vaults any more, and for the same reason no more of the bandits who used to share them with the bats.

We never found the remains of the Great Theatre – it sounds as if we were not really trying – the diameter of which was 252 feet, where we would have found enough subterranean vaults, apparently, and bats inhabiting them, to satisfy the most romantic tastes; neither did we see the great columns, twenty-seven feet in length and more than four feet in diameter, which Chandler saw somewhere to

---

* Gibbon made amends in a footnote in Chap. LI in which he praises Wood's descriptions of the ruins of Baalbec and Palmyra.

the north-west of the Baths, nor the numerous sarcophagi to the north-west of it, one of which he measured and found to be eleven feet long and six feet wide.

'Mottraye,' he wrote, 'when on the spot, caused one of these tombs to be opened; and found in it two sculls, which crumbled to dust on being touched.'

Nor did we discover, outside the walls but reached by a paved way, 'the largest granite pillar in the world, excepting the famous Column of *Alexandria* in *Egypt*, which it much resembles,' described by Clarke.

It was to this column that Clarke's Greek servant, 'laughing immoderately', led him with the words, 'As you are pleased with the sight of columns, here is one large enough to gratify your utmost expectations.' It was a single shaft fashioned from one entire stone, without base or capital, and it was thirty-seven feet eight inches long, five feet three inches in diameter at the base and four feet five inches at the summit. No nineteenth- or twentieth-century traveller refers to this colossal column, so one must assume that it attracted the attention of the Kaptan Paşa, or some other cannon-ball fancier. It can scarcely have disintegrated completely although Clarke himself was far from sanguine about the lasting qualities of granite, some of that which he had seen exhibiting a very advanced state of decomposition. All we saw remaining of what must have been one of the larger repositories of columns in the Mediterranean was a number of huge, broken monoliths at what had been the port of the city down by the shore, shattered, presumably, in the attempt to transport them to Constantinople.

It was not until after we returned to England and I read about Alexandria Troas that I realized something that all travellers on the shores of the Mediterranean eventually recognize, how much we had missed simply by being unobservant and how much more by being born 150 years or so too late.

From Alexandria Troas we continued southwards along the Aegean shores of the Mediterranean. Great tracts of the coast of Turkey between the Dardanelles and Antalya on the southern Mediterranean coast are in much the same condition as the French and Italian Rivieras must have been before the coming of the railway and the Grand Hotel, a state of affairs that will not endure much longer now that a newly-completed coast road makes it possible to drive uninterruptedly all the way along it to Antakya (Antioch) near the Syrian border.

Here, in early spring, we had the feeling that what we saw was for our pleasure alone. There were no guides to expound and interpret or shoo us back on board a coach so that we could get on to the next place, because at this season there were no coaches. Even the custodians, that is if there were any, had only recently emerged from winter torpor and went home before sunset, leaving us to contemplate their mostly unlockable ruins in company with the bats and owls. Visiting the ruins, which are almost too abundant, time ceased to have any meaning.

After the difficulties we had experienced looking down into the various levels of Troy from Troy I to VIIA we ceased to care what epoch any particular remain dated from. Faced with Assos, for example, a ruined city on the southern shores of the Troad, over-looking Lesbos to the south of it, it was impossible to know what one was looking at. Assos is believed to be Padasos, a city founded during the Trojan Wars and sacked by Achilles. In 1000 BC it was colonized by Aeolians from Lesbos – who themselves came from Boeotia in central Greece – and was successively occupied or dominated by Lydians, Persians, Greeks, Persians again – Alexander of Macedon delivered it – Romans, Byzantines, Muslims, Crusaders, Muslims again.

The acropolis is crowned with the ruins of a Greek temple and an Ottoman mosque which has a gateway that once formed part of a Byzantine church which was itself constructed with bits of a Greek temple. The city is surrounded by medieval curtain walls and towers built with stones originally hewn by Greeks, some of which resemble huge bolsters. Roman tomb chests lie around in picturesque disorder. It was visited by St Paul and St Luke and the people became Christians. Yet according to the author of the locally published guide book, 'during its long existence it never played an important political role in history'. In such circumstances perhaps the visitor may be excused for satisfying what Rose Macaulay described as *Ruinenlust* by enjoying them simply as a highly romantic spectacle.

In search of ruins on these Aegean and Mediterranean shores, many of them far more ruinous and inaccessible than Assos, we fought our way through jungles of vegetation, thickets of thorn and laurel, dense groves of evergreen oaks and, more pleasurably, wandered among endless beds of pink oleanders which, as the weather grew warmer as we moved south, were everywhere in bloom, and we were attacked by hornets and visited ruins built among Chinese-type boulders which rise above the olive groves, where storks and herons drift across reedy inlets and stone sarcophagi lie on the dazzling shingle at the water's edge like stranded white, dug-out boats.

We lingered by green watermeadows in which anemones and giant white daisies grew and drifted through fields of fennel, which goes well with ruins, to find, somewhere east of Antalya, a solitary archway, so fragile and so close to collapse after a couple of thousand years or more that one was tempted to stay on there and be present at the moment of its fall. Everything we saw was broken, but beautiful or memorable in some way or other because it was of stone or marble, not cement or reinforced concrete. We saw shattered aqueducts, forests of columns thrown down as if a whirlwind had roared through a fossil forest, and buildings already damaged by some cataclysm being crushed still more by giant growths of ivy, as if they were being squeezed by boa-constrictors. We saw stadiums and theatres, some of them filled with fragments of friezes and statuary, the rubble left by earthquakes and Goths and other producers of ruins and rejected by eighteenth- and nineteenth-century gentlemen, down here on a visit, as being too ruinous to be crated up and sent home. We saw bath houses hewn from single blocks of stone and a vast necropolis in which tomb-chests, some of them eleven feet long, stove in and with their lids left askew by grave robbers, looked as if some giant had gone berserk among them.

As we travelled through these realms of the now ancient dead, our pockets began to silt up with the debris of their various civilizations – shards, bits of bone, splinters of marble statuary on which parts of the folds of a garment could be seen, fragments of iridescent glass, nothing ever whole, not even a coin. The bone was probably part of a sheep. In this endless quest one of us turned over a marble paving stone which showed every sign of having lain where it was for centuries. Under it, where there was no apparent exit or entrance, was a green and orange, diamond-patterned toad.

Sometimes small boys or shepherds wearing thick, rigid cloaks of whitish felt which had shoulders two feet wide, designed to protect them against the winter blasts, cloaks that made them look as if they had taken up residence in a sarcophagus, would appear from nowhere and hiss '*Kainz, Kainz!*' at us in a conspiratorial manner, the traffic in any sort of antiquity being illegal. Sometimes they were erratically-shaped Byzantine coins, most of them defaced, some of them beautiful, silver-coloured, with bearded gods or rulers on them. 'Copies,' we used to say at first, trying to look severe and knowledgeable. '*Karpiz, Karpiz*,' they all replied, the shepherds revealing awful teeth, not understanding but happy to agree with anything. But they were not copies. If they had been, they would have had to ask more for them. It was a pity that neither of us was mad about coins.

The best ruins were those in which archaeologists, those great ruiners of ruins, had either delved briefly without success or appeared not to have delved at all. Among those presumably too uninteresting to suffer their attentions are the remains of a temple dedicated to Vulcan which stands high above the sea north-east of the Lycian Olympus which, submerged in greenery at the mouth of a rocky gorge on the Mediterranean shore, is perhaps the most romantically situated of all the ruined cities. There on the mountainside burn the fires of Chimaera in an area of calcinated limestone, sixteen of them in all, fuelled by natural gas, overlooking the distant sea from which they can still be seen at night, just as they were by fishermen in the time of Homer and Strabo.

An Encounter with Nomads

The Mediterranean coast of Turkey is very long, and as it is five hundred miles by road from Antalya to Antakya (Antioch), on the Syrian border, we decided to go part of the way from Antalya by ship. This was on a Saturday in February, what passes for winter on these shores. Flowers were beginning to bloom everywhere. Spring was in the air and we had already seen a pair of heavily-armed soldiers whose job it was to protect a nearby ruined city from the locals who augment their slender incomes by digging up the past and selling it in season to the carriage trade, drifting happily among the remains hand in hand with freshly plucked wild anemones between their teeth.

It took almost an entire Saturday morning in Antalya to book a double-berth cabin for Monday with Turkish Maritime Lines who operate a service from Istanbul to Mersin on the coast west of Adana which stops at various places on the way. But it was not until we came to pay for the tickets that we found that they had been made out not for the following Monday, two days hence, but for a Monday in June when the first sailing of the year from Antalya would take place, which was in approximately four months' time.

In view of this we decided not to wait, but to continue by car, although we had enjoyed hanging about in Antalya.

On the travertine cliffs on which the town stands there is an enormous Roman tower that resembles the Mausoleum of Hadrian, which has nothing to do with the fact that it was Hadrian who strengthened the walls in AD 130 while on a visit commemorated by a triumphal gateway, and in the museum there are some fine sarcophagi and the jaw bone of St Nicholas, otherwise Santa Claus. There are many mosques constructed by the Seljuk Turks who took Antalya from the Byzantines in 1207, one of them with a fluted minaret, and an equally old *hamam* which is still functioning, some fine old wooden houses, a nice bazaar (or as nice as bazaars now can be in an age of mass production), and on the other side of the main road from it there is a restaurant which has on its menu the sort of items that make travel fun: 'Crem of Eggolant, Fried Shrips with Spectral Sauce, Viol Rip Shop and Rose Bif', followed by 'Sweat and Firutes', all washed down with 'Bear' if so desired. And it has a very picturesque port off which until recently ships used to lie loading timber and cotton. Now they load it at a newly-built port five miles away to the west at the end of a much photographed beach beyond which rise the mountains which form the south-western extremity of the Taurus Range.

Having visited the ruined cities in the Pamphylian Plain, of which Antalya had been one of the seaports, and as a result having contracted a bad attack of ruin indigestion – for which an effective cure would be twenty-four hours in New York – we found ourselves confronted on our way east by yet more ruins, the whole of this coast being an extended scrap-heap full of the inexhaustible debris of the past with more ancient remains than Britain has filling stations.

Long before we reached Okukcular, a hamlet on the shore just west of Alanya, some sixty miles east of Antalya, the weather had broken. Rain had fallen in torrents accompanied by thunder and lightning. By now it was late afternoon and although the rain had stopped the sky was still as black as night. Occasionally flashes of lightning illuminated the scene, accompanied by thunder. Six miles inshore from Okukcular was Alarahan.

Abandoned, dilapidated but not ruined even after the passage of some 750 years – its construction had taken place in the illustrious reign of the Seljuk Sultan Alaeddin Keykubad – the *han*, a caravan-serai on what had been an important caravan route, stood high on the left bank of the Alara River, which was now roaring seawards in spate. A masterpiece of the stonemason's art, like all Seljuk *hans* it was a fortification as well as being a caravanserai. Its walls, which were twenty feet high, enclosed a courtyard in which camels and other beasts of burden could be accommodated, entered by a magnificent gateway from which the gates had long since disappeared. Around this courtyard there was a dark warren of storerooms and cells for the accommodation of the drivers and what had been a mosque in which they could perform their devotions, all either flooded, or deep in mud, and tenanted by bats.

This was one of a chain of *hans* which awaited the caravans at the end of each day's march on the seven-day journey from the Seljuk capital at Konya on the Anatolian Plateau to Alanya, the Seljuk port on the Mediterranean, which followed a spectacular route across the Taurus Range, each one of them a minor masterpiece of Seljuk architecture. The roof was flat, grass-grown and riddled with gaping holes, what had once been primitive chimneys to let smoke out, through which it was only too easy to fall into the depths below.

The Seljuks, pre-Ottoman Turks, were originally nomads from central Asia. They first set up a Sultanate in Persia whose rule extended as far eastwards as Herat. In the latter part of the eleventh century they established themselves briefly in western Anatolia, to the north of Cappadocia, but were defeated there in 1097 during the First Crusade by the Crusaders, who gave back the territory they had taken to the Byzantine Emperor, Alexius I Comnenus. Later, in the twelfth century, the Seljuks made Konya their capital, and there they set up what was called the Sultanate of Rum, which endured until 1242 or 1243, when they were overrun by the Mongols who had arrived in eastern Anatolia two years previously, after which they became, nominally at least, their vassals, although their Sultans continued to rule until 1308.

The Seljuk period sounds as if it might have been slightly more agreeable to live in than most other periods of Muslim occupation of the eastern Mediterranean lands. Although Muslims, they were tolerant of other religions and their own women went unveiled in public. Mysticism flourished and Konya became the seat of the *Mevlevi tarikat*, otherwise the Whirling Dervishes, whose founder was Celahedin Rumi, one of the great Muslim mystics.

The Seljuks were remarkable builders: of mosques, religious colleges, *hamams*, the cylindrical tombs with pointed roofs called *türbe*, and of roads and *hans*. And they were the first to introduce glazed tiles into Anatolia.

At Alanya, their port on the Mediterranean, which Sultan Keykubad, who had taken it from the Armenians, also used as his winter quarters instead of freezing in Konya up on the plateau, he employed a Syrian military engineer, Ali Bey of Aleppo, to make the fortress rock, which is nearly 800 feet above the sea, impregnable. Ali Bey also built the shipyards and arsenal (known as the *tersane*) in tunnels running nearly a hundred yards into the base of the rock, and an enormous octagonal red tower, the Kizil Kule, to defend the outer harbour. As at Antalya, their other seaport, they carried on an extensive trade with the Aegean Islands, the eastern shores of the Mediterranean and with Alexandria.

The view from the roof was memorable. Immediately beyond the *han*, where all that remained of a Seljuk bridge that had once spanned the river was a single abutment, the road ended at the foot of the Taurus Mountains which here rose from the coastal plain in what would have been an unbroken wall if the river had not chosen this particular spot to break through it in a deep gorge, with the caravan route to Konya running along the mountainside above it. Rising in the mouth of this gorge was an immense rock many hundreds of feet high with a castle on its summit, to which a series of curtain walls wriggled their way up over the bare rock like giant, fossilized snakes. There was no visible means of getting to this castle – no gateway, no staircases, not even a footpath.

Down near the river bank opposite the *han* a goatherd had built himself a hut and by doing so had become, simply because he was there, whether officially appointed or not, *de facto* guardian of both the *han* and the castle.

We sat outside his hut in a freezing wind that had now begun to blow, together with a Turkish gentleman who had also come here to see the *han* and who spoke excellent French, drinking sweet tea and eating honey mixed with raisins, an unimaginably delicious dish concocted by Yürüks (the word means wanderer), nomads and semi-nomads of Turkoman ancestry whose women, some of them astonishingly beautiful, are renowned weavers of rugs and saddle-bags. The Yürüks, of whom there are large numbers throughout Asia Minor, spend the winter in the plains, when possible the plains near the Mediterranean, and in summer migrate with their herds and flocks to the *yaylas*, their camps in the high mountain pastures, where they live in goat-hair tents.

'He says that will be 800 Turkish liras,' the Turkish gentleman said when he had finished eating the mixture and were feeling slightly sick.

'Isn't that rather a lot?'

'It is a lot. It is much too much. It is disgraceful. I shall tell him so.'

A prolonged conversation ensued.

'He is a Yürük, although he no longer wanders. He now says he is ashamed of having asked so much. He now says he wants nothing at all, and will also take us to the castle. I think we should give him 400 liras for the tea and the mixture, which is also too much, and another 400 liras and some cigarettes for the castle, which is about right. He says we should leave immediately as it is going to snow and if it freezes it is a dangerous route. He also hopes that we have a torch as part of the way to it is very dark.'

The part of the way to it which was very dark was a steep tunnel, in parts nearly vertical, impenetrably black and with hundreds of steps cut in it which the heavy rain had turned into a series of waterfalls that made us extremely wet. Eventually we emerged from it into what had been the lower ward of the castle, where there were some water cisterns cut in the rock. Here, we were already several hundred feet above the river. From it what was left of a track, after innumerable rock falls had obliterated entire sections of it, led to the foot of the final pyramid on which the castle stood.

The last part was a rock face up which we hauled ourselves with the aid of spiky bushes. As the Yürük said, it would have been no place to be if it became glazed with ice.

At the top we had expected to find a walled courtyard with living accommodation leading off it, similar to the *han*, but there was no room for anything like that. The mountain simply ended in a sharp point like a pencil with a sort of guard house and a tiny domed building stuck on top of it.

Up here in the clouds, with the snowflakes already beginning to whirl about it, it was difficult to imagine the determination that must have been required by the Seljuks not only to build such a fortress in such a place but to build this little building at the top. What was it for, this once elegant little building, with a dome, the inside of which had originally been a brilliant cobalt blue, as minute fragments of colour which we found among the plaster on the floor testified, and so small that it could not have held more than three people at any one time with any degree of comfort? Had it been a miniature mosque, a shrine to some saint, or had it once been a pleasure dome to which the commandant of the castle retired with a couple of companions when things got too much for him in the lower ward of the castle far below? The Turkish gentleman didn't know, no one in the Tourist Office at Alanya knew when we asked there subsequently, the Yürük didn't know, or care, and the only guide book which specifically mentioned Alarahan got all mixed up about it.

East and west of Alanya sand beaches stretch away to what looks like infinity; but much of the coast immediately behind them has been ruined for ever by ribbon development. If such indiscriminate building continues, it will soon be impossible for the traveller to see the Mediterranean at all on the entire seventy miles or so of coast between Antalya and Alanya, just as it has been impossible to see it on great tracts of the French and Italian Rivieras since long before the First World War.

Eastwards of Alanya, at the far end of one of the long beaches, the plain ended at the foot of some outliers of the Taurus and the road climbed above the coast which is steep and rocky. We were now in Cilicia. On these mountainsides goats whose luxuriant coats have from time immemorial provided the hair used to weave the tents of the Yürüks eked out a living. In this region, the inhabitants, who are very poor, live in low, single-storey cabins, and here they cut terraces one above the other in the cliff-sides, which they use not – as they do in some other parts of the Mediterranean, such as the Cinque Terre, on the Ligurian coast of Italy – for cultivating the vine, but for growing bananas which must be, with the spume of winter gales drenching them, a salt-cured variety. Here at Selinus, now the fishing village of Gazipaşa, in AD 117, the Emperor Trajan died while returning to Rome, having quelled a revolt in southern Mesopotamia and after an expedition against the Parthians in Armenia, a year of ferment in the Empire when the Jews rebelled everywhere on the eastern shores of the Mediterranean, in Cyrene, in what is now Libya, in Egypt, in Cyprus, in the Levant and in the Holy Land.

Further on, near Silifke, in 1190, the Emperor Barbarossa was drowned in the gorge of the Calycadnus River, now called the

Goksü, while on his way to the Third Crusade. Unpickled, his corpse was carried on to Antioch by the Duke of Swabia, to be interred in the cathedral there. His death so upset some of the German knights that many of them turned back and the Crusade fizzled out.

By now it was snowing hard, but fortunately here on the coast it didn't settle. Meanwhile up in the mountains and beyond them on the Anatolian plateau the temperature fell to −16°C, into the −30°s in the Palandoken Mountains up in northern Anatolia around Erzurum where the bears live and the wolves come down from the mountains in search of sustenance. Here on the coast we visited a café built on stilts over the water in which young male Turks, identically moustached, sat gloomily listening to the booming of the surf beneath it which threatened to wash it away, at the same time watching a powerful waterspout which had appeared offshore, spinning out their glasses of tea and talking about Germany. What with snow, thunder and lightning and now a waterspout, 1983 looked as if it was going to be an *annus mirabilis*.

'Come to the Mediterranean for vinter sunshine,' Wanda said.

Night fell unnaturally early because of the weather and all we could see in the light of the headlamps or when the lightning flashed, momentarily illuminating the Mediterranean crashing on the rocks below, were the snowflakes hurtling towards the windscreen like tracer bullets. One particularly powerful discharge lit up a couple of ghostly-looking castles, one on a headland, the other standing in what looked like an inlet of the sea offshore. These were the Corcyrian Castles, built in 1151 by the Rubenids, an Armenian dynasty who founded a Christian kingdom in Cilicia and married their daughters to the rulers of Crusader kingdoms in the Levant, which was extinguished in 1375 by the Karamanoglu Turks who took Konya from the Seljuks.

We spent the night at Mersin, and early the following morning followed the road through the Cilician Plain, the principal city of which is Adana, the fourth most populous city in Turkey, where we did not linger either. The plain is really a large delta created by the silt brought down from the Taurus by three rivers, all of them more famous by the names bestowed on them in antiquity than they are today. All of them, like the Po, are wayward and capricious, forming new estuaries just as the local pilots had learned their way about the earlier ones, forming large lagoons which teemed with fish, swans, pelicans, geese, duck and turtles which they then equally capriciously obliterated at the moment when the local inhabitants, having pondered the idea, perhaps for centuries, of fishing in them, had finally built themselves flat-bottomed boats, but leaving behind just enough water to turn them into malaria-ridden swamps inhabited by innumerable frogs whose incessant croaking ensured, even if the mosquitoes failed to make their presence felt, that no one got a decent night's sleep in these parts of the Cilician Plain.

The first of these rivers, the Cydnus – the other two are the ancient Sarus, now the Seyhan, and the Pyramus, now the Ceghan – flows through the outskirts of the town of Tarsus. Although it is a very pretty river above the town, where there is a series of water-falls, here, where the main Mersin–Adana highway crossed it, it was difficult with snow falling intermittently to think of this as one of the arcadian reaches of a river up which Cleopatra, dressed as Aphrodite, a bit one imagines like Diana Cooper at her best, but darker, floated in her purple-sailed galley on her way to lay Mark Antony in the aisles at Tarsus in the autumn of 41 BC, fanned by what Plutarch described as 'pretty boys bedight like cupids' and propelled by oarsmen who pulled together on silver oars, encouraged not by the whistle of the lash descending on their backs but by the sound of pipes and harps and flutes; a spectacle that would have given St Paul, who was a native of Tarsus and spent the first fourteen years of his life here before being sent to study in Jerusalem, something to write about if he had only been born a century or so earlier.

Travelling through what to anyone brought up in England would seem like the endless expanses of what is known as the Cukurova, the Sunken Plain, but to a North American or a Russian would be more like a large back garden, seeing flocks of sheep and herds of goats nibbling their way along the verges of the dead straight road, seeing an occasional grass-grown tumulus housing the remains of some long-forgotten king or chieftain, rising from the endless cotton fields and here and there a small village, or a bigger one with a mosque and minaret, standing at the foot of the Misis Dagh, the miniature mountain range to the south of the road that separates the Sunken Plain from the Gulf of Iskenderun, it was difficult to believe that as long ago as 1500 BC, when it was occupied by the Hittites,* this was one of the most populous regions of Anatolia. And it continued to be so until fever and malaria, which have been such a scourge almost until the present day, brought about its depopulation. Now, once more efficiently irrigated with the help of concrete aqueducts which stretch out in every direction across the plain, it has become prosperous again, its fertile soil yielding enormous crops of citrus fruits and cotton.

At Toprakkale, about forty miles east of Adana, a village which takes its name from a nearby Byzantine castle, the E5, a road which begins at Calais, turns sharp right for Iskenderun and Antakya, beyond which, at Yaylodagi, where it ceases to be the E5, it crosses out of Turkey en route for Latakia in Syria, and beyond that for Tripoli in Lebanon. If you go straight on at Toprakkale without turning right you end up at Mosul in Iraq. Both roads are awful; infested with great stinking lorries and Turkish traffic police who set up road blocks all along them to harass their drivers, some of whom can do with a bit of harassment.

By now there was a lull in the bad weather. The black clouds had rolled away seawards, taking with them their loads of snow, which they were now probably dropping in the Mediterranean and on Cyprus in the form of rain, and although they were still thick and threatening over the Taurus, here in the plain the sun shone down from a cloudless sky.

A mile or so south of Toprakkale the road passed through a gap in what in the south-western USA would be described as a *mesa*, a steep-sided, flat-topped escarpment in this case composed of rocks and earth and shingle which looked as if it might have been thrown up by some colossal flash flood. Here, we left the Cilician Plain and entered the Plain of Issus.

It was a romantic spot, at any rate for anyone with a spark of romance in their make-up. Above us on a mound loomed Toprakkale, a castle built by the Byzantine Emperor, Nicephorus II Phocas, in AD 969 on his way to take Antioch. He failed to take it but it later fell to his successor, John I Zimisces, who murdered him, or caused him to be murdered, that same year when he returned to Constantinople, and it remained in Byzantine hands, together with a large

* An ancient people of Anatolia, who built a great empire in Northern Syria and Asia Minor in the second millennium BC.

part of the Syrian coast, for more than a hundred years. His partner in crime, Theofano, described by Gibbon as 'a woman of base origin, masculine spirit and flagitious manners', besides helping Zimisces, who was her lover, to murder her second husband Nicephorus, poisoned two emperors, the first of whom was her father-in-law, Constantine VII, the second his son, her first husband, Romanus II. Later, Zimisces himself was also poisoned, but not, it is thought, by Theofano.

To the north was the escarpment we had just driven through, which together with the Misis Dagh, the miniature range to the west, effectively isolated the Plain of Issus from the Cilician Plain. To the east were the steep-sided Amanus Mountains, now white with snow, running away south in a great curve towards the Gulf of Iskenderun. And to the south was the Plain itself with the railway line from Toprakkale to Iskenderun running through it for some thirty miles, with the remains of an aqueduct built by the Seleucids dark against the sun, running out westwards from the railway line through the flat fields to what remained of the Seleucid city of Epiphania, founded in about 175 BC by Antiochus the Mad, Antiochus IV Epiphanes, who was, in spite of his title, the most brilliant of the Seleucid kings, one of a royal dynasty (312–64 BC) that at the height of its power ruled over an area extending from Thrace to India. And beyond that there were the glittering waters of the Gulf, glimpsed between the sand dunes. Dunes over which, in 401 BC, the 20,000 Asian and Greek mercenaries of Cyrus, younger brother of the recently enthroned King of Persia, Artaxerxes II, had tramped on what was to be one of the greatest marches in the history of the world, one which, in its later stages, when the 20,000 had been reduced to 10,000 Greeks, after Cyrus had been defeated and killed at Cunaxa, near Babylon, had become the March of the Ten Thousand, a journey of discovery through regions unknown to the Persians themselves. And this route through the dunes was the one followed by the right flank of Alexander's army at the end of October 333 BC, on its way from Mallus (now Karataş), a coastal city of the Cilician Plain, to the Syrian Gates.

And here in the plain, at the beginning of November, 333 BC, after a series of marches and counter marches, Alexander joined battle with the army of Darius III Condoman. The battle took place on the banks of a river that it has been the pleasure and despair of *savants* to attempt to identify – there are three rivers and five streams for them to choose from that flow down from the Amanus

Mountains into the Gulf of Iskenderun – across which the opposing armies now faced one another on an approximately one-and-a-half-mile front between the mountains and the sea, Alexander's Macedonians numbering between 25,000 and 35,000, the infantry in a long line with his Shield Bearers on the right flank, the Foot Companions in the centre and his foreign mercenaries on the left, the seaward side, with the cavalry on both flanks. The army of Darius, probably a superior force in numbers, consisted of Persian archers, Greek mercenaries of various sorts, light and heavy cavalry and infantry and oriental slingers. Medes, Armenians, Hyrcanians, North Africans as well as Persians were some of the troops which the last of the Persian kings assembled and counted at Babylon when the news of Alexander's irruption into Cilicia became known.

The battle began on the afternoon of 1 November with both sides moving to the attack and meeting in head-on collision in and on both sides of the river, which Darius had fortified with palisades. On the Greek right, below the mountains, the Persian archers, light infantry and cavalry, gave way before Alexander's horse, the Companion Cavalry, the Thessalians and the Lancers, who then turned left and drove into the Persian centre, taking the foot soldiers, the tough Greek mercenaries of Darius, who were heavily engaged with Alexander's Foot Companions, in the rear.

Meanwhile Darius had put in a massive cavalry attack on his right down on the seashore. It failed and his cavalry, as were those on his left, were thrown back on the centre, causing indescribable confusion, although the actual centre front where his mercenaries had had to fall back was still intact.

By this time night was falling. Believing the battle lost, Darius fled the field in his chariot, leaving his brother, Oxathres, and his nobles to carry on the struggle, until the time came when the Persians and their truly heroic Greek mercenaries broke and scattered.

It was a great cavalry victory and Alexander was magnanimous, sparing Oxathres and the nobles, sparing the wife, mother and children of Darius, treating them with great honour. Later he married Darius's daughter.

By defeating Darius, Alexander had opened up the *Pylae Syriae*, the Syrian Gates, otherwise the Beilon Pass, across the Amanas mountains to Antioch and the Plains of Syria; the route which would take him and his army to Egypt, then into Asia as far as the borders of China and Tibet, as conqueror of the world. Here on the banks of the river he erected, as was his custom, temples to Zeus, Athena and Heracles and down on the shore the first of the cities he was to build to commemorate his victories and his name was erected on the site of what is now Iskenderun.

In the Plain of Issus, in a sandy waste below Toprakkale Castle, there was a Yürük encampment. As it was impossible to reach it with anything but a four-wheel drive vehicle, the three of us, the third member of the party being a Turkish girl with whom we had previously travelled extensively in other parts of Turkey, set off on foot to visit it. The wind was bitter from the north and in the hollows there were little drifts of snow.

It is never easy to approach a nomad encampment unless accompanied by a member of the tribe or clan because of the appalling ferocity of their guard dogs. In the not-so-distant past, when the majority of travellers in such outlandish places as the one in which we now found ourselves were armed, they often only saved themselves from being torn to pieces by shooting their attackers dead.

The dogs in this encampment were no exception. While we were still a hundred yards or more away half a dozen of them, pale-coloured brutes with manes, having instantly identified us as strangers and therefore a potential danger to the community, came racing out towards us uttering the most blood-curdling roaring noises. Then, as no one in the camp showed any inclination to call them off, we turned and fled for the shelter of the car, just reaching it in time to get in and slam the doors on ourselves before they arrived and began to rage up and down, looking like miniature lions. And there we sat, wondering what to do next.

Fortunately, as in a play in which no time can be wasted, a middle-aged Yürük appeared, driving a pony cart from the direction of Toprakkale village, where he had been selling yoghourt which the Yürüks are considerable artists at preparing. He uttered a single word and the dogs became as good as gold; another and they all six went loping off back to the camp.

Most of the male Yürüks we had seen in Turkey, apart from the one at Alarahan, had been picturesque figures, often dressed entirely from head to foot in materials spun and woven from the wool of their own animals, even their shoes sometimes being made from the skins of their own goats. This one was a bit of a disappointment. He was wearing what was now the almost universal male uniform of rural Turkey – the shiny black suit, the black peaked cap, the white shirt, in this case made of nylon – an outfit that, apart from the fact that he was wearing scuffed black loafers, made him look a bit like an off-duty mute at the Rampe del Campo in Naples.

'You did well,' he said, when Ince, our Turkish friend, told him what had happened, 'to reach your *arabiyeh* [the picturesque word in Turkish for motor car]. If you had not done so at least one of you would probably now be dead.'

And he invited us to accompany him, which we did, following his cart on foot as it lurched through the scrub, a by-now-rather apprehensive little party of visitors.

The encampment consisted of half a dozen goat-hair tents, some of them covered with plastic sheeting as a further protection against the dreadful wind which was howling about them and each with its guard dog now sitting primly in front of it. There were some enclosures made with thorn bushes for the sheep and goats, which were somewhere out in the plain with whoever was looking after them, a couple of large pens fenced with cane, full of young lambs, some hobbled horses and a tank on wheels which provided drinking water for the community.

He took us to his own tent and introduced us to his younger brother, who was dressed in the same subfusc way; then to his wife, a tall, lithe, beautiful woman in her early thirties, a queen among women, and to their daughter, who was half her age and although good-looking, showed less promise of becoming as impressive as her mother. Both were dressed in flower-patterned *salvar*, the baggy trousers and short jackets of wildly contrasting colours which somehow contrived to look as if they had been carefully co-ordinated to go with one another. On their heads they wore what looked like hats, or rather the sort of helmets worn by the Crusaders, but were, in fact, neither hats nor helmets, being simply tightly wound scarves ingeniously arranged and knotted. On their feet they wore thick woollen socks with a red and green pattern knitted into them, and rubber sandals made from old motor tyres.

They sat us down in a depression in the ground on a couple of kilim rugs, alongside one of the lambing-pens where, miraculously, there was no wind. There was a fire going and all the primitive artefacts of the Yürük kitchen, made of wood and horn and iron and copper, including an enormous shallow vessel more like one of King Darius's chariot wheels than a cooking receptacle, were lying

against the wall of the pen. There was also a wooden bowl scooped
out of the trunk of a tree, full of recording tapes.

Now the daughter stirred the fire, put on some more *tezek*, dried
animal dung, and began to boil water for the tea. At the same time
she switched on the radio and got Ankara.

Yürüks are not gypsies – some are settled permanently in the
plains near Tarsus and Adana. They bear no relationship to them in
any way, except perhaps in their hardiness and love of movement,
neither in appearance, behaviour – Yürüks do not beg – or in their
way of life, which is pastoral, and, among the women, exceptionally
creative.

The men, because of their exceptional powers of resistance,
make good soldiers; the women, who are often extremely beautiful
as well as faithful, are reputed to make excellent wives, so excellent
that they are often sought out by less mobile Turkish gentlemen
who marry them and make them sedentary. They are notable
weavers of rugs and saddle bags, using designs that are never
committed to paper but are memorized and handed down from
generation to generation. Some of the colours they use are still
produced with vegetable dyes, blues with indigo or a plant containing a similar substance, madder for reds, cochineal for pink reds,
and a number of plants producing yellows, although now more
rarely because chemicals have been widely used for almost a
century. There are many thousands of Yürüks and other nomads in
Turkey, and those on the borders, especially those on the Iranian
and Syrian borders, but to a lesser extent on the borders with the
USSR, have always tended to cross them when the spirit moved
them without asking anyone's permission.

The wife took us into the tent. It was beautiful in its neatness,
everything not needed being stashed away in woven saddle bags.
Next to it there was a smaller tent with a vertical weaving loom
against one wall on which she had just finished making a kilim,
what is known as a weft-faced tapestry woven rug, otherwise a
flat-woven rug. The loom was nothing but a simple frame made
with two side-pieces and a couple of cross-pieces from which the
warp threads hung. It had been used for this special method of
weaving, in which the spools bearing the different coloured wool
for the weft threads for the motifs, are made to pass back and forth
through the warp threads. The result is a smooth-faced carpet
woven like tapestry, without any knots.

The kilim was hanging there on the loom, a thing of primitive beauty, glowing in the semi-darkness of the tent, a wonderful medley of green, orange, wine-red, white, dark indigo and black, disposed in grouped arrangements constantly reiterating themselves, some five feet wide and eleven feet long.

Later, sitting outside in a hole in the Plain of Issus, drinking the sweet tea made with water from the tank which had been boiled over the dried dung, the *tezek*, eating their yoghourt which was like sharp-tasting clotted cream with great glogs of yellow stuff in it, listening to the wind, Radio Ankara and what I now called the Queen of the Yürüks describing to Ince how she had made the carpet and how her daughter would now never make one as she wanted to live in a town, looking out over the plain past the ruins of aqueducts and cities to the snow-clad mountains on one hand and to the distant Mediterranean on the other, I knew that eventually, quite soon, a moment would come in which we would offer to buy the kilim and the offer would be accepted, and we would take it away from these wild shores to enliven the greyness of an English winter. And thinking of this I experienced a feeling of pure, ephemeral, unadulterated happiness.

Hemmed in by young Turks and old Turks as anxious as I was in such weather to get some steam up I sat on the *göbek tasi* in a *hamam* in the bazaar quarter of Antakya, the ancient Antioch, the hottest seat in any Turkish bath, now rapidly thawing out after a mad attempt to make a circuit of the walls in a blizzard. Somewhere round the corner Wanda had taken refuge in a similar establishment for ladies only and I hoped for her sake that her navel or belly stone was as hot as ours was in the men's department.

Meanwhile outside, the snow continued to fall in enormous flakes which down here in the valley of the Orontes River immediately turned to slush on what must have been, in its several heydays, Hellenistic, Roman, Byzantine and Crusader, which had continued off and on until it had been completely destroyed by the wretched Egyptian Mamelukes, if not among the most beautiful cities on the shores of the Mediterranean, one of the most splendid, one of the most fascinating, and certainly among the most profligate. It fell in the Bazaar where at the street corners the *hamals* crouched over fires fuelled with bits of broken packing cases in the gathering gloom, waiting to be commissioned but not caring much as they are paid whether they work or not, and very well by Turkish standards. 'The ruin-seeking traveller pushes on to Antioch,' Rose Macaulay, here at some more clement season, wrote in *A Pleasure of Ruins*, one of my favourite travel books. 'He is exalted, almost intoxicated by the magnificent mountain path through the oleandrous glen of Daphne, whose gushing streams and aromatic odours and smiling ghosts from the richly licentious past set the right mood for the ghosts of the glory and luxury of ancient Antioch.'

We, too, ruin-seeking travellers, had pushed on to Antioch through the Plain of Issus and over the Beilan Pass in the gathering darkness and by the time we reached the city it had begun to snow again. The next morning the oleandrous glen of Daphne, five miles from Antioch, where the colossal image of Apollo erected by the Macedonian kings of Syria had looked down on what some writer had described as 'an unending festival of vice', was frozen solid and even the famous waterfalls and rivulets that poured down through it were muted. Here, one suspects that in ancient times, when it snowed and the temperature fell to freezing point, even vice, used to flourishing in the open air, must have had a close season.

Inspired by Miss Macaulay's description of the wall of ancient Antioch and what amounted to a challenge to follow in her vigorous wake, 'The great wall which it is the tourist's duty and pleasure to walk round will have with its seven-mile circuit over crag, mountain and ravine, a bracing, tonic effect, counteracting the enervating mood of voluptuous luxury', we set off to make the tour of what is left of it after a succession of earthquakes and innumerable invading armies have done their worst. Although great tracts had been flattened of a wall that in early times had been broad enough to allow a four-horsed chariot to be driven along the top of it and in subsequent ages had risen to a height of fifty or sixty feet, what remains is one of the wonders of the Mediterranean world. Said by Miss Macaulay to be seven miles in circumference, the wall seemed longer as we followed in her long-lost footsteps up a steep mountainside to a plateau filled with ruins over which the blizzard was raging, then along the edge of precipices, passing huge hulks of masonry, all that was left in some places of the great square towers that had stood in profusion along the length of it until they were thrown down by an exceptionally violent earthquake at the end of the eighteenth century, providing the Turks, the last invaders, with a further supply of ready-shaped building blocks with which to build their mosques and minarets down below on the banks of the Orontes, of which there was already a superabundance.

We followed her and the wall to a point where, still unbroken, it spanned a deep and narrow river gorge with a caravan route, perhaps to Aleppo, running through it. Beyond this it was lost to view in the whirling snow on a mountainside so steep that it was impossible for us to climb it. We decided to give up. We had already been more than the five hours she had allotted for the purpose, we were soaked to the skin, and there was more to come.

'I bet she never did that next bit in spite of writing all that stuff about counteracting the enervating mood of voluptuous luxury,' Wanda said as we went down the gorge to the city, passing on the way a church in a cave in which St Peter had preached to the always dissolute Antiochians.

Here in Antakya, so far as the Turkish shores of the Mediterranean and proceeding any further south from it were concerned, we were to all intents and purposes at the end of the line. A few miles away to the south was Syria which, in spite of having exchanged visiting cards with Dr Abd el-Aziz Alloun, Director of Tourist Relations at the Ministry of Tourism at Damascus, we were still as far off visiting as we had been when we had swapped them at a party in London, one of the reasons being that there was a war on. And beyond Syria was Lebanon, where there was a total war on, which neither of us was particularly keen to visit.

Instead we went back to Istanbul and took a plane to Tel Aviv.

V
THE LEVANT

Jerusalem

On the way to Israel in an El Al plane, Wanda asked me what I most wanted to see, to which I replied that I thought it a damn silly question, and this led to a certain coolness between us up there for a couple of hundred miles or so which was eventually overcome when I suggested that we should play a game called 'What I most don't want to see in Jerusalem', using as source material a couple of magazines entitled *Hello Israel: The Only Country-Wide Weekly Guide*, and *This Week in Jerusalem*, now in its twenty-second year, with which we had been presented gratuitously by the airline – no wonder they were in a financial mess – the players to choose alternately and the game going on until one or other of us got bored, Wanda to have first service.

'I don't want to see the Jerusalem Biblical Zoo,' she announced. ' "The Biblical Zoo" ', quoting from the *Guide*, ' "attempts to bring to life the powerful imagery of the Bible, with living creatures that run, jump, eat and play against the backdrop of Jerusalem, in their natural setting . . . cages are equipped with plaques quoting the most appropriate Biblical sources in the original Hebrew and in English translation. The verses of the Bible suddenly take on a new meaning and vividness after seeing the animals mentioned in their natural habitat . . . Tickets for Saturday should be purchased in advance".'

'OK, what about this? Arieh Klein's Olive Wood, at 34 Bar Ilan Street: "The selection of items ranges from key rings and coasters to rare carvings, mostly from exquisitely gnarled and whorled olive wood, dried by a unique method" – it sounds like I feel – ". . . Klein has achieved the great distinction of being invited by Israeli and foreign governments to make special olive wood gifts for presentation to visiting dignitaries and heads of state".'

'I don't want to visit his Olive Wood either,' Wanda said. 'My next selection is the Chung Ching Kosher Chinese Restaurant, "under the supervision of the Jerusalem Rabbinate-Catering service for all addresses in the city: Beit Hakerem, by the Smadar Gas Station".'

'My next selection is a visit to Ben Gurion's Hut. "Next door to the Sdeh Boker Inn".'

'You can't have that,' Wanda said, after studying the appropriate page in *Hello Israel*. 'It's in the Negev, half an hour's drive from Beersheba. Why do you always have to try and cheat?'

'Alright, smartyboots,' I said, 'try this for size. If I can't have a presidential hut, a visit to the Tomer Company on Herbert Samuel Street, "Now is the Time to invest in 'The Jerusalem You Love', 4½ and 5½ Room Apartments in the Exclusive Residential Quarter, Kiryat Isaac Wolfson, THE LAST HIGH RISE NOW COMPLETED, with a Panoramic View of rolling gardens, the Knesset and the Valley of the Monastery of the Cross. Don't hesitate to call".'

'I'm fed up with this game,' Wanda said. 'In spite of having been there I can't remember how many times, I really want to go back to Jerusalem. That's why I came. Now it's putting me off.'

'I know you do,' I said. 'So do I. It's only a game.'

Having been extruded through the security checks at Ben Gurion airport that leave one feeling like toothpaste squeezed from a tube, but which nobody in their right mind blames them or any other airport for carrying out, we were transported into Tel Aviv, a seething city by the sea which, when I first saw it in 1942, when it was still seething although smaller, I compared, quite irrationally, not having ever seen one, to some eastern European city, whereas, in fact, it is like no other city but itself. Whatever it was now, I knew that it was too much of a handful to write about. So instead of trying to wrest its secrets from it we spent a rewarding but sometimes rather harrowing afternoon in the Beth Hatefutsoth, otherwise the Nahum Goldmann Museum of the Diaspora, which is on the outskirts of the city, on the University campus.

The following morning we caught the 08.18 train for Jerusalem from the Beneii Beraq station, choosing to do so because it was something we had never done before, which is always a good reason for doing anything.

The only guide book we had about us which describes this journey in any detail, most of the rest of the inhabitants having abandoned it long since to travel to Jerusalem by road, the most modern of which, a four-lane highway, cuts the distance from sixty miles by the train to about thirty-five by road, is the extremely rare Baedeker's *Palestine and Syria, with Routes through Mesopotamia and Babylonia and the Island of Cyprus*, published in 1912. This guide book was produced during the reign of Sultan Mehmed V, who had succeeded his brother, Abd ul-Hamid II, in 1909. At that time he still ruled over an empire which included Syria and Palestine with Jerusalem, Mesopotamia and immense areas of Arabia including the holy cities of Mecca and Medina.

The only disadvantage of this otherwise excellent book was that names of places then rendered in Arabic were now in Hebrew. This meant that I found some difficulty in identifying the various places along the route as we chugged along, at first through what in 1912 had been orange groves and sandy wastes inhabited by Beduin, snakes, lizards and jackals, now occupied by enormous buildings, then through the coastal plain towards the Judaean Hills, blue in the distance. What the Israelis called Lod, for example, the Arabs called Ludd and everyone else called Lydda. It had been sacked by the Mongols in 1271 and according to the Prophet was the place at the gates of which Christ will slay Antichrist.

It was an interesting journey. We passed Er-Ramleh, now Ramla, which its Christian inhabitants firmly believed was the site of Arimathea but Baedeker, equally firmly, said wasn't, a town in which Napoleon had once spent the night and which had a mosque with an enormous tower beneath which Muslims believe forty companions of the Prophet, and Christians believe forty martyrs, repose in the vaults. We had views, more or less distant, of Akir, otherwise Ekron, one of the five cities of the Philistines, where Baron de Rothschild founded a Jewish colony in 1881; of the ruins of Gezer, on a hill with cave dwellings in its lower levels that were occupied between 3000 and 2000 BC, a city later captured by the Pharaoh Psusennes, who reigned *c.* 984–950 BC, and who gave it to Solomon, his son-in-law. And we rode past the site of the city of Bittir, in which the Jews were besieged by the Romans for 3½ years after Simon Bar-Cochbar's great insurrection in AD 132, before it was finally taken and they were put to the sword.

After all this the train began crawling up what used to be known as the Wadi el-Werd, the Valley of the Roses, the line of the old caravan route from Jerusalem to Gaza and Egypt, past Philip's Well, in which the apostle baptized a eunuch in Palestine on a visit from Ethiopia where he was in charge of all the treasure of its queen, Candace; past the Well of the Magi, where they saw for the second time the guiding star; past another well at the Monastery of Mar Elyas, from which the Holy Family drank, where there is also a depression in the rock said to have been made by the Prophet Elijah when he lay down on it to rest. After all this, the train, more or less on the level now, ran through an industrial zone and a series of enormous suburbs, and across the plateau confusingly known as the Rephaim Valley, on which the Philistines were defeated by David, finally coming to rest, Cook's Overseas Timetable says 60 miles, Baedeker says 54 miles, and two hours and seventeen minutes from Tel Aviv in the Central Railway Station, built by the Turks in 1892 as the terminus of what was the first railway line in the Middle East. Here, outside the walls of the Old City, across the Valley of Hinnom from Mount Zion, and only three-quarters of a mile from the Jaffa Gate, we parked our baggage to be collected later.

How King David, a thousand years before Christ, came to choose such a site for his capital, having captured it from the inoffensive Jebusites, is a bit of a mystery. One of the reasons must have been because it was isolated and therefore free from corrupting outside influences, something that would have been inescapable down on the shores of the Mediterranean, where every ship that arrived was a harbinger of innovation and change. Two thousand five hundred feet up in the air on an almost bare plateau, more than thirty miles from the sea as the crow flies, it was devoid of almost every amenity. The only cultivation that could be said to flourish on these rocky hillsides was of the grape and the olive, almost everything else grew better elsewhere. There were no minerals, just endless limestone of varying degrees of excellence, and it was this proliferation of stone and the absence of anything else for the inhabitants to do, other than build and think, which made the city a place where architecture shot up in much the same way as wheat would have done in a more hospitable environment, and where ideas came into being, some of them extremely dangerous ones.

The greatest problem was the complete absence of any drinking water up on the plateau on which the city stood. Nearly 1000 years were to pass before the first aqueduct was built in the time of Herod and another 130 years or more before Hadrian, having obliterated Herod's city and rebuilt it, at last constructed aqueducts and cisterns that were more or less adequate for the needs of the inhabitants.

The nearest drinking water was outside the walls in the Valley of the Kidron, deep down at the foot of Mount Ophel, at the southern end of the plateau on which the Jebusites had perched their city, a spot also used since the beginning of recorded time as a rubbish dump. From this spring, the Spring of Kidron, known to Christians as the Spring of the Virgin, and from other sources, the water was either carried up into the city by what must have been endless files of women balancing pitchers on their heads, or, less picturesquely, on the backs of camels and donkeys. There was also a steeply inclined tunnel leading down from within the walls and ending in a perpendicular shaft above the spring, which enabled the inhabitants to draw water from it in times of trouble without exposing themselves to danger, and this is perhaps the route by which Joab, David's commander, was said to have gained access to the city, surprising the Jebusites.

Later, in the time of King Hezekiah, who reigned from about 715 to 687 BC, a tunnel more than 580 yards long, which still exists, called the Siloa Canal, was cut which carried the water into what are known as the pools of Siloa which were then within the walls. Even today drinking water is pumped to the city from miles away on the shores of the Sea of Galilee, which is itself nearly 700 feet below sea level, more than 3000 feet below the Jerusalem plateau.

Once the city was in his hands, which was in about 1000 BC, David transferred to it the Ark of the Covenant and at the same time acquired a threshing floor from Araunah the Jebusite on which to set up an altar to the Lord. By doing so he made it the federal capital of the Twelve Tribes of Israel and set in train the process by which Jerusalem was to become, under his son, Solomon, the Holy City.

The city was not only difficult to get to, as the Israelis were to find in 1949 when they themselves had to fight their way up to it; it was also difficult to hang on to, as successive waves of invaders, many of them intent on destroying what they found and starting again with, as it were, a clean slate, discovered: Egyptians in 922 BC; Assyrians in 700 BC; the Babylonians who, in 586 BC, destroyed the city and Solomon's Temple and led the people into a captivity that lasted for fifty years from which they returned to build the Second Temple; Alexander the Great, whose Macedonians took it in 332 BC without any blood being shed on either side; the Seleucids, the abominably cruel Hellenized Syrians, who took it in 198 BC; the Maccabean Jews who, after a short but bitter campaign, freed Judaea and Jerusalem from the Seleucids in 164 BC; the Romans who took it twice, in 63 BC and AD 70; the Byzantines who first arrived in the fourth century; the Persians who sacked it in AD 614; the Muslims who took it in AD 638; the Frankish Crusaders in 1099; the Muslims again in 1187; the Egyptian Mamelukes who began to rule over it in 1250; the Mongols who sacked it in 1271; the Turks who took it in 1517; the British who entered it in 1917 and the Israelis themselves who finally occupied it in 1967.

Even the Romans avoided making Jerusalem a capital, sickened of it, perhaps, by too much bloodshed. They preferred Caesarea, built by their deputy Herod in 13 BC, in a magical situation down on the foreshore where to this day a great aqueduct stretches away along it among the encroaching sand dunes and the ground underfoot still sparkles with the fragments of their iridescent glass, a site still more or less unchanged since I had last seen it forty years previously, apart from an enormous industrial plant which looms over it now to the south. It was Herod, who reigned from about 37 BC until 4 BC, to whom the Romans left it to rebuild Jerusalem after the enormous damage done to it in 63 BC by Pompey's legions when the question of who among the Hasmoneans (the dynasty of Jewish priest-kings) was to succeed to the throne led to a civil war.* In Herod's lifetime it became one of the most splendid cities in the Middle East.

These splendours were to endure for little more than seventy years after the death of Herod. In AD 66 the Jews revolted against

---

* It was the Hasmonean commander, Judas Maccabeus, who was to a great extent responsible for ridding Israel of the Seleucids.

their Roman masters. In the course of a five-month siege of the city by Titus, which was defended with what one historian described as 'all the grim tenacity of which the Semite race is capable when on the defensive', 1,000,000 of the 3,000,000 inhabitants of the country are estimated (by the Jewish historian Josephus) to have died, and a further 100,000 were sold into slavery when the city finally fell and was left a heap of smouldering ruins, after which Jerusalem became nothing more than a camp for the Tenth Legion. These events are recorded on the Arch of Titus in Rome, on which the Jews are depicted being led into captivity and the famous seven-branched golden candlestick, the Menorah, is being carried up to the temple of Capitoline Jove. And it is this date, AD 70, that the Jews regard as the traditional beginning of their world-wide dispersion, the Diaspora.

Sixty years later, Hadrian began to rebuild Jerusalem as the pagan city of Aelia Capitolina, a Roman garrison town with a temple to Venus and a statue of Jupiter rising sacrilegiously on what had been the site of the most sacred Jewish Temples of Solomon and Herod.

This gross affront to their religious sensibilities led in 132 to the second Jewish revolt, headed by Simon Bar-Cochbar who succeeded in regaining Judaea and Jerusalem and there recommenced the practice of the sacred Jewish ritual on the site of the Temple, which had been forbidden. But his success was only temporary and the revolt was eventually crushed, although Hadrian had to recall Septimus Severus from Britain and twelve legions from the Danube in order to do it.

After leaving the railway station we walked down past the fort-like buildings of the Miskenot Sha'ananim, the 'Home of the Unworried', the first Jewish settlement outside the walls of the Old City, built here in 1857 at the top end of the Vale of Hinnom by the English Jewish philanthropist Sir Moses Montefiore, while Palestine was still under Turkish rule, to encourage Jews to leave the confines of the Old City and create a new life outside the walls. Then we went on down to the Pool of the Sultan, rebuilt in the sixteenth century by Suleiman the Magnificent as a reservoir for rainwater on the site of an earlier pool at which the Crusaders used to water their horses; after which we went up along the foot of the west wall of the Old City, past David's Tower, through what had been between

1948 and 1967, when Jerusalem was partitioned and the Arabs held the Old City, a very dangerous no-man's-land, to the Jaffa Gate.

The Jaffa Gate is one of the seven gates of the city, all of which were shut at night well into the twentieth century, leaving anyone outside who was not within four walls at the mercy of marauding Beduin. It was this gate which was used by the victorious General Allenby when, on 11 December 1917, having received the Turkish surrender, he entered the city on foot.

Next to the Jaffa Gate there is a large hole in the wall, made in 1898 by order of Sultan Abd ul-Hamid II to enlarge it so that Kaiser Wilhelm II could ride into the city on a white horse and dressed in shining armour in order to attend the consecration of the Lutheran Church of the Redeemer. Here we climbed up on to the Wall.

The first wall was built by David and enlarged by Solomon; the second was built, or rebuilt, in fifty-two days, by Nehemiah, a Jewish cup-bearer to Artaxerxes I, King of Persia, who became Governor of Judah after the return of the Jews to Jerusalem from their captivity. Later walls were built by Herod and the Romans. The present one, which enclosed a far larger area than any before it, was built by Sultan Suleiman. The work took five years and the Sultan had the builder in charge put to death for omitting to include within it what was for long presumed to be, but some boring experts now say isn't, the burial place of David.

Whether it is or not, and it would be difficult to persuade any practising Jew that it isn't, the tomb is very impressive, hidden away in a labyrinth of courts and separated by railings from the remainder of the small room in which it stands. During the years when they were denied access to the Wailing Wall, the Jews used to come here to pray in large numbers, and many still do, grasping the railings and leaning yearningly towards the tomb and the great silver crowns of the Torah, the Law, which rest on it. It would be a pity if some wiseacre succeeded in proving that it is not the Tomb of David. There is already enough to be unsure about in Jerusalem, a strange, beautiful, yet to me somehow not altogether lovable place, not the sort of place to which I would come to seek the peace that the world cannot give, perhaps because it is one in which almost everything has a variety of meanings and interpretations, many of them wildly at variance one with another, and one in which no one is absolutely sure where anything is, even Calvary.

Up on the Wall we were afforded previously undreamt-of views, undreamt-of because the last time we had been in Jerusalem we were not allowed on it. Now you can walk round it on every side except the east where the Golden Gate was and where the Muslim burial grounds are at the foot of it, above the Valley of the Kidron, opposite the Mount of Olives. A few years ago, if you had been an Arab and had exposed your noddle above this western section of the Wall where we were now standing, an Israeli sniper on the other side of the Hebron Road would have drilled a hole in it. Now you can safely look out over the amazing panoramas that make up the modern city: the endless builders' developments that follow the contours of the hills, all faced with limestone that is a golden honey colour in the sunlight; the appalling tower blocks, hotels many of them, that have been allowed to ruin what was once a beautiful landscape, buildings that have also ruined the incomparable view of the Old City from the Mount of Olives, all of which appear to be sprouting up behind it like a lot of rotten teeth.

The best vistas are all on the inside of the Wall, nearly forty feet below in the 210 acres of the Old City; vistas of whitewashed mosques, synagogues, churches, convents, monasteries, noble old houses and unspeakable hovels – all overgrown with a dense forest of TV aerials – forgotten alleys that have somehow got sealed off from the rest of the city and are now knee-deep in grass, secret gardens stocked with carob, pine, fig and peach trees, acacias, oleanders; vegetable gardens behind impenetrable hedges of prickly pears, in which are cultivated onions, artichokes and gooseberries; scrapyards, one of them full of old iron bedsteads, worth a fortune; butchers' shops catering for various religious sects; cook shops from which rise the smells of outlandish dishes that we will perhaps never eat. And from down there in the Old City there rises what is the murmuring of a vast, polyglot company of Ashkenazim Jews from Russia, Rumania, Galicia, Poland, Moravia, Germany, Austria and other parts of western Europe, the Americas and the Commonwealth who speak Yiddish; Sephardim, Ladino-speaking Spanish and Portuguese Jews who fled here and to other places on the shores of the Mediterranean after the introduction of the Inquisition and their expulsion from Spain in the reign of Isabella I; Arabic-speaking Jews; Maghrebim from Morocco (some of them Berber speakers from the Atlas Mountains), Algeria, Tunisia and Libya, Iraqi Jews who before coming here had lived in Iraq ever since the Babylonian exile, the oldest community outside Israel; Urfali Jews from southern Turkey and Musta'rabim, descendants of Jewish families who never went into exile and adopted the life but not the creed of their Muslim Arab neighbours; Yemenite Jews and Baghdadi Jews; Iranian Jews who speak Persian; the Benei Israeli who speak Marathi and the strictly observant Jews of Cochin who speak Malayam and are divided into three castes who do not marry or even dine with one another – White Jews at the head of the hierarchy, Brown Jews and Black Jews the most numerous; Syrian and Lebanese Jews; Georgian Jews; Bokharan Jews; Kurdish Jews; Karaite Jews, fundamentalists from Iran and Iraq who believe in a literal reading of the Scriptures and reject all rabbinical interpretations; Dagestani Jews, who once spoke an Iranian dialect known as Tat; Crimchake Jews from the Crimea who speak Judaeo-Tatar. And this is just the Jewish portion of all the different people down there in the Old City whose murmurings can be heard up here on the Wall.

There are Sunnite Muslims and Christian Arabs and Christian Armenians, and Jacobites and Copts, and Greek and Russian Orthodox and Roman Catholics and an infinite variety of Protestants, and Melchites and Marionites and Abyssinians. All of these are currently giving tongue, buying and selling, praying, reading sacred and not-so-sacred works, listening to taped music, teaching the living, tending the dying, calling the faithful to prayer, quarrelling, picking pockets, smoking water pipes, playing *sheshbesh*, a form of backgammon, begging, cooking and eating, digging their plots, feeding their hens, their flocks of sheep, their donkeys and their camels – all of which are also from time to time giving tongue – or simply waiting for the Second Coming.

Dominating everything from up here, rising into the air from its platform opposite the Mount of Olives like some exotic space vehicle waiting to take off, is the Qubbat es-Sakhra, the Dome of the Rock, the masterpiece of the Umayyad Caliph Abd el-Malik, one of a dynasty which ruled from its capital, Damascus, from AD 661–750. He built it in about 691, at a cost of what was said to be the equivalent of seven years' revenue from Egypt, in order to attract Umayyad pilgrims who could not make the pilgrimage to Mecca because at that time they were being refused admission to the Kaaba (the most sacred Muslim pilgrim shrine into which is built the black stone believed to have been given by the Archangel Gabriel to Abraham, in the direction of which Muslims turn when they are praying). He also built it in order to outdo the dome of the Emperor Constantine's original church, which had been raised over the Holy Sepulchre in the fourth century. The walled platform on which it stands is known to Muslims as the Harām es-Sherif, the Place of the Temple. It conceals within it the Holy Rock on which David erected his altar, having bought the threshing floor on which it was to stand and the oxen to make his first sacrifice for fifty shekels of silver. And it is the site of Solomon's Temple, and the Second Temple built when the Jews returned from Babylon to find Solomon's Temple destroyed, and of the Third and last Temple, built by Herod.

According to the Talmud,* the main authoritative compilation of ancient Jewish law and tradition, the Rock covers the entrance to the Abyss in which the waters of Noah's flood can be heard roaring. It is also the Centre of the World, a title it shares with a point in the nave of the Greek Cathedral in the Church of the Holy Sepulchre, the place where Abraham was about to slay Isaac, the Rock anointed by Jacob, and the Stone of the Foundation, the *eben shatyâ*, on which the Ark of the Covenant stood and beneath which Jeremiah concealed it at the destruction of Jerusalem, where it still lies buried. It was also the Rock on which was written the great and unspeakable name of God (*shem*) which, once Jesus was able to read it, allowed him to perform his miracles.

According to Muslims the Rock is without support except for a palm watered by a river of Paradise, which hangs in the air above the Bir el-Arwah, the Well of Souls, where the dead assemble to pray weekly. Others say it is the Mouth of Hell.

It was Mohammed, who prayed here before being carried away to heaven on his mare, al-Burak, who said that one prayer here was worth a thousand anywhere else; and in the underside (the ceiling) of the Rock there is the impression made by his head and the handprint of the Archangel Gabriel, who managed to hold on to it and prevent it from following the Prophet to Paradise. Here, on the Last Day, the Kaaba will be transported from Mecca, to await the sounding of the trumpet which will announce the Judgement, when God's throne will be set up on the Rock, the scales will be suspended for the weighing of the souls, and a horsehair tightrope will be set up between the Rock and the Mount of Olives, spanning the Valley of the Kidron, otherwise the Valley of Jehoshaphat, which Muslims believe will be the Mouth of Hell, across which the Faithful will walk without falling into it. The same valley devout Jews believe to

---

* The Talmud derives from the laws of Moses and comprises the Mishnah, a compilation of precepts passed down by an oral tradition and collected in the late second century AD, and the Gemara, the later main part of it, which is a commentary on the Mishnah.

be the place to which the Messiah will come first, and on the eastern slopes of which, below the Mount of Olives, they exert all their efforts to be buried.

Also within the Dome of the Rock is the marble cover of Solomon's Tomb, into which the Prophet drove eighteen gold nails, one of which falls out at the end of every epoch – when the last one goes it will be the End of the World; the footprint of the Prophet – displayed by the Crusaders during their tenure of the city as the footprint of Christ – some hairs from the Prophet's beard, and one of his banners.

Below the Harām es-Sherif, on its west side, is a section of the Western Wall of the Second Temple, nearly sixty feet and twenty-four courses high, with sixteen more courses invisible beneath the ground, its nine lower courses composed of enormous blocks of stone fifteen feet long and between three and four feet high, one monster being sixteen and a half feet long and thirteen feet wide.

This section of the Wall, which is just over fifty yards long, is the Wailing Place of the Jews, in Hebrew the Kothel ma'arvi, to which they come to bemoan the downfall of their Temple, the destruction of their City and the Diaspora, the Dispersal of their Race. It is also sacred to the Muslims, being part of the wall of the Harām where Mohammed tethered his mare, al-Burak, after his miraculous over-night journey from Mecca. In 1929 this conflict of interests led to rioting and bloodshed all over Palestine because the Muslims suspected that the Jews were trying to turn the area in front of it into an open-air synagogue.

There are always Jews to be found at the Wall, both men and women, who use separate sections of it, some with books of prayers, kissing it, weeping, inserting small pieces of paper with prayers written on them into the interstices of the stones and rocking backwards and forwards on their feet, but around 4.00 p.m. on a Friday evening, the evening of *Shabbat*, the Sabbath, and on the Sabbath itself and other feast days, it becomes crowded.

On the evening of the Sabbath, with the sun sinking and only the upper part of the Wall still illuminated by it, we heard the chanting of one of the cycle of Hebrew dirges on Zion:

> *For the Palace that lies desolate,*

the Leader lamented, to which those taking part responded:

> *We sit in solitude and mourn.*

For the Temple that is destroyed; for the Walls that are overthrown:

For our Majesty that is departed; for our Great Men who lie dead:

For the Precious Stones that are burned; for the Priests who have stumbled:

For our Kings who have despised Him:

To each of which separate lament the response was:
We sit in solitude and mourn.

This was followed by another litany:
We pray Thee, have mercy on Zion:
to which the response was:
Gather the Children of Jerusalem.

Haste, haste, Redeemer of Zion!
to which the response was:
Speak to the Heart of Jerusalem.

May Beauty and Majesty surround Zion!
to which the response was:
Ah, turn Thyself mercifully to Jerusalem.

May the Kingdom soon return to Zion!
to which the response was:
Comfort those who mourn over Jerusalem.

May Peace and Joy abide with Zion!
to which the response was:
And the Branch of Jesse spring up at Jerusalem.

What used to be a narrow alley in which the Jews prayed in front of the Wall was now a large open space, what was left of the dwellings of the Maghrebim, fanatical Muslims from north-west Africa, who used to make the visitor's life a misery, having been bulldozed to form an open space that could accommodate tens of thousands instead of a few hundred persons. Now the whole of the Jewish Quarter, which had been destroyed during the street fighting of 1948 when the Jews had held it against the Arab Legion for six months before being forced to surrender, was being reconstructed and the great open space in front of the Wall, with its infinite variety of Jews from all quarters of the earth, on this Sabbath evening, was a memorable spectacle.

Of all the Jews at the Wall the most fascinating to a gentile were the Ashkenazim, the ultra-orthodox central and eastern European Jews who originally came to Jerusalem at the beginning of the nineteenth century with the intention of 'Enticing the Divine Presence to Return'. There, nearly a century later, they were joined by those who had fled the pre-1914 pogroms, then by those who fled the Eastern *shtetlach*, the ghettoes, between the two world wars, and finally by survivors of the Holocaust.

The men wore the *shetraimel*, a big, now very expensive, circular black felt hat, trimmed with beaver, or else a similar hat, untrimmed but bigger still; long, dark overcoats with huge, square shoulders, made of silk or velvet or gabardine, and beneath them long black trousers which were slightly short, black shoes and socks, or else black knickerbockers and long black stockings. They were all extremely pale and most of them had full beards – red ones, which suggested that they might be of Tartar origin, brown, blond or black. Younger, beardless men and boys were distinguished by the *peyot*, side locks of hair worn forward of the ears. The younger boys wore black knickerbockers or long black shorts reaching below the knee and long black or white stockings so that no flesh was visible. Ashkenazim boys, their parents usually being poor, often wear their elder brother's long trousers cut down to make these long shorts. Their women, in the matter of clothes, were unremarkable when they appeared in public, as were their daughters, wearing ordinary frumpy clothes and thick lisle stockings.

The effect of seeing, especially from the back, a number of these tall, black clad, solemn men with their enormous square shoulders and stilt-like legs standing immobile in the open space before the Wall in the gloaming, together with their pale, delicately featured, black clad, equally solemn male children, was most extraordinary. It was like looking at a flock of giant black-feathered birds of prey and their young which, at any moment, might take off and fly away with long, slow wing beats across the Holy City to their nests. And when this flock, as if by some secret agreement, suddenly began to break up, by which time the sun had disappeared behind the buildings in the Jewish Quarter to the west and the whole Wall was in shadow, we followed three of them as they set off homewards along the Tariq el-Wad. Tariq el-Wad is the long street, part of it forming a section of the Via Dolorosa, which runs through the Old City to the Damascus Gate, and following them along it was exactly like pursuing three birds which are about to take off but never quite do so, as they scurried along its length, past the Moslem Orphanage, the Fourth Station of the Cross where Jesus met his mother, the House of the Rich Man, Dives, the House of the Poor Man, Lazarus, the Third Station of the Cross where he sank under the weight of it, the Armenian Catholic Church of Our Lady of the Spasm, which is on the site of a Turkish bath on the site of a Crusader church, on the site of a Byzantine basilica, past the Red Mosque and the Greek Praetorium to the Damascus Gate with us literally cantering after them. Then, with the end almost in sight, up Hanevi'im Street through what used to be open country, leaving to starboard the Terra Sancta Tourist Co. Ltd, on Nablus Road, the Franciscan Sisters' Convent, taking a right fork by the Italian Hospital on to Me'a She'arim Street, leaving the Rumanian Patriarchate and various Jewish institutions, such as the Toldot Aharon Yeshiva,* the Batei Hungarim, the Shomrei Hachomot and the Beth Abraham Yeshiva to port and starboard, the Ashkenazim coming up with a very strong finish now as the sun began to set and the Jewish *Shabbat* was about to begin, before suddenly disappearing under an archway into the fastnesses of their dwelling place, Me'a She'arim, having covered something over a mile in just over fifteen minutes, leaving us on our knees.

Me'a She'arim means 'hundredfold' in Hebrew and the name is derived from the text in Genesis which was read in the synagogue when the final decision to found the community was arrived at in 1875: 'Then Isaac sowed in that land and received in the same year a hundredfold and the Lord blessed him.'

This enclave was founded by Shelomo Zalman Beharan, and one long house on the south side of it covers an entire block of a street named after him. Me'a She'arim itself is in the form of a rectangle surrounded by parallel rows of one- and two-storey tenement buildings that face inwards into courtyards rather than outwards, the outer walls of the buildings which form the perimeter presenting a largely windowless front to the outside world, the only way into it being through one of six narrow gateways which can be swiftly barred, as they often needed to be when it was built in what was then the wilderness beyond the city walls. Deep wells, now no longer in use, provided water and could do so again in time of need.

* A *yeshiva* is a school devoted chiefly to the study of rabbinic literature and the Talmud, or a school run by Orthodox Jews for children providing religious and secular instruction.

The place is a fortress, but one with a market place, some minute shops selling everyday necessities and ritual objects, and with its own free food kitchen for the poor and its own resident letter-writer for those who cannot write.

These long low buildings, which bear a remarkable resemblance to the married quarters in a Victorian barracks, are what are known as Warsaw or Hungarian Houses, and they are of the same kind in which the ancestors of the present occupants used to live in in the *shtetlach* of eastern Europe. They were built with the help of donations from Jews in many distant countries and the individuals within it, who inhabit different parts of it according to where they came from originally, Russia, Rumania, Poland or wherever else, and who embrace various sects, more or less extremely orthodox, are still supported, as they always have been, by donations from *Halukah*, fellow Jews abroad. The most extreme of these groups is Neturai Kartah, an ultra-right-wing, anti-Zionist group whose members believe that only the Messiah can establish a State of Israel and that everything that stems from the present administration of the State is therefore invalid and illegal. Its members are forbidden to vote in elections, to do military service or any other kind of work that benefits the State, and their children are forbidden to attend state schools, or make use of swimming pools in which mixed bathing takes place. Post-mortem examinations of the dead are also forbidden and the corpses of members of Neturai Kartah are often literally stolen from mortuaries in order to prevent them taking place.

Everywhere in Me'a She'arim there are admonitory graffiti on the walls inveighing against Zion, and everywhere there are placards, such as the one prominently displayed near the Torah ve'irah, the synagogue of the most orthodox, which reads:

'Jewish Daughter, the Torah obligates you to dress with Modesty. We do not tolerate people passing through our streets immodestly dressed.'

All of this is a source of acute displeasure to modern, free-thinking Israelis, fighting for survival in a modern world, who consider the Ashkenazim who live in Me'a She'arim and other similar enclaves in Israel as idle layabouts and anachronistic impediments to political and material progress, if not as an actual menace to the State.

In fact, if study can be regarded as a form of activity, the Ashkenazim work as hard as anyone. Male children begin at an early age to study Hebrew and the Bible in what is called the *cheder*, literally 'a room', exactly as they did in Europe before the Holocaust. As grown men most of them spend their entire lives studying and expounding the Torah, which is the whole body of the Jewish sacred writings and tradition, including oral expositions of the Law.

The lingua franca is Yiddish, the vernacular language of European Jewry and of emigrants; a dialect of high German with admixtures of words of Hebrew, Romance and Slavonic origin that developed in central and eastern Europe during the Middle Ages, Hebrew being regarded as too sacred for secular use, although it is now the official language of the State of Israel.

By now, although the sky overhead was still bright after the sunset, here in Me'a She'arim it was quite dark. We were standing in a triangular courtyard in the heart of it, surrounded by various communal buildings devoted to religious use, the Yeshivaman, the principal place of assembly and study, behind which was the building where chickens were killed in strict accordance with the requirements of *kashrut*, the Jewish dietary laws, various *chedarim* and the synagogues, now all illuminated within, from which came the sounds of the scriptures being read in unison by the worshippers as they rocked rhythmically backwards and forwards on their heels, worshippers whose entire world revolved about their faith, the limits of which had been fixed immovably by the laws of the Talmud, and who regulated every moment of their lives by the minutely detailed laws of the mediaeval codex known as the *Shulchan Aruch*, otherwise 'The Table Prepared', which was based upon and elaborated from the decisions of the Talmud. They were men whose minds, in spite of having lived for centuries in eastern Europe, were closer in spirit to those of their predecessors who had gone into captivity after the destruction of the Temple 2500 years ago, men whose constant prayers were for the coming of the Messiah and the rebuilding of Zion.

It was also very quiet in Me'a She'arim. This was because the streets that pass near and through it, Shelomo Zalman Beharan Street and Rabbi Abraham Mislonim Street, had, when the sun went down, been closed to traffic. Anyone who now attempted to drive through it until the Sabbath ended on Saturday evening would find himself and his vehicle being pelted with rotten fruit and stones by Ashkenazim boys, who are much tougher than their fragile appearance might lead one to think, all shouting accusingly, '*Shabbat! Shabbat!*'

Meanwhile, inside the houses the women and girls and small children waited for their men to return from the synagogue. Ever since the morning of the previous day, Thursday, until now, at the setting of the sun on Friday, the housewife would have been cleaning the house inside and out and cooking the food in readiness for the Sabbath, during which no work of any kind could be done, taking the twisted loaves sprinkled with poppy-seed in memory of the manna from heaven and making the most important dish of all, the *shalet*, known as *cholent* in Russia, and *chulet* in Bohemia, meat stewed with potatoes and fat, or else with peas, beans and barley, which she would place in the oven or on the top of the stove on Friday afternoon. It would then be hot enough to eat at midday on the Sabbath after the protracted service in the synagogue.

By now she would long since have covered the dining table with a white linen cloth, placed at the head of it the two twisted loaves, symbolic of the double quantity of manna gathered in the Wilderness of Sinai on another far-off Sabbath eve, covering them with a dark velvet cloth with a Hebrew benediction embroidered on it in yellow. Near it she would have put the ritual bottle of raisin wine and at the other end of the table the candles in their candlesticks, after which she would light them before covering her eyes with the palms of her hands and offering up the Hebrew prayer, 'Blessed art Thou, O Lord our God, King of the Universe, who hast sanctified us with His commandments and commanded us to kindle the Sabbath Light.'

She performed all these actions just as her ancestors had done in Jewish towns in Russia and Lithuania within the Russian Pale of Settlement, which no Jew might ever leave, and to which if he did he could never return, a form of imprisonment which began in 1769 in the reign of Catherine II and which endured until the First World War. Her forebears had done exactly the same in such Jewish towns as Mohilev on the bank of the Dniester in White Russia, the sort of town that had an unpaved main street, ankle deep in mud or dust according to the season, with crumbling houses on either side of it in which they lived and ran their businesses. Just as they had done in the Warsaw ghetto, which between the two wars had a population of 300,000 souls, in the cities of Lemberg, Vilna, Kovno, Cracow and Bialystok where, in the 1920s, out of a total population of 90,000 people, more than 50,000 were Jews, a world from which some had escaped to see the lights of Broadway and worked for a living on the Lower East Side, or in Berlin or Vienna, or in the sweat shops in Whitechapel, or down the Mile End Road, or else had escaped to Palestine, or had stayed on in the ghettoes and been taken to the gas chambers. A world that is no more.

We sat in the sunshine on the roof of the Church of the Holy Sepulchre, on chairs kindly provided by the Abyssinian monks. Through it the dome of the Chapel of St Helena sprouted up like some enormous mushroom. The roof forms part of the courtyard of the Abyssinian Monastery, the most hidden away of any of the various sectarian constructions in and around the Church of the Holy Sepulchre and one of the comparatively few places in the city where you can have a bit of quiet.

Far below it, sixteen feet below the level at which the Sepulchre stands, probably in what was the moat of the second city wall, is the site of the original basilica built by Constantine, the first Christian Emperor, in 336, after the discovery of the tomb of the Saviour, 'contrary to all expectation'. In this chapel of St Helena there are two apses. One is dedicated to St Dysmus, the Penitent Thief, which the Armenian Catholics pinched during the plague of 1835 from the Abyssinians, the least bellicose of all the sects which congregate about the Holy Sepulchre, who had jurisdiction over it. The other contains a stone seat said to have been used by the Empress Helena, Constantine's saintly mother, while watching the diggers who eventually, by which time she had already left Jerusalem, unearthed the True Cross of Christ and the crosses of the Two Thieves, the True Cross being identified because it raised a woman from her death bed; the nails being subsequently used to make for the Emperor a priceless horse-bit.

The best way into this courtyard is by a ramp which runs up from Souk Khan es-Zeit, the Market of the Oil Caravanserai, part of a very long, very narrow street which under various names bisects the Old City from north to south, from the Damascus to the Lion Gate. This ramp climbs up between what was once a Russian hospice when pilgrims from Russia still came to Jerusalem, which they did until 1914 in large numbers, and Zalatimo's pastry shop, in which Zalatimo, his descendant or whoever is currently running the business, whirls great sheets of dough round his head, preparatory to plunging them in boiling oil, which is a step on the way to producing a delicious sweet pastry; and in his shop you can see part of the second enclosure wall attributed to Hezekiah, built before the Neo-Babylonian invasion led by Nebuchadnezzar, round 600 BC. Here, too, you can see part of the wall of the atrium, the courtyard of Constantine's original basilica.

Sitting with us on the roof, but in the shade afforded by the dome, were three or four of the Abyssinian monks, who get quite enough sun in the summer months when the roof becomes an inferno, now recuperating from a service in their chapel that is so minute and full of religious equipment that when all those officiating are inside it there is scarcely room for a congregation.

These particular monks – it would be difficult to say whether we had seen the whole lot at the service we had attempted to attend – were typical Abyssinians of the sort I had met in Abyssinia. That is to say they had regular features, long black hair, lively eyes as bright as if they were lit by electricity, and were of various hues from dark olive to jet black. They were also extremely friendly, although it was difficult for any of these particular monks to do anything but smile and make reassuring noises as none of them spoke any tongue with which either of us were acquainted.

Sitting with these kindly, well-disposed men, looking across the roof at the primitive hutments in which they lived under the trees on the periphery of what is one of the two most revered places in Christendom (the other is the Church of the Nativity in Bethlehem), there were so many things that I would have liked to have asked them.

Why, for example, during the service, had the priest, at some particular part of the proceedings, changed his brilliant silk and brocade vestments for even more flamboyant ones? Was their Abbot, the Abouna, Our Father, still appointed by the head of the Coptic Church, 'The Most Holy Pope and Patriarch of the great city of Alexandria and of all the Land of Egypt, of Jerusalem, the Holy City, of Nubia, Abyssinia, and Pentapolis (Cyrenaica), and of all the preaching of St Mark'? St Mark being the founder of the Coptic Church, the native church of Egypt.

I would also like to have known why they kept holy the Jewish Sabbath; why they celebrated Christmas once a month; what the Jewish rites were they had contrived to mix in with their own Christian ones (was this the reason why circumcision was practised and no graven image allowed in their churches?); why it was that they would only eat the meat of animals that did not have cloven hooves or chew the cud; why they had made Pontius Pilate a saint, and why they reverenced the Virgin and a very large number of saints more than the Almighty. Were they still allowed to have wives, providing that they already had them when they were ordained? I would like to have asked these men, members of the smallest and poorest of all the religious communities at the Holy Sepulchre and one without a square foot of territory within the church, a distinction they shared with the Protestants.

Far below us, and what was probably the only monastery on a roof in the entire world, was something unique: a church, or rather a number of churches, in the possession of a number of on the whole mutually antagonistic sects – Greeks, Latins, Armenians, Syrians and Copts – the greater part held by the Greeks, the keys to which were held in perpetuity by a Muslim family to whom they had been entrusted during the time of the Ottoman Turks.

The only parts of this rambling and in some places ramshackle construction common to all these sects – the Protestants are only allowed inside on sufferance – are the vestibule, where the custodians sit, and one aisle of what would otherwise be part of the Greek Cathedral, in which there is the stone, actually a replacement put there in 1808, on which Jesus was laid to be anointed by Nicodemus, a stone that was owned by the Copts in the fifteenth century, the Georgians in the sixteenth century and afterwards by the Greeks. It is now owned by the Latins, who originally paid the Georgians 5000 piastres to be allowed to burn candles over it, a privilege which they now share with the Armenians, the Greeks and the Copts.

Common ground, too, is the Rotunda of the Sepulchre, built in 1810, with a hideous dome added in 1866, and the Holy Sepulchre itself which was reconstructed at the same time by the same architect who worked on the Rotunda, and which contains within it, in the interior chapel, what is said to be the actual tomb, six and a half feet long and six feet wide, now roofed with marble, and which is also the fourteenth and last Station of the Cross, the outer room being the place where the angel rolled away the stone from the mouth of the tomb.

The Greeks, besides having a perfectly enormous church, their so-called Katholicon, own, among other places, the place where St Longinus, the soldier who pierced Christ's side, was cured of blindness; the Place of the Raising of the Cross, of the Mocking and of the Crowning of the Thorns. They also own Calvary, which is fourteen and a half feet up in the air above the level of the Holy Sepulchre and which has a silver-lined cleft in it in which the Cross was set up and, down at ground level, the burial place of Adam's skull on to which Christ's blood dripped, restoring him to life, which is in a cavity which communicates with the Centre of the Earth.

They are also the proprietors of the Stabat, the Place where Mary received Christ's body, while in their church, the Katholicon, they have a stone marking the Centre of the World. They also possess the Place of the Invention, or Discovery, of the Holy Cross and the stone seat in which St Helena sat.

The Latins own the Place of the Nailing, the Place where Mary Magdalene stood, the Place where Our Lord appeared to her in the Guise of a Gardener, the Place where He appeared to His mother after the Resurrection, the Place of the Recognition of the Cross, part of the Pillar to which He was Bound and the Altar of the Franks in the Chapel of St Helena.

The Armenians own the Place where the Virgin Mary stood when the Body of Christ was Anointed, the Chapel of the Parting of Our Lord's Garments, the Chapel of St Helena and the Chapel of the Penitent Thief.

The rest are more modestly endowed. The Copts have what is an extremely lucrative altar attached to the back of the Chapel of the Holy Sepulchre and a chapel adjacent to the Syrians' only possession, a dark, mysterious and highly romantic chapel behind the Sepulchre which communicates with the Tomb of Joseph and Nicodemus. The Copts used to own the Fissure in the Rock of Golgotha, but whether they still do or not is not clear.

There was enough down there in the semi-darkness, whether fact or inspired fiction, to keep any normal intelligence whirling for an eternity, enough even to content the Greeks, Latins, Armenians, Syrians and Copts. The only ones left out were the Protestants and the Abyssinians, and the Abyssinians seemed quite happy up on the roof.

VI

NORTH AFRICA

In and Out of a Pyramid

As no one at the El Nil Hotel, one of the less expensive caravanserais, seemed to have any idea what time rosy-fingered dawn occurs over Cairo in mid-January, we settled for a 4.45 a.m. departure to get us to the Pyramids in time to witness it.

At 4.15 a.m., rather like a *corps-de-ballet* all taking off on the same foot, everything began to happen at once. The alarm clock went off. The telephone waking system jangled into action, operated by the night porter who a few seconds later – we were five floors up – was thundering on the door with what sounded like an obsidian sledgehammer, announcing, 'Your limousine, Mister!' I opened it a couple of inches to tell him that we had got his message and would he kindly desist, and a chambermaid the shape of a scarab beetle slipped in through this chink and began dusting my hat. She was followed by three humble but dogged-looking men, the sort I imagined who had been forced to build the Pyramids. They began shutting our bags, apparently under the impression that we had already had enough of Cairo and were on our way to the exit, although we had not checked in until midnight, having come straight from a party that was probably still going on. In the face of all this, still dressed in pyjamas, I felt my reason going.

'*Ma fish bakshish.*' ('There is no baksheesh.') 'Try again Monday,' I said, the last bit in English, when we were finally ready to go.

'*Mas es-Salama!*' 'Go with safety,' they said, hoping that I would be preserved that long, raising some sickly grins.

Take plenty of baksheesh, ladies and gentlemen, when visiting Egypt under your own steam, unprotected by couriers. Wonderful how it softens the hardest Muslim or Coptic heart, better than any nutcrackers. And do not begrudge it; most people, even those quite far up the social scale, are poorer than it is possible for most of us to imagine.

Then in the limousine, an immense, black, air-conditioned Mercedes, we howled up the road to the Pyramids, the six-mile-long, dead straight Shari el-Ahram, built by the Khedive Ismail for the visit of the Empress Eugènie of France on the occasion of the opening of the Suez Canal in 1869. Then, having traversed it at more than a mile a minute, we climbed on to the escarpment on which the Pyramids would have long since been descried if it hadn't still been pitch black night with a sandstorm in progress.

After a bit we stopped and the driver, a distinguished-looking Egyptian of fifty-odd on whom constant intercourse with the limousine-using classes had conferred the manners of a Firbankean cardinal, assisted us out of the vehicle by the elbows as if we were antiques.

'Good place, Sir,' he said.

'Good place for what?' Apart from a small segment of flying sand, illuminated by the headlights, one could see nothing. The only thing it seemed adapted for was a witches' coven.

'Good place for seeing Pyramids,' he said, gently, as if humouring a couple of loonies, which I suppose, thinking about it in retrospect, was what we were. 'From up there,' pointing into the murk. 'Up there, where there are weruins, broken buildings in the desert, Sir.'

'Is it safe?' I asked. 'I mean for my wife and I to be here alone? It's horribly dark.'

'Safe, Sir, safe? What is safe?'

'I mean are there any bad people?'

'No bad peoples, all good peoples here,' he said, raising his hands in an expansive gesture, as if embracing the teeming inhabitants of the Valley and all those scattered over the three million-square-mile expanse of the Sahara Desert, then dropping them and entering his vehicle.

'Here, I say,' I said, genuinely alarmed at the thought of being left alone in such a spot. 'What time's dawn, actually?'

'Dawn, Sir, actually? About dawn, Sir, actually, I do not know. Will that be all, Sir? Thank *you*, Sir, Madam!' receiving from me a generous helping of closely folded baksheesh which a lifetime of experience told him was an ample sufficiency without actually counting it. And he drove away.

It was now 5.15 a.m. and bloody cold with the wind that was raising the sand around us coming off the snowbound High Atlas in Morocco, 2500 miles to the west, with nothing in between to slow it down as it droned over the debased 'weruins' up to which we climbed. Underfoot they felt like what they were (I had forgotten to bring a torch), a bulldozed brick barrack block with sheaves of those metal rods that are used to keep reinforced concrete together protruding from them, and lots of broken glass, all of which made it impossible to walk or even run about in order to keep warm. We tried running on the spot but it was exhausting. Then we tried slapping one another, but I did it too hard and we had a row.

Then, around 6.15 a.m., the terrible wind suddenly ceased, as if whoever was in charge had switched it off at the main, the sand fell back to earth where it belonged, the sky over the Gulf of Suez and Sinai turned an improbable shade of mauve, overhead the morning star shone down brilliantly out of a sky that had suddenly become deep indigo, and the Pyramids of Giza – two huge ones, of King Cheops and King Chephren, a lesser one of King Mykerinos and three little ones, one behind the other – appeared to rise up out of the ground with the rapidity of mushrooms in a slow-motion film, the only Wonders of the Seven Wonders of the ancient world – first designated by Antipater of Sidon in the second century BC, six of which were on the shores of the Mediterranean (the other, which was not, was the Hanging Gardens of Babylon) – to survive more or less intact.

Looking at them, under a sky that was now rapidly turning from mauve to apple green and lower down was the colour of honey, with the lights of Cairo glimpsed shining between them until they were either switched off or made invisible by the strengthening light of day, there was no doubt that these were among a select body of man-made wonders of any date which in spite of having all the attributes of follies and having suffered severely from over-exposure, actually came up to expectations, if for nothing else, for their shapeliness.

The Great Pyramid was built by King Cheops, Kheops or Khufu, who is thought to have begun his reign in about 2690 BC. It is the first of the three Pyramids built at Giza by the kings of the IVth Dynasty which lasted from 2720–2560 BC. The Great Pyramid was known to the Egyptians by the enigmatic name Ekhet Khufu, the Horizon of Khufu. The other two have more prosaic names.

The Second Pyramid, called Wer-Khefré, Great is Khefré, was built by the king of that name (Herodotus called him Chephren as do most people today), who reigned from about 2650–2600 BC. The Third Pyramid, Neter Menkewré, Divine is Menkewré, was built by the son of Chephren, referred to by Herodotus as Myker-inos, and according to Herodotus its construction was inspired by the Greek courtesan, Rhodopis.

The Great Pyramid is the most famous, the largest, the highest, the most visited, the most written about, the most scrupulously measured and the one that has attracted more crackpots than all the other pyramids put together.

The limestone plateau on which it and the other Giza pyramids are built is roughly a mile square, about forty acres, of which the Great Pyramid covers thirteen acres, the equivalent, according to an American source, of seven New York mid-town blocks. An area large enough, according to an even more assiduous calculator, to contain the Houses of Parliament and St Paul's Cathedral, or the cathedrals at Florence, Milan, St Peter's at Rome, Westminster Abbey and St Paul's.

Napoleon, in a rapid calculation made after he had defeated the Mamelukes at the Battle of the Pyramids, while his generals and savants were on top of the Pyramid admiring the view, worked out that the amount of stone in the Three Pyramids of Giza – what another of his savants, Baron Denon, described as 'the final link between the colossi of art and the colossal works of nature' – was sufficient to build a wall ten feet high and one foot thick round the whole of France (the effect of which would have been incalculable), and this did not include the casing stones.

The Pyramids of Giza remained undamaged externally until 1196, when Malik el-Kamil, a nephew of Saladin, who later became ruler of Egypt, made, for what was otherwise a prudent man, a mad attempt to demolish the Pyramid of Mykerinos. But after months of frenetic activity his demolition workers had only succeeded in stripping part of the casing, which was of granite in the lower courses, limestone in the upper ones, from one of the sides.

In 1356 Sultan Hasan began work on the great mosque which was to bear his name and stone quarried from the Pyramids was used to build what is accepted to be, if not the most beautiful, the finest example of Mameluke architecture in Cairo. Forty years later the Seigneur d'Anglure, on a pilgrimage to the Holy Land, reported 'that of these stones are built, and have been built these many years, the finest constructions to be seen in Cairo and Babylon'.

In a century or so the Arabs succeeded in removing the entire twenty-two acres of limestone casing, eight feet four inches thick, from the Great Pyramid, apart from a few courses at the base which escaped their attentions because they were covered with rubble, and used it not only to build architectural masterpieces but to construct bridges over irrigation canals, walls, dwelling houses and for other mundane purposes.

The last serious plan to destroy the Great Pyramid, some say all three, was made by Mohammed Ali, the viceroy of Egypt, in 1833. He issued an order that the proposed Nile barrages, north of Cairo, which were to control the flow of water through the Delta, should be built with stone from this source. This meant, now that the casing stones had all been used up, removing the backing stones which made up the four faces, and attacking the core, which would have turned it from a pyramid into a shapeless heap of rubble. It was Linant de Bellefonds, the French engineer who initiated the construction of the barrages, who persuaded the viceroy that it would be less expensive to quarry fresh stone than to dismantle a pyramid.

And now, across the mist-filled Valley of the Nile, the sun came roaring up from behind a black rampart of cloud that was resting on top of the escarpment of the Mukattam Hills, turning what is a seven-hundred-foot limestone escarpment into what looked like a colossal mountain range. It shone palely at first on the southern faces of the three big pyramids, but diagonally so that the countless thousands or millions of stones that composed them stood out in such a way that each individual one was distinct from its immediate neighbour and one had the crazy feeling that with enough patience one could have counted them.

As the sun rose it shone down into the thick white mist that filled the valley and illuminated the tops of what must have been some immensely tall palm trees which rose up through it, producing an unearthly effect, as it would be, I imagined, to look across the Styx.

It also illuminated the hideous 'weruins' in which we were imbrangled, and for a few moments it filled the whole of this vast landscape, in which, apart from ourselves, there was not a living thing to be seen, with a vinous, purply light. Then everything turned suddenly golden. It was like the springtime of the world and we set off downhill into the eye of this golden orb for what must be, for no one has so far come up with a scheme to make you pay for looking at them, the greatest free show on earth.

Then, just as the Pyramids had seemed to rise out of the earth, so when we were at last among them, did a picturesque, elderly, shifty-looking Beduin, mounted on a camel and with a donkey in tow, close in to the Pyramid of Chephren. Perhaps he had spent the night in one of the innumerable, lesser tombs with which the plateau is riddled.

'Good morning, King Solomon,' he said, dismounting from the camel which made a noise like a punctured airbed as it sank down, 'I kiss your hand,' seizing it and doing so before I could stop him. 'Good morning, Queen of Sheba, I kiss your hand also.'

'Oh no you jolly well don't!' said the newly-elevated Queen, dexterously avoiding this attention. 'You kiss your own.'

To tell the truth, he was a distinctly smelly old Beduin. If he had come out of a IVth Dynasty rock tomb then he needed a re-embalming service. He was a Nagama, one of a highly sophisticated tribe of Beduin who for uncountable centuries (they may have commissioned the pyramids as a tourist attraction) have descended like swarms of gad-flies on visitors in order to suck them dry of life-giving baksheesh, in return offering their victims camel, horse and donkey rides and, until recently, when some kill-joy forbade the practice, assisting them up the outside of the Great Pyramid, at the same time contriving to manoeuvre female ones wearing skirts into positions of peculiar indelicacy, not all of them fortuitous.

Now he offered us a selection of these various services, including the opportunity to take his photograph in one of the stylized poses the Nagamas permit themselves in this traffic with the infidel. To all of which, not wishing to hurt his feelings but enjoying being called 'King Solomon' as much as I enjoy being addressed as 'Squire' by London taximen, I replied, 'Later, later!'

'Laters, laters! See you laters, alligators! In a whiles, crocodiles!' said the Son of the Desert, getting the message finally that we were a no-show, fishing a transistor designed to look like a military transmitter out of his saddle bag, plugging in to Radio Cairo and departing in a blast of harem music round the south-west corner of the Pyramid of Chephren, which was now the colour of Kerrygold butter but with added colouring, with his donkey in tow.

Close in under the cold, sunless north face of the Great Pyramid, looking up its fifty-one degree slope to a summit eighty-five feet higher than the cross on top of St Paul's, I had the impression that a petrified seventh wave to overtop all seventh waves was about to fall on us and rub us out. Outside the original entrance and another forced entry made by the Caliph al-Mamun in AD 820, which made it look as if it had been gnawed by giant mice, there were two notices: NO SMOKING IN THE PYRAMID and NO CLIMBING THE PYRAMID. Across the way from these holes in the Pyramid two young Japanese, a man and a pretty girl, and an elderly American couple were hovering indecisively outside an office advertising trips to the interior at £2 ($2.80) a head. '*O-nayo-gozaimasu!*' the Japanese said, bowing as if welcoming us to a tea ceremony, baring what looked like a couple of upper and lower sets of silicon chips.

'They don't open till ten,' said the American gentleman whose name, he told us, was Henry Haythorn. 'Can you beat it? Rosie and I got up specially to be here before the coaches. I guess now we'd better go on back down to the Mena House, grab breakfast and come back up again.'

Guarding the entrance to the still-locked interior was a Tourist Policeman, member of an admirable force specially recruited to protect visitors to Egypt from being defrauded and other forms of molestation.

'Gom on,' said this resourceful representative of law and order. 'No need of a ticket. You go now. Many peoples later. Give me one half pound each. Gom on!'

We went in through al-Mamun's forced entry to the Great Pyramid. Abdulla al-Mamun was Caliph of Baghdad, the highly cultivated son of Harun el-Rashid. In AD 820, while on an expedition to Egypt to subdue the Copts and Beduin, he initiated a search for a secret chamber in the Great Pyramid reputed to contain maps and spheres, long-forgotten information about the earth and heavens, rust-proof weapons and glass that would bend without breaking. At that time the glittering white limestone casing that must have made it a truly wondrous sight in sun and moonlight was still in position, as it had been in the time of Herodotus in the fifth century BC, Diodorus Siculus of Agyrium in the first century BC and Strabo, who visited it on a trip up the Nile in 24 BC. Strabo had described a hinged door in the north face which when closed was indistinguishable from the rest of the casing and which led into a low, narrow passage which descended into a vermin-infested pit a hundred and fifty feet below the level of the plateau, on the ceiling of which Greek and Roman trippers had used the smoke of torches to write their names.

Unable to discover the door, which had presumably once more become a secret with the passing of nearly eight and a half centuries, al-Mamun ordered great fires to be banked against the casing stones at the seventh course, which eventually proved to be ten courses lower than the actual entrance. Then, when the stones were red hot, vinegar was poured on them and they shattered. What he and his men found within was remarkable enough architecturally, but they appear to have found no treasure, and the Arab workers employed on the project were extremely displeased.

Inside, the Pyramid was surprisingly hot. The smell was not what we had steeled ourselves to support, what someone had described as being like the inside of a public telephone box. Instead it was the stench of the deodorants with which mad humanity now sprays its nooks and crannies in order to suppress more natural, feral odours. The going was hard. Anything that isn't horizontal in the Pyramid has a gradient of twenty-five degrees, one in two, and I was carrying a suitcase which contained cameras, quantities of baksheesh, passports and some great tomes about pyramids, everything I felt we might need in a pyramid and which I was reluctant to entrust to a policeman, even a Tourist Policeman, as I had no key with which to lock it.

One belief held by some pyramidologists is that the Great Pyramid is an enormous allegory in stone, built under the influence of Divine Revelation, and that every part of it that can be measured has some particular significance.

What is perhaps the finest flowering of this belief was produced by David Davidson, a structural engineer from Leeds. An agnostic when he began his researches in the 1900s, he soon took off more or less completely and published an enormous book *The Great Pyramid: Its Divine Message*, which was one of the volumes inside my suitcase. A best-seller, it is nevertheless one of the most difficult books to read, which is not to denigrate it, as indeed it must have been to write and print. (In case the reader was not getting the message, the author paraphrased whole paragraphs and had them printed in small type in the margin.)

'The Great Pyramid of Gizah,' Davidson wrote, 'is a building well and truly laid, perfect in its orientation, and built within five points symbolising the five points of the fulness of the stature of Christ . . . four define the corners of the base square – symbolising the foundation of Apostles and Prophets – the fifth point the Apex of the Pyramid . . . the Headstone and Chief Corner Stone, Jesus himself as the Head of the Body; the Stone rejected by the Builders.'

Because we had entered the Pyramid by al-Mamun's forced entrance we had failed to travel down the Descending Passage as far as the First Ascending Passage, a stretch which for Davidson symbolized 'The Period of Initiation into the Elements of the Mysteries of the Universe in a Spiritually Degenerate Age, from the time of the Pyramid's construction to the time of the Exodus of Israel', which he dated 2625 to 1486 BC. By doing so we had avoided one of the worst fates in Davidson's Pyramid Game, which was getting into the dead-end of the Descending Passage. This passage began below the First Ascending Passage and, once into it, any member of the human race descended irrevocably towards Ignorance and Evil. We had missed it because al-Mamun's forced entrance had carried us across the Entrance Passage on what was the equivalent of a spiritual fly-over.

However, by missing the way down to Eternal Damnation, we had also missed the entrance to the First Ascending Passage which begins at the date of the Exodus, 1486 BC, ends at the Crucifixion and is symbolized by the granite plug which blocks its lower end, 'sealing up all the Treasures of Light, Wisdom and Understanding'. It was also the 'Hall of Truth in Darkness' up which 'Nation Israel progressed under the Yoke of the Law towards the True Light, the coming of which was to lighten the Darkness of the World'.

There was no doubt about the fate of those who rejected the Messiah. It was awful. Borne swiftly along the horizontal passage leading off from the top of the Hall of Truth in Darkness, symboliz-ing 'The Epoch of Spiritual Rebirth', they found themselves in the Queen's Chamber, otherwise the 'Chamber of Jewish Destiny' and, the way Davidson interpreted it, a spiritual dead-end.

But by now we were no longer engaged in what had been beginning to resemble a game of snakes and ladders, with rules invented by Davidson, played out on an evolutionary, spiritual plane. Instead we were plodding on foot what seemed interminably upwards in al-Mamun's most awesome discovery, the Great Gal-lery, which leads into the heart of the Pyramid. Nearly thirty feet high, a hundred and sixty feet long, its walls of polished granite seven feet apart at their widest point but diminishing in width towards the ceiling, and so finely jointed that it is impossible to insinuate a hair between them, it is a place of nightmare.

It was also Davidson's 'Hall of Truth', a direct route, symbolizing the Christian Dispensation, up which we were climbing at the rate of one pyramid-inch a year, with no chance of taking a wrong turning, from the Crucifixion (7 April AD 30 according to the Old Style, Julian Calendar), to the first day of the Great War (4–5 August 1914, according to the Gregorian, new one). It was rather like being on a moving staircase in a chic department store which normally takes you to the restaurant on the roof without stop-offs but has ceased to function so that you have to foot it.

At the top, having hauled ourselves over a monolith known as the Great Step, which symbolizes 'The Great Epoch of Science for the Consummation of the Age', we passed, bent double, through 'The First Passage of Tribulation' which led from 4 August 1914 to 11 November 1918. From there, after the Armistice, we successfully negotiated 'The Chamber of the Triple Veil' which would have been a continuous period of woe and tribulation, lasting until 1936, if Divine Intervention had not shortened it so that it ended 29 May 1928.

With the goal almost in sight we passed through 'The Passage of Final Tribulation', which extended from 1928 to 1936 – a period (was it a coincidence?) that almost entirely covered my schooldays – after which came the end of all toil and pain and the end of human chronology in 'The Chamber of the Mystery of the Open Tomb', better known as 'The King's Chamber' to non-pyramidologists.

It was a tense moment, the one before entering it. In theory it should have disappeared on the night of 15–16 September 1936, and everything else with it, but it was still there, an astonishing construction at the heart of an edifice in which the epithet loses force from sheer over-use.

In it is what archaeologists believe to be the empty, lidless tomb chest of King Cheops, cut from granite so hard that saws nine feet long with jewelled teeth and drills tipped with diamonds or corundum had to be used to cut it and hollow it out; what some pyramidologists believe to be a symbol of the Resurrection in a chamber in which 'The Cleansing of the Nations in the Presence of the Master of Death and the Grave' should have taken place back in 1936, a happening I would have dearly liked to witness from a safe distance, and judging by the smell inside it something of which they still stood in need. Others believe that it embodies a standard of cubic measure left for posterity to do what it will with.

And above this chamber, which is entirely sheathed in polished granite, unvisitable, are five more chambers, one above the other, with floors and ceilings each composed of forty-three granite monoliths and two enormous limestone ones at the very top, each of the granite ones – many of them badly cracked by an earthquake thought to have taken place soon after the presumed burial of the King (those in the King's Chamber, including walls and ceilings, are all cracked) – weighing between forty and seventy tons. Here, 300 feet or so below the apex of the Pyramid, 200 feet from the nearest open air (the King's Chamber is connected with the open air by two long ducts), and with the ever-present possibility that another earth tremor might bring down something like 4000 tons of assorted limestone and granite monoliths on our heads, I felt as if I was already buried alive.

There was a sudden flash, brighter than a thousand suns as it bounced off the polished walls, caused by the Japanese gentleman letting off a fully thyristorized, dedicated AF 200-type flash on top of a Pentax fitted with a lens that seemed more suitable for photographing what lay on the floor at our feet than the actual chamber. Perhaps this was what he was photographing, this unsuitable human offering on the floor.

'Holy hat!' said a fine hard voice that I recognized as that of Rosie, the Girl from the Middle West. 'Who in hell laid that? Don't say it was the cop. They got a sign outside, "No Smoking". What they want's one saying, "No Crapping".'

'Well, it wasn't one of us,' I said, beginning to suspect that Rosie must have had some more lively incarnation before settling down to life entombment with Haythorn in Peoria, or wherever.

'Let's get out of here,' Wanda said, who in some ways is disappointingly sensitive for one who prefers to travel rough. 'I think I'm going to be sick.'

Whatever the reason, she was not the only visitor to find the King's Chamber too much for her. In it, or on the way to or from it, Abd el-Latif, the chronicler of al-Mamun's excavations, who taught medicine and history at Baghdad, had fainted away. Napoleon, left alone in it on 12 August 1799, at his own request, as Alexander the Great is said to have been, refused to speak of what happened while he was in it, and said that he never wanted the incident referred to again. 'What's the use. You would never believe me,' were his last words on the subject to Count Las Cases on St Helena, shortly before his death.

'I'm with you all the way, honey!' said Rosie. And to me, 'Lead on, Macduff!'

Having set Henry and Rosie safely on course, toddling down the road towards the Mena House, we went to visit the Nagamas, down at the place below the plateau where they relaxed and fed their animals bright green forage. There they didn't try to sell you anything. They sat looking noble by their dung fires, surrounded by couched camels, donkeys which occasionally let loose volleys of hysterical, spine-chilling shrieks, and hobbled horses, belly-aching about the state of the nation and particularly of the tourist trade. It was like being in the worst sort of London club.

'No more Yumbos,' they said, which was all Sadat's fault, getting himself assassinated. 'No more English! No more Germans! No more Americans! No more French!' one elder intoned. It sounded like a dirge, or an end-of-term hymn. We tried to persuade them that it was a world recession that was keeping people at home and the jumbo-jets half empty and shouldn't they be thinking of putting a few of their fellow Nagamas in mothballs until things looked up, but it was no good and we left them listening to their soothsayer and nodding in gloomy acquiescence.

> The *Ascent* of the Pyramid though fatiguing is perfectly safe. The traveller selects two or three of the Beduin. With one holding each hand, and the third pushing behind, he begins the ascent of the steps. The ascent can be made in 10–15 minutes but, in hot weather especially, the traveller is recommended to take nearly double the time . . .
> *Egypt and the Sudan*, Karl Baedeker, 8th edition

Later that afternoon I climbed the Great Pyramid from the north-west corner in Baedeker's ten minutes without any Beduin to push, pull and support me. The easiest way is from the north-east corner, but as it is now forbidden to climb it from any corner I wanted to be out of sight of the Pyramids police station which is situated in what used to be one of King Farouk's pleasure houses on the edge of the plateau below the east face. The top, truncated by the removal of the limestone, is about twelve yards square, and I was the only one on it.

The view could scarcely have been more extensive. To the west, the north-west and to the south, where the stepped Pyramid of Sakhara, prototype of the Giza Pyramids, stood on the edge of the plateau above the valley, was the Libyan desert which in the late afternoon sunshine looked as if melted chocolate had been poured over it. Across the river, below the cliffs of the Mokattam Hills, from which so much of the 6,000,000 tons of stone used to build this single pyramid was quarried, were the mosques and spectacular minarets of Muslim Cairo, the largest city in Africa, and the great labyrinthine cemeteries, now also occupied by the poor. And the other cities: the secretive remnants of Old Coptic Cairo which also conceals within it the first known city on this site; the Roman, pre-Christian fortress called Babylon, and out beyond it, lapped by smoking rubbish dumps that may soon engulf them, the burnt brick and stone remains of El Fustat, the oldest Arab settlement, established in AD 641. And down towards the Nile, to the north of Old Cairo, was the modern city with the high buildings rising above it, not enough of them, as in Manhattan, to form groves and forests which gives them an air of majesty, but as they are in London, in melancholy twos and threes, or completely isolated.

And out beyond the road to the Pyramids which we had traversed what now seemed a long time ago, lined with rickety-looking apartment blocks and night clubs and hoardings advertising enormous belly dancers, was rural Egypt, full of fields of dark Nile silt intersected by canals with the tall palm trees soaring overhead. Fields in which the *fellahin*, the peasants, who still make up some 80 per cent of the population, men with big bones, yellowish complexions, wide mouths full of excellent, intensely white teeth, rather thick noses, and dense black eyelashes shielding brilliant almond eyes, use wooden ploughs drawn by bullocks and raise water from one level to another using the *shâdûf*, a bucket suspended by a rope from a swinging beam suspended between two uprights with a counterpoise weight at the other end, just as their ancestors are shown doing on the walls of the ancient tombs. Men who for working in the fields wear nothing but a skull-cap, cotton drawers and a sort of apron. Their women wear the *burko*, or face veil of black crepe, which conceals everything except the eyes, beautified with *kohl*, made with smoke-black which is produced by burning a sort of aromatic resin. In some cases the *burko* reaches almost to the feet which, like the hands, are stained with henna. Some have tattoo marks in blue or greenish colours tattooed on their foreheads, hands and feet. They live in single-storeyed houses that are simple rectangles of Nile mud thatched with straw in which the hens roost. By nature home-loving, despising persons of every other faith as children of perdition, submissive yet obstinate, cheerful, hospitable, temperate yet licentious, quarrelsome, terrible liars (falsehood was commended by the Prophet when it tended to reconcile persons at variance with one another and in order to please one's wife, and in Egypt has long since reached a point of development that entitles it to be regarded as an art form) and hard-working by necessity rather than nature.

Long ago their ancestors migrated from western Asia to the Valley of the Nile, which they called Atur. There they settled on its banks and mingled their blood with that of the indigenous Africans and, by the construction of a complex system of irrigation works which relied on the *shâdûf* or on long lines of men simply passing buckets from one to another, they succeeded in winning from the deserts which hemmed the river in closely on either side, a thin green line of oasis which extended downstream to the point below the present city of Cairo where the waters of the Nile expand to water a fan-shaped area of constantly replenished alluvium, the Delta, which, together with the region between the Tigris and the Euphrates, was the richest farm land in the whole of the ancient world.

They were the first recorded people to sail the waters of the Mediterranean, but not the first to do so. In about 2600 BC the Pharaoh Seneferu, the immediate predecessor of Cheops, the builder of the Great Pyramid, ordered the cutting of a hieroglyphic inscription at Medum on the left bank of the Nile in Lower Egypt, where he was subsequently interred in a great, stepped pyramid. It announced the bringing of forty ships of one hundred cubits with cedar wood from Byblos on the coast of Lebanon, the oldest known city, for the furnishing of temples and palaces, the first recorded sea voyage in the history of the world, although by that time men had already been sailing in the Mediterranean for at least four thousand years.

The Egyptian ships were little more than scaled-up river boats with punt-shaped hulls. They were equipped with a single sail and were propelled by a dozen or so oarsmen on either side and they were steered with oars lashed to upright posts.

By the time the voyage to Byblos took place Egyptian civilization was highly developed and extremely sophisticated. The Egyptians had the advantage of living on the banks of the Nile, the only really navigable river that debouched into the Mediterranean; but in spite of this they were basically freshwater rather than deepwater sailors, using river boats, the smaller ones made of papyrus reed, for internal communication and depending for their prosperity on intensive farming rather than on external trade.

But in spite of knowing these things, and in spite of what someone in London before we left on this trip had said about the top of the Pyramid being a good place to collect my thoughts about the Mediterranean, it was no good at all. For one thing I couldn't see it. For another, however fine the view and what it conjured up, for me it was the Pyramids themselves, and particularly the one I was at present standing on, that dominated everything. In the mind's eye it was the embodiment of what can only be described as an insane and misplaced expenditure of human effort which for the protagonists, except those of the ruling and priestly caste who initiated it, can have had little or no religious significance and have given little hope of personal salvation, or even of an afterlife.

According to what seems a more or less generally accepted opinion based on the writings of Herodotus, the only author of ancient times to have left an account of their construction, 100,000 men were employed each year for three months from July to the end of October (the period when the Nile flooded and the mass of the population would have been idle) on the building of the Great Pyramid for a period of twenty years. In addition there would have been a large force of quarrymen and stonemasons, estimated at some 40,000, who would have worked all the year round. It has also been estimated that a further 150,000 women and children, dependants of the workers, would have encamped around the site, and that a large proportion of the 400,000-strong standing army would have had to be deployed as guards.

The number of stones transported was approximately 2,300,000, including 115,000 glittering white limestone casing stones, with an average weight of two and a half tons. About 115,000 blocks a year which, if each one was handled, as they are thought to have been, by gangs of eight men – inscriptions recording the names of individual members of such gangs have been discovered – would have meant each gang moving ten or twelve blocks every twelve days, from the Mokattam quarries to the right bank of the Nile on a causeway, then across the river by boat and up to the plateau on another causeway. Ten years alone may have been devoted to the construction of this colossal causeway on the left bank, and if this is so then the figures given may be completely wrong.

If they are not wrong (the figures are Sir Flinders Petrie's) and are not a gross underestimate, this meant, assuming 7300 work-days, delivering 315 stones a day, 26 stones an hour, working 12 hours a day. However this does not take into account the granite monoliths used in the construction of the King's Chamber and the others above it, some of which weighed 70 tons, the weight of a locomotive. They were cut in the quarries of Syene, near Aswan, 500 miles upstream, and transported to the site in reed boats. To drag such blocks, and there were limestone blocks used for the same purpose of commensurable size, up a simple incline of one in twenty-five, the gradient of the Giza causeway, would have required at least 900 men for each block, disposed in double ranks and hauling on four ropes to raise them 120 vertical feet to the plateau. Once they reached the plateau the stones had to be lifted into position, and some experts suggest that a simple, straight, inclined ramp, of the sort referred to by Herodotus, would have been impracticable as it would have had to be increased in height constantly as the building progressed, with a consequent increase in gradient. To carry a one in ten ramp to the top of the Pyramid would have meant starting it more than 3000 yards from the foot of it, down in the river valley, and this would have required more than 75,000,000 cubic feet of mud bricks, four times the number of cubic feet of stone in the entire Pyramid. Various suggestions have been made as to how it was done: by the use of tapering ramps or with ramps with slanting sides which wound up around the Pyramid, encompassing it on all four sides. The refuse from the cutting of the stone at the site, which was thrown down over the escarpment, amounted to half the bulk of the entire Pyramid, and this was only one of three.

So far as is known all that has ever been found in the Great Pyramid is the single, empty tomb chest, vermin and huge bats. It may have been pillaged as early as the XIIth Dynasty, 2000–1790 BC, the most prosperous period in the history of Ancient Egypt.

What was it, if it was not a tomb, or besides being a tomb? Our suitcase also contained a giant paperback version of a book entitled *Secrets of the Great Pyramid*, written by an American, Peter Tompkins, who first visited it in 1941. His book sums up more or less everything known about it. Without Sir Flinders Petrie, Tomp-kins and Davidson, none of whose books are really suitable for reading in the field, to me the Pyramid would have been a pyramid built that way because the builders liked the shape.

Is it, Tompkins asked, to quote him, pure chance that its structure incorporates a value for *pi* (the ratio of the circumference of a circle to its diameter) accurate to several places of decimals; that the King's Chamber incorporates the sacred triangles which Pythagoras embodied in his theorem, triangles which Plato said were 'the building blocks of the Cosmos'? Does its shape incorporate the fundamental proportions of what is known as the golden section (the proportion of the two divisions of a straight line, or the two divisions of a plane figure, such that the smaller is to the larger as the larger is to the sum of the two, known by the Greek letter *phi*)? On the other hand were *pi*, Pythagoras' Theorem and *phi* known about at the time the Pyramid was built?

Was it built as an almanac, by means of which the length of the year could be measured accurately; a giant theodolite, used for surveying the Delta and the Nile Valley; an accurately adjusted compass; a geodetic marker from which the geography of the world could be extended; a celestial observatory from which maps and tables of the stellar hemisphere could be accurately reproduced; a depository of an ancient system of weights and measures, left for posterity; a scale model of the northern hemisphere, incorporating the geographical degrees of latitude and longitude; or a building constructed under the influence of Divine Revelation, an allegory in stone?

All the various and almost innumerable theories seem to depend on the meaning attributed to such terms as 'accurate' and 'precise', and whether the various sorts of measures used, such as 'British inches', 'sacred inches', 'pyramid inches', 'sacred cubits', 'profane cubits' and other variations, have been manipulated to achieve a desired result.

As one American coarsely put it: 'If a suitable measurement is found – say versts, hands or cables – an exact equivalent to the distance to Timbuctu is certain to be found in the roof girder of the Crystal Palace, or in the number of Street Lamps in Bond Street, or in the Specific Gravity of Mud . . .'

I was now joined by a host of little Nagamas, fiends in night-shirts who had seen me climb the Pyramid and now, with their insatiable demands for baksheesh and their constant tugging at my clothing, very nearly succeeded in driving me round the bend.

Before retreating I took one more look over the edge. It was a

Friday, the Muslim day of rest, and the lower courses of the Great Pyramid and to a lesser extent that of King Chephren were filled, although the sun was setting now, with happy bands of modern Egyptians, couples and families and bands of students, most of whom had come out from Cairo or Giza by bus, car, shared taxi, or on motorcycles to spend the day picnicking, singing, sometimes to the accompaniment of musical instruments, or listening to transistors, while others played football on the level expanses at the foot of it. Almost all, without exception, if we passed close enough to them, had welcomed us to Egypt, had asked us if we liked the country, if we liked them, and, if they were eating or drinking, had invited us to join them. The proximity of these Egyptians also ensured in some mysterious way freedom from the attentions of the Nagamas. What a difference, I thought, it made in one's relations with them, to be no longer a member of an occupying army, as I had been, who referred to them one and all collectively as 'wogs'.

When I reached the bottom I was met by the same Tourist Policeman who had admitted us to the Pyramid.

'No climbing of the Great Pyramid,' he said severely. It was as if we had never met before. 'Fine is fifteen Egyptian pounds.'

'I haven't got fifteen Egyptian pounds,' I said. It was true. I imagined he wouldn't want a cheque on American Express.

'OK,' he said. 'You give me one Egyptian pound.'

'OK,' I said. I liked this policeman. He reduced justice to a level of extreme simplicity, if not absurdity.

'OK,' he said, pocketing the money, saluting smartly and moving off, having successfully solved yet another problem for a foreign tourist in distress.

Return to Tobruk

To Colonel Muammar Al-Qathafi,
The Socialist People's Libyan Arab Jamahiriyah. Tripoli
Al-Jamahiriyah Al-Arabia Al Shabiya Al Ishtirakiya
Tarabulus.

Dear Colonel Qathafi,
    I am engaged in writing a book about the various
countries on the shores of the Mediterranean and I would
very much like to visit the Socialist People's Libyan Arab
Jamahiriyah.
    I have a particular reason for wishing to do so, which is
as follows:
    I am an ex-officer of a British Infantry Regiment, The
Black Watch (The Royal Highland Regiment). On the
morning of 20 November 1941, the Second Battalion of the
Regiment which had previously taken part in the defence of
Heraklion Airfield in Crete was ordered to break out of the
Tobruk fortress which at that time had been invested by the
Axis forces commanded by General Rommel for more than
seven months and take a strong point to the south-east of
the perimeter. Although the battalion succeeded in reaching
and taking this objective the cost was very high. In the

course of two hours 456 men and 24 officers were either killed or wounded.

Those who died that morning and many who died subsequently are buried in the British and Commonwealth War Cemetery at Tobruk. I am sure that you, as a soldier, will understand how much I would like to visit the Cemetery, and also Tobruk itself of which I have so many vivid memories even after more than forty years have passed.

I do hope that you will give this request your sympathetic consideration, and if you do grant it I would also very much appreciate being given the opportunity to meet you personally. I would also like to bring my wife with me.

As we are at present in Italy, at the above address, may I ask that if permission is granted, it is relayed to your Diplomatic Mission in Rome, rather than to London.

> Yours sincerely,
> Eric Newby, ex-Lieutenant, The Black Watch
> (The Royal Highland Regiment)

There was nothing in Rome at the People's Bureau when we went there to find out. The Libyans do not refer to their missions as Embassies any more. Nothing in London when we returned there. Then one day an envelope arrived with a Libyan stamp on it. It contained a letter typed on a flimsy sheet of paper with bright green edging and in the margins two of what were presumably the Leader's *obiter dicta* in Arabic, French and English. One of them read 'To Dispense with The Natural Role of Women Is Start In Dispensing With Human Society', the other 'The Blacks Will Prevail In The World', which seemed a rather mysterious statement by someone who was quite rightly proud of the fact that he was a Beduin.

The letter read as follows:

Dear Sir,

This is to acknowledge receipt of your letter addressed to Brother Colonel Muammar Qathafi, Leader of the 'ELFATA' Great Revolution.

We are pleased to inform you that we have no objection to the visit you wish to pay to Al-Jamahiriyah, in the context of your request.

> With best regards,
> Revolution Leader's Bureau

Jamahiriyah, a word difficult to translate really, means the People being the Source of Power (the State of the Masses, the Authority of the People, People's Polity, are other ways of expressing it, all of which have official blessing). It is synonymous with El Fatah, The Great Libyan Revolution, which took place in 1969 when the then ruler of Libya, King Mohammed Idris Al-Senussi, was deposed by a group of army officers, twelve of whom formed the Revolutionary Command Council, one of whom was Colonel Muammar Qathafi, the man who formulated the principle of Jamahiriyah, which he expressed in his definitive work on the subject, *The Green Book*, which has the same authority as a source of good in Libya today as did until recently the *Thoughts of Chairman Mao* in China. These abstractions were given concrete-form by the creation throughout the country of People's Committees which make their feelings known at what are known as Popular Congresses. Their propositions are then submitted to the General People's Congress whose members debate them and then propose a series of amended draft propositions, which are then sent down the line again and submitted to the Popular Congresses, People's Committees, Syndicates and Unions and so on, that make up this apparently democratic way of doing things. Once this has been done, and the motions to go ahead carried, the People's Committees responsible to the Popular Congresses can then start executive action. This, in its simplest form, is, so far as I can make out, the revealed Theory of Jamahiriyah.

But what at that particular moment interested us more, not yet having been able to lay our hands on a copy of *The Green Book* which had been out of stock in Rome when we were there, was from whom this unsigned letter emanated.

We were left in no doubt about this when we went, armed with it, to apply for visas at the Libyan People's Bureau, next door to William Waldorf Astor's old town house in St James's Square, and handed it to the Secretary of the People's Committee, the Head of the Mission, otherwise the Ambassador.

'It really is quite a rare letter,' he said, having perused it closely. 'Why don't you frame it? Meanwhile I will have it photostatted.'

'I wonder if he's going to frame the photostat,' Wanda said when we were once more out in the street on English soil.

A couple of weeks later we arrived in Libya, whether as guests of Leader or not was uncertain. Whether we were to blame or whether his executives were to blame was also uncertain, but whoever was at fault we had somehow contrived to slip into this at the best of times difficult-to-get-into country unnoticed. No mean feat, having survived three successive passport checks and an inquisition by the teenage customs officials. It was only when we went to the bank to change some money that it was discovered that we had somehow failed to be given a currency declaration to fill in, and were sent back through immigration control to go through the whole process of entering the country again, as if we had been playing snakes and ladders and had landed on a particularly long snake. By the time we made our second debut in Libya more than an hour and a half had passed since our first visit and if anyone had been meeting us they would by now have long since given up and gone home. As a last resort I rang the only telephone number we had in the entire country, which was that of one of the Leader's advisers who had at one time fallen from grace but had now apparently been reinstated in favour, but there was no reply.

Three hours after landing at Tripoli airport – 'How time flies!' as Wanda said – we set off for the city, which some people call Tarabalus, in a bus loaded with genial, moustached Turkish labourers, all as tough as old boots, who were on their way back from the wilds of Anatolia to complete what for them was a three-year, wifeless stint building apartment blocks in what had been, until 1912, when the Italians took over the country, part of the Ottoman Empire in North Africa. Meanwhile, outside in the open air, a cloudburst was in progress, accompanied by thunder and lightning which lit up the shells of some of these apartment blocks in the western suburbs, which from what one could see of them in such conditions looked surprisingly well designed and robust, as were a lot of the buildings we subsequently saw in Libya, many of which had been designed by distinguished foreign architects and apparently constructed without thought of expense. From time to time the bus stopped to allow little bands of Turks to get down and stagger off to their billets in the rain and darkness with bulging suitcases, and by the time we reached the centre of the city the bus was Turkless.

By this time, too, the rain had almost ceased, and in the absence of any taxis and with the help of a kindly Libyan boy who was a conscript in the navy and just like conscripts anywhere in the world hating every minute of it, we lugged our luggage half a mile or so through waterlogged streets to the Libyan Palace Hotel, the sort of hotel to which people like ourselves naturally gravitate when travelling at their own expense round the shores of the Mediterranean but which, modest though it appeared, still cost the equivalent of something like £28 ($40) a night for a double room with breakfast, having previously tried, without success, to locate a Youth Hostel which is said to exist somewhere in the city.

There we were allocated a succession of rooms on various floors. The first had no electric light bulbs; the second had lights but they could not be extinguished; the third had no lock on the door; the fourth, which we finally accepted, was reached by a carpetless corridor from which the paint had been stripped in preparation for redecoration and looked down out over a gloomy well on to the windows of other similar rooms. By the time we got to the fourth room, dinner was off. Told that we could dial room service for dinner in our room, I did so. We instantly received an iron tray covered with newspaper which bore a soggy bread roll sliced in half, two cubes of Lurpak Danish butter done up in silver foil, and two small segments of Pingouin pasteurized French cheese packed in a similar fashion but with no knife to spread it, presumably in case we might be tempted to use it to do away with ourselves, no plates, no glasses, but with a festive magnum of Pepsi to celebrate what was my birthday. Outside the storm had returned, the thunder rolled and the rain fell into the well outside our window in such torrents that I wondered if we ought to move to the top floor in case it filled it.

After this repast, principally because it was my birthday which had not been going all that well up to now, Wanda suggested that we might descend to the foyer and mingle with the other guests, most of whom were in Libya to fulfil the 1981–5 Five-Year Plan on behalf of their hosts. Among them we identified, and in some instances spoke to, Italians, here regarded as the best of all foreign workers, Southern Irish, South Koreans, Canadians, Filipinos, members of the Eastern bloc impossible to identify because they hardly ever spoke, and Cubans, regarded by the Libyans as the worst of all foreign workers. Some were drinking what was really excellent coffee, others were going to pieces as I had already done on Pepsi Cola drunk straight from the bottle. All those we spoke with were counting the days, months or years that would have to elapse before they could finally go home and never return. Possession of alcohol in Libya, quite apart from drinking it, is a criminal offence, even for diplomats in the seclusion of their embassies, yet according to a Canadian who seemed well informed about such matters, some of the Eastern bloc countries financed the entire day-to-day running of their embassies by smuggling Scotch into the country and then trading it at £100 a bottle, £1200 a case.

All in all it was an appropriate end to a drinkless birthday on one of the wilder shores of the Mediterranean. After the best part of half a magnum of Pepsi I felt as if I was the Graf Zeppelin, about to float out over the Gulf of Sirte where I would be shot down by the Sixth Fleet. I decided to take up smoking.

The following morning we asked to be moved and they took our luggage to the room without any lights. Then they put it in another room and couldn't remember which one. By this time we felt our reason going. All the telephones in the hotel were out of action because of the storm which was now blowing out of a cloudless sky, hurling the sea over the harbour mole and threatening to uproot the palm trees, and so we set off for the British Embassy, which was not much more than a biscuit's toss away on the waterfront, in order to try and find some way of getting into communication with some members of the Libyan administration. Fortunately for us, the Chargé d'Affaires was, besides being an Arabic speaker, a kindly, hospitable man and after a lot of telephoning which thoroughly disrupted his morning, he succeeded in handing us over to them.

Apparently, the Libyans had been searching for us high and low but could not conceive that we would have stayed in anything as sleazy as the Libyan Palace Hotel; and now we were instantly transferred to the recently completed Grand Hotel, a lap of luxury if ever there was one, in which double rooms were £100 ($140) a night, built by the Swedes and equipped by the East Germans with such sophisticated bugging apparatus that every time we went to the lavatory we felt we ought to apologize for the noises. It was a pity that by the time we checked in, which was about 3.30 in the afternoon, there was hardly anything left to eat in the restaurant. So instead of eating, having been told that there was a fifty-fifty chance of meeting the Leader in the course of the next few days, I sat down and began to formulate the sort of questions that leaders tend to get asked when they grant interviews, and pretty feeble they sounded when I read them back.

But I was never to meet the Leader, whose guests we now were, and who acted throughout our stay in his country rather like a fairy queen in a pantomime, although in this case an invisible one who continued to be invisible, because, as it later transpired, he had other more pressing matters on his mind (what may have been the prelude to an assassination attempt – if it was an attempt, it was the ninth since December 1982).

Invisible he may have been, but he appears to have waved a magic wand which enabled us to get to Tobruk, and it was a strange sensation being back there after so long, a near miracle it seems in retrospect. I had been there in the winter of 1941, one of a detachment of the Special Boat Section, a little force set up in 1940 to land behind the enemy lines, which were out in the desert forty miles west of Tobruk at Gazala. From Tobruk we operated with a flotilla of MTBs which was using the port as a base. They were glamorous craft armed with torpedoes, twin Oerlikon guns, Lewis guns, depth charges and so on and it was fun roaring about in them at thirty knots or so, but they were not ideal for the sort of clandestine operations we were endeavouring to engage in. They were incredibly noisy: each boat was equipped with three 1000 h.p. aircraft engines and they could be heard dozens of miles away. For this reason, returning from some long abortive sortie westwards of Gazala towards Derna, with the sun already up in the east and ourselves just abreast of the enemy line, it always seemed a miracle to me that we were not given the Stuka treatment.

Tobruk was extremely noisy too. The Germans were intent on rendering it unusable as a supply port for the Eighth Army and each afternoon Stukas, sometimes in very large numbers, would come screaming down out of the sun with their sirens going full blast and with everything in and around the harbour firing flat out at them: Bofors guns, Oerlikons, 3.7s, machine guns, rifles, rockets linked to one another with piano wire. When these raids occurred, living on board one of the MTBs, each of which was deep loaded with high octane petrol, or on their minute depot ship with the bombs roaring down into the harbour on all sides, one felt horribly exposed.

Next to being on board a ship in the harbour, one of the most exposed positions in Tobruk was occupied by what was called Navy House, the former Italian Port Office which was situated on an eminence above it. Navy House was equipped with an excellent bar which served Plymouth gin, and the naval officers who patronized it used to keep a rack of Lewis guns, stripped of their cooling jackets to make them more manageable, in a rack in the vestibule, just as they might have left their umbrellas in the vestibule of the Naval and Military Club in London before the war. And when the Stukas were announced as '20 plus' or '30 plus' or whatever the number was coming in from the west up the length of the harbour, they would drain their pink gins, pick up their Lewis guns, offer their guests one if there were enough to go round and would then take to the caves in the cliffs from where they would spray away at them as they came diving in.

Now I had come back, forty-two years later, with the intention of following the course of a battle on foot, a battle that had started at six-thirty on a November morning.

It was about six forty-five, and the sun was shooting up over the edge of the desert just as it had done what now seemed long ago behind the Mukattam Hills beyond the Nile, in doing so ending our freezing vigil in the darkness among the 'weruins' at the Pyramids. Only now it was a blood-red sun not a golden one and it was coming up beyond the barbed wire fence, sixty miles away on the frontier between Egypt and Libya, that General Graziani built back in the thirties to keep out the gun-running camel caravans from Egypt that were supplying the Libyan Beduin with arms to fight the Italians. A fence five feet high, thirty feet wide and 250 miles long that extends from the Mediterranean to the edge of the Great Sand Sea.

It was very cold, as it always is in winter until the sun has been up for a few hours, here in what geographers and historians call the Marmaric Desert and what everyone else who has been here as a soldier or in the desert on the Egyptian side of the wire calls the Western Desert, a desert which is not really a desert but a semi-desert. This semi-desert, composed of clay or limestone dust, was now very sticky from the rain that had fallen during the last weeks. It was dotted with small tussocks of the dry, pale green scrub called *agam* on which camels of the Beduin browse as if it was some undreamt of luxury, and with some shrubs that were something between a bush and a miniature tree, called *hillab*. In fact with this sparse vegetation apparently floating on its wet surface the desert here looked more like the Sargasso Sea than terra firma, stretching away to what appeared to be a limitless horizon, the only features in this apparently vast expanse an occasional *hillab* slightly larger than its neighbours, but in this context of near nothingness something which drew the eye.

In fact the horizon was only three miles off. Beyond it the terrain began to slope away gently away downhill for another three miles or so before rising equally gradually to a low escarpment a little less than 200 feet above the sea. Along this escarpment for more than a hundred miles ran the Trigh Capuzzo, one of the old caravan routes and one of the most famous and fought-over tracks in the whole of North Africa. The place names on the Trigh Capuzzo are mostly those of wells, the tombs of Muslim holy men, or are the meeting places with other tracks, or some point that originally had few if any features at all but was one that had been chosen by a commander of one of the contesting armies as a place to hold. One of these was Knightsbridge, an eight-figure map reference (37984118) on a piece of corrugated iron supported by empty oil drums which indicated the existence of a defensive box hemmed in by wire and minefields. All these named places – Sidi Azeiz, Gasr al Areid, Bir Harig, Sidi Rezeg, El Duda, El Adem, Sidra, Knightsbridge, Sidi Muftah and Mteifel – were as well known to those who were actually fighting around them as their own native high streets and to those who survived these battles as well remembered as La Haie Sainte, Rorke's Drift and Delville Wood had been to earlier generations of soldiers in other wars.

Here in the 4500 yards of featureless terrain between the south-eastern perimeter of the Tobruk fortress, where we were standing, and the point where the ground begins to slope away downhill before beginning to climb again to the Trigh Capuzzo, the destruction of the 2nd Black Watch had taken place in the two hours between 6.30 and 8.30 on the morning of 20 November 1941.

Looking at it, one of the smaller of the battlefields in which the desert abounded, I felt my blood run cold. I had spoken to friends who had taken part in this battle, immediately afterwards. I had read the regimental history,* and I now for the first time viewed it from the point of view of what I would probably have been if I had been present at the battle, a lieutenant commanding a platoon of perhaps thirty men.

In the simplest terms – this is not a military history – the aim was to break out from the Tobruk fortress, then surrounded by Axis forces, and to link up with the Allied armour which was sweeping up from the Egyptian frontier. The immediate aim of the Black Watch was to attack and carry an advanced German post known as Jill which was about two miles out from the perimeter across the

---

* Bernard Fergusson, *The Black Watch and the King's Enemies* (Collins, 1950).

terrain I had compared to the Sargasso Sea. Having taken it they were to carry on and take Tiger a mile further out, a very heavily defended strongpoint which was both wired and mined.

In support the Black Watch had what was generally conceded to be one of the finest gunner regiments in the British Army, the 1st Royal Horse Artillery, who had long since given up using horses to take their guns into battle, and three squadrons of a tank battalion. One squadron was to attack Tiger from the right rear and another would make the frontal assault on Jill and Tiger. Without the tanks an attack on such terrain using infantry could not possibly take place. To attempt it would be suicide. In fact, on the morning of the attack, the tanks failed to emerge from the fortress on time and when they did, at 6.34, four minutes late, they immediately advanced in the wrong direction, north-eastwards towards Butch, another position on the left flank, which was to be attacked by the King's Own, another British infantry regiment, instead of south-eastwards, straight ahead, towards Jill. Perhaps their commander was not altogether to blame. Enemy positions such as these were notoriously difficult to identify at a distance, even with binoculars. At this point the tanks got stuck in a minefield and four of them were blown up.

Meanwhile, B Company of the Black Watch, the company selected to take Jill, with only the memory of the hot tea and rum they had been issued with two hours previously to sustain them, set off on its two-mile advance towards it, completely unprotected in the face of heavy machine-gun fire from the Germans in Jill and also from machine guns on their left flank, which caused appalling casualties. Eventually they reached their objective and took it with the bayonet, but by the time they had succeeded in doing so they had to all intents and purposes ceased to exist. Of the five officers, three were dead, one was dying and the last was seriously wounded, and of what had been a hundred NCOs and men only eleven remained, ten men and the Company Sergeant Major, to carry on to Tiger a mile away to the south-east. This they did when the rest of the battalion came up, also unsupported by tanks, to attack it.

In and around Tiger there was the best part of a German machine-gun battalion supported by mortars and artillery and the battalion, led by its pipers, advanced into what the survivors described as being like a hailstorm, but a hailstorm of lead. Before setting off the men had been told that if they were hit they must bayonet their rifles in the ground so that the stretcher bearers could find them. Soon the field in the wake of the advance began to look as if a whole forest of rifles had been planted in it.

It was the Pipe-Major and the Pipe-Sergeant who played the battalion in on to their objectives with the regimental march, *Highland Laddie, Lawson's Men* and the music called *The Bear*. The Pipe-Major, hit three times, after which he was taken back to a dressing station, astonished German prisoners there by continuing to play while his wounds were being dressed by a captured German doctor, in order to put heart into the other wounded.

Finally, at around 8.30 a.m., Tiger was taken with the bayonet and large numbers of prisoners with it. But at what a cost. Of the 32 officers and something over 600 men who had crossed the start line two hours previously only 8 officers and 160 men were left.

In the face of such discipline and heroism displayed by friends and comrades dead and gone, and by those who survived, I had not even the courage to ask myself if the action had been necessary at all, and if it had been necessary whether it had been worth it. Looking at the long lines of headstones in the Tobruk cemetery, which we visited on our way back, each with its beautifully carved regimental crest, a cemetery that was so magnificently kept by its Muslim custodian, I could only pray that it had been.

That same afternoon we sat in the dining room of the hotel in which we had been put up, eating a very late lunch of Libyan soup and roast chicken of which there are inexhaustible quantities in Libya and which might well, just as the meat does, come from Bulgaria, and washing it down with a strange, gaseous, non-alcoholic bright red drink called 'Bitter'. Altogether we formed quite a mob. There was our horribly fast driver who had just admitted to having six children but was not a day over twenty-six, nothing compared with the manager of the hotel who told us he had twenty-four brothers and sisters (we didn't ask how his mother was); there was Mr Seddik Mabruk Jedalla, the head of the Press Office in Benghazi who although he spoke very little English managed to give us the impression that he didn't like us; there was Mr Khalid Ziglam, our absurdly juvenile chain-smoking bodyguard with a beaky nose and a huge shock of hair, who had just showed Wanda a quantity of gold jewellery which he was carting about until an appropriate moment presented itself to give it to his 'love'; and there was Mr Keralla and his elder brother, Mr Jedalla, both of whom were

Beduin of the Shavar, a tribe whose territory is on the shores of the Mediterranean, west of Derna and north of the Jebel Akhdar, the Green Mountain. Beautifully dressed in well-worn tweeds and anoraks, they now worked for an oil company.

'Tell me,' I asked Mr Jedalla, 'why do they call this hotel the Yala? It's a funny name for an hotel.'

'I would rather not tell you,' he said.

'Oh, come on, don't be silly!' I said. 'You, a Shavar Beduin, whose ancestry goes back to the Ark? What's the world coming to?'

'Well, you see, it wasn't always called Yala,' he said. 'It used to have another name when the British used to come here when Tobruk was a military base but then, after the Revolution, the name was changed to the Yala, the Go Home British Hotel.'

'Don't worry,' I said, 'I can take a hint. We're leaving tomorrow.'

'On the contrary,' said Mr Jedalla, 'we should like you and your lady to stay with us for ever.' He was genuinely shocked and upset. It was against all the established rules of Beduin hospitality.

Outside, a continuous procession of Toyotas, Nissans, Mazdas and every other sort of Japanese vehicle, plus Macks, Peugeots and a few Land Rovers, ground up the hill, driving dust through the open door into the dining room, which was decorated in an astonishing mixture of virulent shades of green, pink and yellow, adding additional layers to those which already lay within. Upstairs there were plugless bathrooms in which the water was so hot that it came from the taps in the form of steam, and lockless lavatories hung with rusty chains that looked like mediaeval torture chambers that the torturers had forgotten to clear up after use. The last time I had seen such a set-up was in a hotel in Siberia, in Novosibirsk. Now we were billeted next door to one of these appalling latrines in a bedroom lit by a forty-watt bulb that was so cold that we had run the beds together and even then had had to go to bed almost fully clothed. Tobruk hadn't changed much.

On the last evening we gave the zealous Mr Ziglam the slip and made a surreptitious tour of the town on foot. There was scarcely anyone to be seen in the streets of what was now a place with reputedly 100,000 inhabitants. It was an empty shell. What had once been the *souks*, the markets of the town, where the little shops had been which had sold all the various artefacts necessary to life in Muslim countries, the *souks* of the metal- and the wood- and the leather-workers, of the makers of clothing, the merchants selling pottery and rugs, were padlocked and closed, apparently for ever. Their place had been taken by large supermarkets set up by the Leader in which almost everything, from food to furniture, was imported. It was the same everywhere we went in Libya. With the apparently total cessation of any kind of manufactory, one trembled to think what would happen to Libya and the Libyans when the present generation of craftsmen had died off.

Into a Minefield

Tobruk, with its shuttered shops and dusty streets full of garbage, which made it look as if a civil rather than a world war was going on in it, was still the noisy, unlovely place it had always been, the only real difference being that now there was more of it. It was also still extremely dangerous. Even in the town people were still being blown sky-high by mines and booby traps, reminding me of the day when a corporal had gone through the roof of a dwelling, having sat on a long-unused lavatory seat that had been booby-trapped way back by some member of the opposing side with a grotesque sense of humour. 'Must have been something he'd eaten,' was the comment of someone with an equally macabre idea of what was funny who had witnessed his ascent.

So, not believing for a moment that we would be allowed to, I asked if we could make an expedition to Bir Hakim, one of the so-called boxes, the desert fortresses that had been the scene of one of the many big battles that had preceded Rommel's capture of Tobruk in June 1942, the biggest disaster suffered by the Allied armies since Dunkirk.

Bir Hakim, which, depending on where you put the accents, means either the Well of the Ruler or the Well of the Doctor, and can also be spelt Hacheim or Hukayyim, according to taste, lies about fifty or sixty miles. south-west of Tobruk and about forty miles south of the Gazala Inlet on the Mediterranean which is, itself, about forty miles west of Tobruk.

Neither of the Beduin brothers had ever heard of Bir Hakim but they were thrilled at the prospect of getting away from the town even for half a day, although they did say that the whole area was infested with mines and terribly dangerous; and they immediately set off to talk to the Secretary of the Tobruk People's Committee, the equivalent of a mayor, a courteous, intelligent man who had welcomed us on our arrival, to ask the police for the loan of a couple of four-wheel drive vehicles, to find a Beduin in whose tribal area the place lay to act as a guide through the minefields to it and save us all from being blown to pieces, and to organize a picnic, all of which kept them occupied for a bit.

The following morning we set out in a couple of Nissan patrol cars and out beyond the anti-tank ditch at El Adem, about twenty miles south of Tobruk, we picked up the Beduin who was to take us through the minefields. He was waiting for us at one of the new supermarket-type *souks* which had been set up here in what was the middle of nowhere.

The Beduin, whose name was Adem Gamary, was a member of the Omar Mukta, a tribe whose territory, the large area of desert on which its members grazed their camels, sheep and goats and to some extent raised crops, was bounded to the east by the land of the Obeidad Beduin, a boundary invisible to an outsider but one that by them is very accurately delineated. All Beduin are extremely jealous of their possessions and land boundaries are one of the principal causes of the innumerable quarrels that are always breaking out between them, a characteristic that extends to all Arabs and makes unity of purpose almost impossible among them except for relatively short periods.

He was about thirty years old, had a drooping moustache and wore a long overmantle made of the same goat-hair material as the Beduin tents are made from, for which his wife had spun and dyed and woven the wool; on his head he wore a white kerchief known as a *mandil*. The only European items were his shoes. When he wasn't living alone in the desert, tending his camels and his sheep and goats, he lived in a small, single-storey house not far from the Commonwealth cemetery on the outskirts of Tobruk. As the man who was to take us to Bir Hakim and, one hoped, back again, without being blown up, he sat next to the driver in the first Nissan.

It was a brilliant morning, almost windless, with a few tattered rags of cirrus high in what was otherwise a cloudless sky, in which from time to time one of the Leader's Migs or Mirages made a sudden ear-splitting appearance, streaking low across the northern horizon. Everything was crystal clear, the air dry and cold, like a morning in early spring in England. What we were in was a treeless steppe, here and there slightly undulating, in which the tussocks of vegetation were interspersed in some places with expanses of scattered stones. This was the terrain in which the opposing armies fought, fly-infested and horribly hot in summer when the temperature sometimes rose to around 120°F and the vehicles churned the powdered limestone into a fine, stifling, penetrating dust which often, when the wind blew, for days on end became a pea-soup fog, halting everything. In winter it could be bitterly cold and when it rained in some places the surface turned to mud that could bog almost any sort of vehicle, wheeled or tracked.

Although apparently endless, this semi-desert was only about fifty miles wide. Beyond it to the south was the real desert in which the main bodies of the armies never operated, well beyond the range of their armour. The real desert was left to such specialist organizations as the Long Range Desert Group which carried out long-range reconnaissances and took agents behind the enemy lines, and the SAS on their way to attack Axis airfields.

Down there the only flies were the ones these intruders brought with them, the only rain a freak thunderstorm, otherwise it might not rain for ten or twenty years, down in the *hammadas* and the *serirs*, the stony and gravel deserts, and among the massifs, some of which were up to 6000 feet high. Down in the sand seas it never rained: in the Great Sand Sea, the one that was as big as the whole of Ireland, the Calanascio Sand Sea, the Rebiana and the Murzuk Sand Seas, in which there is not even a stone, let alone a shrub, seas in which when one of the storms called the *quibli* arise the sand sometimes moves across the face of the desert in what appears to be a solid wall up to 2000 feet high.

Knowing these things it is difficult to believe that 10,000 years ago, before the water failed, what is now desert was not desert at all but a region in which men kept cattle, hunted ostrich and depicted these happenings of their day to day life on the rocks.

Here, in the semi-desert, travelling through the middle of what is probably the most mine-infested battlefield in the world on a track that because of them was for most of the way only one vehicle wide, there was ample evidence of life. Little bands of wagtails, perhaps attracted by the rain that had fallen in the last few days, were flying low in search of insects, and wherever one looked there were big herds of sheep and goats, and hundreds of Arabian camels, dromedaries with single humps, all browsing the *agram* and *hillab* bushes. From time to time we passed a place where the Omar Mukta Beduin had scraped the surface and planted it with wheat or barley, fencing it in to keep the animals out with barbed wire that had been lying about for forty years or more, crops that were already turning the land a brilliant green and would be ready to harvest in what in Europe would be springtime. And soon, if it rained again, it would be alive with wild flowers. Occasionally, in the distance, but few and far between, we saw one of the Omar Mukta herdsmen who, like their kinsman in the leading Nissan, would stay out here in the wilderness for anything from ten days to a fortnight at a time, wherever there was water for the animals, subsisting on camel's milk, sleeping on the bare earth wrapped in their mantles, after which they would return to their families for a while, like sailors coming home from the sea.

The Omar Mukta who owned these herds were rich. Camels that in the 1960s had changed hands at the equivalent of £60–70 ($84–98) now fetched £250–600 ($350–840) in the camel markets, while sheep sold for around £120 ($168) and lambs £60 ($84) or so. If, as sometimes happened, a herd of camels walked into a field of pressure mines or tripped a wire on an anti-personnel mine, the loss could be disastrous. And sometimes the herdsman walked into one, too.

It is not difficult to understand why the camel is so prized by the Libyan Beduin now that so many of them who had previously taken jobs as cheap, unskilled labour with foreign companies carrying out contracts in Libya have gone back to living a semi-nomadic, pastoral life on the edge of the great deserts, as their forefathers did before them.

Every summer they shear the valuable, long, fine, woolly hair from the underside of the animals' necks, from their humps and from the upper parts of their legs. The hide is thick and tough and it used to be said that the best leather for making sandals came from the camel-hide sacks that had been used to keep dates in. They eat and enjoy the flesh. The meat of a young camel is rather like veal. The hump provides them with lard. They drink the milk, the dung provides them with fuel, and the urine is, or was, used by men and women to wash their hair, and also to wash their babies. A camel costs nothing to maintain, lives for between forty and fifty years, can carry loads of up to 1000 lbs, 25 miles a day for a total of three days without water, and can continue to do so provided that it is given water every fourth day. Carrying nothing but a rider and his waterskin it can travel anything up to 50 miles a day for five days, or 100 miles a day if given water daily.

They are incredibly hardy. A camel can support itself on a diet of dry sticks or twigs while other animals die of starvation. A camel will never sink down, even when heavily laden, except on the orders of its master, unless to die. Even when ordered to rest, at a halt in the journey, it prefers to do so in the full heat of the sun, never in the shade. A camel can never be left alone to find its own fodder in areas where there are plants that are poisonous to it as it is unable to distinguish between what is poisonous to it and what is not, as a band of explorers discovered when they crossed the Australian continent from east to west with camels. On the other hand, they have a highly developed sense of smell, especially for water, which enables them to detect its presence up to a mile away. Untameable in the sense that a wild horse can eventually be tamed, even though born in captivity, a camel never deigns to admit that it recognizes its owner even after forty years have passed, although in fact it must be able to do so. Quite often it will develop such a violent, malevolent and totally irrational hatred for him that it can only be assuaged by the owner taking his clothes off and getting a third party to offer them to the camel, which satisfies its feelings by trampling on them and kicking him to death, as it were, *in absentia*, while the owner remains concealed at such a distance – presumably something over a mile – that the camel cannot smell him. So much for the Arabian camel, or dromedary, which, commonsense suggests, should be left to the Beduin to deal with.

And that was all that there was to be seen in this part of the desert, apart from old, rusty cans that had contained bully beef, jam, Lusty's Meat Loaf (one of the deadlier secret weapons used in the Second World War), German *Leberwurst* and suchlike, some barbed wire, a few bust-up motor tyres and mines.

I had expected the desert to have been more or less as it was when I was last in it, a graveyard, or rather a series of graveyards full of smashed and burnt-out tanks that had not been worth recovering, vehicles, guns and crashed aircraft and all the other imaginable and unimaginable debris of war. The tank graveyards were particularly sinister. I once passed through one of them south of the Trigh Capuzzo, near El Adem, but because derelict tanks sometimes still had the remains of their crews inside them, the driver perhaps sitting at the controls, the commander still gazing into what was left of the periscope, I never looked inside them. Later, in a prisoner-of-war camp in Germany, I met a gunner officer who told me he knew a man who, when he passed a knocked-out tank with its hatches closed, used to open them, to free the spirits locked up inside.

Now, apart from the wire and the tins and the mines, the desert was almost as empty as it had been before the fighting began. This was because, some time in the fifties, a scrap metal merchant, said to be an Israeli named Nahoum, had appeared at Tobruk and offered the Beduin the prospect of unheard-of wealth, something like 20 piastres, for every 500 lbs of scrap metal they could bring in on their camels; and in order that they could reduce the metal to manageable proportions he had them taught how to lift anti-tank mines, extract the explosive and use it to blow the tanks apart. This led to a spectacular increase of loss of life among the Beduin who now, in addition to stepping on mines and being blown to pieces while engaged in the everyday work of looking after their herds and flocks, began to blow themselves up, either in the process of constructing their home-made bombs, or when setting them off, often together with their women and children whom they had roped in to help in the business. One of those killed while engaged securing a straying camel was an uncle of Mr Jedalla, one of the Beduin brothers, who stepped on a mine a few yards to the east of the road from Tobruk to El Adem. Hearing the explosion at a distance his nephew at once set off in search of him, but by the time he reached the place what was left of his uncle was already being eaten by birds of prey.

As the sun rose higher and the land began to warm under its influence, it became the subject of mirage. Away on the southern horizon, what looked like plantations of bushy-topped trees, magnified versions of the *agram* and *hillab* bushes, came into being to be glimpsed momentarily across equally transient lakes of shimmering, non-existent water, while the camels were subject to the same distorting process, alternatively expanding and contracting as if they were inflatable toys.

As the sun rose, so did the wind. It raised dust devils, thin columns of dust twenty or thirty feet high, miniature whirlwinds that looked like long corkscrews and went chasing one another across the face of the desert until they reached some stony or damp expanse in which there was not enough dust to fuel them, where they fell dead in their tracks.

By now I was beginning to wonder when, if ever, we would reach Bir Hakim.

Just at this moment the vehicle in front stopped and the guide came loping back to exchange a few words with Mr Keralla, the younger of the two brothers, who was driving our vehicle.

'He says that we are now at the point where the main Gazala minefield curves round Bir Hakim to the south of it and then turns north. From here it is about a mile through the minefield to the southern entrance. We are now going to leave this track and from now on for some way there is only one very narrow track through the minefield and he has told me that I must follow in his wheel-marks exactly as there are mines on either side.' At this a certain feeling of tension made itself felt in our vehicle as we turned off the main track and followed the other one into what appeared to be trackless, virgin desert. There were no more camels on the horizon, no more goats, no more sheep, no more Beduin, nothing but little bands of wagtails who were strutting about on the main Allied minefield, now on our right and left, with what can only be described as contempt. All very well for them – lightweights.

'I say,' Wanda asked Mr Jedalla, something I had wanted to do myself ever since leaving the track, but hadn't the courage. 'Do you think this is safe?' (I would also have liked to have asked his brother if he would mind slowing down a bit and leaving a slightly larger gap between our patrol car and the one in front, which might give us a slightly better chance of not going with it if it blew up.) But all Mr Jedella said was something about us all being in the hands of Allah.

Then, having travelled about a mile, just as the guide said we would, and having gained a few feet in altitude, with the second minefield presumably to our left front now, we drove through some vestiges of what had been wire entanglements, through a gap in the remains of what had been a wall made of piled up stones, to a place where there was the well, the Bir, from which Hakim took its name, and the ruins of what was called the Ridotta Bir Hakim, a pre-war Italian desert fort. We were in Bir Hakim, and like all the other boxes in the Gazala Line it was a hell of a place to be stuck in.

On 21 January 1942 Rommel had attacked the British and driven them back to this Gazala Line. The following months were spent by both sides in preparing to attack one another and by the Eighth Army in further strengthening the Gazala Line. The Line was forty miles long and up to fifteen miles deep. It consisted of a number of heavily fortified boxes largely manned by motorized infantry with artillery support. Behind this line the Allied armour was disposed. Of these fortified boxes the southernmost and perhaps the most heavily fortified was the one held by the Free French at Bir Hakim.

The main minefield was sixty miles long. It extended from the Gazala Inlet on the Mediterranean forty miles south to Bir Hakim, enclosing it on three sides and then extending another twenty miles northwards again. Although no mines were sown to the immediate north of Bir Hakim to allow the space between the eastern and western fields to be used as a sally port, the French had sowed an estimated 50,000 mines around the perimeter, creating what they called *marais de mines*, mine swamps in which the mines were only just over a yard apart. They didn't bother about wire entanglements. There was no need. The only time they put down wire was to remind themselves where the mines were.

This vast fortification system in and behind the Gazala Line, which Rommel estimated to contain a million mines, nothing to the 200,000,000 he ordered to be put down in the Atlantic Wall in France when he was in charge of the defences in 1944, or the 400,000,000 he would have put down if the invasion had been postponed, gave even him the horrors, although he himself realized the inherent defect of such a defence system, which has the effect of limiting the offensive capabilities of whoever is occupying it.

'This form of defence is extraordinarily impervious to artillery fire or air attack,' he wrote subsequently, 'since a direct hit can destroy at the most one slit trench at a time. An immense expenditure of ammunition is necessary to do any real damage to an enemy holding a position of this kind.'

At eight-thirty on the evening of 26 May 1942, Rommel ordered Operation Venezia to be set in train and together with a striking force comprising the 15th and 21st Panzer, the 90th Light Divisions, and two Italian armoured divisions, the Trieste and the Ariete, he set off to the south-east together with 10,000 vehicles in brilliant moonlight, an astonishing sight to those who witnessed it. His intention was to turn the southern flank of the Gazala Line, bring the British armour to battle and destroy it, and to take Bir Hakim.

Travelling through the night and raising great clouds of dust that made navigation extremely difficult, by dawn on the 27th this vast armada was twelve miles to the south of Bir Hakim, with the exception of the Trieste Division that had gone off course and got itself imbrangled in the minefield between the British 150 Brigade Box (the next box to the north of Bir Hakim) and the French position. By half past ten the 90th Light was at El Adem, some forty miles to the north-west, and subsequently the 15th and 21st Panzer Divisions became involved in the first of a series of tremendous armoured battles that were to continue for a fortnight behind the Gazala Line, and which on this first day caused the loss of one-third of the total Axis armour.

We sat with our backs against the wall of some unidentifiable ruin inside the perimeter of Bir Hakim, listening to the wind droning over it and eating the delicious picnic of cheese and the hard-boiled eggs, crisp French bread, dates and oranges that the two Beduin brothers had conjured up, and drinking the strong, orange-coloured tea laced with sweetened condensed milk of which they must have learned the secret of making from some long-departed British soldier; the tea that every British soldier, including myself, firmly believed contained bromide to keep his mind concentrated on killing people and not fooling about with girls, and without which the entire British army and all the Dominion armies, and the war with them, would almost certainly have come to a standstill.

We were on the southern edge of a bare and, apart from the ruined fort, featureless plateau totally devoid of natural cover, that was scarcely a plateau at all in the accepted sense of the word but, nevertheless, because it was a few feet higher than the surrounding desert, gave whoever held it the advantage of being able to bring to bear a murderous fire on anyone who didn't.

Forty years or so ago it had been a very skilfully planned system of combat positions – gun emplacements for French 75mm guns and Bofors guns, small pillboxes, machine-gun and anti-tank gun nests and lots of slit trenches, all small works but incredibly numerous; there were 1200 of them within the approximately ten-mile perimeter of the fortress.

Now they were mostly silted up and the whole area was littered with the debris of the Free French Brigade's occupation of it: broken wine bottles (did they actually have wine at Bir Hakim coming up with the rations?), bits of leather equipment, very brittle after more than forty years, shells, exploded and unexploded, and lots of mines. From time to time, now that the wind had got up, all this unlovely material was hidden from view in clouds of dust.

The regiments that made up the First Free French Brigade that had been given the job of holding Bir Hakim under General Koenig were the Bataillon du Pacific, No. I, which was made up of natives from Tahiti and other French islands in the Pacific; the IIe Bataillon de la Légion étrangère (anti-tank), made up of various nationalities, including Germans; the Bataillon de March No. II, which had been founded in the Congo and was made up of recruits from French Equatorial Africa; and two artillery regiments: the Ier Régiment d'Artillerie, which was armed with French 75mm guns, and the Ier Bataillon de Fusiliers-Marins. There was also an anti-aircraft regiment, an anti-tank company, engineers, signal, medical and administrative troops. Altogether the strength of the garrison was about 3600 men and one English girl, Susan Travers, who was General Koenig's driver. The officers and NCOs were mostly French. The majority of the men were natives of the French Colonial Empire including their islands in Papua.

Here, at Bir Hakim, mines not only formed the perimeter. They were inside it, too. A few yards from where we were sitting sheltered from the wind, eating our picnic, a large crater marked the spot where two members of the Omar Mukta had recently lit a cooking fire on ground which had a mine planted in it and had blown themselves to pieces. Some were on the surface. Most of them had been rendered innocuous. Others, still active, could be seen half buried in the ground. The majority were still below the surface. Most of them were anti-tank mines designed to explode if a weight of 100 lbs or more was imposed on them but after forty years or so all the evidence seemed to be, according to the guide, that a lot of them would go off if you even looked at them. There were also a lot of anti-personnel mines, and the long trip wires which activated them were an additional hazard; they were to be found stretched all over the plateau.

On that May morning forty years ago, eighty tanks of the Ariete, the best Italian armoured division in the desert, had attacked the south-east perimeter here at Bir Hakim, the section held by the Foreign Legion with its anti-tank guns. They failed to take it, although they tried very hard, and they lost 32 of the tanks employed in the attack.

Then, in the course of the next fortnight, the German 90th Light Division, the Trieste Division, specially trained sappers, and combat groups of the Afrika Korps, supported by heavy artillery and the Luftwaffe, who made 1300 sorties against it using Stukas and JU87s and 88s, all tried to reduce it. During this battle Rommel issued three ultimatums calling on General Koenig to surrender. One he wrote in his own hand on a sheet of paper torn from a message pad; another was delivered by word of mouth by an Italian officer whom General Koenig either couldn't or didn't want to understand. The third was communicated to one of Koenig's Légionnaires, who happened to be German, by a German officer who, when greeted distinctly coolly in his own tongue by an enemy compatriot, asked rather plaintively, 'Doesn't anyone here speak English?'

It was no good. The French had too much firepower, and they were too well dispersed behind too many mines. They were also very well supported by the Desert Air Force, who flew close on 1500 sorties in thirteen days, losing nineteen fighters in the process, and by the 7th Motor Brigade which brought in convoys of supplies and ammunition to them through the minefields.

Nevertheless, on 8 May 1942, after the fortress had been attacked by 45 JU87s, 3 JU88s and 10 ME 110s escorted by 54 single-engined fighters, the first of three similar attacks that day, and had been subjected to heavy shelling and repeated infantry attacks, the Germans succeeded in occupying an important French artillery observation post at the north-west corner.

On the 9th, using waves of infantry supported by more than 60 bombers and yet another special combat group, the Germans succeeded in getting within 220 yards of the Ridotta, and on the following day, the 10th, after a raid by 20 JU88s and 40 JU87s escorted by 50 ME 109s and 110s, in the course of which 130 tons of bombs were dropped, the same combat group, commanded by a Colonel Baade, succeeded in the face of the most desperate resistance by the Negro Tirailleurs (Skirmishers) of the Bataillon de Marche d'Oubangui and by the gunners of the Ier Régiment, in breaking through the north-western perimeter and establishing itself within it. Late that night Rommel reported to Kesselring that he was confident that he would take Bir Hakim the following day.

Meanwhile, earnest entreaties to Churchill and others had been made by General de Gaulle, who was extremely loath to allow this *corps d'élite* to go into captivity, and that same day, the 10th,

General Ritchie decided that Koenig and what remained of his garrison, about 2700 men – accounts differ – of the original 3600, including 200 wounded, should break out of the fortress that night, something which had not been allowed to 150 Infantry Brigade who, in their box north of Bir Hakim, had fought until overrun. This they did, under cover of darkness, from the south-west side against some opposition.

Five miles out, they were picked up by a large convoy of lorries and ambulances brought in by the British 7th Motor Brigade, which had many times throughout the siege brought in supplies of water and provisions for them through terrain infested with mines and enemy. General Koenig himself was driven out of the fortress by his English girl driver, who had remained in it throughout the battle. The next morning, by which time it no longer had any importance to them, the Germans occupied Bir Hakim. On 20 June, after an extremely heavy air and artillery bombardment, troops of the Afrika Korps broke through the outer perimeter of the Tobruk fortress in the south-east corner. The following day the general in charge of the defence of Tobruk sent out emissaries and, to the amazement of many of the defenders, they were ordered to lay down their arms. Last to surrender were the Gurkha Rifles and the Cameron Highlanders who only did so after being told that they would be exterminated if they refused. Some isolated parties never surrendered at all. They included one led by a major of the Coldstream Guards, who succeeded in taking out 198 officers and men of his own battalion, 188 men of various other units and all his remaining anti-tank guns.

At Tobruk Rommel took 33,000 prisoners and enormous quantities of ammunition, fuel and provisions, as well as 2000 vehicles. Altogether it had been a famous victory.

Before we left Bir Hakim we visited the cemetery. It lies on the south-east side which the Foreign Legion held against the Ariete, a large enclosure, swept by dust storms, out in the minefields, with a memorial bearing the Croix de Lorraine and planted with hundreds of crosses bearing the names of that heterogeneous collection of men from far-flung places who came here to fight the Germans, the first French soldiers to do so since the fall of France, names which every year become more difficult to decipher as the crosses are either blown down by the wind or broken by the camels and goats of the Omar Mukta.

Here, one feels, it is a long way to Tahiti.

Not Quite Leptis Magna

My letter to the Leader had said nothing about us wanting to see anything except a cemetery, part of a battlefield and, if possible, he himself in person, and if I had asked for more in all probability our request to come to Libya would not have been granted at all. Now, as we travelled westwards on the long haul back to Tripoli, through the hill country called the Jebel Akhdar, terrifyingly fast and in pouring rain, for a meeting with him which was destined not to take place, I began to wish that I had taken the risk and not been quite so literal about what we wanted to see and what, by implication, we didn't. Rendered desperate by the thought of seeing nothing at all between where we were and Tripoli, not even stopping except to drink tea, take on petrol and snatch a few hours' sleep, I asked Mr Seddik Mabruk, a small, dark, touchy, fanatical man, the representative selected to be one of those accompanying us, if we might at least see the ruins of Cyrene, which we had failed to visit on the outward journey, the reason he had given us then being that as it was not on the schedule there was no time to see it.

By the time we got to the turn-off for Cyrene, it was pitch dark as well as raining cats and dogs, and all we were able to discern by the light of the car headlights of what had been one of the five cities on the Libyan shore of the Mediterranean founded by Greeks from Thera, Crete, the Peloponnese and its islands, which together made up what was known as the Cyrenaican Pentapolis, were some indistinct masses of pale-looking masonry on the side of a hill, 2000 feet above the sea and ten miles inland from it.

We had wanted to see Cyrene ever since we had given ourselves as a Christmas present a large, sumptuous and very expensive coffee-table book full of photographs of these and other remains on the Mediterranean shores.* It had first been colonized in 630 BC by Greeks from the island of Thera, now known as Santorin, one of the islands of the Cyclades in the Cretan Sea. They had been inspired to emigrate there partly because the Oracle of Delphi had urged them to do so, partly because their island was not only earthquake-ridden but was becoming increasingly waterless.

Some of these Greek colonists intermarried with what they called the *barbari*, otherwise the Berbers, a light-skinned people, members of a race which inhabited the whole of the North African hinterland from Egypt to the Atlantic. They spoke, and still speak, Hamitic, a very ancient form of which is preserved in the inscriptions and papyri of ancient Egypt and of which 47 languages and 71 dialects have been identified in Africa north of the Equator.

After Alexander the Great had occupied Egypt in 332 BC, he made an ally of Cyrene. Later, in 304 BC, Ptolemy I Soter, one of Alexander's generals, the first of what was to be a line of Macedonian kings of Egypt, annexed Cyrene and it remained subject to Egypt, governed by what were known as Libyarchs or ruled by vassal kings, until 96 or 97 BC. In 74 BC it became a Roman province, as did most of North Africa, producing corn, olive oil and wine; its steppe country, in which the Allied and Axis armies were later to fight their great tank battles, became famous for its sheep, its splendid horses and for its silphium, a much-prized plant yielding a gum resin used as a condiment and a medicine. By the time of Nero, who reigned from AD 54 to 68, silphium had become so rare, destroyed by excessive grazing, that only one plant in the entire country could be found to be sent to him, although less than a century previously, at the beginning of the Civil War, Caesar had 1500 lbs of it stored in the state treasury. Cyrene also carried on an extensive caravan trade with Equatorial Africa across the Sahara.

---

* Roloff Beny *et al.*, *Odyssey, Mirror of the Mediterranean* (Thames & Hudson, 1981).

Its population at this time was mostly made up of Greeks, Hellenized Berbers and a large colony of Jews. In AD 116 in the reign of Trajan, the Jews rose in revolt as they did that same year in Egypt, Palestine, Cyprus and other parts of the Levant. Cyrenaica never recovered from the effects of this insurrection, in the course of which 240,000 persons were slaughtered, although Hadrian, after a visit of inspection in AD 125, in an attempt to fill the gap in the population left by these massacres, imported peasants from Italy to work the soil, as Mussolini was to do some 1800 years later, also after a period of bloodshed.*

The end of Cyrene as a Roman city came, as for so many other Roman cities in the Mediterranean, with the arrival of the Vandals from Spain in the fifth century, Germanic-Scandinavian predators who moved and fought on horseback.

In 533 the Vandals were attacked and defeated on both land and sea by the Byzantine general Belisarius, who routed them completely, taking Carthage and carrying their king captive to Constantinople. They left behind them, after more than a century of occupation and the most horrible persecution of Catholic Christians, nothing but ruins, defaced statuary and general misery.

From now onward the Byzantines ruled in North Africa until well into the seventh century, by which time the Arab onslaughts were at their height and battle had already been joined in the course of the incursions they made from Egypt.

The third of these incursions was the most lasting in its effects. It took place in 670 when the Emir Oqba ibn Nafi penetrated deep into what was later to be known as Ifriqiya, present-day Tunis and eastern Algeria. While doing so he received a mystical revelation and this impelled him to found Kairouan, a city that was to become, after Mecca and Medina, the most venerated in the Muslim world.

Now as we roared on again westwards through the red earth and limestone uplands of the Jebel Akhdar, knowing without seeing that they were there because we had seen them on the outward journey, through groves of olive trees, uncountable thousands of newly planted fruit trees, fields of cauliflowers, wheat, barley, grapes that

* Italian military operations against the Libyans began in earnest in the 1920s and continued into the 1930s when the first peasant colonists arrived from Italy. By 1938 the native population of the country had been halved from 400,000 to 200,000.

would be eaten here in Libya but never crushed and fermented unless clandestinely, greenhouses full of ripening tomatoes, we sensed the palpable disapproval of Mr Seddik Mabruk, who, if it had been left to him and not the Leader, would not have admitted us to his country under any pretext, a feeling of disapproval which hung over our heads like a cloud of poison gas.

Gratefully we accepted a couple of Mr Khalid Ziglam's, our bodyguard's, apparently inexhaustible supplies of Marlboros with which, silly boy, he was apparently trying his best to smoke himself to death.

Now I knew that unless God worked in an even more mysterious way *vis-à-vis* ourselves than he had done up to now not only would we never see Cyrene, but we would never see Leptis Magna either, which I had wanted to visit ever since as a small boy of five and a half I had been taken to see some of its marble columns and other masonry in Windsor Great Park. They had been plundered in 1817 by a British naval commander of antiquarian tastes, who excavated them from the dunes which at that time engulfed the city, fortunately choosing as the site for his depredations the middle of the vast forum where he could do comparatively little damage. Having done so, and having a ship handy, he sent them to England where the Prince Regent, a suitably cultured recipient, had them re-erected or otherwise left about in picturesque disorder on the shores of Virginia Water, an ornamental lake, where they make, surprisingly, a rather lugubrious impression.

I longed to see this Roman city over which everyone who has seen it goes into ecstasies. Formerly a Carthaginian, and before that a Phoenician, settlement, it had been brought to its final state of splendour and perfection by the Emperor Septimius Severus, a very dark, almost black, bearded native of Leptis, son of a noble father and a black concubine, who spoke Latin with an African accent and died at York on 4 February 211.

It must have been a wonderful, perhaps not beautiful, possibly vulgar city, if only for the extraordinary variety of marble, porphyry, granite and other more or less exotic rocks which Severus imported from all over the empire, either in the form of enormous monoliths which weighed so much that more than two of them put aboard a ship of the time would probably have sent it to the bottom instantly, or as facing stone for what had previously been a city mainly built of a not very inspiring mixture of brick and porous limestone.

I wanted to see the Severan Forum, the most splendid of its kind in existence – finer, according to Sacheverell Sitwell, whom one feels ought to know, than that of Rome because less cluttered – and the Medusa heads on what remained of the arcades that surrounded it, and the headless figures of the Muses on the house of a man called Jason Magnus, whose robes were so lightly carved that one could imagine them to be moving. I wanted to see the enormous temple that the Byzantines had turned into a basilica, and the wonderful white marble statue of Venus Aphrodite with the bracelets on her gleaming upper arms and her plaited tresses, noseless as every other statue the Vandals ever came within striking distance of, striking off these and other natural protuberances which for them perhaps had some curious iconoclastic significance associated with their Arianism, noseless but still beautiful.

'It's funny to think, isn't it,' Wanda said, as we travelled in through the outskirts of Tripoli to the centre of the city, 'that the only way you'll probably ever see anything of Leptis Magna now will be by going down to Virginia Water on a bus.'

Back in Tripoli, feeling that we had trespassed on the Leader's hospitality sufficiently for the time being, and having received an invitation from him to come back in a couple of months and see him in the flesh as it were, by which time it was hoped that things might have quietened down a bit up at the top and that he would send us a couple of return air tickets (they didn't and he didn't, being heavily involved in the nightmare activities in St James's Square), we decided to press on to Tunis by bus and train and any other means of transport that suggested itself.

To tell the truth, not being accustomed to it except in strictly regulated doses, we were beginning to become sated, even after a couple of days of it, of the sort of luxury which his aides lavished on us on his behalf: the beef which if you hadn't got a spoon you could practically suck through a straw, the sumptuous lavatories in which we didn't dare fart, let alone speak, for fear of putting all that delicate East German listening apparatus out of joint, not to mention giving the operators of it the equivalent of shell shock, the provision of which, including all other accommodation, transportation and the constant presence of one mad driver, one bodyguard and one accompanying official, was estimated by Old Libya Hands whom we met in the equivalent of the bar, swigging Pepsi as if it was methylated spirits – Old Hands anywhere being notoriously inaccurate – to have cost the Jamahariyah some £3000 ($4200).

'You,' they all said, 'are the first British tourists.'

They also said that we were insane to go to Tunisia by bus, which further emboldened us to do so, but we began to think that they might be right after having spent a couple of hours down at the bus terminal, which is located in a large puddle outside the walls of the Old City, buying our tickets for the following morning, a Saturday, only to find when we got back to the hotel that they had been made out for the following Wednesday, which was rather similar to what had happened at Antalya in Turkey. After this, worn down by our efforts to be independent in late-twentieth-century Libya, we scuttled off in search of our Libyan nanny, Mr Abdussalem Abouaza, a senior official who himself accompanied us to the bus station and fixed everything for the following morning in ten minutes, which in Britain would be the equivalent of getting a fairly senior ministry official to come down from Whitehall to book us a couple of seats at Victoria Coach Station on a bus going to Aberdeen. He did this at a cost to us of about £8 ($11.20) a head for a journey of 387 miles which would get us as far as Sousse in Tunisia. There we planned to board the 19.27 train operated by the Société Nationale des Chemins de Fers Tunisiens for the last 90-odd miles to Tunis, travelling as a treat in what the SNCFT described as *grand confort*, otherwise *luxe*, meantime sampling the light refreshment facilities, drinking one hoped Tunisian wine and arriving at Tunis at 22.14, with luck still in time for dinner.

Not only this. Taking pity on our Libyan ruinless state Mr Abouaza drove us that day to Sabaratha, the Carthaginian/Roman city down on the shore, forty miles west of Tripoli which, like Leptis Magna, for so many centuries, until the Italians excavated it, lay buried in the sands down on the sea shore, more Greek, more Oriental than Roman, conceived not by a emperor but by some unknown genius or genii, now being buried once more not in sand but under mesembryanthemum.

By the time we reached it, the custodian was already locking up, but he was prevailed upon to let us in and we saw in the last of the sunset, its masonry turned a deep orange by it, a theatre that was itself a stage set, with tiers of colonnades one above the other towering eighty feet or so in the air and with its exits and its entrances reaching out through enfilades of corridors, each one giving a vista of what was a foam-flecked sea. An architecture which has few, if any, parallels in the ancient world, except perhaps in the Nabatean city of Petra; but nearer in spirit, with its tricks of perspective, to those wooden structures of the Renaissance, Palladio's Teatro Olimpico at Vicenza, the Teatro Farnese at Parma or, nearer our own time but in a miniature version, the museum house of Sir John Soane in Lincoln's Inn Fields.

And so, at eight o'clock the following morning, we said goodbye to Tripoli, where the Roman Catholic Cathedral is now a mosque and the bell tower is a minaret which even the most devoted muezzin might jib at climbing five times a day but has no need to, as he has installed a loud-hailer in it. A city in which there are shops selling almost every known foreign newspaper but not much else, and in which the Old City, now that the *souks* have been closed and replaced by super-*souks* on the outskirts, is now more like a City of the Dead.

We also waved goodbye to Mr Abouaza, who had not only got up early on what was for him a holiday to take us to the bus station an hour before the bus left but had also gallantly insisted on waiting until it left, presumably to make sure that we didn't abscond from it, which was a great trial for all three of us for there is nothing worse in life than either being seen off or seeing someone off. And we had invited him to come and stay with us the next time he visited the family who had put him up while he was learning English in Bournemouth, which is where most Libyans appear to learn it.

Then, with a complement, but not a full complement, of twenty-two passengers, all of them Tunisian workers returning to their country, the bus lurched out of the enormous puddle in which all the buses were parked and trundled gently through the suburbs as though we had all the time in the world to get to Tunisia and Tunis. It was a fine sunny morning with a strong onshore wind blowing and the sea when it momentarily hove into view was navy blue with little white caps on it.

Altogether, apart from a ten-minute halt at a roadside café, we drove for about two and a half hours, past Berber villages, endless olive groves, little farms that had once been worked by Italian peasants who at weekends, when they went into Tripoli for the day in their best clothes with their wives, transformed its main square into a piazza in some Italian provincial town, past orange groves and long lines of stalls strung out along the roadside where there were so many oranges for sale that it seemed impossible that they could all be disposed of before they went bad. Then the country became more arid. There were fewer trees, more prickly pears, more thorns, fewer houses, and there were scuts of sand blowing across the road from the dunes to the right and beyond them was the beautiful blue sea. To the left of the road an immense saline lake shimmered in the sun. The frontier was straight ahead, with the Libyan border post astride the road, an ugly modern building like border posts everywhere except that no one had apparently cleaned the plate glass windows of this particular one since they were put in. There was a queue of cars in front of us, but not more than half a dozen. It was a quarter to eleven.

'It looks as if we're going to be lucky,' I said.

At five o'clock the following morning, twenty-one hours and some 480 miles outward bound from Tripoli, our bus entered the coach station at Tunis.

It was not a journey either of us would be anxious to repeat. It was certainly not one that we would ever forget. And sometimes since making it I have found myself wondering whether, if given the choice, taking into account my age and everything, I would choose to make it again or be guillotined. Obviously we had been spoilt. Travel under the auspices of the Leader, at the speed of light, had rendered the more lumbering methods of moving about under our own steam intolerable. I realized what Cinderella must have felt when deprived of her crystal coach.

The Libyan frontier when we reached it had proved to be in the hands of characters from Kafka, most of whom, most of the time, remained invisible behind the expanses of smeared frosted glass which enclosed them and prevented them from being reminded of the outside world, and in which they could be heard but not seen, except in the form of exaggerated and distorted shapes dimly perceived against the glass, like the shadows of reality cast on the wall of Plato's Cave. Invisible, that is, unless you bent double and peered into their office through what the French-speaking Tunisians on the other side of the frontier called a *guichet*, a small, oval hole in the glass, where they could be perceived for what they were, teenaged males with seven o'clock shadow and with hair that aped but failed to emulate the Leader's inimitable coiffure, chatting animatedly with one another, greeting comrades coming on shift with a lot of back slapping and other forms of false bonhomie, smoking Marlboros, drinking the noxious cola or Chinese Gun-

powder Tea made with leaves extracted from the ten-pound pack-
ages of the stuff seized from travellers en route for Tunisia by their
comrades in the customs department, great mounds of which lay
around in a special pen in the customs hall. Occasionally, apparently on impulse, one of them would rise to his feet, languidly select
three or four passports from the large pile on the table before him
(for by now an ever-lengthening queue of vehicles was building up
behind our bus), rather as if he was taking cards from a conjuror
doing a boring trick, before switching on his official, menacing
scowl for the benefit of the customers and sallying forth to order the
owners of the passports to present themselves, be identified by him
as such, and begone to form another queue, this time for customs.
Sitting on a packing case which some unfortunate was later ordered
to prise open so that its contents could be examined, I had a fine
view of these fiends and their goings-on through the *guichet*, until
one of their number, unhappy that anyone not actually employed
on the premises should be enjoying himself, shouted at me to go
away.

After the stamping of the twenty-two passports, which took
until some time after midday, came the customs examination,
carried out under a canopy by one customs official, all the others
having gone off to eat their dinners.

I must say it was a new experience, at least in a Mediterranean
country, to pass through a customs in which every traveller, in this
case including a one-legged Tunisian lady on crutches who was
travelling with her husband in an old car loaded inside and out with
all their household possessions in cardboard boxes, was required
not only to remove everything they had with them from whatever
vehicle they happened to be travelling in, but were then required to
lay their luggage out open on the road under the canopy outside the
customs house, where eventually the one official on duty inspected
the contents simply by placing his hands beneath them inside the
bag, lifting them up, then turning them upside down and allowing
them to run through his fingers, an operation which took, even with
the help of those full of fight who had come back to help him after
eating their midday meal, another two and a quarter hours, by
which time it was quarter past two in the afternoon.

After which we were free. Free to drive in the bus another
hundred yards or so across a bare expanse to the Tunisians and their
border post; there once more to remove everything we possessed
from the bus, wait another hour and a half to have our passports

stamped, and another three quarters of an hour to have our possessions made to loop the loop once more, but this time in the middle of an enormous, sand-swept open space, and to watch the one-legged lady as she hopped about, opening cardboard boxes, stoically supporting these fresh indignities. By the time we left it was four o'clock. Altogether we had been on the frontier for more than five hours.

I asked the conductor, who made the same journey twice a week in both directions, whether he thought we had been unlucky, but he said it had been comparatively quick.

'I wonder what it would be like,' Wanda said, 'if they were going slow.'

Then, after trundling through a succession of check-points at each of which a policeman boarded the bus and inspected all twenty-two of our passports, the driver put his foot down and we zoomed away down a dead straight road, with drifts of sand across it in places, straight into the eye of the setting sun. We were travelling through the Gefrara Plain, an almost treeless steppe desert with the great saline lake, the Sebkhet el Adibate, which forms part of the northern frontier between Libya and Tunisia, to the left, seeing no one along the way except a few ragged herdsmen tending their goats and camels, until we reached what seemed like an oasis in which there were small villages with box-like white houses with little beehive huts of reeds built on to them standing beneath the trees. Women wrapped up to the eyes were drawing water from the wells and carrying it away in earthenware pots balanced on their heads. Then, just as we were congratulating one another on the good progress we were making, the bus came to rest in Ben Gardane, a small town in which the houses were painted in shades of blue and ochre where the bus conductor announced to our dismay that there would be a half-hour lunch break.

After this enforced rest once again onwards into the wilderness, after the first bottle of wine for what seemed weeks and some delicious lamb chops. Occasionally we passed the empty shell of a building at the roadside and sometimes a well, with what my map said were the jagged peaks of the Jebel Dahar range looming up on the port bow, running away southwards, the sun going down behind them in a cloudless sky over the Grand Erg Oriental, a part of the Sahara, silhouetting them so that they looked like the temperature chart of someone suffering from undulant fever. After this we entered a more fertile country that until recently had also been part of the wilderness, but was now covered with immense olive groves which stretched away as far as the eye could see. Here and there among them little rectangular whitewashed barns or farmhouses with barrel-topped roofs gleamed in the last of the light. Along the roadside, women were going home dragging bundles of olive twigs for their cooking fires, raising the dust. How beautiful the world could be, at least to look at, I thought. '*Com'è bello il mondo!*' I would like to have shouted out, but didn't for fear that my fellow passengers might think I'd been driven round the bend by the events of the day and might start clamouring for me to be dropped off at the next convenient *hôpital psychiatrique.*

Then, after passing through the fifth road block, suddenly it was quite dark and there was nothing more to be seen except the headlights of the bus tunnelling through the darkness ahead between the eucalyptus trees, occasionally illuminating signposts. Some of them indicated places that had once been world famous as the scenes of battles – Mareth, Gabes, Wadi Zigzaou, the Wadi Akharit in the Plain of Arad where the Italians and the Afrika Korps had made a stand between the sea and the marshes of the Chott el Fejj – places on a map, places on signposts, places now largely forgotten, that having come to them with not inconsiderable difficulty even now we couldn't see.

On 6 April 1943, it had taken two British and one Indian division to force the Wadi Akharit, a narrow river bed nowhere more than fifty yards wide. The following day, a patrol of the 4th Indian Division met up with one from the US 2nd Corps advancing from the west, who greeted the Indians with the words 'Hello, Limey', a greeting which they appreciated although they did not understand it. This was the historic moment at which the two armies, which had started nearly two thousand miles apart, were united. Just over a month later the Axis armies laid down their arms.

At 9 o'clock that night we arrived at Sfax.

One of the other passengers on the bus, who was an inhabitant of Sfax, had told us that if we got down there we were still in time to catch the last train to Tunis. Knowing that we had missed the 19.27 from Sousse, not having a timetable and not really believing this kindly disposed man, I arranged with the bus conductor that he would halt the bus at the station at Sfax, where it stopped anyway, long enough for me to find out if there really was a train. If there was not we would stay on the bus and try and get a shared taxi from Sousse to Tunis.

Now, while Wanda waited on the bus with our luggage, ready to disembark, I raced into the station. The *guichet* was open.

'*Quand part le prochain train pour Tunis?*' I asked the man behind it.

'At half past ten,' he said in near perfect English.

'It's OK,' I said to Wanda, back at the bus, where the other passengers were becoming slightly restive at this sixty-second delay after thirteen hours on the road. 'We're in luck, there's a train at half past ten.'

Both the conductor and the driver waved to us as the bus drew away, leaving us on the pavement. By this time I felt as if I had known them all my life. We had been through a lot together in the last twelve hours or so. How they both managed to endure the Libyan/Tunisian customs torture twice a week, each way between Tripoli and Sousse, without going bananas was a mystery, especially as the conductor told me that very often an entire day was consumed crossing from one country to the other.

'Let's get the tickets first, then we can eat at that place round the corner the driver recommended,' I said, as soon as the bus had disappeared from sight.

Inside the station the man in the ticket office was just closing his *guichet*, apparently preparatory to going home.

'Here,' I said, 'I say. What's going on? We want two tickets to Tunis, for the half past ten train. The one you told me about.'

'You don't need them now,' he said, closing the *guichet* and switching out the light, thereby rendering himself invisible, no doubt relishing the effect. 'You can get them tomorrow. It's at half past ten tomorrow morning.'

'We seem to be a bit stuck now,' I said to Wanda, out in the yard into which we had been hurried by a soldier whose job it was to guard the station and who wanted to lock up. It was a bitter night. According to the radio in the restaurant at Ben Gardane where we had eaten five o'clock lunch, snow had fallen at Nabbeul on the shores of the Gulf of Hammamet.

'Yes, we are a bit stuck, my husband,' she said. 'You certainly are some famous traveller. Even I know that anywhere you want to catch a train at 10.30 at night it leaves at 22.30.'

'Perhaps there's a bus,' I said, but I didn't really believe there would be.

The restaurant round the corner was a very jolly place, although it had an awfully sinister proprietor, like someone invented by Genet. It was full of French-speaking Muslims, all of whom were drunk and getting drunker every minute on what appeared to be the good red Tunisian wine with which they were washing down prodigious quantities of what also looked to be excellent *agneau en brochette*. The only table left was one in the direct line of a terrible draught of cold air that was entering through a gap in the swing doors, which nevertheless, not feeling particularly choosy at this moment, we decided to occupy.

The head waiter, a moustached fellow, proved to be a mine of information. According to him there was *pas de problème*. There was a mini-bus leaving from a café across the road at ten o'clock, otherwise 22.00, and a bus at 22.15 from the station yard.

'Don't order anything,' I said to Wanda, leaving her to thaw out in the draught, and raced what proved to be not just across the road but a couple of blocks to the café from which the mini-bus was due to leave in about forty-five minutes from now, where nobody had ever heard of it, but from which I was sent to the office of a shared taxi service where the proprietor told me (he was shutting up, too), that one of these vehicles would be setting off, if a quorum could be found to fill it, at 03.00 the following morning. After this I walked back to the restaurant where the head waiter said he couldn't understand it but there was *pas de problème* for the bus which stopped at the station yard every night at 22.15. We then ordered a dinner for two, which made the 17.00 lunch the Tunisian equivalent of a British high tea.

At 22.05, by which time Wanda was rigid with cold in spite of having been filled up with *agneau* and the good Tunisian red wine which turned out to be deep frozen rosé, having paid our modest bill which amounted to the equivalent of £7 ($9.80) for two, we set off, lugging our bags, for our tryst with the head waiter's bus at 22.15 which, like the mini-bus due to leave at 22.00, proved to be a figment of his imagination. There, in the station yard, we waited until 22.30, by which time it was obvious to anyone, even me with my peanut brain, that it wasn't coming.

Back at the restaurant we found it on the point of closing, the atmosphere no longer jolly, our table cleared with the chairs stacked on it, the now acrimonious drunks being ejected, having paid their bills, and the previously almost too friendly head waiter now unaccountably hostile, presumably because we hadn't caught his non-existent bus. However, an under-waiter, who actually lived over the premises and therefore might be presumed to know, said that there was definitely a bus at 12.15, otherwise 00.15, the following morning and he suggested that the best place to wait for it, in fact the only place now in that they were closing, was an all-night café about fifty yards away, round the corner and in full view of the station where the bus would stop.

The only occupants of the café, which appeared to have no doors, was like a tomb and served no alcohol, were a very old, nice man who was the proprietor and his friend who was younger but equally nice and looked like an emaciated version of Omar Sharif. Both of them were wearing thick overcoats and the friend of the proprietor said that he came to the café every evening in order to pass the night with him and keep an eye on things if he wanted to have a nap. I told him about our bus trouble and he took me round the corner and showed me a notice on the wall, more or less outside the restaurant in which we had had dinner, which stated quite distinctly that the next bus to Tunis was at 00.45, not 00.15.

Meanwhile Wanda was feeling so ill that she had retired to the upper floor of the café, which was equally cold but slightly less public, to lie down. Feeling heroic I took off my coat and put it on top of the blanket in which she was wrapped, now apparently fast asleep, which had presumably been lent to her by the proprietor, who had disappeared. By now it was midnight, 24.00 hours, and not believing anyone in Sfax any more so far as buses were concerned, I began to queue outside in the station yard for whatever might turn up. The 00.15, the brain-child of the under-waiter, failed to appear and so did the officially-accredited-on-the-notice-board 00.45, by which time I was practically dead and went back to the café for what I felt was a well-earned rest, where I promptly fell asleep with my head on one of the tables, only to be woken at 01.30 hours by the friend of the proprietor in a high state of excitement to say that a real bus had arrived in the station yard on its way to Tunis and that he had managed to persuade the driver to wait for us.

I rushed upstairs to wake Wanda, cocooned in her blanket and further hidden by my coat, only to find that it was the proprietor whom I had tucked up and that Wanda was lying on a table at the far end of the room without any sort of covering at all. Followed by him and his friend manfully bringing up the rear with residual bits of our baggage, we ran to the station and boarded what proved to be a big, luxurious and warm bus just at the moment when the driver was about to leave, no doubt fed up with waiting for potential passengers who in this part of the world at this time of night were probably as ephemeral as the buses appeared to be which were supposed to carry them. This time it was we who waved goodbye, to the owner of the café and his insomniac friend who had saved us from travelling on the almost certainly non-existent shared taxi to Tunis at 03.00, otherwise 3 a.m.

We arrived at Tunis at half past five on a Sunday morning, while it was still dark, and in a sort of coma picked up a prowling taxi and ordered its driver, who wasn't very full of fight either, to take us to a railway station from which we could catch a train to a village called Sidi Bou Said on the northern outskirts of Tunis where we had booked a room in a hotel. He took us through deserted streets past what looked like abattoirs to an equally deserted station where we boarded a train which appeared to have no guard and certainly had no other passengers besides ourselves, and which halted obediently at each station until we reached Sidi Bou Said which was the fourteenth or the fifteenth stop, I forget which. There we lugged our bags a mile or two uphill, finally reaching the hotel just after six o'clock, 06.00. There we had a hot bath and went to bed. We were whacked.

We were whacked because the nice warm bus we had been so happy to board had turned out to be a mobile oriental torture chamber. Its interior, brilliantly illuminated by fluorescent lights that were never for a moment extinguished, was also equipped with a short wave radio capable of picking up every Arab radio station in the Mediterranean basin as well as those in the Arabian peninsula, but all of them imperfectly and to the accompaniment of dreadful noises that one could only suppose were atmospherics, and this functioned at full blast throughout the night, the conductor of the coach moving along the wave bands from one station to another every few minutes as the spirit moved him.

'Do something,' said Wanda, who was feeling terrible, putting on her outraged, Marguerite Dumond/Marx Brothers act. 'Tell him to stop it.'

So I did, and he looked at me just as a British coach conductor would look at a Tunisian who told him to switch off a coach radio; and I had to tell her that she would either have to learn to live with it or, if necessary, die with it or get off the coach in the middle of darkest Tunisia, for we live in cruel times.

Knowing that what remains of ancient Carthaginian Carthage, which is almost nothing, was going to be a let-down, yet unable to sleep, at ten o'clock after about three hours in bed we got up and dressed and walked downhill from Sidi Bou Said in a nippy wind to view the various sites, through miles of streets, past filling stations and round roundabouts in modern, Sunday-morning Carthage which was full of bijou villas protected by wrought iron fences and savage Alsatian dogs, imported at Allah knows what cost to protect the Tunisian bourgeoisie from whatever fate they deserved.

Later, looking down at the only ruins of Carthage that really merit the journey, the Roman ruins of the Antonine Baths on the seashore which, like most of the ruins of Carthage, are displayed in what looks like a sort of municipal park, closed because it was Sunday, I realized why Rose Macaulay, that most masterly exponent of ruin writing, who could make even a disused gasworks sound exciting if she put her mind to it, found herself up against it when she came to write about Carthage not as it was but as it is. For there was nothing to go on, nothing to tell one what the city and its port had looked like in its pre-Roman glory before the three Punic wars with Rome.

The first of these wars, which began in 264 BC, she fought to maintain her position in the central Mediterranean. It ended with the partial destruction of her fleets, the loss of her bases in Sicily, and, after peace was made with Rome, the evacuation of Sardinia which was one of her colonies.

The Second Punic War, which lasted from 218 to 201 BC, she fought to regain the position she had lost in the first one. It began with Hannibal and an army of 90,000 infantry, 20,000 cavalry and 40 elephants crossing the Pyrenees from Spain, the Rhone Valley and then the Alps into Italy, probably somewhere near the source of the Po on Monte Viso, defeating the Romans in a series of actions and taking his armies as far south as Taranto, before being forced to return to Africa to defend Carthage, having spent fifteen years on enemy soil with his armies unconquered. It ended in 202 BC with his defeat at Zama, a site in Tunisia, never accurately determined, by Scipio Africanus, who had already driven the Carthaginians from Spain in 206 BC, after which he fled to Carthage. As a result of his defeat Carthage lost all her overseas possessions, her trade monopolies in the Mediterranean, her entire fleet apart from ten ships and was forced to agree to pay an enormous indemnity over a period of thirty years and an annual tribute, rather like Germany after 1918. All the Carthaginians retained was their autonomy within what were called the Phoenician Trenches, which more or less approximated to present-day Tunisia.

For the next six years Hannibal ruled Carthage as a suffete, a magistrate, encouraging constitutional reforms, diminishing the powers of the oligarchs in the Carthaginian Senate, earning their undying enmity by doing so, and putting the financial affairs of the state in such good order that the city was able to pay off her indemnity not in thirty years but eleven (in 191 BC), and without any great increases in taxation. Alarmed by his success and the rapid resurgence of Carthage, Rome demanded that he be handed over and in 195 BC he was forced to flee, first to Tyre, the mother-city of Carthage, then to Ephesus where Antiochus, King of Syria, was planning what proved to be a disastrous campaign* against Rome, then to Crete and finally to Libyssa on the Asiatic shores of the Sea of Marmara, where he died by his own hand to avoid being handed over to the Romans by a King of Bithynia in 183 or 182 BC. Thus perished one of the greatest soldiers of his or any other age, who was also a great statesman.

There followed a long period in which Rome encouraged her ally, Masinissa, the ruler of the neighbouring Berber kingdom of Numidia, who had been brought up in Carthage and had fought with her armies against the Romans in Spain, to goad the Carthaginians into attacking him, thus breaking the non-aggression treaty they had made with Rome, which he succeeded in doing in 150 BC, defeating them in the ensuing battle. The following year, which saw the opening of the third Punic War, the Roman armies invaded Carthage and the Carthaginians agreed to surrender, give hostages and lay down their arms, revoking this decision, however, when the terms, which included the total destruction of their city, became known. A three-year siege followed which ended in 146 BC after a most desperate resistance by the defenders, the wife of Hasdrubal, the Carthaginian commander (not to be confused with Hannibal's brother of the same name), choosing death for herself and her

---

* He was defeated at Magnesia in Lydia in 190 BC by Scipio Africanus and his brother Lucius.

children rather than capture and leaving Hasdrubal to surrender and become part of Scipio's triumph.

'*Delenda est Carthago*,' the elder Cato told the Roman Senate; 'Carthage must be destroyed,' and so it was. It burned for seventeen days and when the fires were finally extinguished there was nothing to be seen of what had been a great city except an immense heap of ashes, a gigantic version of the funeral pyre of Queen Dido, the legendary founder of Carthage, who immolated herself, having failed to deflect Aeneas from his destiny, which was to be the forefather of Rome. Only an enormous aqueduct fifty miles long remained, and no one is sure whether this was Carthaginian or Roman. After this site was levelled, ploughed and the earth in what had been its fields drenched with salt as a sign, if nothing else, that this land which had been officially cursed should remain for ever sterile, this being the first task performed by the 50,000 survivors of the siege, all of whom were condemned to slavery. However, 117 years later, in 29 BC, it was colonized by Hadrian with 3000 veterans of the Roman legions and it eventually became, with its population augmented by Phoenician-speaking and Libyan subjects, not only the capital of Africa Proconsularis but, with Alexandria, one of the three most important cities of the Roman world. Later still it became an important centre of Christianity, its bishop regarding himself as the equal of the bishop of Rome, and was also famous for its orators and lawyers.

What therefore could one learn about the Carthaginians from looking at the remains of a Roman city that had subsequently been destroyed by Vandals, besieged by Byzantines, further destroyed by raiding Arabs, quarried, and, as a final indignity, had what was left of its marble walls taken to build a railway line? Nothing. Although they are known to have produced historians and geographers, the Carthaginians have left no written works. Even a work on agriculture, written by a Carthaginian named Mago, which became a standard work on the subject throughout the Roman Empire, has not survived in the original. It is known that they were very religious and frightfully cruel with it, at Carthage sacrificing hundreds of children to their god Baal Ammon and the goddess Taanit, strangling them or cutting their throats before consigning them to a fiery furnace that stood before the image of the god. Among the few artefacts that have come down to posterity from the Carthaginians are the urns in which they buried the ashes of these children. They themselves were buried in sepulchres in a vast necropolis far from the habitations of the living for fear of contaminating them.

Adept with their hands, the Carthaginians were not creative in the artistic sense. Although they manufactured rugs and tapestries and textiles and pottery and jewellery, their inspiration was Greek, Syrian or Egyptian. They were great carriers of merchandise and dealers in raw materials as were their ancestors, the Phoenicians, who had founded a trading station here and on other parts of the Tunisian coast, such as Sousse and Bizerta, early in the ninth century BC. They bought metal from Spain, Gaul and Britain, marble from all over the Mediterranean and from other parts of Africa timber, ostrich feathers and ivory.

If little belonging to the Carthaginians remains in these excavations, even less pertains to the Phoenicians, of whom very little is known at all. A dark-skinned, Semitic people, in about 1300 BC they moved westwards from Canaan, later to be known as the Holy Land, and occupied a narrow, cultivable strip, no more than 120 miles long and nowhere more than 30 miles wide, between the Lebanon mountains and the Mediterranean. Finding it too small to support them as agriculturalists, and being at the meeting point of the caravan routes from Mesopotamia, the Caucasus, Asia and the Persian Gulf, after trading in cypress and Lebanon cedar wood for a while, they took to the sea. On the coast they built themselves a number of strategically sited ports, among them Aradus, otherwise Ruad, on an island, Byblos on a cliff, Sidon on a headland and Tyre, raised on some offshore rocks and tenuously linked with the mainland by a neck of sand. Here, they became the ancient world's greatest ship-builders and sea-carriers of other people's merchandise in the Mediterranean and beyond.

By the beginning of the seventh century the Phoenicians controlled the whole of the trade with the Persian Gulf by way of the Red Sea. However, disaster was soon to overwhelm them on their own shores, where the Assyrians, advancing westwards to the Mediterranean, captured their cities one by one, driving out their inhabitants who sailed westwards to found colonies on the shores of the Gulf of Sirte (in Tripolitania), in Sardinia, in the Balearics, near the Pillars of Melcarth, otherwise the Pillars of Hercules, and at what was to be Carthage. In 666 BC, Tyre, the last of their cities, fell to the Assyrians, lamented by the Prophet Ezekiel, and the Phoenician domination of the eastern Mediterranean was at an end. But they survived, being known as the Kinaahu, the 'People of the Purple'. They were so named because they manufactured a deep purple dye from a liquid secreted by *Murex brandaris* and *Purpura haemastoma*, shell fish that existed in vast quantities on the Mediterranean shore of what had been their kingdom. Their expulsion from their own land drove them to seek new sources for the dyes, and these they found in the Canaries and Madeira.

It was about this time that the Pharaoh Necho II despatched a Phoenician fleet to find a way round Africa. It is not known whether they succeeded or not, but Herodotus, writing 150 years after the voyage took place, recorded that on returning to Egypt by way of the Strait of Gibraltar, in the third year of their voyage . . . 'they reported a thing which I cannot believe, but another man may, namely that in sailing round Libya [then the name for Africa], they had the sun on their right hand', which although it must have sounded incredible to the Greeks, offers the most conclusive proof that the voyage took place, as a ship sailing west while south of the equator would find that the midday sun was on the right, that is to the north.

A similar voyage, better documented, but one undertaken basically for reasons other than discovery, took place *c.* 500 BC when Hanno, one of the suffetes of Carthage, set off with a fleet of sixty ships, each with fifty oarsmen and a large number of men and women – to settle them in new colonies along the west coast of Africa and so safeguard the Carthaginian trade route to the Canaries and Madeira, their newly-found sources of dyes. After founding a colony and building a temple on the site of present-day Mehediya on the Atlantic coast of Morocco, north of Rabat, Hanno continued to sail south, establishing six more colonies, the last of which, Cerne, possibly Herne Island on the Tropic of Cancer, was to be the leading trading centre on the West African coast for 400 years. Hanno left an account of his voyage, from which he had to turn back because of lack of provisions, in the temple of Baal Ammon when he and his men returned to Carthage. This journey was not to be emulated again for some 1900 years, when the Portuguese, with all their modern navigational aids, set out to find a trade route to India, and even then it took them over forty years to accomplish what Hanno achieved in a single voyage of more than 3000 miles and only a few months.

'Listen,' Wanda said, in a voice which told me, having been married to her since practically before the Flood, that something pretty shattering was looming up for public presentation in her Slavonic mind, something I could have done without, as peering down into these excavations under what looked like a snow-filled sky had given me a bad dose of what the Tunisians might call *la tristesse du dimanche*, reminding me of similar grey, featureless Sunday mornings in Barnes, SW13, as a boy before the war.

'I'm listening,' I said.

'What I want to know,' she said, 'is what have you got in mind after Tunisia? You said you wanted to go to Morocco, but there's Algeria in between. What are you going to do about Algeria? It's enormous.'

'Well,' I said, and it sounded pretty feeble, 'I suppose we ought to follow the coast, looking into all those coves the Barbary pirates used to lie up in, that sort of thing. Besides, I thought it would be a good place to have a look at the Sahara. We may never have a chance again.'

'Tell me,' she said, trying to ignore a man who was trying to sell her an enormous, trendy birdcage, big enough to hold a vulture, one of the local products from Sidi Bou Said, 'how far do you think it is from here to Morocco?'

'I don't really know,' I said. 'I suppose about 1300 miles or so if you followed the coast. I'm not sure. Perhaps more.'

'And how far have we travelled in the last seven days?' She was like some inquisitor screwing up a heretic on the rack.

'About 2500 miles. Something like that.'

'And how are you proposing to travel to Morocco?'

'Well, I hadn't really thought. Even you said we can't afford to hire cars any more. There's a train service, I looked it up. It's something like 1000 miles from Tunis to Fez but you have to keep on changing and most of the time it doesn't go anywhere near the coast, except at Algiers and Oran. I suppose we'd have to go by bus.'

'I don't know how you can bring yourself to say that after yesterday,' she said. 'Sometimes I wonder if you're all there. Aren't you done in? I am. Anyway,' she said, changing the subject in a typical Wanda way, 'how long has this book of yours got to be?'

'I don't really know,' I said. 'The contract said about 120,000 words. If it's any bigger it will be so big that no one will be able to lift it, let alone afford to buy it.'

'How many words have you written up to now?'

'About 250,000, and we still have to go to Algeria, Morocco, Spain and France.'

'Well, something's going to have to go,' she said. 'I should start by leaving out Algeria.'

So I did.

On the Edge of the Sahara

After this, having made the momentous decision to give Algeria a miss, something that was hardly likely to break any Algerian hearts, we walked to the nearest station, which some imaginative fellow had named Carthage Hannibal, and boarded one of the now-that-it-was-broad-daylight no longer creepy trains back to Tunis.

There, Wanda was just in time to participate in the last part of a Catholic mass which was being performed in the Cathedral of St Vincent de Paul, a splendid neo-Gothic building put up by the French in 1882. There was quite a large congregation on this Sunday morning, seemingly made up (one could scarcely ask them) of converted Tunisians, what had once been *colons* and their descendants, French colonialists, who had somehow managed to stay on after 1964 when the government of Bourguiba, the President,* now into his second five-year term of office, had instituted a programme of nationalization and confiscation which had deprived them of their *domaines*, some Italian-speakers, including some

---

* By now, 1983, having attained the more than ripe old age of eighty years, most of his subjects believed he had filled the post long enough, a feeling which many inhabitants of all the other countries of the North African shores of the Mediterranean currently have about their heads of state.

rather gloomy-looking Maltese and various other Christian foreigners who, like us, had ended up on these exotic shores. One old Italian lady who stood next to Wanda during the service said that she disliked Tunis and the Tunisians intensely but had nowhere else to go.

Once the service was over the air became thick with the sort of salutations with which people tend to greet one another after church on Sunday mornings anywhere:

'*Madame, Monsieur, je vous souhaite le bonjour. Comment portez-vous, Madame? J'espère que vous êtes en bonne santé.*'

To which Madame replied, '*Merci, Monsieur, je me suis portée parfaitement*' (or if only so-so '*passablement*'). Or, if she was an Italian-speaking lady, '*La ringrazio, Signore, sto bene* (or '*sono stato mediocremente bene*'), which conjured up visions of someone who, rather like a cheese, was in the process of going off. They were jolly lucky to have a cathedral to grumble in and make *plaisanteries* to one another. If it had been in Libya it would long since have been turned into a mosque and there would have been no opportunity for such unbridled intercourse between the sexes.

After this, by which time it was raining heavily, we went into the Medina, the Old City, which had a pork butcher's shop in one of its outer walls, with a sign depicting an enormous pig above it, something I had never seen before in a Muslim city, but with nothing about being by appointment to anyone. Then through miles of what would have been wonderful *souks*, many of them covered ones. If only it hadn't been Sunday – it would have been the same on Friday – when all the booths in them, apart from a few religious ones selling Korans, one or two selling tourist junk and an entire *souk* selling furniture, were shuttered and barred, as they were outside in the modern city, apart from the street markets and the food and vegetable markets, which were thronged with people.

Then to the food markets behind the dead-straight Avenue Habib Bourguiba which, if you persist in following it to its conclusion, lands you in the off-colour waters of the Lac de Tunis, otherwise El-Bahira, which is the nearest approximation in Tunis to the sea. There we ate in an open-fronted restaurant, well wrapped up against the cold, a delicious Tunisian repast, *Brik à l'oeuf*, triangular sheets of very thin pastry with a seasoned egg inside it, deep fried at such a high temperature that the outside becomes crisp while the egg remains runny, which when it is ready looks like the sort of letter that ought to be sent to the *Good Food Guide*. Then we had a delicacy called *harghma*, stewed calves' feet, to keep the cold out, and a bottle of a good red wine called Morag which cost 1.3 Tunisian dinars, the equivalent of £1.30 ($1.80), a bottle.

After all this we felt strong enough for a visit to the Bardo Museum, half price on Fridays and Sunday afternoons; photography extra (no flash or tripods to be used except with special permission); transistor radios, parcels, etc., to be left at the entrance. And no jokes about the President being past it either, as he might quite easily be upstairs listening in, in what is now the Tunisian House of Representatives. Until the last one abdicated in 1957, this was the palace of the Hosainid Beys of Tunis, who for 200 years ruled the country with only nominal acknowledgement to the Turkish sultan whose vassals they remained.

The contents of this museum are remarkable. There are the most brilliantly-executed Roman mosaic pavements from the ruined cities of Tunisia, some of them enormous; depictions of bacchanalian processions of Neptune and his cortege, of fishing, hunting and maritime scenes, one showing every sort of Roman trading vessel, banqueting scenes of the greatest liveliness, heads of river gods, of Oceanus, Apollo and Diana, rural scenes, a country seat with park, stable, granary, sheds and wine cellar, Virgil writing the *Aeneid*.

Equally if not more memorable are the sculptures in bronze and marble and other artefacts including beds, most of them dating from the third and second centuries BC, found in the hold of a Roman ship sunk in 100 feet of water in the Gulf of Mahdia, south of Sousse, which is thought to have been returning with these wonders looted at the sack of Athens by Sulla in 85 BC, among them a bronze statue of Eros, perhaps a replica of one carved by Praxiteles in the fourth century BC. By now we were beginning to suffer from both cultural and gastronomic indigestion – the calves' feet hung heavy on us – and not having slept for two days and a night, we took the train back to Sidi Bou Said and went to bed.

The next day, having overcome Wanda's scruples about making use of a car, we set off in one to satisfy what can only be described as my irrational desire to see the Sahara, which I could only justify by telling myself that it was, like the Kras, one of the frontiers on which the Mediterranean world ended.

To tell the truth I was not all that happy about driving in a country in which I had already noticed, in the brief hours of daylight after we had entered it from Libya, that the rural inhabitants regarded the more dangerous bends in the roads as being good places to settle down for a leisurely discussion with one another about the state of the country, surrounded by their flocks, and neither was Wanda, who was going to have to stand her tricks at the wheel so that I could absorb the atmosphere of Tunisia without hurtling off the road into some *wadi*. This was a country that still, I felt sure, punished any transgression of the law, such as running someone over, with the utmost severity. It was only comparatively recently that the practice had fallen into disuse of dropping offenders from the walls of Tunis on to hooks embedded in them, there to die a lingering death. Or it may have been Algiers, in which case I am doing the Tunisians an injustice. Anyway, it is now only a matter of academic interest, as the whole of the apparatus, with only too life-like figures hanging on the hooks, has long since been transferred to Madame Tussauds where it can be seen, on payment of a supplementary fee, in the Chamber of Horrors.

From Tunis, following a circuitous route to the Sahara so that we could see more of Tunisia on the way, we drove north-westwards through country which had once been one of the great granaries of Rome, crossing the valley of the Medjerda River, the only perennial river in the whole country, which has its origins in the Jebel Zellez in Algeria. This valley was one of the places where the French *colons* had engaged in intensive farming, using the local people as cheap labour, and where, after the land nationalization of 1964, young Tunisians were trained to carry on where the French had been encouraged to leave off, after which, when they were judged to be sufficiently competent, they were given their own farmhouses and freehold land.

Beyond the valley of the Medjerda the road entered an enormous fertile plain with big herds of cattle and sheep grazing in it and here and there one of the barrel-roofed buildings brilliantly white in the afternoon sunlight, for by now the clouds that had looked to be full of snow had rolled away. The plain partly encircled the Jebel Ichkeul, an isolated mountain, and also a lake of the same name, a large, reed-fringed expanse on which what looked like rafts of waterfowl floated too far out to be identified. Its waters were partly rain, partly sea water which entered it from another lake, the Lake of Bizerta, which is connected with the Mediterranean.

Here, above the shores of the lake, on the stony slopes of the Jebel, there was a primitive village of stone huts roofed with reeds from the lake and hemmed in by enclosures of thorn, which prevented the animals from straying and on which the women, who were dressed in brilliantly-coloured clothes, hung their equally brilliantly-coloured washing.

Down by the lake itself, which at this point was an expanse of mud with scarcely any water in it, there were two little buildings with whitewashed walls and domes that looked like the tombs of holy men, but which inside were full of the jolly-looking men-folk of the women up the hill, all sitting contentedly up to their necks in the waters of a hot spring, their day's work presumably done, for by now it was late afternoon and the sun was rapidly sinking. But what sort of work could they do here, on the slopes of a stony mountain, cut off from the rich grazing lands beyond by miles of mud, for they were certainly not fishermen?

Perhaps there were no fish. There were a lot of questions I would have liked to ask these friendly men, but they spoke nothing but Arabic, or perhaps Berber, and there was no one else to ask, and this is what travel anywhere so often leads to, the traveller being confronted with a series of what are often unsolvable mysteries while out in the sticks and then, once he or she has returned to civilization, where the answers are often available, forgetting to ask.

That night we slept at Tabarka, a small port on a wild coast, whose inhabitants lived mainly by fishing for fish and twigs of coral and by processing cork from the forests, in a hotel full of Frenchmen, mild-looking little men, all dressed in camouflage clothing and armed to the teeth, who had come here to shoot wild boar in the nearby Khroumerie mountains on the Algerian border. Tabarka had originally been a Phoenician, then a Carthaginian port and then, after the fall of Carthage, Roman. At the mouth of the harbour there was a rock which had once been an island but was now joined to the mainland by a causeway. On it stood the shell of a Genoese castle where the wife of the lighthouse keeper, whose lighthouse rose above the walls, kept her chickens and dried her washing. The island had been given to the Genoese by the Holy Roman Emperor, Charles V, in 1542, to thank them, it is said, for having betrayed to him the great Turkish corsair Dragut; but this seems unlikely, as at that date Dragut still had a long and active life ahead of him.

This occupation of Tabarka by the Genoese, and other foreign infidels equally antipathetic to the Muslims, continued until 1741, when the Bey, Ali Pasha, a bloodthirsty, unbalanced despot (not to be confused with his equally bloodthirsty Albanian namesake), whose mercifully short reign came to an end when he was strangled in the Bardo, took Tabarka and the island with it, and consigned the inhabitants to slavery.

Tabarka was a pleasant place, apart from a rather weird off-licence to which the proprietor of a supermarket, not at that moment having any stock himself, sent us to buy a bottle of wine which we wanted to drink in our room, not liking the wine in the hotel. It turned out to be situated in an almost pitch black room packed with large numbers of very drunk and not particularly friendly Tabarkan Muslims, all brandishing large receptacles they had brought with them to get topped up with the stuff which was available from barrels on draught, and all pushing and shoving as if they were outside a bank that was about to go bust.

It was here, at Tabarka, in 1952, that the now President Bourguiba, then a revolutionary trying to liberate his country, was kept under house arrest before being transferred to France; and here, in the Hôtel de France, in the main street, we were shown the astonishing dining room in which he took his meals, a hecatomb of dead game, its walls covered with stuffed birds and the heads of other trophies of the chase, now past their best, all illuminated by candelabra ingeniously constructed from the legs of wild boar. Now a national monument, the table at which he used to sit is never allowed to be occupied.

The next morning we left the shores of the Mediterranean and drove southwards away from it over the Khroumerie Range, home of the Khroumir Berbers, wild mountaineers who were such a thorn in the side of the French that they made them the excuse to invade Tunisia from Algeria, after the Khroumirs had made a raid across the border into Algeria in 1881. The road wound up the west side of the gorge of the Oued Kabir, at first through a tunnel of huge eucalyptus trees that were in the process of being cut down, then through woods of cork trees, evergreen oaks and pine trees with ferns and bracken growing beneath them, part of an immense and dense forest that was still the abode of wild-cats, civets, jackals, foxes and the wild boar, in which the last Tunisian lion was killed in the early years of the 1800s, in which the last panther survived until 1932, and in which boys now stood at the roadside, apparently miles from anywhere, selling wooden hatstands, eggs and objects made of cork. Finally we arrived at Aïn Draham, a little mountain resort with red-roofed houses that was more like some place in the Balkans than in North Africa. Here, at around 3000 feet, still below the watershed, we were only a few miles from the Algerian border.

Then we drove down the southern, sunny, less wooded flank of the range, passing through fruit orchards before entering the wide green valley of the Medjeda River, where, in what was like spring-time, men were ploughing with wooden ploughs and others were sowing the seed, broadcasting it by hand. How beautiful Tunisia was. How lucky we were to be in it, in what would have been in England the depths of winter. There, at the foot of a rocky slope, in the side of which, according to the custodian, slaves had been doomed to live in shallow caves, were the ruins of Bulla Regia, originally a Carthaginian city, then a city of the Numidian ruler Jugurtha, the grandson of Masinissa, who had successfully pro-voked the Carthaginians to break their non-aggression pact with Rome. Then, in the first century AD, the Romans annexed it after Jugurtha had been defeated, and it continued to flourish as a Roman city during the second and third centuries.

An extraordinary site for a city, in the middle of nowhere, but built here originally because it was on the main road from Carthage to Hippo Regius in Algeria, which was the port of western Numidia until it was added to the Roman province of Mauretania. St Augustine was bishop of Hippo Regius from AD 396–430. The inhabitants of Bulla Regia, a place cold in winter, enormously hot in summer, later became Christians (from the third until the seventh centuries it had its own bishop). They constructed a city in which a large part of the accommodation was underground. Some of these subterranean rooms have mosaic floors, perhaps the most beautiful of which shows Amphitrite, wife of Poseidon, the god of the sea and earthquakes, and mother of Triton, bestriding a sea monster and attended by cherubs who are surging through the water on the backs of dolphins.

We crossed the valley of the Medjerda and beyond it climbed through immense olive groves, vineyards and fields of sprouting wheat, a vast *domaine* of the White Fathers, French missionaries who still continue to administer it under Tunisian control, to the escarpment of the Teboursouk Range, lunching in a small place called Dougga where we were given omelettes and hot peppers, salad made with delicious olive oil and wine vinegar, presumably a by-product of the White Fathers' wine-making, and, strange in a place with large numbers of Muslims eating in it, jugged wild boar.

Then to the ruins, at Dougga, of ancient Thugga, a city with more or less the same history as Bulla Regia, but more beautiful, unravaged by earthquakes and less troubled by vandals of any date, with a theatre looking out over beautiful rolling country; a magnificent temple built of golden stone, dedicated to Jupiter, the Roman Zeus, Juno, otherwise Hera, his queen, and Minerva, the Goddess of Wisdom, otherwise Athena; and, more astonishing, if less beautiful, the Mausoleum of Atebamn, a Numidian prince, who was buried here in this, one of the only Carthaginian buildings still standing, at the end of the third or the beginning of the second century BC, and built in the style – it is certainly very Asiatic in feeling – of the tombs of the Syrian kings. Neither very well executed nor very beautiful, it originally rose to a height of more than fifty feet, a pile of huge limestone blocks, each successive storey of which was decorated with pilasters, the whole construction being crowned by a small pyramid with the figure of a lion on top of it. The top sections of this rare monument were destroyed not by Vandals, or even by equally iconoclastic Arabs, but by Sir Thomas Reade, British Consul in Tunis, who, in 1842, obtained the permission of the then Bey of Tunis to knock it down in order to obtain an inscription in Phoenician and Libyan which states that Atebamn was the son of Iepmatah, who was the son of Pallu, which he then presented to the British Museum. The mausoleum then had to wait for more than sixty years before it was restored, but only as a shadow of its former self, by M. Poinssot, a distinguished French archaeologist who was responsible for a great deal of the excavation and restoration within the city. After all this we felt that so far as Tunisia was concerned, and for that matter as far as the entire Mediterranean basin was concerned, we had had enough of ruins, by this time having seen an innumerable quantity.

So we struck south to the interior and went down some 250 miles to the edge of the Sahara.

We stood on an escarpment above Nefta, in southern Tunisia, looking down into what is called in Arabic the Kasr el-Aïn, the castle of the springs, what the French called la Corbeille, the Basket, a deep basin behind the ridge on which the town stands, at the head of which, hidden from view in a small but dense oasis of palms, hundreds of sweet water springs, said to be 152 altogether, erupt from the sands to form delicious, bubbling pools. No men are allowed near this place, and the women go down to it to bathe with their children in the early mornings and evenings, when the little grove resounds with the happy sounds of their laughter. From the pools the waters snake away downhill, still hidden beneath the palm trees which here form a narrow tunnel, eventually emerging by way of a miniature gorge into another pool, formed by a dam built by the Romans who lived here, or perhaps by the Numidians, or even by the Carthaginians before them, in which the men and boys from the town make their non-ritual ablutions, after which it disappears into the depths of the great Nefta Oasis.

The Nefta Oasis is the finest in all this region of the Djerid. It waters some 187,000 date palms and gives life to what grows beneath them, pomegranates, avocados, quinces, almonds, pears, olives and vines, and what in turn and in season grows beneath the palm shade, masses of flowers. This system of husbandry was invented by a man named Ibn Chaddat who is buried in a *zawiya*, an honoured shrine, in a village called Bled el-Haddar, near Tozeur, another oasis town of the Djerid.

Here at Nefta, and at Tozeur, where there are said to be 420,000 palms, the oases, perhaps the most fertile plots in northern Africa between the Nile Delta and the Atlantic Ocean, stand on the very edge of one of the most infertile land tracts anywhere in the world, the Chott Djerid, a saline marsh devoid of life and vegetation, fifty miles long and fifty wide at its widest point, the biggest of a whole series of dozens of similar *chotts* which extend for something like 1000 miles in a great arc across North Africa from the Gulf of Gabès on the east coast of Tunisia, across the whole of Algeria and into Morocco.

Not only were the Oasis of Nefta and the valley of the Kasr el-Aïn and the springs that watered them beautiful; so also was the town itself, but of a more rare and strange beauty, which, although it was intensely Islamic, was a beauty compounded of worldly and other worldly ingredients that had very little about it of the picture postcard, pop-art visions of what might constitute paradise. Its narrow, often unpaved streets, which were nothing more than alleys, especially those high up on the ridge exposed to the winds that blew in from the desert, which here lapped it on all sides, were full of driven sand, and into them the sewage ran from the houses on either side down little channels that had been made in the sand either with a foot or a human hand. The houses themselves were mostly single-storey, built either with blocks of gypsum or more often with thin, sand-coloured bricks, the walls curiously ornamented with whole networks of them forming geometrical patterns in high and low relief, houses that I could not imagine anyone ever building in the ordinary sense of the word, but looking as if they had been brought into being by some magician waving a wand over a heap of dust.

It is a holy town. Its people are Sufis, members of a strict mystical and pantheistic sect within Islam which originated in Persia, the earliest exponents of which lived and died in the ninth century. It is said, although we found no evidence of it, that its inhabitants, of whom even the most closely wrapped ladies never failed to say '*Bonjour*' as they swayed past, are not happy when infidel visitors show too great an interest in what are reputed to be, and it is a relatively small place, its twenty-four mosques and hundred *zawiyas*. Of these the most revered is the Zawiya el-Kadia, which is both a shrine and a religious school dedicated to the much-revered Sufi Persian saint Sidi Abd el-Kader el-Djilani, the founder of the Kadria brotherhood, who is buried in a *marabout*, a chapel, near Oran, in Algeria.

The sun set while we were looking at this scene and when it was down, in the last of the light everything – the town, up to which the heavily swathed ladies were now hurrying homeward from the springs, the Oasis and the Chott beyond – was the colour of pearls.

The Chott stretched away for what seemed to be for ever into the distance, fifty miles of mud and salt, pale and mysterious, which when it rained turned into a sea that could and did engulf men and animals, across which, until the building of a causeway, the only way was along the line of a caravan route, used originally by the Romans, called the Trigh el-Oudiana. And beyond the Chott, due south from where we stood, there was nothing. If you drew a line due south from where we were standing and travelled along it you would be in absolute wilderness for the first 1250 or so miles, and by the time you reached Calabar in southern Nigeria on the shores of the south Atlantic you would have made a journey of some 2000 miles without encountering a town even as large as Nefta, which has about 14,000 inhabitants.

It was big, the Sahara, there was no doubt of that. More than 3,000,000 square miles. The biggest desert on earth. Six times as large as the next largest desert in the world, the Gobi. You could put India and Pakistan into it and lose them. If you knocked off Alaska you could get the United States into it. It extended from the Atlantic to the Red Sea, and southwards from the Mediterranean to the Sudan in the east and in the west to the River Niger.

I felt that I had come far enough for someone whose interests were supposed to lie on the shores of the Mediterranean.

View from a Hill

It is not the *muezzins*, the regular summoners to prayer, who are the first to sound reveille in Fès el-Bali, Old Fez, which they do with such notable effect at the first intimation of light in the east. Long before there is any suggestion that the *fejer*, the dawn, is on the way, back in the middle watches of the night, the Companions of the Sick, ten devout Muslims chosen, like the *muezzins*, for their voices and provided for by a bequest made long ago by one who was himself sick and required moral sustenance in the night, begin their weird and hauntingly beautiful chanting, changing over throughout the night at half-hourly intervals. Failing this, half an hour before the dawn, there is the *ábad*, the thrice-repeated cry of praise to God which begins, 'the Perfection of God, existing for ever and ever'.

Haunting and unforgettable though these chants are when taken up and echoed from minaret to minaret, they also have a fearful capacity for murdering sleep. This is one reason we are here. The other is because we want to see the sun rise over Old Fez, just as we had seen it rise, in greater discomfort, beyond the Pyramids. So we are out beyond the northern walls, up on the hill called el Kolla, among the *kubbas*, the tombs of the Merinid Sultans, the nomad

Berbers from the Sahara, looking in the direction of Old Fez and also of New Fez, which stands beside and above it.

Now cocks crow and packs of dogs howl and bark and bite one another on the outskirts, just as they did on the outskirts of Cetinje in Montenegro, just as they still do on the outskirts of any oriental city, which they are welcome to do, just so long as they don't bite me. We can hear them out beyond the walls, in the orange, apricot, pomegranate and olive groves which now invest them at an ever-increasing distance, out there in the *msallas*, the great open-air praying places, out on the stony hillsides where the prickly pears grow, around the strongholds built by various conquerors to dominate the Old City without the necessity of getting too close to it, out among the *kubbas* and the *zawiyas*, the tombs and shrines of the illustrious and saintly dead, tombs around which cults, some of them rather strange cults, have arisen, such as that at the tenth-century tomb of Sidi Boujida, where young wives, swathed in white, who have lost their husbands' esteem, pray to recover it.

Eventually, after what seems an age and the *ábad* has been repeated for the second time, first light seeps into the world away to the east over the northern outliers of the Middle Atlas, and the *muezzins* go into action from the minarets, the only really tall edifices in a city in which there appear to be no buildings of European inspiration at all (apart perhaps from some now long-disused foreign consulates), announcing that 'Night has Departed . . . Day Approaches with Light and Brightness . . . Prayer is Better than Sleep . . . Arise And to God Be Praise!' The whole cry is repeated in its entirety four times, once to each cardinal point of the compass, in parts twice.

And now the Old City is revealed behind its crenellated, turreted walls. It is a city set in a valley, an amphitheatre or an open shell, tilted so that its western end is higher than its eastern and its northern end higher than its southern, with a river and other streams, most of them invisible until you actually stand on their banks or fall into them. All of these streams run down from the plateau up at the western end on which New Fez, Fès el-Jedid, which is not new at all, was founded in 1276.

The walls of Old Fez, thirty or forty feet high, twelve or thirteen feet thick at the base, are made of *tabia*, clay mixed with chalk and cement which sets rock-hard, and their angles are reinforced with masonry. They were built by Christian slaves for their masters, the Almohads, in the twelfth century. Many more centuries were to pass before there was any pressing need to import Negroes as slaves, to supplement what seems to have been an unending supply of Christian captives taken by Barbary corsairs or in battle – who, when they breathed their last, usually from over-work, were often added to the mixture to give it more body.

A completely Muslim city, one of the most revered in the Muslim world.

At this moment the city is still quiet. There are no motor vehicles, no motorcycles, not even a bicycle within its walls now, or at any time. Almost the only wheels to be found in it are water wheels, wheels that form parts of machines and the wheels of wheelbarrows. Now, with the coming of the day, even the dogs have fallen silent and dispersed. Apart from the *muezzins*, and some of them may be on tape, it could be a city of the dead.

But not for long. In a few minutes the sun comes racing up behind the tall, modern houses perched on an escarpment above the lower, eastern end of the amphitheatre in which the city stands and floods it with brilliant light, at first honey-coloured, then golden, transforming houses that a moment before were drab rectangles of a shade that someone, rather unkindly, compared to unwashed bed-sheets, into golden ingots. It illuminates the green-tiled roofs of the mosques, the *médersa*, the Islamic colleges, and the tall, square minarets that are so different from the tall, slender, circular minarets of Cairo and Istanbul, some of which have golden finials and are embellished with ceramic tiles. And it shines on the leaves of those trees that have managed to force their way up into the open air from the courtyards of the houses, like grass forcing its way through concrete.

And as the city is drenched with light that is more and more golden as the moments pass, it comes to life. The air fills with the haze of innumerable charcoal fires and with what sounds like the buzzing of innumerable bees, the noise made by some 250,000 human beings telling one another that night has departed, prayer is better than sleep, wishing one another good morning across the deep, cobbled ditches between the buildings that serve as streets, or else having the first row of the day in Berber or Arabic.

There is perhaps no other city in the western world which exists so much out of time as Old Fez. There are few that so resemble a beehive and, like a real beehive, once the sun is up and the air becomes warm, the closer you get the more danger there is of being stung. At one time it was only too easy to be stung to death in it, as many an intruder who had the misfortune not to be Muslim discovered. Now one is only in danger of being driven insane.

In fact two sharply-dressed stingers have already spotted us from the ring road and are even now weaving their way up towards us among the tombs and other debris of past civilizations on a motorcycle. How *unfair* Islam is to non-members, in spite of all that is in the Koran about respecting the beliefs of others. If *I* rode a motorcycle through even an out-of-date fourteenth-century Muslim cemetery, I would be hung, drawn and probably quartered. They turn out to be identical, juvenile twins with identical, embryonic moustaches and identically dressed. In Britain they would be thinking vaguely about not taking O-level examinations at some still distant date. In the United States they would still be in the tenth grade. Here, they seem as old as the surrounding hills and are planning retirement at our expense and other unfortunates like us.

They are not from Old Fez, it transpires, or New Fez. Nor are they from Modern Fez, which is something altogether different again: a colonial-type city, founded by Marshal Lyautey in about 1916, after the French had set up a Protectorate, to allow the two older cities to continue unchanged in a way of life which was already showing signs of becoming anachronistic. Enlightened though such an aim then was, it has not altogether succeeded.

They live, we later discover, in what was known when it was built as 'The New Indigenous Town', the brain-child of the French town planner Ecochard, which is sited, with the fine contempt for the potential inhabitants which characterizes town planners everywhere, on a bare and arid hillside, the sort of site traditionally reserved for the poor everywhere. It preserves little or nothing of traditional Muslim town planning which might make life in it more comprehensible to the 60,000 inhabitants who find themselves hoiked into the twentieth century in this dreary place. And it has solved none of the problems it was supposed to solve in the Old City. In fact it has produced worse ones. One of these problems is talking to me now, the one who is riding pillion. The driver is the quiet one.

'Hallo, Sir! I will be your guide, Sir! You cannot visit Fez alone, Sir! Bad mens, Sir, in Fez!' And so on, similar tosh. Fez may be confusing but it is not dangerous, unless you play the fool at some shrine or mosque, or openly eat ham sandwiches in its streets. In fact we are speaking to two of the most dangerous people we are likely to meet.

'Thank you. We have already had a guide. With him we have seen everything we wish to see with a guide.' It is true. We have already spent an entire day with a highly cultivated guide, arranged for us by the Tourist Office, the only sort worth having. Now we want to retrace some of the routes we travelled together, but alone.

We both want to do this, but in our hearts we know that it is going to be very difficult, if not impossible. By climbing up here in the early hours we had hoped to escape, at least temporarily, the hordes of self-styled, self-appointed guides and touts, most of whom know less than the most ignorant visitor armed with the most primitive guide book can learn about Fez in twenty minutes. They invest every hotel and every place of interest, waiting for their prey to emerge, and their maddening and, if thwarted, threatening attentions make life such a misery that for many visitors travelling by themselves, as opposed to travelling with a group, the memories of innumerable encounters with these pests become the most enduring of all their memories of Morocco. The rest of this band, presumably, have not yet risen from whatever they spend their nights on – I for one hope it is a red-hot griddle – otherwise there would be other motorcyclists up here among the Merinid tombs. No need to travel as far inland as Fez to suffer their attentions. They have branches in all the principal towns and cities and they do their basic training in Tangier, down at the approaches to the Strait of Gibraltar.

Eventually we escape, but only at a run, swerving among the tombs of lesser men than Merinid sultans to the ring road which encircles the Old and New Cities where, by a miracle, we manage to board a bus in which the passengers are so crushed together that if they adopted the same positions in the open air they would be arrested.

It lands us in the Place du Commerce, outside the royal palace in Fès el-Jedid, to the south of which lies the Mellah, our next refuge, and there we find the twins waiting for us astride their motorcycle, and the whole boring business begins again.

From about 1400, in the time of the Merinids, the Mellah has been inhabited by Jews, descendants of those from the Holy Land and those who had arrived from Spain with the Vandals when they

invaded the Maghreb in the second century. The great majority of
Jews had fled the Inquisition and first settled in the Fondouk el
Ihoudi, the Jews' Caravanserai, up in the north-east corner of Old
Fez inside the Guissa Gate, but after a violent attack on them by the
Muslim population, in the course of which numbers of them were
killed, the Sultan gave them the choice of apostatizing and remaining where they were, or removing themselves outside the walls of
the New City. The majority chose to move to the Mellah, but others
chose to become Muslims, which is why in Fez there are still, or
were until recently, numerous Muslim families of Jewish origin,
identifiable as such because their names all begin with Ben –
Benshokron, Benjeloon, Benguessos, and so on. In fact Moroccans
from other parts of the country, who are always happy to make fun
of the people of Fez, the Fasi, say that half the Berber and Arab
families have Jewish blood.

Mellah is the Arabic word for salt and the ghetto was so-called
because one of the tasks the Sultan set the newly-installed Jewish
butchers, although they may have already been doing this work for
centuries in their *Fondouk*, was pickling the heads of his innumerable victims in brine so that they could remain on public display
longer than would otherwise have been possible, work which kept
them and their successors busy into the early part of the twentieth
century. When Lawrence Harris, a journalist who worked in the
1900s for *The Graphic*, a then-popular illustrated magazine, entered the city in 1908 by way of one of the gates, 'two sun-dried
ghastly objects grinned down to warn us of the fate of rebels . . .'

Indispensable to their Muslim masters in matters of external
commerce, finance, the clandestine manufacture of wine and other
alcoholic beverages, the consumption of which, if not the manufacture, was forbidden by the Koran, the Jews had a virtual monopoly
of the working of gold and silver – they made the needles used by
Muslim women to set their hair and fasten their garments, their
finger rings, their bracelets and their heavy silver ankle rings – and
the coining of money in the Sultan's mint, which formed part of the
Dar el-Makhzen, as the Palace of the Sultans was later known. They
also had a reputation, which they were not at any pains to dispel,
that they were magicians, magic and necromancy being, as it still is
to this day, a major industry in Fez and throughout Morocco.

Yet in spite of, or perhaps because of, being so indispensable, the
Jews were hated, and it is a remarkable testimony to their capacity
for survival that they did survive. They were made to go barefoot,

although according to Leo Africanus, the great African traveller who was a native of Fez, they were allowed to wear 'sockes of sea-rushes'; they were forced to ride mules bareback and wear black, a colour abhorred by most Muslims; they were given the job of clearing obstructed drains and of disposing of the bodies of animals when they fell dead in the streets; they had to be in the Mellah by sunset when the gates were locked, and were forbidden to defend themselves. The rule of the Sultan was not always strong enough to protect them from religious extremists; when one of the more enlightened sultans of the nineteenth century, Abd el-Rahman, who reigned from 1822–59, gave permission for Jews to dress as Muslims, the first and last to do so, and some of them appeared in public wearing the hooded white *jellab** and the yellow slippers called *babouches*, they were instantly stoned to death.

By now most Jews, not altogether surprisingly, have left the Mellah and gone elsewhere, and on this day, while admittedly on the run ourselves, and subsequently, we saw no one we could positively identify as being Jewish. Of the last two of the original seventeen synagogues in the Mellah, the Sefati and the Fasiyin, we were only able to find one, and it had its doors and windows boarded up as if for ever. On our guided tour, the guide, either by accident or design, had steered us clear of the Mellah.

What still remain are the Jews' tall, pale-washed, balconied houses, like the town houses in Spanish Andalucia, from where so many Jews fled to Morocco. They could be of any age, although most of them were probably built in the nineteenth century. In the great cemetery on the slope above the valley outside the walls, to which they were required to carry their dead at a brisk trot, their horizontal tombstones are still kept whitewashed by the custodian.

'You do not like Moroccan peoples,' says the pillion-riding twin, a cunning ploy at this stage of the torture, when the victim, now nearly insane, may quite easily hoist the white flag, fall on his knees and blubber, '*Please, please*, be my guide.'

'I *do* like Moroccans,' I shout. 'We *do* like Moroccans.' By this time a small crowd has collected and is looking at me as if I had

---

* The *jellab* is hooded and made from a single rectangle of material. It is joined down the front and has armholes set in the upper corners with sleeves made from the remnants of material left over from making the hood.

committed some misdemeanour. There is not a policeman in sight. 'We're just fed up with *you*! NOW FOR CHRIST'S SAKE GO AWAY!'

And to escape them we set off together at a shambling trot which eventually leads us into the Mellah.

'FUCK YOUR MOTHERS!' shouts the boy on the pillion, before dismounting and setting off in leisurely pursuit.

'AND FUCK YOUR FATHERS ALSO!' shouts his brother at the helm, the one who up to now had preserved a sombre silence, doing a kick-start and revving up preparatory to heading us off in case we make a swerve in some other direction. All of which seems to prove that in Fez, among the motorcycle-owning classes at least, there has been a marked decline in the use of religious imagery, if not in the actual practice of the religion. A few years ago they would have called us Christian dogs and hoped that our parents' bones might rot in their graves.

Now, with a twin dogging our footsteps, we briskly cross the Rue du Mellah, which with the neighbouring Rue des Orfèvres Juifs (The Street of the Jewish Gold and Silversmiths) had contained the only European shops to be found in Fez before the modern town was built by the French, and enter New Fez by the Semmarin Gate.

The builder of New Fez, Fès el-Jedid, and the royal palace near where we had been standing, was Abu Yousef Yaacub, first of thirty Merinid sultans, a dynasty which endured from about 1240 until 1471. The Merinids dominated Barbary and the western Mediterranean and their pirate fleets terrorized the Christian lands on its northern shores. Yet, in spite of the savagery with which they treated their enemies, they were great patrons of the arts and literature.

It is difficult to contemplate the royal palace on account of the vocal twin interposing himself between us and it. The Palace of the Sultans was the royal and administrative centre of the country, and it was built of the same mixture as the walls of Old Fez by Christian slaves, many of them British. Hidden within its walls – no admittance – are two hundred acres of gardens (one of them planted with forty-foot-high myrtle trees), huge courtyards paved with highly glazed ceramic tiles, of a sort for which Fez has been famous since the earliest times, a now disused harem commodious enough to house a thousand women, which puts it almost in the same class for this type of accommodation as the imperial harem at Topkapi, numerous pavilions, some prisons, a mosque, several parade grounds, one of which covers twenty-one acres, and a barracks. There is also a menagerie which until comparatively recently housed a variety of wild animals.

The palace and the menagerie were described by Harris, who was sent to Fez in 1908 to interview and sketch – photography was forbidden – the new Sultan of Morocco, the revoltingly cruel Moulay el-Hafid, who at that time resided in the Dar el-Makhzen.

In the course of his visits to the Sultan who, to an embarrassing extent as the days passed, came to regard him as a sort of diplomatic adviser, a role which he did not relish, Harris was taken to see the menagerie by its owner.

' "Wait," ' said the Sultan to Harris, ' "and I will show thee something for thine eyes to feast upon. . . ." Soon a live sheep was brought. I naturally thought they were going to kill the sheep, cut it up and feed the animals. But to my astonishment, the sheep was not killed, and struggling and bleating it was thrust alive into the cage of a fine tiger. The sight was most nauseating, and I had to turn my head away. As I did so I caught sight of Mulay Hafid. Such a cruel look of enjoyment I had never seen before on a human face: with glistening eyes and open mouth he thoroughly enjoyed the horrid spectacle, as the poor sheep was rent in pieces . . .'

Later, Harris was invited by the Sultan to be present at a public ceremony in the course of which a sheik, torn from sanctuary in a mosque, had his head and beard shaven without the use of soap or water, the palms of his hands slashed with a knife, salt rubbed into the wounds, a round stone placed in each hand and a leather gauntlet drawn tightly over each clenched and mutilated fist, before being led off to prison with a rope round his neck, to die a lingering death. 'Now he will write no more letters,' the Sultan remarked with a smile.

In the Grande Rue, we stop to buy a very large tray of beaten aluminium with a folding stand which took our fancy during our guided tour. A Fasi craftsman's answer to the problems of the air-age, previously it would have been unthinkable to make such an object in anything but solid copper or brass and therefore untransportable. It would, nevertheless, give Air Maroc a few headaches. I only hope they won't fold it in half to get it into the machine. While we are negotiating this purchase, a twin arrives and, in a decidedly threatening manner, demands commission on the sale, in which he has taken no part, from the shopkeeper. One would have expected the shopkeeper, who is twice his size and age, to give him a thick ear and send him packing, something I have been longing to do for some time myself, being something like four times his age and three times his size. Instead, the shopkeeper shows every sign of being cowed and frightened. Is there a protection racket? If so, is this the result of putting too sudden a brake on the head-pickling business? We leave them to it.

The Grande Rue leads into a big open space, a *mechouar*, enclosed by high, crenellated walls, at the far end of which is a gate, the Bab es-Seba. Above this gate, a larger order than was customary for the picklers, but they could do it, the Infante Ferdinand of Portugal was exposed naked and upside down in his entirety for four days or years, no one seems quite sure which, six years after he had been taken prisoner while on an unsuccessful expedition against Tangier in 1437: after which he was exhibited, this time stuffed as well as pickled, in an open coffin, for another twenty-nine days, or years. It was here, also, that the Franciscan, Andrea of Spoleto, far from home, was burned to death in 1523. Here, too, a Merinid sultan is said to have had himself walled up above the gate after his death. The Bab es-Seba is not a particularly cheerful spot, but then very little of either Old Fez, New Fez or Modern Fez can be said to be exactly jolly.

The Bab es-Seba leads into the Old Mechouar, another walled courtyard, with, so far as can be made out with the aid of an old map, the Oued Fès, the principal river of Fez, flowing secretly beneath it.

Like the square at Marrakech, the Old Mechouar has always been a gathering place for story-tellers, snake-charmers, who carry coils of snakes wound round their necks, jugglers and such like, but now in decreasing numbers. A gate in the wall to the right leads into the Bou Jeloud gardens, which are a kind of no-man's land between New Fez and Old Fez.

In these gardens the Oued Fès emerges to form a series of pools among groves of bamboo, weeping willows, olives and cypresses, all of which flourish here. From them a waterwheel, said to have been brought here by the Genoese, scoops up water and distributes it into conduits lower down, which take it down through the gardens of the palaces in what was the Belgravia of Old Fez. Here the rich and cultivated used to live, families who kept their own bands of musicians, and here the consulates, around which the always very small foreign colony would congregate in the hope of not being slaughtered, used to be found.

In the Bou Jeloud Gardens, looking down on the abundant waters of the Oued Fès before it continues through the amphitheatre in which the old city stands, one begins to understand why the two cities came to be built where they were. Enormous quantities of water were needed for drinking purposes, for watering pleasure gardens, for fountains, for all the other more mundane domestic uses and for the ritual ablutions of countless thousands of Muslims.

These headwaters and the springs outside the walls also had a strategic importance, for whoever controlled them held the key to the Old City, which was why Sultan Yousef built his palace, a garrison for his Christian mercenaries and a *kasbah* (fort) for his Syrian archers, upstream of the Bou Jeloud Pools. From this vantage point he could cut off the water supplies to the Old City, or even flood it if he wanted to, which was what the Almohads had done when they captured it from the Almoravids in 1145.

The whole of the Old City, from the highest to the lowest part, is watered by means of canals from the Oued Fès, many of them subterranean. From these canals, conduits lead off to every house. Any waste water is taken off by other conduits to flow back into the same canals that delivered it in the first place, but lower down, by which time the canals have become sewers. And from them the by now filthy waters are discharged into the Bou Khareb, a stream which eventually enters the Sebou, a river in the plain eastwards of the city.

This system, worked out in its present form in the twelfth century, with its maze of separate veins and arteries, has been compared to the circulatory system in a human body, but although it certainly makes Old Fez a city of superabundant water, it does not need a sanitary engineer to divine that there are certain problems when it comes to providing water fit to drink.

In fact why the entire population was not wiped out ages ago would be a mystery if not for the fact that anyone wishing to survive in the city either, if he was well enough off, had drinking water delivered to his door from some unimpeachable source, on mule-back or by water-carriers who brought it in goatskins, or, if not, became immune to it from constant use.

Our twins appear to have deserted us. Presumably they have lost interest. There is certainly no possibility of a foreigner giving anyone the slip in Fez. Perhaps they are still engaged in putting the screws on the shopkeeper. Nevertheless, lingering in the blessed shade of the Bou Jeloud, we have already acquired several more of a similar sort, two of them, although not twins, even nastier than the originals, if such can be imagined. One can see why they work in pairs. It is less easy for someone like myself to murder two of them.

'I wish to God I was a member of one of those groups outside the Palace wearing a label in case I get lost, with guides and leaders who would protect me from them,' Wanda says.

'I'd like to be Moulay Hassan II, the King. I'd have them flown to Iran and dropped in the back garden of an ayatollah by parachute,' I say, knowing that I should be ashamed of expressing such sentiments, but I am not.

Up to now we have not opened our mouths to these new men. Now, as a last, desperate resort, Wanda begins to speak to them in Slovene, a language with which it appeared they are not *au fait*. It works. Puzzled, angered, knowing in their black hearts that they are being taken for a ride, but unable to prove it, and finally half-convinced and certainly somewhat alarmed by her, they go off in search of more intelligible prey with much fucking of our mothers and fathers.

The way into Fès el-Bali, the Old City, is through the Bab Bou Jeloud. A fine gate with an arch in the form of a keyhole and embellished with brilliant blue and green tiles, it looks old but isn't. It was only built in 1919, but like almost everything in Morocco made or built by craftsmen using traditional methods and materials, it is an instant and total success.

Through the Bab Bou Jeloud two minarets can be seen. One has what look like a couple of golden apples speared on a finial on top of it., The other, which is disused, has a stork's nest. Storks, the Moroccans believed, were a mysterious people from islands beyond the seas and as such were the only foreigners they really approved of. When the secret service agent, Prince Ali Bey el-Abbasi, otherwise Domingo Badia y Leblich, born in Barcelona in 1767, who learned to speak Arabic so well that he was able to pass as a Muslim, visited Fez – having previously taken the additional precaution of having himself circumcised in London – he found there a hospital for injured storks.

Some say that Old Fez, Fès el-Bali, was founded by Moulay Idriss II in 809, and others that it was founded by his father. His father, who was also named Idriss, was a potential successor to the

Abbasid Caliphate at Baghdad, and it was because of this that he had been forced to flee Arabia and take refuge with a tribe of pagan Berbers in what was known as El Maghreb el-Aqsa to the Arabs, the Furthest West of the Setting Sun, otherwise Morocco. These Berbers invited Idriss to become their ruler – this was in 785 or 786 – and were themselves converted to Islam. Some six years later he was poisoned by an emissary of the ruling Abbasid Caliph at Baghdad, Harun el-Rashid.

Two months after the death of Idriss I his wife gave birth to a son, Idriss II. Idriss, it was said, could read at the age of four, write when he was five and knew the whole of the Koran by heart by the time he was eight. His father was buried in a mausoleum some twenty-five miles west of Fez. Around it a town called after him sprang up and to this day, together with the tomb of Idriss II in Old Fez, it is the most venerated shrine in all Morocco.

The Idrissid dynasty was destroyed in 973 by the Umayyad Caliph of Cordoba, Hakam II, whose dynasty presided over what was the Golden Age of the Moors. The whole Cordoban Caliphate, which included El Maghreb el-Aqsa and Fez, was in turn overrun in the eleventh century by the Almoravids, religious Berber warriors from Mauretania, known as the Veiled Ones, the Lemtounline. Their leader Yousef ben Tachfin made Marrakech his capital in 1063 and captured Fez in 1069. In 1087 he invaded Spain.

The Almoravids were in turn destroyed by the Almohads of the High Atlas who crossed into Spain in 1149. From Fez, for nearly a hundred years, the Almohads ruled an empire which extended as far north as Castille in what was for the Moors a second Golden Age, until they, too, were worn out; by 1244 they had lost Andalucia to the Christians and had been forced to ask the Merinids, nomad Berbers from the Sahara, for assistance. It was among the tombs of the Merinids we had been exercising ourselves earlier in the day. They finally took Old Fez in 1250.

Once inside the Bab Bou Jeloud you are in the Souk of Talaa (Talaa being one of the eighteen wards into which the city is divided), and as if by the waving of a wand, back in the Middle Ages. In it a street is an alley about 9 ft wide, in which five people might with difficulty walk abreast, off which lead innumerable alleys, no wider than trenches, in which it is often impossible for two people to pass one another without one of them turning sideways. For long stretches of their courses, these various ways are roofed with rushes, through which the sunlight, if it reaches into them at all, filters down on the crowds moving purposefully and apparently endlessly below, casting on them a tremulous light, as if they were underwater. It falls on men wearing a fine variety of clothing: skull caps decorated with geometrical designs, felt caps called *shashia*, like sugar loaves, with silk tassels hanging from them, turbans, hooded *jellabs* and *selhams*,* and on their feet yellow *babouches* with their backs turned down exposing heels as hard as rawhide.

It falls equally fitfully on men in rags lugging bunches of live chickens in either hand as if they were bunches of bananas, or pushing wheelbarrows, the only wheeled vehicles to be seen; on porters bent double under the weight of huge sacks and packing cases; on donkeys loaded with charcoal, brasswork, brushwood, maize, newly-fired pottery, mounds of pallid, slimy goatskins on the way to the dyeing vats down at the bottom of the hill, or else on the way back from them to some drying ground on the outskirts of the city, now a brilliant red, dyed with what may still be, if a dye of the highest quality is required, the juice of a berry. And it dapples the boys balancing boards on their heads, loaded with round loaves which they have collected unbaked from the housewives and are taking to the ovens for them, and on the bearded merchants perched on corn-fed mules, dressed in a sort of fringed, cream-coloured toga, six yards long and nearly two yards wide, made of woollen gauze, which they wear with one end lapped over the head, a garment, called the *k'sa*, which gives them – for they are already stern-looking – a really awesome air.

The noise is incredible. All of them, riders, porters and boys with boards on their heads and anyone else in a hurry, are shouting at the tops of their voices, '*Balèèèk! Balèèèk!*' 'Make way! Make way!', and if you don't they or their animals simply shove you out of it.

Here, men with more time to spare, having prudently made way, greet one another by pressing their fingertips together, then to their lips, then to their hearts, crying 'God be praised!' meanwhile gazing into one another's eyes. From then on the air is full of cries of 'Peace be unto you.' 'And to you be peace.' 'How art thou?' 'Thy house?'

---

* The *selham* is the Moroccan version of the burnous. It is made from a rectangle of fine woollen material, white or dark blue, with a hood made from the trimmings cut from the fronts, which are not joined together as they are in the *jellab*. The *selham* is a much more aristocratic garment than the *jellab* and is, or was, the only one permitted to be worn in the presence of king or sultan. It is sometimes worn over the *k'sa*.

(an enquiry which contrives to include the women without actually naming them as such). 'Thy relatives?' To which the reply is, 'All well, thank God.' Or, if it isn't, 'God knows; everything is in the hands of God.'

There are many women. Those squatting in the rare open spaces selling bread and vegetables are often fairly negligent about the veil, or do not wear it at all. Those who are better-off, who are buying rather than selling, are dressed in the *häik*, the equivalent of the *k'sa*, a long, white, fine rectangular woollen wrapper. They also wear the *litham* – as do some of the men but for a different reason – which is a white veil bound round the face, hiding what to the Muslim is the sacredness of the nose, ears, nostrils and the mouth, but not the huge almond eyes with the edges of the lids blackened with antimony, which are left uncovered like huge, old-fashioned car headlamps, to dazzle and disturb the beholder.

Most of these people are Arabs and Berbers, people of the Atlas, the indigenous inhabitants of the Maghreb, or a mixture of both. Some Berbers are light skinned, so pallid that romantic theories are advanced about their antecedents: that they are descendants of Vandals, some 80,000 of whom crossed the Strait of Gibraltar to North Africa from Spain in 429, taking Carthage from the Romans, and thus depriving them of their principal granary, as a prelude to their attack and sacking of Rome itself; or that they are descendants of the tribes expelled from Palestine by Joshua; or that they were of the race of Shem, Amelekites descended from Esau, or kinsmen of the Agrigesh (Greeks), or are from the Baltic, or are descendants of Celts.

Other Berbers are as black as Negroes from Central Africa. Some have blue eyes and rosy cheeks, which may be due to the familiarity of their women with Christian mercenaries and slaves.

There are many Negroes. Men and women dressed as Moorish Muslims, descendants of the slaves, who, when the supply of Christians began to flag and long before that, made the awful hundred-and-fifty-day journey across the Sahara with the slave traders to Morocco, as well as to Algeria and Tunis, from Timbuktu and Bornu in the western Sudan, with their children slung on either side of mules, their price a block of salt large enough for one of them to stand on, six or seven inches thick.

And there are ourselves. To tell the truth, now that we have succeeded in casting off our shadows, we feel a little lonely, going down into the souks of Fès el-Bali. Few of these Fasi even deign to notice us, however outrageous we must appear in their eyes, both in our behaviour and in our dress. If they do look at us at all, it is incuriously. Then they put us out of mind. They do not want us in their holy city, or anyone else like us, unbelievers from the far side of the Mediterranean.

We could assume their dress, as a sort of compliment to them – but the result would be a parody, the very opposite of the effect intended. As it is, our presence reminds them that although their city is physically preserved, with assistance from UNESCO – itself another alien presence, largely financed by unbelievers – the way of life that they have cherished and pursued here for more than a thousand years will soon be no more.

I wish we could speak with them, these Fasi, perhaps become friendly with one of them, that is as much of a friend as a Nasrany (Christian) or any other sort of unbeliever can ever be with followers of the Prophet. They, the most reserved of all Moroccans, are known for their intelligence, their skill in business, their particular intonation – which is made fun of by other Moroccans who intone less well – the niceness of their natures, their argumentativeness, their avoidance of sunlight which might darken their skins, their alleged lack of courage, their appreciation of the pleasures of conversation and of, what some say is the best of all, their food. Facets of their characters that casual visitors, such as ourselves, can never know or experience, pursued as they are by westernized Fasi (themselves the living embodiments of the change they fear so much), and locked in the equivalent of a prison by ignorance of all but the most basic fragments of their language and divided from them by impassable gulfs of belief and antecedence.

Here, at this upper end of Old Fez, in the Souk of Talaa, you can buy painted hard-boiled eggs, *seksou* or *couscous*, which if dried in the sun will keep for years, *smeen*, green-streaked rancid butter to eat with it, best when it has been buried in an earthenware pot for a year – by which time it smells a bit like gorgonzola – chick-pea paste, the best mint from Meknès to flavour the sweet tea the Moroccans love, and other flavourings: red rose, marjoram, basil, verbena, *toumia* (which tastes of peppermint) and orange blossom.

Here, the butchers display their products, some of them ghastly to look on: flayed sheeps' heads, still with their horns *in situ*, suspended from cords so that the owner of the stall can attract attention by setting them swinging under the light of the paraffin pressure lanterns (this part of the souk is always very dark); miles of entrails, cloven feet chopped off short, with the hair still on them, tongues and eyes and testicles. Who eats eyes voluntarily? Are they bought to be offered to a non-believer at a feast as a *pièce de résistance*, to test his courage? If such sights upset you then steer clear of the abattoirs at the bottom of the hill, astride the river.

Up here, there are minute restaurants in which, if you are not too squeamish, you eat well for next to nothing. We shall return to one of them later on, after midday, to eat *harirah*, meat soup with egg and coriander, or *kodban*, meat on skewers, or *seksou* and the stew made specially to go with it, among the ingredients of which are ginger, nutmeg, coriander, turmeric, saffron, fresh marjoram, onions, bread, beans and raisins or, if we are not really hungry, *seksou* with fruit, such as quinces, or whatever is in season.

Grander restaurants are hidden away in fine old houses in the labyrinths further down the hill. They serve such dishes as *bastilla*, cakes of puff pastry stuffed with minced pigeon, sprinkled with sugar and cinnamon, which is not as sickly as it sounds; and *tajine*, dishes of chicken, pigeon or mutton, either cooked whole or stewed, and dressed with olives, beans, almonds, apples, artichokes, carrots, or whatever else is appropriate and in season.

To dine in one of these beautiful dim lofty silent places populated by grave, equally quiet, picturesquely clad serving men, one needs a companion while the ritual unfolds itself: while the cone-shaped, lidded dishes are lined up, and while, squatting in what is excruciating discomfort on the cushions, one washes ones hands over an elegantly embellished copper pan. Alone, one would feel like an unloved sultan, without even his food taster.

The mosque with what look like two golden apples impaled on a spike on top of it in the Talaa Kebira beyond this *souk* is the Bou Inanya. It was also a *medersa*, a college of Koranic theology, one of twelve such schools in Old Fez that, together with the Kairouyyin Mosque and the Library, made up the University. When its builder, Sultan Abu Inan, read the first pages of the accounts and saw that expenditure had already exceeded the estimate by some 40,000 ducats, he threw them in the river with the words that a thing of such beauty could not be thought of in terms of money. The most beautiful of all the colleges built by the Merinids, and the last to be built by a Merinid sultan, it was finally completed in 1357, after seven years' labour.

To the left of the entrance there is what remains of a carillon of bells or gongs. A pair of wooden doors, embellished with engraved bronze plaques and brass knockers, open into a sort of porch with a cupola above it, ornamented with painted plaster and what look like painted wooden stalactites. These stalactites are not made by carving blocks of wood, as they appear to be, but by binding together smaller blocks of various lengths, then carving the points and afterwards painting them, a work called *muqarnas*, for which the craftsmen of Fez are still famous.

From this porch, which is where the porter's lodge would be in a college at Oxford or Cambridge, a staircase ornamented with faience and onyx leads up into a courtyard embellished with mosaic panelling, decorated plasterwork, arches of cedarwood, and with an inscription in black cursive script around it. From the upper storey the windows of the cells once occupied by the students look down into it.

In 1900 there were still seventy-five *tolba*, students, living in this college, at a time when seven of the twelve original colleges, housing more than a thousand *tolba*, were still active. How did they live, or rather exist, after their parents had paid for the 'key', the equivalent of fees, purchased from their predecessors, at a cost of what at that time was the equivalent of anything from $20–200, two hundred dollars being a very large sum in Morocco in those days, which entitled them to live in the college and study for anything from three to ten years? As they did in every other college in Old Fez well into the 1950s, in exactly the same way as they had done for six hundred years.

They existed, at least the great majority did – we know nothing of how the better-off ones, if there were any, lived – on a monotonous diet of *seksou*, the rancid *smeen* and, if they could come by it, lean, sometimes dried meat, often clubbing together with other students to make a communal stew, a *tajine*. The cooking was done over charcoal fires in their cells. Some had relatives who brought them presents of food from the country, but they always shared what they received with their fellows.

Their cells, cool enough in summer, were cold and damp in winter, and many of the students suffered from tuberculosis. The only item of furniture was a mattress. Often, the only clothes they possessed were the ones they stood up in.

To survive, they earned what they could in the brief intervals between attending lectures and preparing for them, by copying out the Koran for anyone who wished to acquire one, work that could only be done by a Muslim, or by reading to those who could not read and writing for those who could not write. In extremis they even begged for food to supplement their meagre, self-supplied rations and the one daily loaf provided at the expense of the university, which was delivered to each of them through a hole in the door of the cell by the *mukaddam*, the cleaner and caretaker.

Their great day out was their annual visit to the tomb of Sidi ben Ali Harazem, a Sufi, a member of a Muslim mystical and pantheist sect, who died in the twelfth century. It is one of the most venerated of the many tombs on the outskirts of Fez, to which those who are a bit wrong in the head are taken in hope of a cure. There they elected one of their number to be their 'Sultan' for the following year, and he was subsequently taken to pray with great pomp and circumstance in the other great mosque of Old Fez, El Andalus, the Andalucian Mosque. The ceremonies still take place, although in 1953 the University, to the great detriment of the Old City, was moved lock, stock and barrel to a site outside the walls.

What did a *taleb* (literally a scribe), a student, learn at the University? Providing he had mastered the Koran by heart and knew the outlines of grammar and rhetoric he could attend lectures given by the professor of his choice. The professors, the *ulema*, sat on chairs or stools in one or other of the sixteen aisles of the Kairouyyin Mosque, if they were sufficiently eminent. If not, they were divided into three classes of excellence, and sat on the rush matting on the floor.

A student's day began with morning prayers, followed by study of the Koran, commentaries on it, and of orthodox dogma, which took an hour or so, until about seven o'clock.

From then until ten o'clock he would study the *Sunna*, the body of traditional Islamic law, based on the acts and words of the Prophet, and jurisprudence, each with a different professor. A great deal was – and still is in Muslim education – learned by rote. In his dealings with a professor, the student would read a passage aloud and the professor would expound on it, dealing with the meaning or importance of individual words and quoting any commentators. No interruptions were permitted but at the end of the session the student could ask questions. From ten until midday he studied arithmetic or else learnt about the taking of astronomical observations, although the earth was not allowed to move round the sun as this was against the teachings of the Koran. In fact the study was principally important to the student for its astrological rather than its scientific or navigational significance.*

In the afternoon, from one-thirty to two-thirty, grammar and rhetoric were dealt with, followed by science, which continued until the hour of the *'asar*, mid-afternoon prayer.

In the evening the student was supposed to read history, geometry, astronomy, medicine, poetry, or whatever subjects he was interested in, besides preparing passages to be discussed the following day or else pacing, head down, round and round the courtyard of his college or the mosque, to a set rhythm which helped him to memorize texts. This, and the journey to and from the mosque, was about the only exercise he ever got. No wonder all the students looked ill.

Wednesday was a half holiday, Thursday and Friday whole holidays, which enabled him to get on with his copying of the Koran, his public letter writing, sometimes even begging, if necessary.

We are shown their cells by the present *mukaddam*, who no longer has to deliver bread to the students as there are no longer any students to whom to deliver it. He is a fine, venerable-looking greybeard who positively radiates sanctity – often a bad sign in the Muslim world – but when I give him what is really a jolly generous dollop of the Moroccan equivalent of baksheesh he ceases to look either holy or radiant. It is as if someone had turned out the lights in a building, leaving it in darkness.

The Talaa Kebira, the street in which the College stands, continues to descend into the Old City, past mosques in various stages of dilapidation, blacksmiths' booths, a *guelsa*, which is a sort of halting place on the way to the Shrine of Idriss II, with lamps burning before it, some tea houses, and down through *souks* with endless rows of shops on either side of it, shops that are nothing more than cupboards with doors that can be locked at night, each more or less a carbon copy of its neighbour and, in a *souk* selling the same commodities, displaying almost identical goods.

In them the shopkeepers sit – telling the beads of their rosaries, the *tasbeeh*, which can be of amber, fruit stones or simply plastic, ninety-five of them, with five more at the end to record repetitions – hour after hour, year after year, dreaming of money and the *houris*

---

* According to Dr Gerhard Rohlfs, *Adventures in Morocco and Journeys Through the Oases of Draa and Taafilet* (London, 1874).

who will be at their disposition when at last they are wrapt away to Paradise, scarcely moving except to stretch out a languid hand to reach some item of stock in which a passer-by has betrayed some interest. Shops into which the customer hauls himself up, sometimes with the help of a dangling rope, to settle down, slipperless, for – if the object is of sufficient interest to warrant it – a long period of bargaining which usually ends with the shopkeeper feigning despair or exasperation and saying to him, 'Take it and begone!' Shops in which the proprietors take siestas in the long, torrid, insufferable summer afternoons.

This street also has some *fondouks* in it. *Fondouks* were partly caravanserais and partly, some still are, warehouses in which the goods and raw materials for the craftsmen were stored before being auctioned and distributed throughout the various *souks*. At one time there were said to have been 477 *fondouks* in Fez. They are the equivalent of the *han* in Asia. They are built round a central courtyard in which the caravan animals were tethered, with storerooms on the ground floors and with accommodation on the upper floors for the caravaneers where they awaited the auctioning of the merchandise and recuperated from the rigours of the journeys across the deserts. Some of these upper rooms in the poorer sorts of *fondouk* were barely large enough to allow the occupants to recline at full length. The guests provided their own bedding but the landlord supplied each of them with a large brass plate, a teapot, teacups and a receptacle in which to boil water. On either side of the entrance gate to the larger sort of *fondouk* there was usually a coffee stall where what was generally regarded as the best coffee in Fez was to be found.

All trades and crafts, except some specialist or smelly or other-wise disagreeable ones, such as those of the tanners and slaughter-ers, are situated along a main artery such as this. And so we pass, successively, the *souk* of the repairers of *babouches*, the *souk* in which they are made, the *souk* of the makers of rush and horsehair sieves, bellows, the reed mats used to line the walls of mosques and houses, of embroidered and gilded leather and of the sellers of nails and chains. Then the pretty *souk* of the perfumers, filled with scents, spices, sugar, candles and incense, to which the worshippers at the Zawiya of Idriss are as addicted as Roman Catholics and, at least until recently, arsenic and corrosive sublimate, much in demand by wives eager to rid themselves of over-demanding husbands, being easily administered to them in their morning tea.

Then the henna *souk*, where the Moristan, the mad-house built by the Merinids, stands, in the indescribably filthy cells of which, well into the twentieth century, the occupants were kept chained to the walls with iron collars round their necks.

Down here is the glazed white pottery *souk*, the *souk* of the carpenters, a *souk* selling salt and fish from the Sebou, the *souk* of the eggs, a *souk* which sells yarn in the morning and corn in the evening, and the *souk* in which, until the beginning of this century, the slaves were sold, having previously been fattened up, taught some vestigial Arabic, enough of the religion and ceremonial practices of Islam to enable them to be deemed to have embraced it, and having been given one of the particular names reserved for them, such as, for men, Provided for, Fortunate; and for women Ruby and Dear.

And beyond these are the *souks* of the tailors, the *souk* of rugs and fabrics, the *souk* selling *häiks*, *selhams*, *jellabs* and other clothing, a *souk* where antiques are sold, and the *souk* of the coppersmiths.

And there is the Kisaria, otherwise the Market Place, which is not a market place at all, but the final labyrinth within a labyrinth, a network of covered *souks*, with gates which are locked at night, each with its own nightwatchman, as in the Great Covered Bazaar in Istanbul, and, like the Great Bazaar, burned down innumerable times, always to rise once more, phoenix-like, from its ashes.

In Old Fez, the craftsmen are members of guilds according to the particular craft they are engaged in. At the beginning of the century there were 126 of them. Such guilds bear scarcely any resemblance to the trade unions of the western world. Their members think of themselves primarily as belonging to the *Ummah*, the community of believers which, in theory, although it is difficult to know to what extent in actual practice a Fasi craftsman today would subscribe to this, transcends nationality, creed, and even ties of race and blood, a community held together by belief in the Oneness of God. One of the best ways of giving this practical expression was by becoming proficient in a craft, as a member of a guild working first as a *mubtadi*, an apprentice, then for long years as a *sani*, an artisan under a *mu'allim*, a master craftsman. The master of such a guild, who had wide powers – he could order the most draconic punishments for those who behaved dishonestly, for example – was the *shaykh*, the descendant of a line of *shaykhs* going back to two companions of the Prophet, Ali ben Abi Talib and Salman al-Farisi, and beyond them to Shem, the son of Adam.

Here in Fez, looking at the works performed by these craftsmen in mosques and *medersa* and secular buildings, in plaster and cedarwood and stone, in ceramics, firing the amazing, lustrous tiles, forming the bowls and vases decorated with the dark blue and jade green arabesques in the potteries out by the Ftouh Gate in the Andalus quarter on the right bank of the river, working in brass, binding the books in the soft red goat leather which required twenty different operations to produce it, 13 carried out by the master, his artisans and apprentices, the remaining 7 by other specialists, embroidering the single coloured silks, just a few of their abundant skills, one begins to understand that there is no division between religion and secular activity in traditional Islam and that what they were working for, collectively, was the Glory of God.

Behind the *souks*, many of them reached by the narrowest of alleys, many of them spanned by arches which appear to have the function of keeping the walls from coming together and sandwiching between them whoever happens to be using them at the time, many of them concealing the workshops of the craftsmen, many of them cul-de-sacs, are what appear at a distance to be the great honeycombs of houses in which the Fasi live, those apparently interlocking cubes we have seen this morning from the hill, none of which, despite a superficial uniformity, ever quite repeating the form of another, a lack of symmetry which is an inherent part of the Muslim ethos, and one which manifests itself in every sort of art and artefact, from the asymmetry in the design and even the shape of a Berber rug, to the near perfection of a key-hole arch in a mosque courtyard which is ever so slightly but palpably different from its neighbour, partly because the design was not drawn out on paper but retained in the builder's eye, partly because that was how the builder wanted it to be.

These dwellings, large or small, inhabited by rich and poor, but even if poor, here in Old Fez, until recently without the poverty and squalor of the slums, were designed and built, not for the requirements of a husband, wife and children, childless couples, the aged whose families have left home, or even for individuals – no *appartements meublés*, no bungalow accommodation on a single floor, no bachelor chambers – but as centres of family life to house the entire extant hierarchy of a family comprehending several generations. There is no word for 'home' in the Muslim vocabulary and in Morocco the nearest approach to it is *wakr*, which is almost exclusively used to describe the lair of a wild beast.

A typical Fasi house is an irregular quadrilateral, built of mud bricks and clay, the same material that was used to build so much else in Fez from walls to mosques. If there are any windows opening outwards onto the street they are high up and covered with wood or iron gratings. The only embellishment on these outer walls will probably be the hand of Fatimah, the Prophet's daughter, delineated in hen's blood, to ward off evil.

In such a house the courtyard is surrounded with a sort of cloister in which columns, which may be partly tiled, partly decorated with plasterwork, support richly encrusted arches. In the centre there is usually a fountain with a tiled or marble surround into which water splashes soothingly. In the courtyard there may also be orange trees, vines and figs. On the upper floors long, lofty rooms, some of them bedrooms, surround the well of the courtyard and look down on it.

The roof, surrounded by walls and trellises, is the retreat of the women of the house, from which they can look out over the city and down into it without themselves being seen. Like all Moroccans the Fasi use the rooms on the upper floors of their houses in winter, the lower ones in summer. Then during the hot nights the inner court collects the cooler air which descends into it; by day the stifling heated air flows across the mouth of it, leaving the lower floors and the courtyard cool.

Such a house, although it appears to be inextricably locked together with its neighbours, is not. There are no communal stairs. Each windowless, walled dwelling that goes to make up the mass is completely cut off from its neighbour, without any possibility of being overlooked, except perhaps from the roof. Each one is essentially a sanctuary, demonstrating as well as anything material can the essential duality of Islam. The huddle of houses displays the unity of all within Islam, the walled sanctuary, the place where the head of the family is its *imam* and in which his person, and those of his family, are intensely private, inviolable, *harām*, forbidden to others, as inviolable as the Zawiya, the shrine of Moulay Idriss.

The alleys surrounding the Zawiya are packed with Fasi and pilgrims from the furthest parts of Morocco, all of whom come to obtain a *baraka*, the Saint's blessing. They are also crowded with beggars who crouch against its outer walls, demanding alms 'For God and my Lord Idriss!'

Such beggars, men and women, are said in Islam to 'Stand at God's door', and what they receive is described as being 'God's due'. For those who appear reluctant to give them this due, a familiar prayer is 'May God give thee something to give!' To which the hard-of-heart or the penniless may reply, but rarely do, so close to the shrine, 'God open the way for us and thee to prosperity!'

Here, in these outer walls, there is an aperture in the surrounding woodwork, which is richly decorated, in which the pilgrims place their offerings, at the same time pressing their lips to the woodwork, offerings which are distributed, according to immemorial custom, among the descendants of the Saint. Next to the aperture is a *souk* where pilgrims can buy candles to burn at the shrine and incense, dates, nuts, figs and cakes. This is a shrine said to be a *horm*, a place where a fugitive from justice could, and might perhaps still under certain circumstances, gain sanctuary. The lanes leading to it always have chains or bars drawn across them and to pass beyond these barriers for a Jew meant either instant apostasy or death. As late as the 1870s no Christians were allowed in the city at all.

There is no admission either for the non-Muslim to the great Kairouyyin Mosque, founded in 859 by a pious old Arab lady named Fatima, a refugee from Ifriqiya, then the name for Tunisia, in memory of holy Kairouan, then its capital and her former home. She had it built on behalf of her fellow refugees from Ifrekeea who swarmed to live here on this, the left, west bank of the river, in what became known as the Kairouyyin quarter, after the foundation of the city by Idriss.

The population of the right, eastern bank of the river, already occupied by Berbers before the arrival of Idriss, was greatly increased in 818 by a large number of Arab refugees from Spain who had fled from Andalucia after an unsuccessful rebellion against their unpleasant ruler Hakam I in 814. Others, a larger number, fled to Egypt, from which they eventually crossed the Mediterranean to conquer Crete. This quarter was, and still is, known as the Andalus Quarter. The refugees from Tunisia and Spain numbered among them a high proportion of craftsmen and it was they and their descendants whose skills made Fez renowned.

The Kairouyyin Mosque is a world within a world, but one inhabited only during the hours of daylight, apart from by its custodians and those such as the Companions of the Sick, when engaged in their chantings. In it, under sixteen long, white-painted naves, each spanned by twenty-one arches supported by two hundred and seventy columns, more than 20,000 worshippers can congregate on the reed matting which covers the floors, and each component part seems to reflect the other, as if in a giant hall of mirrors.

The Mosque was until recently the seat of a University older than the Sorbonne, which was founded in 1257, older than Oxford, founded 1227, older than Bologna, founded 1119, although none of its colleges were built at the time of its foundation, the date of which no one is quite sure. It is so old that Pope Sylvester II, who was Pope from 999 to 1003, is said to have attended it before his elevation to the papacy, one of the only known unbelievers ever to have done so. Here he learned the principles of Arab mathematics and was able to introduce the study of them into Europe. Well into the 1950s some three hundred students still attended lectures in the Kairouyyin Mosque.

As it grows dark, which it does very early here, we go up through the Fondouk Ihoudi, what was the old Jewish quarter, slipping on the greasy cobble stones, greasy because the sewers are being dug up in this area, and for a moment look down into their unimaginably awful depths. Then up to the beautiful Jamai Palace built by the half-barmy Sultan Abd ul-Aziz on the steep slope inside the walls by Bab Guissa, the gate in the north-east corner which we went out through in the small hours of the morning.

The Palace is now an hotel with a terraced garden filled with palms, cypresses and willows, and, as hotels go, a very good one.

Difficult to believe, sitting in the bar, ordering a very expensive drink, something you cannot obtain for love or money otherwise inside the walls of Old or New Fez, and something that we are at present much in need of, that as late as 1908 Sultan Abd ul-Aziz – who that year was deposed by his equally revolting brother, Moulay el-Hafid – sat in judgement here on prostrate figures stretched out before him against a backdrop of the salted, pickled heads of those whom he had already judged and found wanting, impaled on spikes, the equivalent of an 'out' tray in the western world.

VII
RETURN TO EUROPE

Imperial Rock

We crossed the Strait of Gibraltar from Africa to Europe in a car ferry, and the sight of the Rock, with a long plume of thin cloud streaming away from what is invariably compared to a lion's head, because that is what it looks like, filled me with the same feelings that I had experienced previously either when passing through the Strait or approaching it, of excitement, awe and barely suppressed feelings of stubborn pride at the thought that we, we being the British, were somehow still contriving to hold on to something we really didn't want any more – just as we hadn't really wanted Malta any more, but had finally succeeded in disentangling ourselves from it, leaving it to the Maltese, at the same time managing to convey the impression that to get rid of it was the last thing we wanted to do. Now we were supposed to hand Gibraltar and its inhabitants over to Spain, something which we displayed a dogged reluctance to do on account of Spain's bad track record, and something we were not entitled to do, Gibraltar being a British Crown Colony, which can in fact only be handed over to its occupants who will then have the alternatives of holding it or losing it.

Leaving the ship we went out through the customs on the Mole on which policemen in shirt-sleeves and tall London helmets stood

around looking keen and helpful, and along it to terra firma where
two or three enormous prostitutes were sitting on park benches
waiting to catch some hot-blooded arrivals from the Land of the
Moors, like us straight off the 10.30 p.m. boat, and bear them away
to their dens. Then we went on through Old Mole Gate and
Waterport Gate into Casemate Square where a butcher's shop in the
market advertised itself in Spanish and English as 'Importers of Best
Quality, Fresh Frozen, Prime Cuts', and through the Waterport
Gate into Main Street in New Town, which is a compound of
eighteenth- and nineteenth-century architecture with extravagant
additions, Main Street itself being long and narrow and full of
buildings, the upper parts of which are partly Andalucian in inspiration, partly Genoese, and the lower floors shops filled with, because
this is a duty-free port, all the stuff normally on sale in a duty-free
shop in an airport, over which you can haggle in a thoroughly
un-British way with the Gibraltarians. The Gibraltarians, otherwise
known as Rock Scorpions, are mainly of Italian, Spanish and
Portuguese descent, and they flourish like exotic plants bedded out
in the midst of what is a British garrison town and naval base, full of
naval outfitters with hardly anyone left to outfit and barber's shops
in which you can get the worst sort of British army haircut if you ask
for it.

But even if they are keen shopkeepers, the inhabitants are a loyal
lot in a curiously British way. They have long memories of regiments and ships' companies, some popular, some less so, all now
dead and gone. When the battle cruiser *Hood* was sunk by the *Bis-
marck* in the Denmark Strait in 1941, the Gibraltarians were in
tears. They loved her because she was a beautiful ship, and her
crew because they had such a good football team.

The Rock is historic. It makes you feel its history as powerfully
as any other great ruin in the Mediterranean, for it is a ruin of what
it was constructed for. Everywhere there are dismantled batteries
and the dark embrasures of long disused forts. There is not a single
coastal defence gun on the entire Rock with which it could be
defended. Men who died of wounds after Trafalgar lie buried here,
outside the gates in a tree-shaded cemetery beneath monuments
decorated with cannonballs.

Otherwise life went on here in what was early spring exactly as it
had done in another spring when I was last here, only the regiments
and the organizations taking part were different. On the fifth of
May there was a ceremonial parade of the Royal Engineers com-

memorating the tenth anniversary of the granting to them of the Freedom of the City of Gibraltar, followed by, on the sixth, the Drum Platoon of the 1st Staffordshire Regiment with 1/4 Marquis of Milford Haven's Own Scout Band giving a concert in the Piazza, and all through the month of March there were other diversions: jumble sales and dinner dances and the Women's Corona Society Card Evening, all of which took place at the Catholic Community Centre, and a Girls' Comprehensive Drama Week and a Gibraltar Youth Theatre Dance Drama, and a Mental Welfare Exhibition at the John Mackintosh Hall and a Motor Cycle Trial at Catalan Bay and the Gibraltar Automobile Club Hill Climb at Lathbury Barracks, both of which seemed rather risky projects on a 2½-square-mile rock. On the twenty-eighth, Double Summer Time would begin, leaving the Rock two hours in advance of Greenwich Mean Time, and everyone would get out their swimming costumes and rush off to Easter Beach and Catalan Bay on the east side of it. And every Monday there was the ceremonial Changing of the Guard outside the Governor's residence by the resident battalion, and the meeting of the Gibraltar Photographic Society. Tuesday saw the meeting of Rotary at the Rock Hotel, and a Whist Drive at the Queensway Club. The Judo Club met on Tuesdays and Thursdays, and on the second Wednesday of every month Lions International met at the Holiday Inn. On Thursday the Philatelic Society met at the John Mackintosh Hall – all stamp collectors welcome – and the Gibraltar Art Society also met at the same venue. There was also Old Tyme Dancing at the DSA Hall, Queensway. On Saturday the St Joseph's Blue Disco (opposite South Barracks) welcomed all sixteen-year-olds or under. On Sunday there was Clay Pigeon Shooting on Europa Point and, on the first and third Sundays of every month, the Round Table met at the Garrison Library.

It would be difficult to think of another similar size plot offering such a variety of activities, or anywhere else in the world for that matter.

We sat on the main ridge of the Rock, some 1200 feet up but below the highest point, which is 1396 feet above the sea. The long plume of cloud had vanished and the sun shone from a cloudless sky. To the west was what was presumably the Atlantic, although where the Atlantic begins – the Strait being 36 miles long – and the Mediterranean ends I am still unsure. To the east, where one could see for ever but there was nothing but water to be seen, was undoubtedly the Mediterranean. To the south, fifteen miles away across the eastern end of the Strait, only dimly visible in the haze was Almina Point near Ceuta, the southern of the two Pillars of Hercules, in what was still a small foreign enclave on Moroccan soil, all that remained of Spanish Morocco which the Spaniards appeared to be as reluctant to leave to the Moroccans as we appeared to be to leave Gibraltar to the Spaniards. In between, in the Strait, which for centuries was the limit of enterprise for the seafaring peoples of the Mediterranean world, the surface waters of the Atlantic flowed eastwards into the Mediterranean, while deep below the surface, in complete contradiction to the waters of the Bosphorus and the Dardanelles flowing to and from the Black Sea to the Aegean, it flowed westwards to the Atlantic.

It was beautiful up here. Looking at the Rock from out to sea it seemed to be nothing but a barren expanse. Here where we were, at the head of a steep and rocky descent by what are known as the Mediterranean Steps to the north side, which was already in shadow, it was covered with vegetation, including some of the 400 flowering plants and ferns that are indigenous to Gibraltar, not to speak of others which have been subsequently introduced, and among which the bees were now humming busily.

It was also a singularly quiet and lonely place, something for which, after a comparatively short stay on it of twenty-four hours, we were beginning to crave, just near O'Hara's Tower where Joyce's Molly Bloom, wearing a skirt opening up the side, tortured the life out of Lieutenant Mulvey before deftly putting an end to his misery. He had a good eye for country, Joyce.

After this we went back to Africa by hydrofoil, which at that time was the only way, short of flying to London and then flying back to Spain, of getting to Spain from Gibraltar.

After this money-consuming journey – back to Tangier, then back to Algeciras by ship, the sea by this time being too rough for the hydrofoil from Tangier to Tarifa – we travelled westwards along the still wild and beautiful coast of southern Andalucia, with little beaches far below hidden between bluffs covered with scrub and broom, behind which rose rocky hills covered with cork and eucalyptus trees, to Tarifa, the most Moorish town in Andalucia with an *alcazar*, a Moorish castle from which, beleaguered by the

Moors in 1294, its commander, Alonzo Perez de Guzman, saw his nine-year-old son put to death, allowing this to happen rather than surrender, throwing down his own dagger from the walls for the purpose with the words, 'I prefer honour without a son, to a son with dishonour,' for which act of fortitude he was subsequently ennobled by Sancho IV of Seville who created him Duke of Medina Sidonia, one of whose descendants some 300 years later commanded the Spanish Armada.

Here, down on the shore at the end of an isthmus at the end of a road covered with drifted sand, there was a castle and a lighthouse on the Punta Marroqui, the southernmost point of mainland Europe, on 36°N. It was an inspiring place. Only a few miles away across the Strait to the south was Africa, mysteriously and romantically wrapped in what was a mixture of mist and the fine spray that was being raised on its shores by a strong breeze, and westwards an enormously long beach extended as far as the eye could see to where the coast became more hilly out towards Cape Trafalgar and the sand piled up against it in huge dunes.

It was here that the Moors first landed from Africa, and it was probably in the plain beyond that they won the first of a series of battles with the Visigoths who had been masters of the peninsula for some 250 years, having finally put to an end the dominion of the Romans and defeated the Sueves, another Germanic tribe who had marched with the Visigoths and the Alans into Spain, whom they subsequently absorbed.

Here, the Mediterranean world came to an end. Westwards, where the rollers fell on other similar enormous beaches of gleaming white sand, the traveller was on the shores of the Atlantic. Beyond this point even the shops in the little villages were different, shops which sold gumboots which hung from the ceiling on strings, shops which were exactly the same whether they were on the coast of Portugal, or at the head of one of the long *rios* in Galicia, or in Brittany, or on the coasts of Kerry, Clare, Galway, Mayo and Donegal, or in the west of Scotland and the outer isles, as far north as the Butt of Lewis and Cape Wrath.

As our business was with the Mediterranean, we turned back towards the west and those parts of Andalucia familiar to the Moors.

The Moorish conquest of Spain was swift and almost complete, meeting with little resistance from the Celtic-Iberian inhabitants who found the Muslims no more disagreeable to live under than they had found the Visigoths or the Romans before them. Slaves found their situation noticeably improved, Muslims having a far more humane attitude to them than owners of other religions, while the Jews, who had been consistently persecuted by the Christian clergy of the Visigoths, also experienced a change for the better.

In 711, Tarik, the lieutenant of Musa, viceroy of Walid I, the Umayyad Caliph who had occupied the whole of North Africa, landed by the Rock of Calpe, the northernmost of the Pillars of Hercules, which was subsequently named Jebel Tarik in commemoration of this event, a name that eventually became corrupted to Gibraltar. There, on the tip of Europe, with a force of between five and seven thousand Berbers, on 26 July 711, he utterly defeated the army of Roderick, the recently crowned king of the Visigoths, either in the Plain of Salado near Cape Trafalgar or near Jerez on the bank of the River Guadelete, Roderick being slain in the action and earning for himself the unenviable title of 'Last of the Goths'.

Tarik subsequently took Cordoba and, in 712, Toledo, with such apparent ease that Musa became both jealous and alarmed at his subordinate's success. Putting himself at the head of an army of some 18,000 men drawn from a variety of sources in the Islamic world, Musa crossed the Strait into Andalucia and took successively Seville, where the widow of Roderick soon married the son of the conqueror; Carmona, which was betrayed to him; and Merida, which capitulated on 23 October 715, a place of such Roman magnificence that the Moors exclaimed when they saw it, 'All the world must have been called together to build such a city.'

Imprisoned by Musa, Tarik was released by the Caliph and both men went on to conquer the Peninsula, their armies, aided by constant dissension among their Visigothic opponents, flowing like quicksilver through the passes in the high sierras, over the burning plateaux of Aragon and La Mancha, along the green river banks where the cattle grazed, until they came to a halt at the feet of the Pyrenees, having conquered all Spain with the exception of Galicia and the Asturias where a Goth, Pelayo, was elected king. Recalled to Damascus by the Caliph and arriving there in 715 in time to see him breathe his last, Musa was fined an enormous sum by the Caliph's successor, Suleiman, and died broken-hearted on the Mecca pilgrimage. What happened to Tarik is not known.

The Conquest led to a period of political confusion, with Berbers, Moors (Muslims of mixed Arab and Berber descent), Arabs, Egyptians and Syrians quarrelling among themselves in the Muslim fashion, and no sooner had the new empire reached its greatest extent than it began to disintegrate. The defeat of the Muslims at Tours in 732 by Charles Martel marked the furthest extent of their advance and by 759 they had been forced to retreat south of the Pyrenees.

They were saved by the arrival in Spain of Abd al-Rahman, the only survivor of the Umayyad dynasty at Damascus. He founded a new Umayyad dynasty at Cordoba and obtained recognition of his new dominion from the Caliph, whose capital had been transferred to Baghdad in 756. It was not until some twenty years later that the Golden Age of the Moors could be said to have arrived and Cordoba became what was perhaps the most civilized city in Europe. But in 1031 the Caliphate of Cordoba disintegrated, fragmenting into several parts under separate dynasties, and in 1085 Alfonso VI of Castile succeeded in taking Toledo for the Christians. It was then that Yousef ben Tachfin, leader of the Almoravids, appeared on the scene. The Almoravids were those religious Berber warriors from Mauretania, otherwise known as the Lemtounline, the Veiled Ones, who under his leadership in North Africa had united El Maghreb, the Muslim West, and had founded Marrakech, from which Morocco takes its name, making it the capital in 1063.

In 1087 the Almoravids entered Spain, and in the space of twenty years their leader, Tachfin, succeeded in imposing his authority on all the emirs of the petty states that had emerged after the break-up of the Caliphate of Cordoba fifty years before – on Granada, Malaga, Tarifa, Cordoba itself, Ronda, Carmona, Seville, Almeria, Murcia, Jativa, Badajoz and finally, in 1102, Valencia, eventually proclaiming himself ruler of Spain and dispossessing the emirs completely.

The Almoravids were succeeded by the Almohads who, in North Africa at least, literally massacred them. The Almohads had their origins in the High Atlas and in the hundred years of their rule (1147–1244/8) they extended their empire to the furthest possible limits in the west. They presided over what was a second Golden Age for the Moors, but after the flight of the last of dynasty, to Africa in 1232, a fearful Muslim collapse took place in Spain.

In 1236 Ferdinand III of Castile, the Saint, captured Cordoba, the great capital of the Muslim rulers; subsequently he took, or forced to submit to him, Murcia, Granada, Seville, Jerez, Medina, Sidonia and Cadiz. When he died in 1252, contemplating the invasion of North Africa, the frontiers of his kingdom, Castille, extended to the southern shores of the peninsula on the Strait of Gibraltar. Nevertheless, 240 years were to pass before Granada fell in 1492 to the forces of the Catholic monarchs Ferdinand and Isabella, and the rule of the Moors was finally extinguished.

Holy Week in Seville

Late in the afternoon of Holy Saturday, 2 April 1983, the seventh and last day of Holy Week, we lay on a rooftop high above the Plaza Jeronimo de Cordoba near the Church of Santa Caterina in the eastern part of Seville, soaking up the sun which was shining down from a deep blue cloudless sky. Although it was still only the first week of April, here it was already as hot as an English midsummer day.

We were exhausted. We had arrived in Seville seven days previously, early on the morning of Palm Sunday, the first day of Holy Week, in time to see the Procesión de Las Palmas, headed by the Archbishop and the Chapter carrying palms which they later placed on a *paso*, a processional float, with a statue on it depicting Christ on an ass entering Jerusalem.

This float, popularly known as La Borriquita, was escorted on its four-hour journey from the Church of San Salvador, where it was housed, to the Cathedral, and back again, by children wearing long white robes, belts of woven grass and hoods embellished with the red cross of Santiago. Many spectators carried olive branches as symbols of peace during this procession of the Archbishop.

During these seven days we had seen at least part, in some cases the major part, of fifty-one processions escorting one hundred and three separate *pasos*; fifty-two if the first part, the children's procession, is considered separate from the second part, the procession of the Sacred Christ of Love, Our Lady of Succour and St James the Apostle, popularly known as El Amor, which is escorted by black-hooded brothers wearing the shield of their Hermandad or Cofradia, as these Brotherhoods are known. None of these processions had lasted for less than four hours. The longest, La Macarena, had lasted for twelve and a half hours, another, Jesús Cautivo, Jesus Captive, had lasted for twelve hours, and that of Cristo de la Sed, Christ of the Thirst, otherwise known as Nervion, after the Barrio, the quarter of Seville from which it comes, eleven and a half hours.

Night and day, except for an hour or so after midday, the great floats, all of them enormously heavy, embellished with silver, some decorated with flowers and bearing sumptuously dressed figures of the Virgin, costing thousands of pounds each year to decorate (the floats and figures are of inestimable worth, a Virgin's clothing and accessories alone valued at £100,000 ($140,000)), other effigies depicting events in the last six days of the life of Christ, had swayed through the streets, those of the Virgins like great ships illuminated by masses of candles, all borne on the backs of hordes of sweating porters invisible beneath the velvet draperies, some macabre, some beautiful, some very old, some made as late as the 1970s. If it rains during the procession, the floats are taken back either to their own churches or the nearest available one and the whole thing is called off.

All these figures, however old or new, have been carved and coloured by what can only be described as a school of artists who have always devoted themselves to producing what the Spanish call *simulacros imagenes*, with a skill that they have inherited from the craftsmen of Greece and Rome, who themselves inherited it from Babylon, Egypt and Phoenicia. This art form is based on such exact observation that the end products have somehow ceased to have the attributes of statuary as we think of it but rather resemble wax-works or dead bodies wearing clothing, for these figures, except those of Christ Crucified, are almost always clothed, usually very richly, with real not sculpted clothing.

Looking at these figures, so many of them similar in intention and execution, it is difficult for the layman to know whether he is looking at a work of the sixteenth century, such as the Cristo de Burgos, the oldest documented image, carved by Juan Bautista

Vasquez in 1573, one by Marcos de Cabrera, carved in 1575, a seventeenth-century work by Juan de Mesa, Pedro Roldán or Juan Martinez Montañes, or a modern work, done in the fifties, such as the masterly figures carved for the procession of Jesús Cautivo by José Paz Vélez.

In the course of these fifty-two processions, besides seeing Jesus riding into Jerusalem, we had seen him instituting the Eucharist of the Last Supper, kissed by a Judas dressed in yellow, the colour of anathema, while watched by Peter, James, Thomas and John, and praying in the olive grove at Gethsemane.

Arrested, presented to the people by Pilate in the presence of Claudia, his wife, and a band of Negro servants, Roman soldiers and Jews. Slapped by a Jew at his trial in the palace of Annas, who is seen seated on a throne flanked by a bearer of false witness, another Jew. Sentenced to death surrounded by Roman soldiers and Jews, while Pilate washes his hands and Claudia looks on thinking of something else (Holy Week in Spain is something to be avoided by practising Jews like the Plague). Mocked by Herod.

Scourged. Having the Crown of Thorns placed on his head. Receiving the Cross and embracing it. Falling to the ground unable to support its weight. Helped by Simon of Cyrene. Carrying the Cross, consoling a number of women, among them St Veronica, who has just wiped his face with a cloth that miraculously retains his image. Sitting on a rock while soldiers gamble for his robe. Waiting to be crucified with the two thieves, meanwhile converting one of them.

Crucified. Raised to a vertical position by four Jews. Speaking his last seven words on the Cross, listened to by the Virgin of the Remedies, St John the Evangelist and the Three Marys, Magdalene, Salome and Cleophas. Dying on the Cross, with Mary Magdalene kneeling at the foot of it. Having his side pierced by a soldier mounted on horseback, while others watch. Dead on the Cross, which rises from a bed of red carnations. Removed from the Cross by Joseph of Arimathea and Nicodemus and slung in a sheet. Held in her outstretched arms by the Virgin, dead below the empty Cross. Taken to the burial grounds.

So many scourgings, so many crucifixions, so much agony. Too much for us, day after day, although there is no commitment to witness any of it. The Brotherhoods gain nothing at all out of the hundreds of thousands of spectators. No collections appear to be made. Only those who set up stands and provide chairs along the route, presumably the Municipality, and those with good points of view to offer, make anything out of it; these and the providers of food and drink, sleeping accommodation and souvenirs. In this way the Semana Santa is rather like an extended coronation; but although there is no obligation to watch the processions one can scarcely ignore them, for they quarter the city with a persistence that is unparalleled elsewhere in the Catholic world, even in Spain, outside Andalucia. Here, even the most devout have been known to confess to a surfeit.

Most difficult to become fed up with, and almost impossible for the Spaniards, who are virtually Mariolatrists, are the fifty-two Virgins we have seen up to now (there are more to come), most of them lone figures, all of them with their own floats, some of them accompanied on these always sumptuous vehicles by a diffident, usually moustached, disciple, John.

There are so many Virgins for both men and women to go overboard about, Virgins of Peace, the Broom Bush, Grace and Hope, the Star, Grief, Succour, of the Dew, the Mercies, Health, the Sadnesses, the Afflictions, of Guadelupe, of the Waters, of Grace and Protection, of the Abandoned Ones, of the Anguishes (two of them), the Incarnation, of the Candles, of the Sweet Name, the Sufferings, the Remedies, of Protection, the Palm Leaf, the Rule, of Charity, of the Palm, of the Good End, of the Angels, the Tears of Victory, of Mercy, of the Conception, of Great Pain and Grief, of Hope, of the Presentation, of Montserrat, of Great Pain in her Loneliness, of Protection, of the O (from antiphons, prayers sung on the Feast of Expectation, all of which begin 'O, Maria . . .'), of Loreto, of Villaviciosa, of Pity and so on, almost *ad infinitum*. As Wanda said, something of a confession for a practising member of the Church to make, 'I've had enough Virgins for a bit.'

Even up here on the rooftops, almost level with the belfries of half a dozen churches, one or two of which had been built by the Moors as minarets, it was difficult to get away from them. From far below and far off, in the deep canyons which were the streets of a city that was still partly Moorish, with its pillared inner patios surrounding fountains that were for them as secretive as anything in Fez (that is if the occupants wanted to be secretive) rose the fanfares of bugles and trumpets and the rolling of drums which accompany the playing of the marches which are peculiar to Holy Week. In this case one of the bands was playing a march called the *Armagura* which was originally composed for the Crowned Virgin of Grief, La

Armagura Coronada, and which is played so often that it might almost be regarded as the theme music of the Semana Santa.

These bands were accompanying two of the Brotherhoods that had both set off at 3.30 p.m. from their respective churches where they kept their *pasos*. One, the Brotherhood of the Order of Servitas of Our Lady of Pain, Sacred Christ of Providence, Holy Mary of Loneliness and St Mark the Evangelist, otherwise known as Los Servitas, was by this time, 5.00 p.m., one and a half hours outward bound from its mother church, the Capilla de los Dolores, near the Plaza de San Marcos in the Barrio of the same name, and was now about to enter the Plaza Encarnaçion on its convoluting course to the Cathedral, which it would reach, unless the procession in front of it was running late, around 6.50 p.m.

The other, La Esperanza de la Trinidad, the Sacramental Brotherhood of the Sacred Decree of the Holy Trinity, Sacred Christ of the Five Wounds, Sacred Mary of the Conception, whose church was La Trinidad in Calle Maria Auxiliadora off the ring road, was now in Calle Juan de Mesa, bound on what appeared to be a collision course with the floats of Los Servitas, an encounter that would take place, unless the organizers averted it, which they would probably succeed in doing, at the entrance to the Sierpes, the narrow tortuous Bond Street of Seville which is also at the beginning of what is known as the Carrera Oficial, Official Route, to the Cathedral, which every procession must follow whatever route it has taken previously. According to the ultra-Catholic, ultra-Establishment newspaper, the *ABC*, which I was at this moment trying to read, they were due to arrive at this point within five minutes of one another, around 6.15 p.m.

It was time to get ready for the procession of El Réal Hermandad Sacramental del Santo Entierro de Nuestro Señor Jesucristo y Maria Santísima de Villaviciosa, which promised to be rather different from those we had previously seen, as I was to be a participant.

'Are you sure you want to go?' I said to Wanda. 'You've seen so many.'

'I'll tell you what,' she said. 'I may have had enough Virgins and crucifixions, and I don't care if I never eat another *pescado frita* or drink another glass of manzanilla, but I wouldn't miss you in the procession for anything.'

With Wanda clasping the *laissez-passer* signed by the Hermano Mayor, the elected head of the Royal Sacramental Brotherhood of the Holy Burial of Our Lord Jesus Christ and Sacred Mary of

Villaviciosa, popularly known as the Santo Entierro, the Holy Burial, in case I lost it, we set off on foot – which is the only way of arriving anywhere on time in Seville in Holy Week – for the church where its images are kept, the Convent of San Gregorio in Calle Alfonso XII.

It was from this same street, or rather a turning off it, that we had seen the floats of the Primitive Brotherhood of Our Father Jesus the Nazarene, the Holy Cross of Jerusalem and Sacred Mary, otherwise known as El Silencio, emerge from the Chapel of San Antonio Abad in the early morning, 1.05 a.m., on Good Friday, Viernes Santo Madraguarda.

The first of its two great *pasos* bore the figure, probably carved at the beginning of the seventeenth century, of Jesus the Nazarene embracing the cross which he had just received into his hands for the journey to Golgotha, with the blood streaming down his face from beneath the crown of thorns. The second bore the Virgin of the Conception standing on a bed of orange blossom, looking down on the dense crowd through a forest of white candles from beneath a gold-embroidered *palio*, a velvet canopy embellished with precious stones. Weeping, with the simulated tears coursing down her face which was framed in fabulous ivory lace beneath a golden crown, her immense embroidered velvet mantle streaming away behind her, she was apparently unconscious of the absurdly young-looking, conventionally moustached St John who stood by her side looking anxiously at her as though she might faint away. And as the thirty-six Costaleros, the porters who were carrying it, invisible beneath the float, made the difficult shuffling turn towards Calle Alfonso XII, the *palio* and the twelve slender silver columns with its hangings began to oscillate, so that the whole construction appeared to be about to take off into the air.

This was the moment when in other processions of a more popular character, such as that of the Sacred Mary of Hope, known as La Esperanza de Triana, or that of her rival, the Sacred Mary of Hope known as La Macarena, the Virgin would have been greeted with cries of '*Guapa! O Guapaguapaguapa!*' ('O beautiful, beautiful, beautiful girl!') and the air would have been filled with fanfares and the rolling of drums. But because this was El Silencio, the Silent, the oldest of all but one of the Cofradias in Seville, founded in 1340, all that was heard was what are known as the Whistles of Silence, a series of eerie sixteenth- and seventeenth-century airs rendered on oboes, bassoons and clarinets.

Then the *paso* had come to a halt and someone had begun to sing a *saeta*, launching it, like the arrow from which it takes its name, from a balcony high overhead, a form of *cante hondo* and a more austere, ancient form of the flamenco which is itself Andalusian. The origins of the *saeta* have been sought, largely unsuccessfully, among the Moors, the Jews, the gypsies and in the Christian liturgy. They are songs which express faith, hope, desire, remorse, repentance and, above all, love. An unearthly performance which here in Seville during Holy Week is received either with extravagant enthusiasm or with derision, according to whether it is approved or not approved. There is no middle way.

Then the Capataz, the foreman of the Costaleros, dressed in a black suit, banged with a gavel on a metal plaque set on the first of the two *pasos*, the one with Jesus the Nazarene embracing the Cross, at the same time shouting, '*Elevar!*' and when the Costaleros had raised it had banged on it again, this time with the words '*Adelante! Marcha!*' (Go on! Forward march!'), and the forty-two Costaleros, having stood up with the dreadful load poised on the napes of their necks, moved forward, together with two files of Nazarenos, the name applied to members of the Brotherhood who were taking part in the procession, wearing black hoods and tunics, wide belts woven from esparto grass and carrying purple candles.

Then the second float was raised and set in motion, that of the Virgin of the Conception and St John, escorted by Nazarenos carrying white candles and preceded by a Hermano, a brother, bearing a drawn sword, a warning that all the members of this Brotherhood are dedicated to defend the doctrine of the Immaculate Conception, even at the cost of their lives, and were so-dedicated centuries before it became dogma. Then the Whistles of Silence began again and the procession swayed out of sight.

There was an elegant crowd in the Convent of San Gregorio when we reached it around six o'clock. There were young men in dark suits and black ties and white collars who looked as if they might be bankers. (There is in fact a Brotherhood largely made up of bank employees, Our Father Jesus before Annas, Sacred Christ of the Great Pain, and Holy Mary of the Sweet Name, popularly and perhaps appropriately known as La Bofetada, The Slap, also as the Dulce Nombre, Sweet Name.) Or they could have been accountants, *negociante de vino*, landowners, lawyers on the way up. Even those who looked as if they might still be on the lowest rungs of whatever ladder they were on, showed unmistakable signs that they would eventually rise to the top of it providing they didn't make a boob of whatever ritual they might be called upon to carry out, in this, El Réal Hermandad Sacramental del Santo Entierro de Nuestro Señor Jesucristo y Maria Santísima de Villaviciosa.

And there were older men wearing morning coats and the sort of grumpy expressions that seem to come as second nature to members of the Spanish upper crust, with the medallions of the Hermandad slung round their necks. They were already at the top, presidents of corporations, and that was what they looked like; one or two of them sufficiently groggy-looking to make one think that they might suddenly fall off their particular ladder, thus giving younger members a chance to go up a rung or two.

Conspicuous among this resplendent band, the younger of whom had not yet started to change into their ceremonial gear, were the wives and girl friends, all dressed up to the nines, some also in black, but all subfusc and as smart as guardsmen. In fact the whole thing was reminiscent of a gathering of officers and their girl friends and madams in the Guards Chapel for a memorial service. They certainly did not look like the sort of women who were employed to dress and undress the Virgin before and after the procession, and they were not, this delicate task being entrusted to those who are usually themselves virgins, but of a certain age. No man is permitted to take this liberty, not even a priest.

This was a Brotherhood of the Establishment, the oldest of all the Brotherhoods of Seville, founded in 1248 by King Ferdinand III of Castile. Known as El Santo, although he was not canonized until 1671 and twenty years after his death, Ferdinand was a Catholic ruler of such extraordinary religious zeal that he not only helped to pile the faggots around the followers of the Albigensian heresy who were sentenced by an early form of Inquisition to suffer the equivalent of the auto-da-fé, but himself applied the torch to them with his own hands. He founded the Brotherhood three hundred years before the Semana Santa began to be celebrated as it is today, which was in the sixteenth century, in order that his newly liberated subjects might have their faith reinforced by an annual procession. The second most ancient of the Brotherhoods of Holy Week was El Silencio, which was founded on 14 March 1340, in what are known as the Carnestolendas, those last three days of carnival when the prohibition against eating meat becomes imminent with the onset of Lent. It was founded with the intention of perpetuating the memory of the journey to Calvary and at that time and for long afterwards its members carried crosses, walked barefoot and wore crowns of thorns, practices which together with flagellation and the wearing of chains did not become extinct among some penitents until after the last war, although all the Brotherhoods always have a number of voluntary penitents who still carry heavy crosses and walk barefoot. The members of El Silencio, by virtue of their devotion to Jesus the Nazarene, were known as Nazarenos, the name by which all members of Brotherhoods who take part in the processions of Holy Week in memory of the penitential progression to Christ to Calvary are known, and notwithstanding the existence of the Brotherhood of Santo Entierro, which pre-dates it by nearly a hundred years, El Silencio is known as Madre y Maestra, Mother and Mistress, of all the Hermandados or Cofradias which make up the Brotherhoods of Seville.

Soon after six o'clock those members of the Santo Entierro who were going to take part in the procession began to transform themselves into Nazarenos in the sacristy of the convent which belongs to the Padres Mercedarios, the Mercedarians, the Fathers of the Order of St Mary. They put on their long black tunics, attaching the long black sleeves, which were separate, with safety pins, of which there were not enough to go round until someone was sent out to buy some. Then they rolled up their trousers so that they would not show below the hems of their tunics, for although the legs of the trousers must not be seen the trousers must not be taken off, as I was told. A host of Nazarenos, emulating the journey to Calvary and escorting the Virgin of Villaviciosa without trousers, would be not only unthinkable but positively scandalous.

When all this was done to their satisfaction, they scrutinized themselves in the one clouded mirror with which the sacristy was provided, crowding round it rather like model girls taking a last look at themselves before beginning to show a spring collection. Then they donned the immensely tall black pointed hoods, which completed the disguise, turning them in an instant from keen, conservative, ambitious young men into strange, unearthly, eerie figures, with only the eyes flickering behind the twin eyeholes in the hoods to show that hidden behind them was not some sort of foul fiend but a human being. These were the Nazarenos. In a sense they were Penitentes; but the real Penitentes wore hoods that hung loose down their backs, walked barefooted and carried heavy wooden crosses on their shoulders.

Of all the Brotherhoods the Santo Entierro was the smallest. Altogether it only had 100 members and of these 80 were taking part in the procession. Some Brotherhoods were enormous. La Estrèlla, founded in 1566 by shipyard workers of Seville, Cadiz and other ports trading with the New World, had 2260 brothers of whom 1000 Nazarenos took part in the procession; El Gran Poder, 4894 brothers with almost a thousand participants; La Macarena had 5893 members, 1007 of whom were Nazarenos; La Esperanza de Triana 3542 brothers, 800 of whom were Nazarenos.

It was now 6.25 p.m. In five minutes the procession was due to begin. It was a strange scene. The body of the church was now crowded with Nazarenos, some swinging thuribles of incense, some carrying wands and silver crosses or else lighting their big four-foot-long candles, bare-footed Penitentes trying the weight of their heavy crosses and the ninety-six Costaleros (others were in reserve) of the Cuadrilla de Domingo Rojas. It was they who would carry the three floats of the Brotherhood. Rough-looking members of the working class, dressed in white vests and wearing canvas shoes, some of them bottle-nosed, some with huge paunches, they were the sort of men who until the introduction of containers and automation into the port area of the city had earned their living as stevedores. What they did now, apart from lugging the *pasos* of El Santo Entierro round Seville once a year, was unclear. Perhaps they had been declared redundant, as had the stevedores at Naples and almost everywhere else, and given such massive severance pay that they no longer had to bother. Or perhaps they were members of a union who were unsackable even if their jobs had disappeared. Whatever they were, they were not the kind of men of whom I was anxious to ask such questions.

On their heads they wore turbans of white cloth wound in such a way that a thick pad, sometimes stuffed with sand and sawdust, protected the nape of the neck on which almost the entire weight of the enormously heavy *paso* has to be supported. The weight is taken on a wooden bar, one of a number of such bars beneath the float, one behind the other, sufficient for whatever number of men are needed to carry it, which varies between twenty-five and forty-eight and exceptionally, to carry the huge first float of the Brotherhood of Sacred Christ of Exaltation and Our Lady of Tears, known as Los Caballos, fifty-four men. These headcloths gave the Costaleros a distinctly biblical air, but of those who mocked the Saviour rather than of those who supported him. Paid to do this work, presumably handsomely, they were a race apart. Few members of the Brotherhood appeared to take much notice of them, but nevertheless they were the most important participants in the entire procession, for without them the floats could not form part of it. They well deserved whatever they earned, for however thick the wrappings, by the time they returned to the church, around a quarter-to-eleven that night, many of them would have deep wounds in the backs of their necks.

In recent years it has become so difficult to recruit Costaleros, and so expensive, that the majority of the Brotherhoods now employ their own members to carry the *pasos*. It was difficult to imagine the brothers of the Santo Entierro agreeing to do this but as it would be impossible anyway, in a Brotherhood numbering only one hundred members, the question does not arise.

One of the first Cofradias to carry its own float was the very large Brotherhood of the Christ of the Good Death (de la Buena Muerte), otherwise known as Los Estudiantes, founded in 1924 by professors and students of Seville University which is housed in what used to be the Royal Tobacco Factory, an immense eighteenth-century building and the scene of the first act of Bizet's *Carmen*. There is a Cofradia of Tobacco-workers, Las Cigarreras, Our Father Jesus Tied to the Column, and Holy Mary of Victory, founded in 1562, which had for its head, its Hermano Mayor, King Alfonso XIII, grandfather of the present King Juan Carlos, who until his abdication in 1930 himself used to take part in the procession. They keep their two floats in the Chapel of the New Tobacco Factory, on the other side of the river in the district called Los Remedios. There is also a Brotherhood of Gypsies, Los Gitanos, whose women dance the flamenco outside their church of San Roman while waiting for the *pasos* bearing Christ walking towards Calvary and the Virgin of the Anguishes to appear; of Negroes, Los Negritos, formed in 1390 by a group of black Africans, although there are very few black Africans now; two Brotherhoods of Bullfighters, one, El Baratillo, named after its church at the bull-ring, the other San Bernardo. There is a Brotherhood of Bakers, Los Panaderos, and of Hotel and Restaurant Workers, known as Santa Maria. There is even a Brotherhood of Judges, Lawyers and members of the Guardia Civil, the Siete Palabras, The Seven Words; and of Travel Agents, Our Father Jesus of Health and Good Voyage, known as Buen Viaje.

High overhead, dominating everything else in the chapel of the Convent of San Gregorio, were the three floats of the Santo Entierro. The first, La Muerte, otherwise known as La Canina, represents the Triumph of the Holy Cross over Sin and Death. At the foot of the now-vacant cross, with the ladders used to lower the body of the dead Christ from it still in position and with long strips of funereal drapery hanging from it, a skeleton, Death, sits on a globe of the world which is enfolded by a serpent bearing in its mouth an apple, the emblem of Original Sin, Death itself in an attitude of despair and dejection, its skull bent, supported by a skeletal hand. This, the most macabre of all the *pasos*, made its first appearance in 1693 and this present skeleton was carved in 1829 by Juan de Astorga. Among all the 112 *pasos* paraded by the fifty-six Brotherhoods in Holy Week, La Muerte is unique, the only one that has this particular allegorical character.

The second *paso* bears La Urna, Cristo Yacente, Christ Recumbent in a great gilded, crystal panelled, Gothic casket, wearing only a loincloth. The figure was carved in the seventeenth century by Juan de Mesa. This is the Santo Entierro, the Holy Burial, from which the Brotherhood takes its name.

The third and last *paso* carries El Duelo, the Mourning. The figure of the Virgin of Villaviciosa carved by Antonio Cardoso Quirós in 1691, tearful, with head bowed, wears a golden halo instead of a crown, a black mantle embroidered with gold thread and carries in her hands the Crown of Thorns. With her are John the Evangelist, St Joseph of Arimathea, Nicodemus and the Three Marys, carved at the same time as La Muerte by Juan de Astorga.

At half past six the great doors of the Convent were flung open and, together with some half dozen Nazarenos, some carrying red candles, one, Guillermo Mira Abaurrea, the Diputado Mayor of the Brotherhood, a tall imposing figure, carrying the leading cross of the Brotherhood, I emerged in the beautiful soft evening light of Seville in spring into a street packed with people who miraculously gave way as we advanced towards them, making a passage for us.

Meanwhile the Costaleros waited invisible beneath the *pasos*. Then the Capataz banged on the metal plaque with his gavel, at the same time shouting, '*Elevar!*', and forty-two Costaleros struggled to their feet beneath their macabre load, bearing the first of the three *pasos*, La Muerte. Then he banged again, this time shouting, '*Adelante! Marcha!*' and they began to shuffle forward. The upright of the empty cross was higher than the archway of the church door and they only cleared it because they bent their knees in what must have been an agonizing position, bowed beneath the awful weight of the *paso*. Then it, too, was in the open air with its funereal hangings moving in the light air and with the skeleton's ribs trembling horribly. There were none of the cheers that would have greeted the successful accomplishment of such a difficult man-oeuvre had this been a less austere, more popular float, such as one of those of the Triana or La Macarena. Instead, as had been El Silencio, it was greeted with silence. You cannot cheer Death, however much you might welcome him. In the 733rd year of its existence the procession of the Santo Entierro was once more on its way.

The main body of the procession had been waiting in the street and now the first part of it formed behind La Muerte. This was composed of hooded Nazarenos from twenty-seven of the fifty-two Cofradias and Hermandados which had already passed through the Cathedral in Holy Week, each in the costume of his Brotherhood, the youngest of these being the Brotherhood of Nuestro Padre Jésus Despojado de Sus Vestiduras, Christ despoiled of his Clothing, which was only 13 years old. The oldest, Los Negritos, was 584 years old.

The Nazarenos were dressed in white and purple for Christ, white and blue for the Virgin, white and crimson, cream with black face-pieces, purple with the cord belt of the Franciscans, white with woven belts of gold cord, and in the black of the Nazarenos of the Gran Poder and Santa Cruz.

I never saw the procession. I was in the worst place to see any procession, in it and at the front of it. I never even saw La Urna or El Duelo leave the Convent, so I do not know what sort of welcome they got from the crowd, whether cheers or silence, for by that time I was already far away, beginning the Carrera Oficial, moving ghost-like through the Calle Sierpes which in places is so narrow that, with chairs placed on either side for spectators, each of which costs 220 pesetas, it fits the processions closely round the hips.

I didn't see the members of the Council or General of Herman-dados and Cofradias, the representative of the Comendador of the Order of Mercy, Padre Luis Cid, the Censor of the Order, or the President of the Council of Cofradias, José Sanchez Dubé, or the Municipal Band, directed by Maestro José Albero Frances, although I certainly did hear it when it entered La Campana, the big square before the Sierpes, when it struck up the march *Cristo*

Yacente, from its position behind La Urna con El Cristo Yacente, when it practically took the tiles off the roofs.

Neither did I see the acolytes dressed in eighteenth-century clothing who were carrying a black canopy raised on silver poles in respect for the dead Christ in La Urna. Neither did I see the troop of Roman soldiers with plumed helmets who preceded it; nor the representatives of the Real Maestanza (whatever that is); the Delegate of the Government of Andalucia (Leocadio Marin); the Second in Command of the Military Government (General Juan Ollero); the President of the Sala de lo Contencioso, Fernando Rubiales, representing the Audencia Territorial; the Chief Inspector of Taxes, Hipolito Hernández; nor the Rector of the University, Guillermo Jimenez Sanchez. Nor did I see Fernando de Queral Müller, Captain-General of the Second Air Region nor his Band and Guard of Honour; he was taking part in the procession as representative of King Juan Carlos. (By a rule of the Brotherhood promulgated in 1805, future kings of Spain would automatically assume the title of Hermano Mayor. In 1940 General Franco took part in the procession, having interpreted the rule of the Brotherhood perhaps too literally.) Nor did I see that indefatigable figure, the Archbishop of Seville, Monseñor Carlos Amigo Vallejo, or the Mayor of Seville, Luis Urfiuela Fernandez, or the members of the Council of the Brotherhood, although I had already seen them, the men at the top of the ladder, in the church before we left. Nor did I see the officials of the Municipal and Provincial Governments of Seville, but I didn't feel any the worse off for that.

Well, what did I see as a pseudo-Nazareno, now one of the supporters of this Real Hermandad Sacramental del Santo Entierro, this Brotherhood with its massive display of temporal and spiritual power which had kindly provided me with their *laissez-passer*, as I walked, one of the front-runners of the procession? I saw a sea of people in front of me which I now knew would open up to let me through without the aid of policemen or the Guardia Civil, would part like the waters of the Red Sea before the Children of Israel, in the circumstances perhaps an unfortunate simile, as I drew near them.

What did they feel, what were they thinking about, these thousands of people, the adventurous people up trees and lampposts, the ladies in mantillas and tall combs on the balconies, some of whom would have been well advised to forgo this way of dressing in which success and failure is measured by a hair's breadth, the bourgeoisie sitting in the seats in the Sierpes, those members of the Establishment not taking part in the processions who were sitting in the boxes faced with red velvet, outside the Casa del Ayuntamiento, the City Hall? What were they thinking about, I wondered, making the most of this heaven-sent gift of anonymity, seeing the Sevillans crossing themselves, drinking beers and manzanillas, picking at their *tapas*, the snacks that come with the drinks, picking their noses, flirting – all in the beautiful Sevillan gloaming? What are *you* all thinking about, I wondered, looking in through what would normally have been an expanse of plate glass, now opened up for the occasion, into a fashionable men's club in the Sierpes, face to face with its assembled members gazing incuriously out at me and the procession, a band of grumpy-looking General Francos, elegantly swathed in dark grey flannel and Harris tweed. Was this the same club referred to as 'Les Laboureurs', the Labaradori, I wondered, that Nancy George, writing in French, looked into through a similar open window in Holy Week, 1931? 'The Labourers have one thing in common,' she wrote. 'They do not labour. It is the best known of all the clubs, the most aristocratic, its members follow the Christ of the Gran Poder barefooted and their wives, filled with ennui, leave them at this hour to run around in their sumptuous automobiles.' Well, if this was what they were still up to, no wonder their husbands looked grumpy.

Such a procession as this was very restful to take part in, at least for the hooded Nazarenos, much less so for the barefooted Penitentes lugging their heavy crosses, but nothing like as heavy as the Cross Christ carried, and much much less for the wretched Costaleros. Hooded, a unique anonymity is conferred on the wearer. Forbidden to speak, a merciful prohibition, the only external distractions are the small boys and girls who continually demand wax from your candle to add to what by now at the end of Holy Week amounts to a large ball of the stuff, and occasionally a girl comes very close who is either brazen or genuinely attempting to identify a friend or relation. The only other obligation a Nazareno has, an unofficial one, is to distribute sweets, of which he should have laid in a large store before leaving on his journey, to children or anyone else who takes his fancy. For the rest of the time he is a privileged voyeur, a ghost arrayed in ghostly clothing.

Halts were frequent. This was because the Costaleros were only able to carry their *pasos* for a comparatively short distance before being allowed to sink down on the road for an obligatory rest. Then they were brought water by an *aguador*, a water carrier, who would lift up the velvet hangings which concealed them from view and give them a drink from an earthenware pitcher. Sometimes during one of these halts one or two of them would rush off to a bar to drink a couple of beers in quick succession and relieve themselves, while others, either overcome by heat or worn down by the enormous weights they were called on to carry, were replaced by reservists.

Our procession was held up because the procession in front of ours, La Esperanza de la Trinidad, was behind time, having been on the road three hours longer than ours. This was because they could not leapfrog over the procession in front of them, that of Los Servitas, which was also running late. These were the two Brotherhoods whose bands we had heard trumpeting away up on the roof in the afternoon. And because of all this we of the Santo Entierro were impeding the progress of the fifty-sixth and last procession, the Papal and Royal Sacramental Brotherhood of Our Lady of Rocamadour, Blessed Souls and Ancient Brotherhood of Nazarenes of Our Lady of Loneliness, La Soledad, which had nothing behind it to hold up. For this was the last procession of Holy Week. There is, in fact, another procession on the morning of Resurrection Sunday, El Resucitado, but it is a new procession, its first appearance was in 1982, and it is not really part of Holy Week.

Now we paced solemnly through the Plaza San Francisco, otherwise Plaza de la Falange, where the top brass were sitting in stands draped in red and no one was going exactly crazy about our austere procession, and on into the Avenida José Antonio and the Avenida Queipo de Llano, otherwise Avenida de la Constitucion (where it got the same reception), wishing that the administration would decide once and for all what they are going to call their streets. The vast bulk of the Cathedral was beginning to loom ahead on the port bow, and the sun was sinking swiftly, for it was now long after eight. It illuminated the float ahead already lit by innumerable candles, which was carrying the beautiful Virgin of Esperanza, the masterpiece of Juan de Astorga, as it halted at the junction of the Alemanes, on the north side of the Cathedral, with Calle Garcia de Vinuesa, the way down to the bull-ring and the Guadalquivir, evoking enthusiastic cries and applause as its Costaleros executed a sort of side step, making the slender silver poles supporting her green and gold embroidered velvet canopy shiver like aspens in a breeze.

How would they have looked at me and any companions I might have had, these people of Seville, if we had been Jews or Moors, the Jews symbols of wealth, the Moors of skill in agriculture, on our way to the Quemadero, the burning place of the heretics in the Prado de San Sebastiano, the flat plain beyond the southern walls where the *auto-da-fé*, the execution of the sentence of the Inquisition, was carried out not by the Dominican inquisitors, the instruments of the Holy Office who would have wrung the confessions from us in the Moorish citadel at Triana beyond the bridge, but by the civil power?

Would they have done what they had done today as El Santo Entierro went by, crossed themselves, shed a tear, applauded, picked at their noses or at their *tapas*, continued to sip their manzanillas, climbed trees to see us, put on their best clothes for the event, while we passed in procession dressed in the *san benite*, the yellow fool's caps and tunics of the condemned heretics, the colour of Judas Iscariot, the colour in those days of the dress of the common criminal on his way to execution?

What I was taking part in here in Seville – and I was impressed by what I was taking part in – is something far older than the processions of the Christian Church. The processions of Holy Week are not only an echo of pagan antiquity. They are a direct continuation, thinly disguised, of the processions of images of gods and goddesses, carried on the shoulders of common men in the ancient world. In ancient times this perhaps was Tarshish, the furthest known habitation in Europe, at the western end of the Mediterranean, the uttermost part of the known world in Europe, as was Morocco in Africa, a place which the Phoenicians wished and tried to keep secret to themselves.

Here, in Spain, these processions continued as a Christian ritual under the Visigoths until they were interrupted by the Moors, but they started up again long before the Muslims left the peninsula for ever.

For us, watching them take place, and at the same time reading accounts of similar processions in the ancient world, time was annihilated. One might have been witnessing the procession of the Phoenician Astarte, otherwise the Egyptian Ashtaroth, goddess of the heavens, the Roman Juno Coelestis, her name everywhere signifying star, imported here in Seville from the eastern Mediterranean to comfort those Phoenician traders who were so far from home. Just as she was worshipped and carried through the streets crowned with stars, as are the Virgins today, in Babylon, Tyre, Sidon, Memphis, Carthage, Rome, in the same way as was the Sacred Boat of Osiris, the Shrine of Isis, the Ark of the Covenant of the Jews, wherever their temples were to be found, so she was here as late as the third century AD.

With a truly dramatic flourish the last of the two *pasos* of La Esperanza de la Trinidad was made to perform a ninety-degree turn by her Costaleros and the Virgin of Hope of the Trinity went swaying up the ramp into the Cathedral through the Puerto San Miguel at the south-west end to the accompaniment of drums and bugles and trumpets and the applause of what here was a vast assembled multitude. We followed her in shortly afterwards with La Muerte, but again it was very noticeable that Death did not have the box office appeal of Virgins, especially Virgins of the calibre of Our Lady of Hope of the Trinity.

The Cathedral was built on the site of the mosque of the Almohad Sultan, Abu Yousef Mansur. He started to build it in 1163 and completed it fifteen years later, in 1178. In 1248 Seville was reconquered by the Christians, and for the next 153 years it was a Christian place of worship. Then, in 1401, it was pulled down and the present building constructed. Nothing was left of the mosque of Abu Yousef to remind the Christian worshipper of the place where his apostatized forefathers had worshipped, suitably circumcised, except for the Patio de los Naranjos, the rather sad-looking Court of Oranges, in which they had carried out their ritual ablutions at what was a fountain originally built by the Visigoths, and the Giralda, the great minaret, soaring more than 300 feet into the heavens, now part of Captain-General Müller's airspace.

Here in Seville a clean sweep was made, and the unknown French architect who built the Cathedral (the influence is said to be that of St Ouen at Rouen, one of the most beautiful Gothic churches ever built) carried out the resolution made by the Chapter at its first conference, 'to construct a church such and as good that it never should have its equal. Let Posterity,' said its members, 'when it admires it complete, say that those who dared to devise such a work must have been mad.'

And indeed, standing in it before La Muerte among the guttering red candles borne by the Nazarenos of El Santo Entierro, all of whose *pasos* were now stationed in it, and those members of all the other Cofradias who accompanied them, awaiting the Blessing at the Station of the Holy Sacrament, hearing the murmurings of what was a vast congregation within its great choir and its chapels, all largely invisible in the ever-increasing murk – for it was now nine o'clock – it would have been difficult not to agree that they had triumphantly succeeded.

And now the Capataces of all three *pasos*, La Muerte, La Urna and El Duelo, banged with their gavels on the metal plaques, and once more the Costaleros, who had profited by this long halt to rush off and relieve themselves in a hard-to-find lavatory in a sacristy on the south side, raised themselves up, some of them bleeding from deep wounds beneath their neck pads, and to the shouts of '*Adalante! Marcha!*' surged forward yet again as they had done innumerable times in the last two hours and a half.

It was now 9.05 p.m. The *pasos* of the Santo Entierro were once more back on time and they had only another hour and ten minutes before re-entering the Convent at 10.15 p.m., for this is a very short procession and all the processions of Holy Saturday have to be back in their temples before Resurrection Sunday begins at midnight.

I went forward with them, the Nazarenos, the *aguador*, the man who walks behind each float with a ladder in case a sudden puff of wind snuffs out the candles, the Penitentes with their crosses causing them real discomfort now, as they intended they should, some of them deliberately carrying them with the lower part of the cross, instead of the point of balance, on their shoulders.

Then we went through the Puerto de los Palos at the east end of the Cathedral into the Plaza de la Virgen de los Reyes with its Christian and Moorish monuments, where the crowds were waiting in the soft night air, leaving behind us nothing but the wax we had spilled on the stone slabs, as had every other Nazareno here and throughout the city in the last seven days and nights. Tomorrow or the day after, no doubt it would be scraped away. Tomorrow afternoon, the afternoon of Easter Sunday, the bullfights would begin, and with them another celebration, the Feria, with dancing and music and feasting and pretty girls carried side-saddle behind their men on horseback. And it would be as if we and our procession, and all the other processions, like the Muslims, had never existed.

Dinner at the Negresco

Summer was over on the Côte d'Azur. Day after day a Force 7 wind blew from the west out of a clear sky. It moaned around the vandalized telephone booths on the long treeless roads outside the marinas in which the yachts, battened down in their thousands until the spring, bucketed at their moorings. It filled the air with flying paper, some of it with *confiture* on it, where the dustmen were ridding the foreshore and *les campings* of the last of the season's *ordures*. All but the hardiest swimmers had goose-pimples. The wind-surfers in wet suits were still out in force but they were locals, not what they called *pingouins* (tourists). The plane trees were peeling. The palms looked awful. The last of the forest fires that had destroyed the usual quota of forest in the Maures and the coverts of the Esterel massif, advancing on anything up to a six-mile front at between two and three miles an hour and rising up to a hundred feet in the air, had burnt themselves out, leaving deserts of white ash punctuated by the blackened skeletons of sea pines and other trees. The bars down on the waterfronts now had only their habitués, caretakers of yachts. Bacon, the restaurant at Antibes which specialized in *bouillabaisse*, had taken it off the menu until the sea, which was cobalt flecked with white, became less rough, as it was impossible to catch the large variety of fish necessary to make it, which have to be absolutely fresh. The museums were already on winter-time opening hours and in some places it was beginning to be difficult to buy English and other foreign newspapers.

The wind was so strong that, falling asleep on the beach at Juan-les-Pins after a delicious, inexpensive luncheon in l'Auberge de l'Esterel, a little restaurant at the back of the town which happened that day to be serving its last dishes of the season, *salade tiède de lotte aux écrevisses* (monkfish salad with freshwater crayfish), *lapin en papillote au beurre de basilic* (rabbit baked in greased paper with basil-flavoured butter), things like that for 75 francs a head (with the exchange at around 12 francs to the pound or 17 to the dollar), we woke to find ourselves buried under mounds of sand, like dead prospectors.

And when, towards evening, we arrived in Nice, it howled down the grey, canyon-like streets behind the Promenade des Anglais. These streets, into which tourists rarely penetrate, reserving their efforts for the old town below the chateau, are as sad and spooky as the back streets of almost any other large resort on the Côte d'Azur, the Italian Riviera or in Atlantic City or Brighton and Hove. It threatened to bowl over the pensioners and the *rentiers*, dressed in their spanking new Burberry trench coats, all ready for *l'hiver*, out for an airing in the gloaming, some of them with a rude-looking little dog in tow.

Nice is the only resort on the Côte d'Azur with a substantial back to its seafront, because it is a city of 350,000 inhabitants, the fifth largest in France, which makes Cannes with 70,000 seem like a village, and the 24,000 inhabitants of Monte Carlo, the Monegasques, a collector's item. This area is filled with workers engaged on a massive scale in pressing olive oil, extruding macaroni, crystallizing fruit, moulding bars of soap, encapsulating scents, exporting carnations, marguerites and stocks and, if all this sounds a little too arcadian, also deeply involved in the tobacco, textile, furniture and garment industries. It also conceals the Músee des Beaux-Arts Jules Chéret, a villa in the Genoese style begun by a Russian, the Prince Kotschouby and finished by an American, the entomologist James Thomson, which contains, besides works by Boudin, Sisley, Renoir, Monet, Degas, Dufy and Van Dongen, the singularly horrible pictures of the Symbolist Gustav-Adolf Mossa (1883–1971), its first curator, whom I would not liked to have met after dark on the Promenade des Anglais or anywhere else.

We had come to stay in an *hôtel-palais*, the Negresco, the only one still in existence at Nice. An *hôtel-palais* is the sort that the *Guide Michelin* used to describe as offering '*un confort princier*' but now describes, in deference presumably to those who disapprove of princes, as '*grand luxe et tradition*'. Here, on the Côte d'Azur, the lights are going out on them, inexorably, one by one, which was one reason why we had decided to stay in this one before it was too late. The other reason was that we had been living rough in the back of a van for what seemed a long time now.

Far into the thirties there were so many *hôtels-palais*. One man, Henri Ruhl, alone built nearly thirty, of which the Carlton at Cannes with its 288 rooms and its 30 suites is the most famous survivor. Of the seven listed in *Michelin* in 1939, only the Carlton and the Majestic remain. At Monte Carlo there are only two, the Paris and the Hermitage.

At Nice the Excelsior-Regina, Queen Victoria's favourite hotel, is now an old people's home, and the Hermitage, the Winter Palace and the Riviera Palace, all four of them on the heights of Cimiez and Carabacel inland from the sea, are gone. Gone, too, is the Ruhl et Anglais at No. 1 Promenade des Anglais, opposite what used to be the Casino de la Jetée – also gone, a casino on what was a sort of mini-pier in the Mediterranean – and also the Plaza et France at 12 Avenue Verdun, opposite the Jardin Albert Ier. And today there is no longer a single casino in Nice.

Only nine *hôtels-palais* are left on the entire Côte d'Azur between Monte Carlo and St Tropez: the Paris and Hermitage at Monte Carlo, La Réserve and the Métropole at Beaulieu-sur-Mer, the Negresco at Nice, the du Cap d'Antibes at Cap d'Antibes, the Carlton and Majestic at Cannes and the Byblos at St Tropez.

The Negresco was the creation of Henri Negresco, a Rumanian émigré with a big black moustache which commended him to his women guests, who had been a violinist in a gypsy orchestra before becoming a renowned *maître d'hôtel*.

It opened in 1912 having been built by Edouard Niermans, described, by whom is a mystery, as 'a Parisian born in Holland by an error of nature'. Architect and embellisher of innumerable casinos, restaurants, theatres, which included the Moulin Rouge and the Folies Bergères, as well as other *hôtels-palais*, Niermans designed it for the same purpose as all the other *hôtels-palais* on the Riviera were designed: for the reception of royalty, which included whole squads of grand dukes (sightings of a dozen at a time were not uncommon; they used to come for the weekend from St Petersburg in special trains),* noblemen, statesmen and millionaires who were also sometimes noble. All these, in various states of decrepitude, used to come to the Riviera in the winter months – those few hotels which remained open all the year used to give low season discounts from May to October – to play at the casinos and be given the kiss of life by such *grandes horizontales* as La Belle Otéro, Gaby Deslys, Liane de Pouget, Cléo de Mérode and, for those who could not afford the astral fees demanded by such high-class operators, a supporting cast of thousands of willing extras. And to show their appreciation of this monumental knocking shop, built on the site of a convent at a cost of 6,000,000 gold francs, eight kings and innumerable millionaires were present at the inaugural revels, in the same year as the Grand Duke Michael of Russia laid the foundation stone of a similar edifice, the Carlton at Cannes, having performed the same office for the Casino there six years previously.

For the period of less than two years before 1914, the Negresco was a tremendous success. In its first year it cleaned up 800,000 gold francs. It then became a military hospital for the duration of the war, as did the Carlton, and in 1920 Negresco died, ruined. It was the end of an epoch. There were no more grand dukes, and kings and queens were on ration. In 1922 two wealthy and sophisticated Americans, Gerald and Sara Murphy, on whom Fitzgerald partly based the Divers in *Tender is the Night* (another wilder part was based on himself and Zelda his wife), discovered a small sandy beach, La Garoupe, while staying at Cole Porter's villa on Cap d'Antibes. 'At that time,' as Murphy said, 'no one ever went near the Riviera in summer. The English and the Germans – there were no longer any Russians – who came down for the short spring season closed their villas as soon as it began to get warm (in May). None of them ever went in the water, you see. When we went to visit Cole, it was hot, hot summer, but the air was dry, and it was cool in the evening, and the water was that wonderful jade-and-amethyst color. Right out on the end of the Cap there was a tiny beach – the Garoupe – only about forty yards long and covered with a bed of seaweed that must have been about four feet thick. We dug out a corner of the beach and bathed there and sat in the sun, and we

* Not only Grand Dukes. They were accompanied by hundreds of courtiers. The Russians were so numerous that an Orthodox Cathedral was built at Nice to take care of their spiritual needs, designed by Michael Preobrajenski.

decided that this was where we wanted to be. Oddly, Cole never came back. But from the beginning we knew we were going to.'

Without realizing it, they had invented a new way of life, or one which if it ever existed had not done so since pre-Christian times, and the clothes to go with it. Shorts made of white duck, horizontally-striped matelots' jerseys and white work caps bought from sailors' slop shops, became a uniform. (A photograph of this period taken on the beach at La Garoupe shows Picasso wearing nothing but a pair of shorts and what looks like a cod-piece of seaweed, festively arranged.)

From now on the rich, and ultimately everyone else in the northern hemisphere, wanted unlimited sun, the sea, sandy beaches or rocks to dive into it from and the opportunity to eat al fresco. Friends of Hemingway and his wife – he introduced them to bull fighting at Pamplona – the Murphys, equally unwittingly, set the scene for him, too. So that, years later, Cyril Connolly could write, without exaggeration, that 'the greatness of Hemingway is that he alone of living writers has saturated his books with the memory of physical pleasure, with sunshine and salt water, with food, wine and making love, and with the remorse which is the shadow of that sun.'

It was the latest in a series of metamorphoses on a coast that before the coming of the grand dukes had attracted well-to-do sufferers from tuberculosis, many of whom died on it, scaring the healthy away, a coast inhabited by a hybrid mixture of peoples: descendants of Ligurians who came to it around 1000 BC, preferring it to their own Italian Riviera; Phoenicians and Phocaeans,* Greeks from the Ionian shores of Asia Minor who colonized Massilia (the present Marseilles) in 600 BC, established trading posts at Nice, Antibes and other places in the fourth century BC, introduced olive, fig and cherry trees, the cultivated vine and the idea of money as opposed to barter, one still firmly implanted in the hard heads of the present-day inhabitants. Their territory, in the second century BC, was invaded by the Celts and then, at their own invitation (to rid themselves of the Celts) by the Romans, who eventually established Transalpine Gaul, which included Provence and its sea coast from Massilia to the Alpes-Maritimes and secured their lines of communication with Spain. And they were followed by Vandals, Burgundians, Visigoths, Ostrogoths and Franks, all of whom invaded Provence in the fifth and sixth centuries; by Saracens

* People of the Seal. Their coins had seals depicted on them.

who sacked its seaboard in the first half of the eighth century and in the ninth terrorized the whole of the mountain area (the Maures) behind St Tropez. Subsequently, in the Middle Ages and the Renaissance, it was at the mercy of any of the foreign mercenary armies which happened to be passing through. Well into the nineteenth century it was a source of women and more durable spoils for Barbary pirates. (The Mission of Lord Exmouth to the heads of the Barbary States – the Bey of Tunis, the Dey of Algiers and the Bashaw of Tripoli – in the spring of 1816 secured, in theory, the abolition of Christian slavery.)

This quest for the sea and sun was not good news for Nice which, like Brighton, has an extremely-uncomfortable-to-lie-on shingle beach, and in 1957, after thirty-seven years which had seen the demise of most of the other palace-hotels, the Negresco, having doddered on under the auspices of a Belgian syndicate, was bought by Jean Mesnage, an immensely wealthy property developer who began life as a charcutier's assistant and made a fortune out of that, too.

The hotel occupies an entire block of seaside Nice. The front of it looks out over a murderous four-lane highway to the Promenade des Anglais, constructed by the local peasantry at the behest of the English colony when the orange crop failed in a great frost in 1822 in order to give them employment, now forming a great arc along the shore of the Baie des Anges. Large, but not as large as it was (the present owners decided to reduce the number of rooms from 400 to 150, leaving the back half of the hotel in disuse), it certainly looks like a *hôtel-palais*: painted a gleaming white like its rival the Carlton – the last time it was done, a couple of years before we arrived on its doorstep, it cost a million new francs to do it – with the railings of its balconies embellished with 24-carat gold leaf, its pink and green cupola of the same shape as two similar protuberances that sprout from the rooftops of the Carlton, which inspired what must have been a very over-excited Frenchman to describe them as '*les boîtes à lait de la Belle Otéro*' ('the milk cans of the Belle Otéro').

We arrived at the Negresco in our Volkswagen van, loaded with battered but good luggage, as good a way as any of determining whether staff can tell sausages by their overcoats, and drew up under a great glass canopy with the name of the hotel spelt out in lights. There we were met by a *voiturier*, what we would call a commissionaire. He was dressed in an extraordinary uniform said by the management to be a facsimile of that of a *pontonnier de l'Empire* – a military pontoon engineer of the Empire – it was difficult to tell which empire by looking at it: top hat with a huge red plume sprouting from it, caped great coat in royal blue, lined in scarlet, and long black boots, all of which initially they had had some difficulty in getting him to wear even though it had been put together by the couturier of Françoise Sagan, but now he loved it and could scarcely be persuaded to take it off. He asked for the keys and parked our not exactly sumptuous machine outside the front door – there is no garage accommodation – where it remained next to a Rolls with Monegasque number plates during our entire stay. Meanwhile *chasseurs* (porters), dressed in riding coats, knee breeches and stockings embodying the same colour scheme and presumably also from the same stable, zoomed our luggage into the building.

Inside, what one might call the foyer was of a theatrical splendour that made one glad not to have arrived shoeless and with a shrimping net. In it other varlets, dressed in what I imagined was the eighteenth or some earlier century equivalent of scarlet track suits, were waiting to take over our bags for what one hoped was the last lap – and the last lot of servitors if we had to tip them all – panting to go like runners in a relay race. Even the high official in charge of reception wore a scarlet suit, albeit a twentieth-century double-breasted one. We did not find him sympathetic and he didn't appear to approve of us, the only man so far who, presumably, didn't approve of Volkswagen Transporters.

Scarcely moving from this glistening marble hall which, when the man in the scarlet suit goes away, is dominated by the *concierge* and a splendid bust by Pron the Younger of Charles Duc de Berry, grandson of Louis XIV, one could see what Niermans and Negresco's indefatigable successor, the present owner, had between them accomplished, which goes some way to explaining why, in 1974, the French Government was prevailed upon to declare the Negresco a national monument.

The present owner is the daughter of Jean Mesnage, who bought it in 1957, Madame Jeanne Augier, wife of a lawyer, its apparently (for we never saw her) red-headed head, who has an insatiable passion for antiques, particularly those of the period of Louis XIV, and an equal enthusiasm for interior decoration and running hotels, which she does with the aid of M. Michel Palmer, an *hôtelier* of genius. Between them they changed large parts of the interior beyond recognition, from Niermans' *style modern* of 1912 to whatever period Madame Augier decreed – not, as Palmer said subsequently, '*une mince* (insignificant) *affaire*'. By doing so they saved it from one of two alternative fates, instant demolition or being turned into a dormitory hotel catering for tourists en masse. Now it is a highly polished museum, animated by its staff and guests. Whatever else inspires the owner it is not the profit motive, although in 1981, to everyone's surprise and possibly alarm, the hotel made one.

To the left, looking into the interior from the entrance, was the Salon Louis XIV, Madame's preferred period (what Versailles would have looked like if she had been alive then and caught the eye of *Le Roi Soleil* can only be a matter of conjecture), used for receptions and such. In it she had installed a monumental stone fireplace which weighed ten tons, two fine seventeenth-century tapestries from the Gobelins workshops and a coffered ceiling from the Château de St Pierre d'Albigny in Savoy which has painted panels recalling the love life of Hortense Mancini, Cardinal Mazarin's niece, with a seventeenth-century prince of Monaco.

And straight ahead was Niermans' masterpiece, the enormous, oval, white and gold Salon Royal with a glass dome supported by several dozen columns with gilded capitals grouped in pairs, from which a whole host of 24-carat gilded putti looked down through the glazing behind which they were more or less innocently disporting themselves on 1196 square feet of white marble floor, half of which was covered by a round Savonnerie carpet which cost Negresco, the automobile manufacturer Darracq and another captain of industry who put up the money for the hotel, 560,000 old francs, about a tenth of the total investment. This salon, as big as an airship hangar, which dwarfs human beings and makes those suffering from agoraphobia scuttle round the edge of it rather than cross it direct, was hung with enormous oils depicting seventeenth- and eighteenth-century French royalty (school of Van Loo) and was illuminated by a Baccarat crystal chandelier six feet high which weighed a ton. In one corner of it there were some luxury shops of the sort that one finds in palace-hotels from which no one ever seems to buy anything, built by the owner and for which she bought the stock, but the Salon was so large they were scarcely noticeable.

And to the right was the bar, glimpsed momentarily as we were escorted by a non-varlet in scarlet to the lift, which one normally worked oneself after the induction ceremony – these boys were slipping, at the Carlton they had a brace of *liftiers* in white jackets and gloves to press the buttons. In the bar, itself now a French national monument, its panelling reminiscent of some epoch or other, a room to me, who finds most palace-hotel bars sad, of monumental sadness, the monumental habitués were already dipping into their first drinks and a distinguished-looking Negro pianist was playing my tune, Scott Joplin's *Solace*.

Upstairs in the corridors on one of the five floors things were much the same but with whiffs of comparative modernity provided by works of Léger, Picasso, Cocteau, Arp and so on, not all of them felicitous, and with boldly conceived carpets signed by a M. Yvaral underfoot.

Of the hundred and sixty or so rooms and suites, each was furnished with what were said to be genuine pieces of a particular period of French interior decoration from the sixteenth to the nineteenth century.

This breadth of choice, one which is not actually offered to the prospective guest, has its disadvantages for those sensitive to their surroundings, especially when they are paying anything from 540 francs for the quietest double room with a view of the well above the glass-domed Salon Royal, to 1495 francs and upwards for a seaward-looking suite, service and VAT included. When they opened the door of ours it was a bit of a shock. 'Golly!' I said, taking it all in as varlets dashed all over the place running taps, looking under the bed for dead guests who might discommode us, opening windows, indicating the view, showing us how to work the lock of the drink cupboard, dusting away non-existent dust, all putting on a similar, more polished performance than the employees at the El Nil Hotel at the other end of the Mediterranean. It was furnished with a bulbous oaken four-poster that had been stripped and was now of an unseemly milk chocolate hue, my unfavourite colour for furniture. There was a lot more scarlet, which was beginning to seem like Madame's favourite colour, and the walls were hung with tapestries. It had a view of the sea and was rather small. Altogether it produced a feeling that Douglas Fairbanks, *père* or *fils*, disguised as d'Artagnan, might suddenly swing into it, on a knotted sheet, waving a rapier. It could have been worse. There was one room we discovered later which was draped entirely *en tricolore*.

What almost all palace-hotels are proud of, and the Negresco was no exception, is their clientele. Wherever possible they leave lying about printed lists of the kings and ex-kings and queens, princes, shahs, maharajahs and their ladies, pretenders, politicians and film stars and 'great names of the artistic world' they have opened their doors to: lists that, taken together, make an ordinary sensitive person think that he is an occupant not of an hotel but of a chamber of horrors. It was the management of the Carlton, not the Negresco, who suggested to the late Aga Khan, head of the Ismaili Muslims, that they would be happy to bottle his bath water for sale to the Faithful as an elixir of life.

We dined at Chantecler, the Negresco's principal restaurant; one of the best restaurants in France; something rare for the restaurant of an *hôtel-palais*. It rates two stars in *Michelin*. Many people think it should have three, but then *Michelin* has never awarded three stars to the restaurant of an *hôtel-palais*. Anyway, it was not *Michelin* that first drew attention to Chantecler. In fact *Michelin* is unable to do so coherently, even if it would like to do so, since it works with symbols rather than words. It was Gault and Millau in their annual survey of French restaurants, *Guide France*. They wrote so extravagantly about the chef, Jacques Maximin, in the 1982 edition, that, reading their advanced and convoluted French, one seriously began to wonder whether they had gone round the culinary bend. They accorded him four chef's *toques* – hats – in red as opposed to black, which indicated that his cooking was '*inventive*' as opposed to '*classique*', and 19 points out of a possible 20 (which no restaurant has ever received), describing the meal as the '*meilleur repas de l'année*'. This put him in a class with five other immortal chefs, four in France and one in Switzerland, all of whom produced, according to Gault and Millau, '*repas exceptionels de l'année*'.

Maximin came to Chantecler by a circuitous route. At the time we ate his dinner he was thirty-three. At fourteen he began to work in the kitchens of a small hotel, Le Chalet, in his native Le Touquet. Perhaps the most important of his formative years were the two he spent working under Roger Vergé in his restaurant le Moulin de Mougins at Mougins near Cannes, which he himself described as '*la révélation de la cuisine*'.

He came to Chantecler in 1979 from what Gault and Millau described as '*un clinquant* (flashy) *restaurant de Marina-Baie-des-Anges*', lured there by Madame Augier and her administrator, who carried out the negotiations, agreeing to give him everything he wanted in the way of assistants and the right to cook whatever he chose, buying all the ingredients himself.

That year he was declared Meilleur Ouvrier de France, together with one of his team, Joël Ray, which made them members of a select band of 24 which includes Paul Bocuse, the late Jean Troisgros and Alain Chapel. That year, *Michelin* accorded Chantecler its first star and Gault and Millau gave it sixteen points out of twenty. In eighteen months business increased by one hundred per cent.

Not everyone, including the Newbys, goes overboard about the décor at Chantecler. The walls covered with flower-patterned, genuine seventeenth-century cotton percale, the chairs upholstered in red velvet, the crystal chandeliers are all the product of Madame's discussable taste; but you can't eat the decorations and the table arrangements were beautifully done, and when course after course arrived escorted by the least forbidding sort of *maître d'hotel*, under silver covers that were whipped away simultaneously to reveal dishes of such insubstantial-looking beauty that one was reminded of eighteenth-century water-colours of flowers and vegetables, everything else was forgotten. Among the dishes that we ate were *courgettes à la fleur et aux truffes*, a dish in which the baby vegetables were scooped out, the orange flowers folded and filled with the purée and then cooked in batter with basil, the courgette from which the flower sprouted being sliced, launched into a butter sauce and surmounted with slivers of black truffle. There was also *galette de pigeonneau aux cèpes et girolles*, a fan of underdone slices of pigeon's breast with almonds and a mushroom sauce composed of fresh *cèpes* and *chanterelles*, and, most wonderful of all, *saumon au gros sel et tous les légumes frais*, fresh salmon flown from Scotland, steamed, surrounded by freshwater crayfish, minute cucumbers, carrots and sliced turnips so small that they could hardly be seen, served with crystals of sea salt, a masterpiece, like no other salmon I have ever eaten. For a sweet we were given one of the creations of Jacques Torres, one of Maximin's adjutants, *gratin de fraises des bois au beurre de Grand Marnier*, wild strawberries in a sort of crême brulée with Grand Marnier. There are two *cartes* for the desserts, one by Torres, the other, with twelve different dishes, by Maximin, all made with chocolate.

This dinner for two, with a bottle of still, red champagne (Pinot France, Laurent Perrier) which cost about 200 francs, produced a bill of £137 ($192) without any liqueurs, twice as much as we had ever spent on a single meal. But in spite of this rudely expensive awakening from what seems in retrospect a beautiful dream, we rose from the table like balloons, thinking about nothing else but where could we lay our hands on a similar amount of money to make possible a return the following day, to eat another version of the best, most imaginative and most beautifully presented meal we have ever eaten in our lives, either on the shores of the Mediterranean or anywhere else.

The Last Vintage

After this scrumptious interlude we set off along the grotesquely overbuilt shores of the Mediterranean through the macabre principality of Monaco and along what the Italians call – with what is now perhaps an excess of Latin imagination – the Riviera dei Fiori, bound for home in Tuscany.

Gastronomically-speaking the dinner at Chantecler marked a fitting end to a protracted journey, little of which could be described as *une route des gastronomes*. Just as we had seen a lot of things and places we never wanted to see again, and with which I hope I have not burdened the reader, we had also eaten a lot of things of which one helping was an ample sufficiency. It is a pity in a way that one could not make a litany or a song about them, as someone once did about hangovers: 'the *cachets faivres* we bought in Sèvres, the *Enos* in Buenos Aires . . .' Instead one must try to think about the more memorable foods for which one has a lingering affection: in Greece, where the food stands or falls according to the quality of the oil, we had eaten *avgolemoa*, delicious rich, spiced soup with oriental affiliations made with chicken, rice, eggs and lemon and served with black pepper, etc., etc.; in Turkey, where the vegetables were the freshest and the meat the best almost anywhere in the Mediterranean, we had allowed ourselves to be fooled into eating *kadin budu*, lady's thighs, which turned out to be pastry and good old unerotic meat croquettes; in Israel we had eaten chickens' testicles and bulls' testicles, described on the menu as 'eggs of adult ox in extent'; and elsewhere in Israel, *kreplach* made with chopped meat and dumplings, and so many *blintzes*, *knishes*, *bagels* and helpings of *lox* that I imagined myself back on Broadway; and in Egypt we had been treated to a meal which took what seemed an eternity to materialize, consisting of *ful*, dried brown beans cooked with red lentils incredibly slowly over a low charcoal fire, eaten with chicken cooked with the aromatic *mulukhia* plant and prickly pears, not all of which had been adequately de-prickled.

Sometimes we thanked our lucky stars that we had decided to give the islands a miss. In Sardinia, where they bury wild boar in trenches before baking them, which means you have to dig for your dinner with a spade, they also, as an afterthought, serve a cheese called *casu becciu* which once seen, let alone eaten, is never forgotten, as it literally swarms with worms. Sometimes there are so many that the cheese is actually seen to move across the platter on which it is served, as if the worms were carrying it in some sort of procession.

After passing Lerici, on the Gulf of Spezia, we turned off the deathtrap Via Emilia, the Roman road to Rome, on to a small straight road that led off it to the foot of a range of hills that are outliers of the Apuan Alps, on the way passing something comparatively rare in this part of the world, a fine Renaissance villa.

When we first came to live here this had been good farmland, but the present owners of the villa, who had taken it over from the feudal lords, were selling it off piecemeal and apartment blocks were being built. Only a few of the former dependants of the old lords, the *mezzadri*, share-croppers who had rendered half their total produce to them in exchange for a roof over their heads, lived on in what remained of their humble but picturesque farmhouses, where they still stubbornly cultivated the pathetic remains of what had once been flourishing vineyards. Beyond the villa the road ran past a little chapel decorated with marble obelisks, in which the old family had gone to pray, and under a high brick archway which formed part of their huge stables.

Here the plain ended and the road began to climb the hillside, winding up among old farmhouses painted in faded pinks and

surrounded by vineyards and groves of olives, and past new
weekend houses – what the owners, most of whom come from
Parma on the other side of the Apennines, call *villette*, constructions
guarded by savage, German-type dogs trained for this purpose.
These holiday houses are hemmed in with wire-mesh fencing, which
the locals, who have gone wherever they wished to go by rights of
way since time immemorial, bitterly resent but do nothing about,
being peasants.

We drove up the hillside, counting the hairpin bends as we
always did, and, as always, failing to come to the same total because
it depends what you mean by a hairpin bend, past our local grocer's
shop and our local butcher's and past what a notice on a rather
decrepit building picturesquely described as a *cellula*, a cell of the
local branch of the Italian Communist Party, to which many of our
friends belong.

Then after another bend or two we turned off along a rutted
track, so steep that for years we had found it worthwhile to own a
Land Rover, running down through a wood of sweet chestnuts
which here, in these hills and mountains, until recently provided the
flour for the staple food, and across a little bridge that spanned a
torrent that was always bone dry in summer unless there was a
sudden storm.

Once across the bridge we saw the house, partly but never really
forgotten, but certainly neglected, like Mole's house in *Wind in the
Willows*; for apart from coming to do the *vendemmia* and to dig
and manure the land, when we had not bothered to open it up, two
years had passed since we had last lived in it. It was autumn 1983
and we were home in time for the *vendemmia*.

It was a pity in some ways that this was the last year we should
make our wine here at I Castagni. Something like eighteen years
ago, I had dug this vineyard with my own hands using a pick and a
spade, at a time when no one remotely considered using bulldozers
or other labour-saving instruments for such a minor project. I
excavated a series of trenches, each more than sixty feet long and
four feet wide and deep, in what was heavy clay embedded with
rocks. Having thrown in a bit of vegetation as I had been instructed,
I solemnly refilled them. This was to give the roots of the vine a
chance to establish themselves in the heavy soil. Then I planted the
vines. By a miracle, of the hundred or so I planted, only one or two
failed to take.

Twice a year, in the spring and in the autumn, we came to work our vineyard, and in the interval, when we were elsewhere, it was looked after by Signor Tarsiero and his wife, our nearest neighbours, he being a real professional who had worked in a very large vineyard for most of his life. He pruned the vines and sprayed them and did everything else that needed to be done except dig them, prune the shoots below ground level when they were young and find the good manure and manure them, things that were in my province. But now he was over eighty, and although still active was unable to look after my vines in addition to his own property, and so from now on we were going to loan the vineyard to another neighbour so that he could make the wine for himself, and we would buy our wine elsewhere. We would do this because we made our wine in a particular way and could not expect anyone else's to be quite the same.

It was perhaps appropriate that this should be our last *vendemmia* at I Castagni, for we had not only come to the end of what had been a very long journey round the shores of the Mediterranean, but had also, at the same time, come to the end of our wine.

Bibliography

A list of some of the interesting, useful and in some cases indispensable books which deal with the shores of the Mediterranean.*

GENERAL

Aharoni, Yohanan and Avi Yonah, Michael, *The Macmillan Bible Atlas*, London and New York, 1968.

Baedeker, Karl, *Baedeker's Mediterranean*, Leipzig, 1911.

Baker, J. N. L., *A History of Geographical Discovery and Exploration*, London, 1931.

Beny, Roloff, Thwaite, Anthony, *et al.*, *Odyssey: Mirror of the Mediterranean*, London, 1981.

Bradford, Ernle, *Mediterranean: Portrait of a Sea*, London, 1971.

Braudel, Fernand, *The Mediterranean in the Age of Philip II*, London, 1972/3.

Cary, M. and Wilmington, E. H., *The Ancient Explorers*, London, 1963.

Chambers's Encyclopaedia, new edition, London, 1950.

Encyclopaedia Britannica, 9th edition, Edinburgh, 1875.

Geographical Handbook Series, B. R503 (Restricted), various countries, Naval Intelligence Division, London, 1942–5.

Gibbon, Edward, *The Decline and Fall of the Roman Empire*, London, 1776–88.

Grollenberg, Luc H., *Shorter Atlas of the Bible*, London and Edinburgh, 1959.

Herodotus, *The Histories*, trans. Aubrey de Sélincourt, London, 1968.

Larousse Encyclopaedia of Mythology, London, 1959.

Macaulay, Rose, *A Pleasure of Ruins*, London, 1953.

Mediterranean Pilot, London, various volumes and dates.

Moore, W. G., *The Penguin Encyclopaedia of Places*, London, 1971.

Murray's Handbook to the Mediterranean: Its Cities, Coasts and Islands, 3rd edition, London, 1890.

Newbiggin, Marion I., *The Mediterranean Lands: An Introductory Study in Human and Historical Geography*, London, 1925.

---

* Dates of publication given for many of the guides and reference books listed are those of my own copies. It does not necessarily mean that these editions are the best. Many of the older works of travel are available in modern reprints.

Newby, Eric, *World Atlas of Exploration*, New York and London, 1975.
Oxford Classical Dictionary, Oxford, 1949.
Peterson, Roger, Mountfort, Guy and Hollom, P. A. D., *A Field Guide to the Birds of Britain and Europe*, London, 1969.
Polunin, Oleg and Huxley, Anthony, *Flowers of the Mediterranean*, London, 1978.
Scullard, H. H. and Van der Heydern, A. A. M., *Atlas of the Classical World*, London, 1959.
Semple, Ellen Churchill, *The Geography of the Mediterranean: Its Relation to Mediterranean History*, London, 1932.
Thomas Cook Continental Timetable, ed. J. H. Price, Peterborough, monthly.
Thomas Cook Overseas Timetable, ed. P. I. Tremlett, Peterborough, bimonthly.
The Times Atlas of the World, comprehensive edition, London, 1973.

NAPLES

Acton, Harold, *The Bourbons of Naples (1734–1825)*, London, 1956.
Baedeker, Karl, *Baedeker's Southern Italy*, Leipzig, 1896.
Barzini, Luigi, *The Italians*, London, 1964.
Blanchard, Paul, *Blue Guide to Southern Italy*, London, 1982.
Borelli, G., *Il Presepe Napoletano*, Rome, 1970.
Burnes, John Horn, *The Gallery*, London, 1948.
de Bourcard, Francesco, *Usi e Costumi di Napoli e Contorni*, Naples, 1857.
de Crescenza, Luccano, *La Napoli di Bellavista*, Naples, 1979.
Evelyn, John, *Diary*, ed. E. S. de Beer, Oxford, 1955.
Fittipaldi, T., *Scultura e Presepe nel Settecento a Napoli*, Naples, 1979.
Goethe, J. W., *Italian Journey (1786–1788)*, trans. W. H. Auden and Elizabeth Mayer, London, 1962.
Gunn, Peter, *The Companion Guide to Southern Italy*, London, 1969.
Lewis, Norman, *Naples '44*, London, 1978.
Michelin, *Green Guide to Italy*, Paris, 1982.
Molajoli, B., *La Scultura nel Presepe Napoletano del Settecento*, Naples, 1950.
Murray's Handbook for Travellers in Southern Italy, London, 1874.
Sitwell, Sacheverell, *Southern Baroque Art*, London, 1924.

VENICE, ITS LAGOON AND THE VILLAS OF THE VENETO

Baedeker, Karl, *Baedeker's Northern Italy*, Leipzig, 1913.
Honour, Hugh, *The Companion Guide to Venice*, London, 1965.

Lorenzetti, Giulio, *Venice and Its Lagoon*, trans. John Guthrie, Trieste, 1975.
Macadam, Alta, *The Blue Guide to Venice*, London, 1980.
Mazzotti, Giuseppe, *Le Ville Venete*, Treviso, 1954.
Mazzotti, Giuseppe, *Ville Venete*, Rome, 1963.
Morris, James, *Venice*, London, 1960.
Murray's Handbook for Travellers in Northern Italy, London, 1901.
Norwich, John Julius, *Venice*, London, 1977/81.
Roiter, Fulvio, *Living Venice*, text by Andre Zanzotto, Udine, 1978.
Sprigge, Sylvia, *The Lagoon of Venice: Its Islands, Life and Communications*, London, 1961.
Tiozzo, C. B. and Semenzato, C., *La Riviera del Brenta*, Treviso, 1968.

THE CARSO AND MONTENEGRO

Baedeker, Karl, *Baedeker's Austro–Hungary, including Dalmatia and Bosnia*, Leipzig, 1905.
Cuddon, J. A., *The Companion Guide to Jugoslavia*, London, 1968.
Venezia, Giulia, *Guida d'Italia del Touring Club Italiano*, Milan, 1934.
Vujosevic, Stanislav-Rako and Jovicivec, *Cetinje and Its Museum*, Beograd, 1972.

ALBANIA

Byron, Lord, *Letters*, ed. Leslie A. Marchand, London, 1973–81.
Foutiou, P. D., *Ali Pasha de Ioannina: Le Lion de l'Epire*, Ioannina, 1980.
Hobhouse, John Cam, Lord Broughton, *A Journey through Albania and Other Provinces of Turkey in Europe and Asia to Constantinople during the Years 1809 and 1810*, London, 1813.
Holland, Sir Henry, *Travels in the Ionian Isles, Albania, Thessaly, Macedonia . . . during 1812 and 1813*, London, 1815.
Leake, William Martin, *Travels in Northern Greece*, London, 1935.
Lear, Edward, *Journals of a Landscape Painter in Albania . . .*, London, 1851, reprinted 1965.
Ward, Philip, *Albania*, Cambridge, 1983.

GREECE

Baedeker, Karl, *Baedeker's Greece, the Greek Islands and an Excursion to Crete*, Leipzig, 1909.
Curzon, Robert, Baron de la Zouche, *Visits to the Monasteries in the Levant*, London, 1849.

de Jongh, Brian, *The Companion Guide to Mainland Greece*, London, 1979.

Fermor, Patrick Leigh, *Roumeli*, London, 1966.

Hachette World Guides: Greece, Paris, 1965.

Hale, John Richard, *Famous Sea Fights from Salamis to Jutland*, London, 1939.

Murray's Handbook for Travellers in Greece, London, 1900.

Nagel's Encyclopaedia Guide: Greece, Geneva, 1973.

Stevens, Alan and Westcott, W. O., *A History of Sea Power*, New York, 1920.

Stournaras, N., *Meteora*, Athens, n.d.

Stuart, Rossiter, *The Blue Guide to Greece*, London, 1967.

TURKEY

General

Boulanger, Robert, *Les Guides Bleus: Turquie*, Paris, 1965.

Freely, John, *The Companion Guide to Turkey*, London, 1979.

Kinglake, A. W., *Eothen*, London, 1844.

Nagel's Encyclopaedia Guide: Turkey, Geneva, 1968.

Schneider, Dux, *The Traveller's Guide to Turkey*, London, 1975.

Gallipoli

Aspinall-Oglander, C. F., *History of the Great War: Military Operations: Gallipoli*, London, 1929–32.

Bennett, Geoffrey, *Naval Battles of the First World War*, London, 1968.

Commonwealth War Graves Commission, Introduction to the *Register of the Helles Memorial*, Maidenhead, 1980.

Commonwealth War Graves Commission, *Notes on the Cemeteries and Memorials of Gallipoli and Greece*, St Albans, 1965.

Hamilton, General Sir Ian, *Gallipoli Diary*, London, 1920.

Herbert, Aubrey, *Mons, Anzac and Kut*, London, 1919.

Moorehead, Alan, *Gallipoli*, London, 1968.

Rhodes James, Robert, *Gallipoli*, London, 1965.

Constantinople/Istanbul

Baedeker, Karl, *Baedeker's Konstantinopel und das Kleinasien*, Leipzig, 1914.

Boyd, H. Sumner and Freely, John, *Strolling through Istanbul: A Guide to the City*, Istanbul, 1973.

Der Amtlicher Plan des Grossen Basars in Istanbul, Istanbul, n.d.

Gülersoy, Lelik, *Story of the Grand Bazaar*, Istanbul, 1980.

Pardoe, Julia, *The Beauties of the Bosphorus, by Miss Pardoe with Drawings by W. H. Bartlett*, London, 1839.

Pardoe, Julia, *The City of the Sultan and Domestic Manners of the Turks*, London, 1837.

Walsh, Rev. Robert, *Constantinople and the Scenery of the Seven Churches of Asia Minor, Illustrated in a Series of Drawings from Nature by Thomas Allom . . .*, London, 1839.

The Harem

Blanch, Lesley, *The Wilder Shores of Love*, London, 1954.

Clarke, Edward Daniel, *Travels in Various Countries of Europe, Asia and Africa*, 4th edition, London, 1816.

Durukan, Zeynep M., *The Harem of the Topkapi Palace* (Guide), Istanbul, 1973.

Hakluyt Society, *Early Voyages and Travels in the Levant*, London, 1893.

Haslip, Joan, *The Sultan: The Life of Abdul Hamid II*, London, 1973.

Köseoğlu, Cengiz, *Harem* (Guide), Istanbul, 1979.

McCullagh, Francis, *The Fall of Abd-ul-Hamid*, London, 1910.

Miller, Dr Barnette, *Beyond the Sublime Porte*, New Haven, 1931.

Penzer, N. M., *The Harem: An Account of the Institution as it Existed in the Palace of the Turkish Sultans with a History of the Grand Seraglio from its Foundation to Modern Times*, London, 1965.

Turkey in Asia

Arrian, *The Campaigns of Alexander*, trans. Aubrey de Sélincourt, London, 1971.

Bean, George E., *Aegean Turkey*, London, 1966.

Bean, George E., *Lycian Turkey*, London, 1968.

Bean, George E., *Turkey Beyond the Maeander*, London, 1971.

Bean, George E., *Turkey's Southern Shores*, London, 1968.

Black, David, Loveless, Clive, *et al.*, *The Undiscovered Kelim*, London, 1977.

Carne, John, *Syria, The Holy Land and Asia Minor Illustrated in a Series of One Hundred and Twenty Views Drawn from Nature by W. H. Bartlett, William Purser and Thomas Allom*, London and Paris, 1842.

Clarke, Edward Daniel, *Travels in Various Countries of Europe, Asia and Africa*, 4th edition, London, 1816.

Cook, Professor John Manuel, *The Troad*, Oxford, 1973.

Denham, H. M., *Southern Turkey, the Levant and Cyprus*, London, 1973.

Homer, *The Iliad*, trans. E. V. Rieu, London, 1950.

Petsopoulos, Yanni, *Kilims: The Art of Tapestry Weaving in Anatolia, the Caucasus and Persia*, London, 1982.

Thompson, Jon, *Carpet Magic: The Art of Carpets from the Tents, Cottages and Workshops of Asia*, London, 1983.

ISRAEL, SYRIA AND LEBANON

Baedeker, Karl, *Baedeker's Palestine and Syria, with Routes through Mesopotamia and Babylonia and the Island of Cyprus*, Leipzig, 1912.
Boulanger, Robert, *Hachette World Guides: The Middle East*, Paris, 1966.
Carne, John, *Syria, The Holy Land and Asia Minor . . .*, London and Paris, 1842.
Cohen, Israel, *Jewish Life in Modern Times*, London, 1914.
Cohen, Israel, *Travels in Jewry*, London, 1952.
Coulbeaux, J. B., *Histoire Politique et Religieuse d'Abyssinie*, Paris, 1929.
Curzon, Robert, Baron de la Zouche, *Visits to Monasteries in the Levant*, London, 1849.
Facts about Israel: The Authorized Handbook, Jerusalem, 1980.
Finkelstein, Louis, *The Jews: Their History, Culture and Religion*, London, 1961.
Josephus, *History of the Jewish War* and *Antiquities of the Jews*.
Kaminker, Sarah Fox, *Footloose in Jerusalem*, Jerusalem, 1971.
Kinglake, A. W., *Eothen*, London, 1844.
Morton, H. V., *In the Steps of the Master*, London, 1934.
Nir, Dov, *New Guide to Israel*, London, 1973.
Sitwell, Sacheverell, *Splendours and Miseries*, London, 1943.
Steinmatsky's Guides: Syria and the Lebanon, Jerusalem, 1942.

EGYPT

Baedeker, Karl, *Baedeker's Egypt and the Sudan*, Leipzig, 1929, reprinted 1974.
Bartlett, W. H., *The Nile Boat, or Glimpses of the Land of Egypt*, London, 1849.
Cook's Handbook for Egypt and the Egyptian Sudan, London, 1911.
Davidson, D. and Aldersmith, H., *The Great Pyramid: Its Divine Message*, London, 1932.
Edwards, Amelia B., *A Thousand Miles up the Nile*, London, 1877, reprinted 1982.
Edwards, I. E. S., *The Pyramids of Egypt*, London, 1980.
Flaubert, Gustave, *Flaubert in Egypt: A Sensibility on Tour* (A Narrative drawn from Gustave Flaubert's Travel Notes and Letters), trans. Francis Steegmuller, London, 1972.

Freeman-Grenville, G. S. P., *The Beauty of Cairo: A Historical Guide to the Chief Islamic and Coptic Monuments*, London, 1980.
Kinglake, A. W., *Eothen*, London, 1844.
Lane, E. W., *Manners and Customs of the Ancient Egyptians*, London, 1860.
Murray's Handbook for Travellers in Egypt, London, 1891.
Nagel's Encyclopaedia Guide: Egypt, Geneva, 1972.
Petrie, Sir William Flinders, *The Pyramids and Temples of Gizeh*, London, 1883.
Seton-Williams, Veronica and Stocks, Peter, *The Blue Guide to Egypt*, London, 1983.

LIBYA

Anon., *Bir Hakim* (in French), Cairo, 1942.
Boillot, Felix, *Bir Hakeim*, Publications de la France Combattante, London, 1942.
Commonwealth War Graves Commission, *The War Dead of the British Commonwealth and Empire: The Register of the Names of Those who Fell in the 1939–1945 War and Are Buried in Cemeteries in Libya*, London, 1957.
Fergusson, Bernard, Baron Ballantrae, *The Black Watch and the King's Enemies*, London, 1950.
Kennedy Shaw, W. B., *The Long Range Desert Group: The Story of Its Work*, London, 1945.
Koenig, General P. M. J. F., *Bir-Hakeim*, Paris, 1970.
Maule, Henry, *Out of the Sand*, London, 1966.
Mordal, J., *Bir Hacheim*, Paris, 1952.
Playfair, Major-General I. S. O., *History of the Second World War, UK Military Series: The Mediterranean and Middle East*, Vol. III, *September 1941 to September 1942*, London, 1960.
Qathafi, Muammar Al, *The Green Book*, Tripoli, n.d.
Rommel, General Erwin, *The Rommel Papers*, ed. B. H. Liddell Hart, London, 1953.
Sitwell, Sacheverell, *Mauretania*, London, 1940.
Thwaite, Anthony, *The Deserts of the Hesperides*, London, 1969.

TUNISIA

Douglas, Norman, *Fountains in the Sand: Rambles among the Oases of Tunisia*, London, 1912.
Sitwell, Sacheverell, *Mauretania*, London, 1940.
Thurston, Hazel, *The Traveller's Guide to Tunisia*, London, 1973.

MOROCCO

Africanus, Scipio (Al-Hassan Ibn Mohammed al-Wezaz al-Fasi), *The History and Description of Africa Done into English in the Year 1600 by John Pory*, revised by Dr R. Brown, Hakluyt Society, Book 3, Vol. II, London, 1896.
Boulanger, Robert, *Hachette World Guides: Morocco*, Paris, 1966.
Bovill, E. W., *The Golden Trade of the Moors*, Oxford, 1958.
Burckhardt, Titus, *Fez: Stadt des Islam*, Freiburg, 1960.
Burckhardt, Titus, 'Fez', in R. B. Serjeant (ed.), *The Islamic City*, UNESCO, Paris, n.d.
Harris, Lawrence, *With Mulai Hafid at Fez: Behind the Scenes in Morocco*, London, 1909.
Harris, Walter, *Morocco That Was*, London, 1921.
Ibish, Yusuf, 'Economic Institutions', in R. B. Serjeant (ed.), *The Islamic City*, UNESCO, Paris, n.d.
Kininmonth, Christopher, *The Traveller's Guide to Morocco*, London, 1981.
Meakin, Budgett, *The Moors: A Comprehensive Description*, London and New York, 1902.
Michelin, *Maroc: Guide de Tourisme*, Paris, 1979.
Ricard, P., *Hachette World Guides: Morocco*, Paris, 1924.
Rohlfs, Gerhard, *Adventures in Morocco and Journeys through the Oases of Draa and Taafilet*, London, 1874.
Selous, G. S., *Appointment to Fez*, London, 1956.

SPAIN AND SEVILLE

ABC (daily newspaper), issues during Holy Week.
Baedeker, Karl, *Baedeker's Spain and Portugal*, Leipzig, 1913.
Butierrez, P. Federico C. M. F., *Semana Santa en Seville*, Madrid, 1975.
Ford, Richard, *A Handbook for Travellers in Spain and Readers at Home*, London, 1845.
George, Nancy, *Les Processions de Seville, Choses Vues*, Paris, 1935.
Michelin, *Green Guide: Spain*, Paris, 1982.
Pritchett, V. S., *The Spanish Temper*, London, 1954.
Robertson, Ian, *The Blue Guide to Spain*, London, 1975.
Semana Santa: Horario e Itinerario Oficial de las Cofradias que hacen Estacion a la Santa y Metropolitana Iglesia Catedral. Aprobados por el Illustrisimo Señor Vicario General el Arzobispardo, Seville, 1975.
Willoughby, David, *Guide to Semana Santa, Holy Week in Seville*, Seville, 1975.

FRANCE AND THE RIVIERA

Baedeker, Karl, *Baedeker's Southern France, including Corsica*, Leipzig, 1914.
Baedeker, Karl, *Baedeker's Riviera, South-Eastern France and Corsica*, Leipzig, 1931.
Cameron, Roderick, *The Golden Riviera*, London, 1975.
Connolly, Cyril, *The Rock Pool*, London, 1935.
Connolly, Cyril (Palinurus), *The Unquiet Grave*, London, 1945.
Guide Michelin, Paris, 1939.
Guide Michelin, Paris, 1982.
Sharman, Fay, *The Taste of France: A Dictionary of French Food and Wine*, London, 1982.
Tomkins, Calvin, *Living Well Is the Best Revenge*, New York, 1971.

Index